Adventures with the Buddha

A Personal Buddhism Reader

Also by Jeffery Paine

Father India: Westerners under the Spell
of an Ancient Culture

The Poetry of Our World:
An International Anthology of Contemporary Poetry

Re-enchantment:
Tibetan Buddhism Comes to the West

Adventures with the Buddha

A PERSONAL
BUDDHISM READER

Jeffery Paine

W. W. NORTON & COMPANY

NEW YORK   LONDON

Copyright © 2005 by Jeffery Paine

Manufacturing by the Maple-Vail Book Manufacturing Group
Book design by Lovedog Studio
Production manager: Andrew Marasia

Library of Congress Cataloging-in-Publication Data

Paine, Jeffery, date.
Adventures with the Buddha : a personal buddhism reader / Jeffery
Paine. — 1st ed.
p. cm.
Includes index.
ISBN 0-393-05906-5 (hardcover)
1. Buddhists—Biography. 2. Spiritual life—Buddhism. I. Title.
BQ843. P25 2005
294.3`092`2—dc22 2004015015

W. W. Norton & Company, Inc., 500 Fifth Avenue, New York, N.Y. 10110
www.wwnorton.com

W. W. Norton & Company Ltd., Castle House, 75 / 76 Wells Street, London W1T 3QT

1 2 3 4 5 6 7 8 9 0

The absence of strictly personal confessions is the chief difficulty to the student who would like to become acquainted with the inwardness of religions other than the Christian.

—William James,
The Varieties of Religious Experience

Contents

INTRODUCTION: Buddhism as Life Adventure   15

Part I
The Era of the Heroic and Almost Magical

Introduction   29

CHAPTER I.   Tibet as It Once Was
Alexandra David-Neel   35

CHAPTER II.   A Himalayan Guru of the Old Style
Lama Anagarika Govinda   77

CHAPTER III.   The Lost World of Chinese Buddhism
John Blofeld   123

CHAPTER IV.   Taoism and/or Buddhism?
Peter Goullart   201

CHAPTER V.   Reality in a Zen Monastery
                Janwillem van de Wetering   233

Part II
The Era of You and Me

Introduction   265
CHAPTER VI.   An African-American Woman's Journey
                into Buddhism
                Jan Willis   267

CHAPTER VII.   In Search of Women's Wisdom
                Tsultrim Allione   317

CHAPTER VIII.   Suffering and Its Partial Cure
                Sharon Salzberg   343

CHAPTER IX.   The Diamond Sutra. The Diamond Business
                Michael Roach   367

Permissions   395
Index   397

Adventures with the Buddha

A Personal Buddhism Reader

Introduction

· · · · · · · · · ·

Buddhism as Life Adventure

I

Once upon a time—and that time not so long ago—it was possible for an American or European child to grow up completely unaware of Buddhism. The Englishwoman Tenzin Palmo (born Diane Perry in 1943) is now a legend for having lived a dozen years alone in a Himalayan cave and then starting a nunnery where she teaches Asian women the dharma. Yet she grew up, as did almost everyone else of her heritage, never encountering Buddhism nor even hearing the word. What a difference a generation makes. Today even complex, complicated Tibetan Buddhism, once thought beyond popular understanding, has become a commonplace subject in the West. A fortunate birth, in Buddhism, is one where the child may be exposed to the Buddha's teachings, and by that measure, contemporary America and Europe have become fortunate places to be born.

Yet some people seem never satisfied. A few readers have complained that they cannot find a certain kind of Buddhist book and half-suspect that it does not exist. Exactly what sort of a book might that be?

Let us suppose you have had a long, hard day, and night has come, and it's time for bed. You are that old-fashioned type who likes to read a few pages before falling to sleep. You reach for a novel or biography to help you fall asleep, but the story is so exciting it keeps you up for hours and you don't mind (till the next morning). Lately, however, you have felt some curiosity about Buddhism, and you think how nice it would be if the book, or some book, wove Buddhist strands into its beguiling night's tale. Many Buddhist books will edify you, but will any entertain you? They, the Buddhist works by your nightstand, can instruct you, soothe you, astonish you—indeed they provide every pleasure, except, it seems, pleasure. "Yes, oh, dear, yes—the novel tells a story," E. M. Forster wrote, humorously apologizing for the novel's age-old function, for its "low atavistic form." Story, narrative, may be the oldest amusement of humankind, but it seems absent from Buddhist literature (at least in English). A Buddhist narrative entertainment to be read principally for enjoyment, that is the book some people suspect that no bookstore or library shelf holds.

But then they may suddenly remember—or someone will mention— Alexandra David-Neel's *Magic and Mystery in Tibet* (1929), in which the author recounted more adventures in that forbidden country than fill *Robinson Crusoe* or *Treasure Island*. Nor is *Magic and Mystery* a solitary hermit on the lonely bookshelf. John Blofeld's *The Wheel of Life* (1959) and Lama Govinda's *The Way of the White Clouds* (1966) are also memoirs transpiring in enchanting, now-lost worlds of Buddhism. But when those books were published, there was little market demand for Buddhist writings, and they seemed doomed not to become spiritual classics but to small sales and premature oblivion. Blofeld was disappointed that there was no popular audience for the autobiography that he worked so hard to make appealing. How different might be the splash today. A few years ago the *New York Times* book critic Richard Bernstein decided to doctor his midlife crisis by retracing a seventh-century Buddhist monk's travels across half of Asia. Bernstein's interest in Buddhism was cursory, yet such is the appetite at present for any "Buddhist" narrative that his *Ultimate Journey* was a best-seller.

The best-seller list was hardly the happy destination for, to take another earlier example, Peter Goullart. Goullart (1902–1978) was a young Russian who escaped the Bolshevik revolution by fleeing to China, where his three decades spent there would condense into books, charming and insightful, about his adopted country and its form of Buddhism. Most of Goullart's books—*Forgotten Kingdom, The Monastery of Jade Mountain,* and *Land of the Lamas*—could not then even find a publisher in America. Yet they, like Blofeld and Govinda and others in this book, offer that oddity, that nonesuch—a Buddhist narrative entertainment—compelling even in the middle of the night or good for beguiling away a long plane flight.

II

Background. Did you ever dream, on a crisp wintry night, of a sojourn among the sages and saints of great Asia? Well, it's probably too late, and before it was too late, it was probably too early. When the twentieth century began, cultural borders and ethnic barriers were such that a refined European could scarcely have dwelled on intimate terms among the good folks of Asia, holy or otherwise. When the century ended, a European or American could live quite neighborly in the Orient, but the experience might not be overwhelmingly different from living among one's neighbors back home. In between those temporal bookends, the writer-adventurers of this anthology were like the members of a small fraternity that, historically speaking, opened its doors one moment and closed them practically the next.

The western world, it's true, had at least heard about Buddhism long before the twentieth century. Marco Polo, for instance, supplied Europeans seven centuries ago with some sketchy knowledge of that religion. In Ceylon he learned the story of "Sagamon Barcon" (Shakyamuni Buddha—that is, the Buddha), and he related it to his readers, generously allowing, "For a certainty, if he had been baptized a Christian he would have been a great saint before God." *But not vice-versa.* No earlier Christians imagined Jesus—or themselves—as resembling in any way good Buddhists.

By the twentieth century, though, Christianity had lost its monopoly hold on the western imagination, and more sympathetic Europeans could look upon Buddhism as an eccentric distant cousin who was, after all, quite harmless and even oddly appealing. During the 1920s Sir Charles Bell, the British political agent for Tibet and Sikkim, was a friend of the Thirteenth Dalai Lama and wrote approvingly of Buddhism. Yet Buddhism was still something "out there," which could not affect his already-fixed-in-place sense of self. To become a Buddhist then required a metamorphosis scarcely more creditable than in Ovid where the person becomes a beast or tree.

Alexandra David-Neel was a pioneer not simply because she became one of the first Caucasian women Buddhists but because she realized that in becoming a Buddhist she was *un*-becoming something else. That one can unshackle oneself from one's inherited or assigned lot in life constitutes a mark of the modern imagination. *Magic and Mystery in Tibet* is not simply an account of Vajrayana Buddhism; it is the record of someone shedding her old skin and remaking herself into a person more in conformance with her ideal image. Buddhism was no longer "out there"; it was *in her,* in even an unhappy bourgeois Frenchwoman—or somebody who would have matched that description, had not Buddhism intervened.

David-Neel thus inaugurated a new sort of Buddhist study. She and, after her, John Blofeld, Lama Govinda, Peter Goullart, and Janwillem van de Wetering plunged, holding nothing of themselves back in their investigation into Buddhism. Before them, ever since Eugene Burnouf's *Introduction a l'histoire du Buddhisme indien* (1844), respectable westerners had discussed Buddhism as an impersonal subject matter in learned tomes, domesticating its wildness with their chronologies and etymologies. But the subjects of this anthology displaced that religion from the academic monograph to the personal confessional: they made it seem less something you objectively *studied* than subjectively *lived.* Their first-person accounts opened a new door into Buddhism for western readers; indeed, for some readers their books opened up a new religion entirely, where before had only existed arcane metaphysics or absurd superstitions. Western Buddhism thus ceased to be an oxymoron, an impossibility.

•   •   •   •

Today. People are still alive who were living when Alexandra David-Neel trekked to Lhasa in the mid-1920s. The youngest contributors here could have, theoretically, met the oldest: David-Neel died only in 1969, receiving visitors till the end. (The novelist Lawrence Durrell visited her shortly before her hundredth birthday, astonished by her youthful appearance.) Yet in the interval since her birth-date, human life on Earth has changed beyond recognition, more so than in any comparable period in history. Alexandra David-Neel made her name by exploring a country, Tibet, where the wheel had yet to be introduced. The Tibetans she chummed with were less citizens of modernity than, in spirit, the contemporaries of Saint Francis or Joan of Arc. Move ahead to the anthology's recent contributors, though, and their contemporaries are Bill Gates, G. W. Bush, cyberpunks, and post-postmodern theorists. As the hypertechnological twenty-first century revs up, Michael Roach (the youngest author here included) envisions new Buddhist communities in America that will support themselves working as electro-commuting computer geeks.

Between then and now, exactly halfway between David-Neel and Michael Roach, there showed up a Dutchman in Japan, Janwillem van de Wetering, who serves as a bridge between the early twentieth century and the Buddhism of today. In 1958, when van de Wetering barged into a Zen monastery in Kyoto, he hardly knew more about what he was getting himself into than Marco Polo would have in the thirteenth century. But, in fact, van de Wetering's experiences proved to be such that a determined young American or European can still approximate them in the (admittedly far fewer) traditional Zen temples and monasteries of Japan today. He inaugurates the chapter on contemporary Buddhism.

In that chapter Michael Roach and Jan Willis, Tsultrim Allione and Sharon Salzberg all followed in the overlarge footsteps of David-Neel, Lama Govinda, and van de Wetering, as soon as they came of age lighting off for Buddhist Asia. But when Lama Govinda and John Blofeld had earlier forged their way there, it was something unprecedented, unknown, and they had to clear their own path through it. A generation later on the Subcontinent, Michael Roach and Jan Willis found the routes demarcated and the places for Buddhist instruction clearly signposted. They traveled there from the late 1960s through the 1980s, as did many others of their generation, with a presentiment that the last of old Asia was disappearing, and, were they to glimpse it, it was now or never. Even more important to them, they were seeking spiritual teachers, which mandated a pilgrimage to Kyoto or Kathmandu, to Bangkok or Bodhgaya, where the gurus of Buddhism were then in residence. And today? Suppose one was seeking a Tibetan guru, say, in the new twenty-first century? The United States boasts perhaps the greatest number, but France or Italy also house the living jewels of the Buddhist lineages. "A journey to the East" (in Hesse's antiquated phrase) tallies but a fraction of the cost it once did; similarly, the ordeals are equally negligible; but in fact one need not now go at all.

Allione and Willis, Roach and Salzberg have more in common, though, than simply their early frolics in India. When young, they seemed part of a new lost generation. American society proclaimed they were the confident, promising youth of John Kennedy's "New Frontier." Yet they themselves felt fairly unpromising, adrift in the great scheme of things. Sharon Salzberg suffered so many childhood sorrows that she concluded she must be a freak to merit such misfortune. Tsultrim Allione was a teenager at loose ends with no particular goals. As an African-American no stranger to injustices, Jan Willis was on the point of joining the Black Panthers. Of the lot, Michael Roach appeared the one golden youth, graduating from Princeton with honors and receiving the President's medal of achievement, but wherever he looked he saw people's struggle for happiness reaping them misery.

Each of them, seemingly by accident, chanced into Buddhism: they plunged into their new discovery, like ugly ducklings into the pond, and from it they emerged as swans. Today Jan Willis is a widely admired professor of Indian and Tibetan religion, whom *Time* magazine called "a philosopher with a bold agenda." Tsultrim Allione became a nun, wrote *Women of Wisdom,* and founded a retreat center, where she is reintroducing the sacred feminine principle into Buddhism. Sharon Salzberg created the Insight Meditation Society through which twenty thousand people have passed studying Buddhism and meditation. Michael Roach has established a monastery as well as teaching centers and put the entire Buddhist canon digitally on computer; in between these activities and going on three-years retreats, he became the first western *geshe* (a "Ph.D." in Tibetan Buddhism, requiring twenty-plus years of study). When young, they all traveled to India to find a guru; today, should one desire a spiritual teacher, one could hardly do better than to go on a pilgrimage and find *them.*

Among their generation they are hardly the only exemplars of western Buddhism (such a list would include B. Alan Wallace, Matthieu Ricard, and, well, too many to name here). But those four have written about Buddhism in the dramatic terms of how you live it out in your own life. Sadly, none of them can escort us back into the lost worlds and strange wonders David-Neel and Govinda once encountered. Rather they serve as guides to a more compromised region; they take us inwardly into the psyche—into the living mess—of ordinary contemporaries, and show us how Buddhist practice can spruce up its ramshackle apportionments. Here is Buddhism looked at, come to terms with, not in grand ideas or theory but in modern day-to-day existences, twenty-five hundred years after the Buddha lived.

III

How Buddhists behave in their off hours—well, that's a rather interesting subject. For what theology is to other religions, biography may well be to

Buddhism. That is because Buddhism looks at human beings through the other end of the telescope, where cause-and-effect appear to happen in reverse order. Tenzin Wangyal, one of the brightest of the post–Tibet-born *rinpoches,* put it thus: "The practices of the spiritual path, if done with correct understanding and application, bring results. Results develop faith." In most religions, though, one needs faith first: believe (though your faith be no greater than a mustard seed), and then you will do and achieve inordinately. In Buddhism, do and achieve, and it will make belief unnecessary or, more likely, inevitable. Consequently, we need to see the results of Buddhism in human lives first, before we can really know what Buddhism is.

In Christianity a humble saint like Padre Pio (Franceso Forgione, 1887–1968) resembles a Tibetan *bodhisattva,* a holy miracle-worker like those who populate Himalayan mythology. He nearly dispensed with food and sleep; he healed the sick by his touch; and he materialized in visions to people far away to divert them from danger. But Padre Pio (in common with all saints in Christian hagiology) had faith first; then he received the stigmata wounds; and only afterward could he perform the miracles he did not understand and for which he had little desire. Two and a half centuries before Pio, in *The Practice of the Presence of God,* Brother Lawrence reported how, despite being a cripple, he undertook long trips for the church, and, absorbed in his faith, he would arrive not even remembering how he got there. For such Christians, faith heralds all things; faith awakens all things; faith makes all things possible.

But faith paved the way to nowhere for the writers in this anthology. From Alexandra David-Neel to Sharon Salzberg, they were exiled (or self-exiled) young from their religion of origin. Nor could they readily believe in another faith, because at some fundamental level *I believe* no longer belonged to their vocabulary of experience. Their half-formed, unspoken thought was: If only—if only one could be buoyed up by belief without actually having to believe anything. If only one could enjoy the consolations of faith without assenting to any divine nonsense. The Dalai Lama hints of precisely this possibility, though, when he jokes that "religion is a luxury item." If the Buddha's teachings and modern science (or, for that matter, one's deepest experience) contradict each other, he has further said, then the former have to go. This seems to suggest that the road to salvation need not detour through theology but can run straight through the experiences of your own life. The adventurers of this anthology have put on display their biographies, Exhibit A, to demonstrate that one can be a Buddhist and not necessarily "religious" at all.

At the start of our story, Alexandra David-Neel, having married unwisely, suffered an undiagnosable ennui, as though her vital energy were ebbing fatally away. But once she began having experiences in, or through, Buddhism (it did not hurt that one included a romance with a Himalayan prince), her vitality began to return and returned with such force to carry her where no white woman had gone before. A purely intellectual understanding of Buddhism was not what reinvigorated her. For example, the key Buddhist doctrine of reincarnation was just that to her, a doctrine, which she had no reason to believe. But then she witnessed, on two separate occasions, young boys spontaneously reciting unknowable details and forgotten facts from their supposed previous incarnations' biographies. Such first-hand observations startled David-Neel into a different conclusion about identity, including her own. Similarly, John Blofeld had no interest in Tibetan Buddhism, until one lama voiced Blofeld's unspoken thoughts and another predicted an impossible turn of events that later transpired. Such first-hand experiences made Blofeld reevaluate Buddhism as something other than theories and principles, something that was somehow printed in the very fabric of life, including his own.

As our story concludes, no uncanny epiphanies like David-Neel's or Blofeld's intrude. Instead, Sharon Salzberg and Jan Willis advance in a slow slog through their own personal history, where at first any relief Buddhism affords comes in installments tentative and irregular. Salzberg, as noted earlier, was cocooned in the misery that an unhappy upbringing had spun around her. At age sixteen, "feeling as lost and afraid as ever," she enrolled at the State University of New York at Buffalo, where she took a course in

Buddhism. It seemed to help a little. SUNY–Buffalo offered a junior year abroad, during which Salzberg traveled to India and studied Buddhism. It helped a little more, and thus inch by inch was the cocoon unspun. Jan Willis, for all her unmistakable intelligence, needed even more years to come through. Her own psychological scarring, suffered when she was an African-American girl in the racist South, left her later unable to trust even Lama Yeshe, the most lovable of Tibetan teachers. Finally one day he exploded at her (see Chapter VI), but only when she realized that this gentle man was feigning anger (painfully, against his own nature) *for her own good*—only then did some age-old knot inside her unravel. Such healing reversals are rarely gained by reading theories and principles.

Willis, Salzberg, Roach, and Allione are hardly the only contemporaries struggling to forge a "spiritual" dimension to their existence. Today's churchgoers and even fundamentalists face a not entirely dissimilar struggle, shaped as they are in the main by influences predominantly secular and worldly, by the materials and social gadgetry of late modernity. Down some forgotten byway an Amish farmer is driving his buggy, determined to shield his offspring from evils like television and computers. Most of the brethren, though, have departed from the olden and sacrosanct ways, and religion and belief become something different from before. An experience of faith has largely yielded, even for the religiously inclined, to faith in experience. In *A Vision* the poet W. B. Yeats composed a work of fantastical mythology but, when asked if he actually believed it, replied: he was not set down on earth to judge but to have his soul and imagination made fertile. Likewise, when Carl Jung was asked if he believed there was a God, he replied mischievously, "I don't believe; I know." Through their encounters with Buddhism, the writers in these pages demonstrate how to replace the majestic credo *I believe* with, instead, the more modest and manageable "I have seen and I have done."

•   •   •   •

Suppose that a party needs to traverse a vineyard where the terrain is rocky, up and down, forbiddingly rugged. If they are tantalized with a taste of sweet grapes beforehand, their reluctance will be overcome and the way made easier. So wrote Sir Phillip Sidney over four hundred years ago in *A Defense of Poetry*, and so possibly for the kind of Buddhist writing included here. Not moral exhortation, but the promise of something sweeter and more tasty is the inducement for traversing these pages (as it is, for some, for entering the dharma itself). What, precisely, is the sweet promise of this particular vineyard? In it, with our pilgrim voyagers, adventure and understanding, enjoyment and effort, passion and clarity join hands and are for an instant united. As for the fruits of their experience, time it is now for you to turn the page and taste them for yourself.

Part I

The Era
of the Heroic
and Almost
Magical

Introduction

As the ship ploughed the rough sea passage, the passengers aboard gradually realized a human puzzle was in their midst. All the other passengers belonged to the grand scheme of things: bureaucratic administrators, military personnel, commercial travelers, they were all being floated to India by the great enterprise of colonialism. But a twenty-three-year-old Frenchwoman was voyaging mysteriously alone—something a woman in the year 1891 did not do—and she remained aloof, so her shipmates had trouble questioning her. When they did, she fobbed them off, replying that in India she intended to study Sanskrit. Many of her fellow passengers looked perplexed, uncertain whether this Sanskrit was a region, a language, or a tribe. Had they divined her real purpose, they would have scratched their heads, worse confounded.

The young woman often remained in her cabin, preferring over her shipmates' company the pleasures of the Bhagavad Gita or some Buddhist text. She should not have been reading such volumes—or at least not in the intense, personal way she devoured them. The proper way for a European to peruse a Hindu or Buddhist tome then was as a scholar, decoding an intellectual problem. But this young woman did not want to explicate texts; she wished to live them. Earlier, when studying in Paris, she had noted, "There are great men at the Sorbonne who know all the roots of the words and the historical dates. But I wish to live philosophy on the spot and undergo physical and spiritual training, not just read about them." This determination would open up unprecedented experiences for her in Asia. She would soon become the first western woman to speak with a Dalai Lama; the first to have a romance with a Himalayan prince; the first to apprentice herself to a mountain hermit at his snowbound cave; the first to enter forbidden Lhasa. Her shipmates would have poo-poo'ed even the idea of such achievements as impossible, as indeed they were until she imported into Asia her personal approach to Buddhism. This woman was, of course, Alexandra David-Neel, to many people as legendary a figure as exists in the annals of travel.

During David-Neel's long lifespan, the century between 1868 and 1969, Buddhism went from being an obscure, occult interest in her native country (and elsewhere in the West) to becoming mainstream, even something of a fad. When, we might ask, did westerners like her first begin to gain an accurate knowledge of that once strange and alien faith?

Eighteen hundred twenty-four is something of a demarcating year. In that year Brian Houghton Hodgson discovered that the original Buddhist canon—instead of perishing when Buddhism perished in India—still existed in Sanskrit and Tibetan manuscripts housed in the monasteries of Nepal. Hodgson was the British assistant resident at the Nepali royal court, and his attitude exemplified the earlier, pre-David-Neel approach to Buddhism. Hodgson devoted his life to preserving and classifying Buddhist canon manuscripts, but Buddhism itself affected him no more than were he cataloging a rare specifies of Himalayan butterfly. As for the value those texts might have for an actual human being, Hodgson insisted that he had "no purpose to meddle with the interminable sheer absurdities of the Bauddha [that is, Buddhist] religion or philosophy."

A half-century later Alexandra David-Neel was interested only in the "absurdities of Buddhist philosophy," which she found not absurd at all. Following in her footsteps, the Englishman John Blofeld (1913–1987) asked questions of Buddhism that were the polar opposites of Hodgson's: like David-Neel, he wanted to know what the religion could and would do for him personally. In Peking, Blofeld met a venerated Tibetan lama, and the lama, amazed that someone from "the Western ocean" was interested in Buddhism, volunteered to answer any of his questions. All Blofeld's queries were on the order of "Which form of meditation is best for a beginner like myself?"—questions that were practically unheard of from a European then but which are quite commonplace today. The door was opened; the western adventure with Buddhism had begun.

●   ●   ●   ●

The writer-adventurers of Part I—Alexandra David-Neel, John Blofeld, Peter Goullart, Lama Anagarika Govinda, and Janwillem van de Wetering—when taken in sequence, reenact in a small chronological span the whole history of religion. Max Weber, the so-called father of sociology, wrote the equivalent of a giant historical canvas. In the beginning was the "age of magic," when nightmare stalked the earth, but for all its terrors, the spacious lack of any scientific boundaries made it seem that anything possible to imagine happening could happen, as in a children's story. The age of magic was followed, in Weber's schema, by charismatic religious leaders. Perhaps in the political arena Franklin Roosevelt or, earlier, Lincoln resembled those heroic visionaries whose very presence changed the chemistry of the times; certainly the great religious figures (Muhammad, Joan of Arc, Gandhi) had personalities that seemingly could replace or embody a better version of the laws. The age of heroes then yielded to the present age of bureaucracy, where religious leader and layman alike subscribe to the common rules. Everyone alive today, attempting to eke out a life among all the cramped regulations, understands this period only too well. To go from Alexandra David-Neel to John Blofeld and Lama Govinda, and from them to Peter Goullart and Janwillem van de Wetering, is to witness these various ages follow one another in quick succession and, in effect, to relive two thousand years of religious history, but compressed into two generations.

Alexandra David-Neel's most important book is *Magic and Mystery in Tibet*. Despite its kooky period-piece title, David-Neel was a Cartesian skeptic who rationally disproved most of the supposed magic she encountered in Tibet. Even so, too much was left over, and she experienced so many scientifically unexplainable phenomena that she half hid them between the lines, to appear credible to modern readers. Indeed, David-Neel's Tibet of the 1910s and 1920s resurrects a kingdom perhaps not uncommon five hundred years ago, and anybody like her, and anything like what she experienced there, will surely never be seen again. Adieu, the Age of Magic.

A generation later, John Blofeld and Lama Govinda (1898–1985) stand halfway between her quasi-shamanic milieu of demi-marvels and our own period of, well, something more tame and mundane. The fabled lamas they met were hardly the unbelievable sorcerers and wizards who populate the outer margins of history; they were ordinary flesh-and-blood men, only with more charismatic presence. Tomo Geshe specifically warned Govinda: "Do not look upon my person as the Guru because every human personality has its shortcomings." Yet Tomo Geshe and Blofeld's Dorje Lama did seem able to read other people's thoughts like magazines casually left open, and if they could not fly through the air they did make all difficulties and worries fly away. "Merely to be in this man [Tomo Geshe]'s presence seemed to be enough to dissolve all problems," Govinda observed, "to make them non-existent, like darkness in the presence of light." Govinda's and Blofeld's adventures still trail clouds from a faintly earlier period, where the inhabitants were not magi but nonetheless wore richer robes and were capable of more surprising actions.

Peter Goullart (1902–1978) never chanced upon spiritual figures possessed of power and numinous aura. He describes instead how courteous and appealing ordinary people and societies become when based on the old esoteric Buddhist teachings. The human interactions he witnessed in out-of-the-way Sino-Tibetan borderlands—full of pleasure, tact, aesthetics, and endearing human foibles—came close, he felt, to making unexpected and unlikely human paradises. (All those societies have subsequently vanished, in the historical conflagrations that transfigured half of Asia.)

Finally, in the late 1950s, the Dutchman Janwillem van de Wetering undertook a spiritual journey, too, but it transpired not quite but nearly in the mundane realm of the everyday. When van de Wetering joined a Zen monastery in Kyoto, he imagined he was relocating to an unknown and unpredictable world of stoic enchantment. And in fact he does execute a deft piece of magic—once: after two years' training in meditation, on a train he attempted to influence a stranger's actions by mental telepathy and briefly succeeded, much to the other person's and his own embarrassment. But, as for anything else magical or charismatic, that was it. The monasteries and temples van de Wetering knew in Kyoto still exist, and one can enter them still; with him we have almost entered the present moment. When he quit the monastery, although he valued his training there, it had not made of him a Buddhist, and his experiences there were, he believed, no different than those that folks in the outside world have.

●   ●   ●   ●

Alexandra David-Neel's Tibet, Lama Govinda's India, and Blofeld's and Goullart's China were separated by immense distances, and their time-periods in Asia did not precisely overlap: those four resemble lonely marbles rolling over vast terrains, where it was all but impossible that they should ever have bumped into each other. Yet, at least on a symbolic level, their stories do connect, almost as though each was unknowingly passing the baton. David-Neel learned Tibetan Buddhism by apprenticing herself to a hermit (or *gomchen*), who reluctantly came out of his retreat and grudgingly agreed to teach her. A score of years later, shortly before the Hermit died, Govinda undertook a pilgrimage to his remote cave: he discovered it littered with newspaper articles and clippings about David-Neel, and Govinda realized that the Hermit had intended her to propagate Buddhism all along. Just as Govinda had sought out David-

Neel's teacher, so at the end of Govinda's life Blofeld sought out him. Blofeld was exhilarated by their meeting, for Govinda offered proof positive that a westerner could go the distance in Buddhism as fully as any Oriental-born sage.

Peter Goullart—nearly nothing is known about Goullart, save what he tells us in his own writings. (No library in America can inform you, for instance, when Goullart died. Only a very, very old gentleman in whose house he died at Holland Park in Singapore; I, the editor; and now you, the reader, know that missing date.) Goullart wound up in so many of Blofeld's haunts in Asia, though, that they surely knew of, even if they did not know, each other, and they had acquaintances in common. Rather than four isolated figures, David-Neel, Govinda, Blofeld, and Goullart seem characters in different acts of the same drama.

Janwillem van de Wetering could read about that drama in their books, but arriving later in Asia, he knew personally none of them. Van de Wetering is very much alive, though, active and involved and writing, and he still gives talks and public readings—so we can, if we wish, meet and know him. The lineage continues, as it were, and in Part II—"the era of you and me"—the circle will come round.

Chapter I

. . . .

Tibet as It Once Was

Alexandra David-Neel

In all those centuries when Tibet was off-limits to foreigners, the first European to penetrate its forbidden terrain and to explore its unknown religion was also the last to do so thoroughly. Alexandra David-Neel (1868–1969) mastered Tibetan fluently and thus could spend a dozen years in and around Tibet, masked in disguises ranging from a learned lama to an old beggar woman. She represented a new kind of religious investigator, the very opposite of those earlier seekers who expected to see monks flying blithely through the air. David-Neel was determined to find rational explanations for supposedly miraculous phenomena, yet for a skeptic she was nonetheless oddly intrigued by religion. Under the guidance of a Tibetan hermit sage at his remote snowbound cave, she studied the tantric arts of Tibet, such as tuomo *(or body heat-control), which later saved her life when she roamed lost in the frozen Himalayas. When she was fifty-five, then considered old age, she undertook a six-month march on foot to Lhasa—with a single companion and carrying no provisions (so to avoid detection and expulsion)—which for near-suicidal audacity equals any daredevil expedition in history.* My Journey to Lhasa *(1927) made her world famous. Today, if a contemporary wants to "visit" the religion of old Tibet, it is mainly through her writings (particularly in* Magic and Mystery in Tibet, *1929) that such a journey can be vicariously made. At a certain point she did throw down her pen and exclaim, "I can write no more," but that was eighteen days before she died, shortly before her hundred-and-first birthday.*

The Beginning:
A Visit with the Dalai Lama

Political reasons had, at that time, led the Dalai Lama to seek refuge in British territory. It had seemed to me a unique opportunity, while he was stopping at the Indian frontier, of obtaining an interview and getting information from him about the special type of Buddhism that prevails in Tibet.

Very few strangers have ever approached the monk-king hidden in his sacred city, in the Land of Snows. Even in exile, he saw no one. Up to the time of my visit, he had obstinately refused an audience to any woman except Tibetans and I believe, even to this day, that I am the only exception to this rule.

As I left Darjeeling, in the early rosy dawn of a cool spring morning, I little guessed the far-reaching consequences of my request.

I thought of a short excursion, of an interesting but brief interview; while, actually, I became involved in wanderings that kept me in Asia for a full fourteen years.

At the beginning of that long series of journeys, the Dalai Lama figures, in my diaries, as an obliging host who, seeing a stranger without the walls, invites him to see over his domain.

This, the Dalai Lama did in a few words: "Learn the Tibetan language," he told me.

If one could believe his subjects who call him the "Omniscient,"* the sovereign of Tibet, when giving me this advice, foresaw its conse-

---

* *Thamstched mkyenpa*

quences, and consciously directed me, not only towards Lhasa, his forbidden capital, but towards the mystic masters and unknown magicians yet more closely hidden in his wonderland.

At Kalimpong, the lama-king lived in a large house belonging to the minister of the Rajah of Bhutan. To give the place a more majestic appearance, two roles of tall bamboo poles had been planted in the form of an avenue. Flags flew from every pole, with the inscription *Aum mani padme hum!*

The suite of the exiled sovereign was numerous and included more than a hundred servants. They were for the most part engaged in interminable gossip, and quiet reigned round the habitation. But on fête days, or when visitors of rank were to be received, a crowd of busy officials and domestics poured out from all sides, peering at one another from every window, crossing and re-crossing the large plot of ground in front of the house, hurrying, screaming, agitated, and all so remarkably alike in their dirty, greasy robes, that a stranger could easily make awkward mistakes about their rank.

The splendour, decorum and etiquette of the Potala [the Dalai Lama's palace in Lhasa] were absent in that land of exile. Those who saw this road-side camp, where the Head of the Tibetan theocracy waited for his subjects to reconquer his throne, could not imagine what the Court at Lhasa was like.

The British expedition penetrating into the forbidden territory and parading his capital, in spite of the sorcery of the most famous magicians, had probably led the Dalai Lama to understand that foreign barbarians were masters in a material sense, by right of force. The inventions that he noticed during his trip through India must have convinced him of their ability to enslave and mould the material elements of nature. But his conviction that the white race is mentally inferior remained unshaken. And, in this, he only shared the opinion of all Asiatics—from Ceylon to the northern confines of Mongolia.

A Western woman acquainted with Buddhist doctrines seemed to him an inconceivable phenomenon.

If I had vanished into space while talking to him, he would have been less astonished. My reality surprised him most; but, when finally convinced, he politely inquired after my "Master," assuming I could only have learned of Buddha from an Asiatic. It was not easy to convince him that the Tibetan text of one of the most esteemed Buddhist books had been translated into French before I was born. "Ah well," he murmured at last, "if a few strangers have really learned our language and read our sacred books, they must have missed the meaning of them."

This was my chance. I hastened to seize it.

"It is precisely because I suspect that certain religious doctrines of Tibet have been misunderstood that I have come to you to be enlightened," I said.

My reply pleased the Dalai Lama. He readily answered any questions I put to him, and a little later gave me a long written explanation of the various subjects we had discussed.

The large number of people who came to Kalimpong to be touched by the Dalai Lama gave me some idea of his widespread prestige.

The procession took several hours to pass before him, and I noticed that not only Lamaists but many people from Nepal and from Bengal, belonging to Hindu sects, had joined the crowd.

I saw some, who had come only to look on, suddenly seized by an occult fervour, hurrying to join the pious flock.

As I was watching this scene, my eyes fell on a man seated on the ground, a little to one side. His matted hair was wound around his head like a turban, in the style common to Hindu ascetics. Yet, his features were not those of an Indian and he was wearing dirty and much-torn lamaist monastic garments.

This tramp had placed a small bag beside him and seemed to observe the crowd with a cynical expression. I pointed him out to my translator Dawasandup, asking him if he had any idea who this Himalayan Diogenes might be. "It must be a travelling *naljorpa*,"* he answered; and

Naljorpa (written *rnal hbyorpa*), literally: "He who has attained perfect serenity," but usually interpreted: an ascetic possessing magic powers.

seeing my curiosity, my obliging interpreter went to the man and entered
into conversation with him. He returned to me with a serious face and
said "This lama is a peripatetic ascetic from Bhutan. He lives here and
there in caves, empty houses or under the trees. He has been stopping for
several days in a small monastery near here."

I had no definite plan for the afternoon, why should I not go to the
gompa (monastery) where he was staying, and persuade him to talk? Was
he really mocking, as he seemed to be, at the Dalai Lama and the faithful?
And if so, why? There might be interesting reasons.

I communicated my desire to Dawasandup, who agreed to accompany
me. We went on horseback and soon reached the gompa, which was only a
large-sized country house. In the lha khang (the room containing the holy
images) we found the naljorpa seated upon a cushion in front of a low
table, finishing his meal. Cushions were brought and we were offered tea.

It was difficult to begin a conversation with the ascetic, as his mouth
appeared to be full of rice; he had only answered our polite greetings,
with a kind of grunt.

I was trying to find a phrase to break the ice, when the strange fellow
began to laugh and muttered a few words. Dawansandup seemed
embarrassed.

"What does he say?" I asked.

"Excuse me," answered the interpreter, "these naljorpas sometimes
speak roughly. I do not know if I should translate."

"Please do," I replied. "I am here to take notes; especially of anything
at all curious and original."

"Well, then—excuse me—he said, 'What is this idiot here for?' "

Such rudeness did not greatly astonish me as, in India also, certain
yogis make a habit of insulting anyone who approaches them. "Tell him I
have come to ask why he mocked at the crowd seeking the benediction of
the Dalai Lama."

"Puffed up with a sense of their own importance and the importance
of what they are doing. Insects fluttering in the dung," muttered the
naljorpa between his teeth.

This was vague, but the kind of language one expects from such men. "And you," I replied, "are you free from all defilement?"

He laughed noisily. "He who tries to get out only sinks in deeper. I roll in it like a pig. I digest it and turn it into golden dust, into a brook of pure water. To fashion stars out of dog dung, that is the Great work!"

Evidently my friend was enjoying himself. This was his way of posing as a superman.

"Are these pilgrims not right, to profit by the presence of the Dalai Lama and obtain his blessing? They are simple folk incapable of aspiring to the knowledge of the higher doctrines—"

But the *naljorpa* interrupted me. "For a blessing to be efficacious, he who gives it must possess the power that he professes to communicate. Would the Precious Protector (the Dalai Lama) need soldiers to fight the Chinese or other enemies if he possesses such a power? Could he not drive anyone he liked out of the country and surround Tibet with an invisible barrier that none could pass? I am only a humble disciple, and yet—"

It appeared to me that the "humble disciple" was maybe a little mad and certainly very conceited, for his "and yet" had been accompanied by a glance that suggested many things.

My interpreter meanwhile was visibly uneasy. He profoundly respected the Dalai Lama and disliked to hear him criticized. On the other hand, the man who could "create stars out of dog dung" inspired him with a superstitious fear.

I proposed to leave, but as I understood that the lama was going away the next morning, I handed Dawasandup a few rupees for the traveller to help him on his way. The present displeased the *naljorpa*. He refused it, saying he had already received more provisions than he could carry.

Dawasandup thought it right to insist. He took a few steps forward, intending to place the money on a table near the lama. Then I saw him stagger, fall backward and strike his back against the wall as if he had been violently pushed. He uttered a cry and clutched at his stomach. The *naljorpa* got up and, sneering, left the room.

"I feel as if I have received a terrible blow," said Dawasandup. "The lama is irritated. How shall we appease him?"

"Let us go," I answered. "The lama has probably nothing to do with it. You, perhaps, have heart trouble and had better consult a doctor."

Pale and troubled, the interpreter answered nothing. Indeed there was nothing to be said. We returned, but I was not able to reassure him.

Conversations with a Prince and with Hermit Monks

The young heir to the throne of Sikkim, Sidkeong Tulku, had met David-Neel in northern India and invited her to visit him in his fairy-talelike kingdom. Sidkeong Tulku was reforming the lax, corrupted Buddhism of his country, and David-Neel, in the robes of a lamina, or lady-lama, joined him in that project: she became that nonpareil, a western woman lecturing Buddhist monks about their own religion. Here began her experience with people—remote hermits, magicians, and lamas—that few, if any, Europeans had ever encountered before.

A *gomchen* whom I got to know when visiting Sikkim was of an uncommunicative character and rather haughty in his manners. Even the customary formulas of politeness which he was compelled to utter were tinged with a peculiar icy coldness. He was called after the place where he lived—Daling *gomchen.*

He always wore the regular monastic robes and toga but with the addition of earrings of ivory, and a silver *dorje* studded with torquoises stuck in his hair. This lama spent the whole summer of every year in a cabin built for him on the top of a woody mountain.

A few days before his arrival, his disciples and the villagers round about would carry into the hermitage enough provisions for three or four months. After this, they were absolutely forbidden to approach the *gomchen*'s dwelling. The lama had no difficulty in getting them to respect his solitude. The country people did not doubt that he practised dreadful rites to trap demons and compel them to give up their mischievous designs against the persons or the possessions of those who worshipped him. His protection greatly reassured them, but they feared that if they went near his hut they might chance to meet some malignant beings answering unwillingly the *gomchen's* summons and not in pleasant mood. Moreover, the mystery which always surrounds the conduct, as well as the character, of the *naljorpas*, inspired them with prudence.

Little inclined as this lama was to answer my questions the desire expressed by the prince—to whom he owed his appointment as head of the small monastery of Daling—compelled him to depart somewhat from his reserve.

Among other subjects that I approached in my talk with him was that of the food permitted to a Buddhist. "Should we interpret the command not to kill sophistically and continue to eat meat and fish?" I asked.

The *gomchen*, like most Tibetans, was not a vegetarian. He expounded a theory on this subject which I heard again in other parts of Tibet and which is not altogether lacking in originality.

"Most men," he said, "eat like beasts, to satisfy their hunger without pondering upon the act they are accomplishing nor upon its consequences. Such ignorant people do well to abstain from eating meat and fish.

"Others consider what becomes of the material elements they absorb when eating animals. They know that the assimilation of these elements involves the assimilation of the psychic elements which are inherent in them. Anyone who has acquired that knowledge may, at his risk and peril, contract these associations and endeavour himself to obtain results useful to the victims sacrificed.

"The question is to find out whether the animal elements which he absorbs strengthen the animal propensities of the man, or whether this man will be capable of transmuting these elements into intellectual and spiritual forces, so that the substance of the animal passing into the man will be reborn in the form of human activity."

I then asked him if this explained the esoteric sense of the belief com-

mon among Tibetans, that the lamas can send the spirits of the slaugh-
tered animals to the Paradise of the Great Bliss.

"Do not think that I can answer your question in a few words," he
replied. "The subject is intricate. Animals have several 'consciousnesses,'
just as we have ourselves, and as it also happens in our case, these 'consciousnesses' do not all follow the same road after death. A living being is
an assemblage, not a unity. But one must have been initiated by a proper
master before being able to realize these doctrines."

Often the lama cut his explanations short by this declaration.

One evening, when the prince, Daling lama and I were together in the
bungalow of Kewzing, the conversation was about mystic ascetics. With
a repressed enthusiasm that was most impressive, the *gomchen* spoke of
his master, of his wisdom, of his supernormal powers. Sidkeong *tulku*
was deeply moved by the profound veneration of the lama for his spiritual teacher.

At that time the prince was full of cares on account of his contemplated marriage with a Burman princess. "I regret very much that I cannot meet this great *naljorpa*," he said to me in English. "For he, certainly,
would give me good advice."

And addressing the *gomchen* he repeated, in Tibetan: "I am sorry that
your master is not here. I really need the advice of some such clairvoyant
sage." But he did not mention the question he wished to ask, nor the
nature of his preoccupations.

The lama with his usual coldness of manner asked: "Is the subject
serious?"

"It is extremely important," the prince replied.

"You can perhaps receive the desired advice," said Daling *gomchen*.

I thought that he meant to send a letter by a messenger and was about
to remind him of the great distance that would have to be covered, when
his aspect struck me.

He had closed his eyes and was rapidly turning pale, his body stiffening.
I wished to go to him, thinking he was ill, but the prince, who had
observed the sudden change in the lama, held me back, whispering:

"Don't move. *Gomchens* sometimes go into a trance quite suddenly. One must not wake them, for that is very dangerous and might even kill them."

So I stayed seated watching the lama who remained motionless. Gradually his features changed, his face wrinkled, taking on an expression I had never seen him wear before. He opened his eyes and the prince made a startled gesture.

The man we were looking at was not the *gomchen* of Daling, but someone we did not know. He moved his lips with difficulty and said in a voice different from that of the *gomchen:* "Do not be disturbed. This question will never have to be considered by you."

Then he slowly closed his eyes, his features changed again and became those of Daling lama who slowly recovered his senses. He eluded our questions and retired in silence, staggering and seeming to be broken with fatigue.

"There is no sense in his answer," the prince concluded.

Whether by chance or for some other reason, it unfortunately proved that there had been a meaning in these words. The matter troubling the young maharajah was about his fiancée and an affair with a girl who had borne him a son which he did not wish to break off when he married. But, truly, he needed not to ponder over his course of conduct toward the two women, for he died before the day arranged for the marriage.

I happened also to see two hermits of a peculiar type which I did not meet again in Tibet where, on the whole, the natives are more civilized than in the Himalayas.

I was returning with the prince *tulku* from an excursion to the frontier of Nepal. His servants, knowing that he liked to show me the "religious curiosities" of his country, pointed out the presence of two hermits in the mountains near the village where we had spent the night.

The peasants said that these men had hidden themselves so cleverly that no one had seen them for several years. A supply of food was placed from time to time under a rock, at a chosen spot where the anchorites would take it at night. As to the huts they had built themselves, none knew where they were, nor did anyone try to discover them. For if the hermits were anxious to avoid being seen, the superstitious villagers were even more anxious to keep at a distance from them and turned away from the wood they inhabited.

Sidkeong *tulku* had freed himself from fear of sorcery. He ordered his servants together with a number of peasants to beat up the forest and bring the hermits to him. The latter should be well treated and presents promised to them, but great care must be taken that they did not escape.

The hunt was strenuous. The two anchorites, surprised in their quiet retreat, tried to run away, but with twenty men on their track they were finally captured. They had to be forcibly made to enter the small temple where we were waiting with several lamas—among whom was the *gom-chen* of Sakyong. Once there, no one could get a word out of them.

I have never seen such strange human creatures. Both men were frightfully dirty, scarcely covered by a few rags, their long hair, thick as brushwood, covered their faces and their eyes shot out sparks like a brazier.

While they looked around them like wild beasts newly caught in a cage, the prince caused two large wicker baskets to be brought. These were filled with tea, meat, barley-flour, rice and sundries. He told the hermits that he meant to give all this to them. But in spite of this agreeable prospect they remained silent. A villager then said that he thought he had understood that when the anchorites came to live on that hill they were under a vow of silence.

His Highness, who was prey to sudden attacks of truly Oriental despotism, replied that they might at least bow to him as it is the custom and adopt a more respectful attitude. I saw his anger rising and, to avoid trouble brewing for the wild "holy ones," I begged him to allow them to retire. He first resisted my request, but I insisted.

In the meantime I had told one of my servants to bring two bags of crystallized sugar taken from my luggage—Tibetans are very fond of it—I placed one bag in each basket.

"Open the door, and let these animals out," the prince commanded at last.

As soon as they saw a chance of escape, the hermits pounced on the baskets. One of them hastily pulled something from under his rags, plunged his claw-like hand in my hair; and then both of them flew away like hares. I found a little amulet in my hair which I showed to my friends and, later on, to some lamas who were conversant in the science of charms. All agreed in telling me that far from being harmful, the amulet secured me the company of a demon who would drive away any dangers on my road and serve me. I could only be pleased. Perhaps the hermit had understood that I begged for him and his companion to be set free, and his strange gift was a token of gratitude.

Meeting a Great Hermit. Becoming a Hermit Myself

There was not much more for me to learn from the lamas. Perhaps in normal times I would have left the country for China or Japan, but the war which had begun in Europe made it rather dangerous to cross seas ploughed by submarines.

I was considering where I should spend the winter, when a few days after my arrival at Tangu, I learned that the *gomchen* of Lachen was in his hermitage, half a day's march from the bungalow. I immediately decided to pay him a visit. The excursion could not help being interesting. What sort of life did he live there?—I was curious to know. No incident marked the trip. Through mountain paths that wound about the woody height, I reached a clearing two days later at the foot of a very steep and barren mountainside that was crowned by an indented ridge of black rocks.

A little farther up a number of flags showed the place of the hermitage.

The lama came half-way down to welcome me. Then he led me through the loops of the winding path not to his own dwelling, but to another hermitage about a mile away below his own. He had a large pot of buttered tea brought there and a fire lighted on the ground, in the centre of the room.

The word room might prove misleading, for it was not in a house that the *gomchen* showed me this hospitality. We were in a small-sized cave closed by a wall of uncemented stones, in which two narrow gaping holes less than ten inches high served for windows. A few boards, roughly hewn with an axe, and bound together with strips of supple bark, formed the door.

My servants spread my blankets on the bare rock, and the *gomchen* took them to sleep in a hut which, he said, was just beside his cave. I went in and lay down. I had scarcely time to roll myself in my blankets before the light flickered and went out. The servants had forgotten to fill the lantern with kerosene. I could find no matches at hand and being unacquainted with the formation of my prehistoric dwelling I did not dare to move for fear of hurting myself on some pointed rocks.

A bitter breeze began to blow in through the "windows" and the cracks of the door. A star peeped at me through the gap facing my ascetic couch: "Do you feel comfortable?" it seemed to say. "What do you think of a hermit's life?"

"Yes, I am all right," I answered. "Thousand times better than all right . . . ravished, and I feel that the hermit's life, free of what we call 'the goods and pleasures of the world,' is the most wonderful of all lives."

Then the star shone more brightly and growing larger, lighted the whole cave.

That I may be capable of dying in this hermitage
And my wish be accomplished,

it seemed to say, quoting the verses of Milarepa.

The next day I went up to the hermitage of the *gomchen*. This too was a cave, but larger and better furnished than mine. The whole ground under the arched rocky roof had been enclosed by a wall of uncemented stones and provided with a solid door. This entrance room served as a kitchen. At the back of it a natural opening in the rock led into a diminutive grotto. There the *gomchen* had his living room. A wooden step led to the entrance, for it was higher than the kitchen, and a heavy multicoloured curtain hid the doorway.

The furniture consisted of several wooden chests piled up behind a curtain which formed the back of the anchorite's couch, which was made of large hard cushions placed on the ground. In front of it were two low tables, mere slabs of wood set up on feet, painted in bright colours. Scrolls of religious painting completely covered the rocky uneven walls. Under one of these was hidden the small cabinet in which lamas of the tantric sects keep a demon prisoner. Outside the cave, half sheltered under protuberant rocks, two cabins had been built that served to store the provisions. As you can see, the *gomchen's* dwelling was not entirely lacking in comfort.

This eyrie commanded a romantic and absolutely solitary site. The natives held it to be inhabited by evil spirits. Such spots are often chosen as dwelling-places by Tibetan hermits. Firstly they deem them a suitable ground for spiritual training. Secondly, they think that they find, there, the opportunity of using their magic powers for the good of men and animals, either by converting malignant evil spirits or by forcibly preventing their harmful activity—at least, simple people ascribe their charitable desire to these "holy ones."

I spent a week in my cave, visiting the *gomchen* each day. Though his conversation was full of interest, I was still far more interested in watching the daily life of a Tibetan anchorite. A few Westerners such as Csöma de Köros or the French Rev. Fathers Huc and Gabet have sojourned in lamaist monasteries, but none has lived with these *gomchens* about whom so many fantastic stories are told. This was reason enough to incite me to stay in the neighbourhood of the *gomchen*. Added to this was my keen desire to myself experience the contemplative life according to lamaist methods.

However, my wish did not suffice, the consent of the lama was needed. If he did not grant it, there would be no advantage in living near his hermitage. He would shut himself up and I could only look at a wall of rock behind which "something was going on."

So I presented my request to the lama in a manner that agreed with Oriental customs. I begged that he would instruct me in the doctrine he professed. He objected that his knowledge was not extensive enough and that it was useless for me to stay in such an inhospitable region to listen to an ignorant man, when I had had the opportunity of long talks with learned lamas elsewhere.

I strongly insisted, however, and he decided to admit me, not exactly as a pupil, but on a trial as a novice, for a certain time.

I began to thank him, when he interrupted me.

"Wait," he said, "there is a condition; you must promise me that you will not return to Gangtok, nor undertake any journey toward the south without my permission."*

The adventure was becoming exciting. The strangeness of it aroused my enthusiasm. "I promise," I answered without hesitating.

A rough cabin was added to my cave. Like that of the *gomchen,* it was built of planks roughly hewn with an axe. The mountaineers of this country do not know how to use a saw, nor did they, at that time, care to learn. A few yards away, another hut was built, containing a small private room for Yongden [a young monk, later her adopted son] and a lodging for our servants.

In enlarging my hermitage, I was not altogether yielding to sybaritic tendencies. It would have been difficult for me to fetch water and fuel and to carry these burdens up to my cave. Yongden, who had just left school, was no more experienced than I at this kind of work. We could not do without servants to help us, therefore an ample supply of provision and a store-house was indispensable since we were facing a long winter during which we should remain completely isolated.

Now these things seem to me small difficulties, but at that time I was making my "debut" in the role of anchorite, and Yongden had not yet begun his apprenticeship as explorer.

The days passed. Winter came, spreading a coat of immaculate snow on the whole country and, as we had expected, blocking the valleys that led to the foot of our mountain.

The *gomchen* shut himself up for a long retreat. I did the same thing.

* To go southward meant to go to Gangtok or to Kalimpong, where a few foreigners reside, or to follow a road sometimes frequented by Western tourists coming to these hills from India.

My single daily meal was placed behind a curtain at the entrance of my hut. The boy who brought it and who later carried away the empty plates left in silence, without having seen me.

My life resembled that of the Carthusians without the diversion which they may find in attendance at religious services.

A bear appeared in search of food and after its first feelings of astonishment and defiance were over, grew accustomed to coming and waiting for bread and other eatable things that were thrown to it.

At last, toward the beginning of April, one of the boys noticed a black spot moving in the clearing beneath us and cried out: "a man!" just as early navigators must have cried "land ahead!" We were no longer blocked in; letters arrived that had been written in Europe five months before.

Then it was springtime in the cloudy Himalayas. Nine hundred feet below my cave rhododendrons blossomed. I climbed barren mountaintops. Long tramps led me to desolate valleys studded with translucent lakes. . . . Solitude, solitude! . . . Mind and senses develop their sensibility in this contemplative life made up of continual observations and reflections. Does one become a visionary or, rather, is it not that one has been blind until then? . . .

What were the fruits of my long retreat? I should have found it difficult to explain, yet I learnt a number of things.

Apart from my study of the Tibetan language with the help of grammars, dictionaries and talks with the *gomchen,* I also read with him the lives of famous Tibetan mystics. He would often stop our reading to tell me about facts he had himself witnessed, which were akin to the stories related in the books. He would describe people he had known, repeating their conversations and telling me about their lives. Thus, while seated in his cabin or in mine, I visited the palaces of rich lamas, entered the hermitages of many an ascetic. I travelled along the roads, meeting curious people. I became, in that way, closely acquainted with Tibet, its inhabitants, their customs and their thoughts: a precious science which was later on to stand me in good stead.

I never let myself be taken in by the illusion that my anchorite's home might become my final harbour. Too many causes opposed any desire of staying there and of laying down, once and for all, the burden of foolish ideas, routine cares and duties to which, like other Westerners, I still fancied myself to be bound.

I knew that the personality of a *gomchenma* which I had taken on, could only be an episode in my life as a traveller, or at the best, a preparation for future liberation.

Sadly, almost with terror, I often looked at the threadlike path which I saw, lower down, winding in the valleys and disappearing between the mountains. The day would come when it would lead me back to the sorrowful world that existed beyond the distant hill ranges, and so thinking, an indescribable suffering lay hold of me.

My Surprising Encounters with Two Reincarnations

With access via India blocked, after leaving Sikkim and India David-Neel entered Tibet through the "back door," through a long arduous route through remote rural China. She soon arrived at the monastery of Kum-Bum. Although Kum-Bum was indeed a celebrated monastery, it lay far enough from Lhasa (a many-months-long journey then) that she could stay there for three years, without fear of expulsion from the central authorities. There she encountered examples of reincarnation so dramatic and seemingly irrefutable as scarcely to be admitted into her rational European worldview.

Countless tales are told throughout Tibet about extraordinary proofs of memory from previous lives and wonders worked by young *tulkus* to testify their identity. We find in them the habitual Tibetan mixture of superstition, cunning, comedy, and disconcerting events. I could relate dozens of them, but I prefer to confine myself to the relation of facts connected with people whom I have personally known.

Next at the mansion of the Pegyai Lama, in which I lived at Kum-Bum, was the dwelling of a minor *tulku* called Agnai tsang. Seven years had elapsed since the death of the last master of the place and none had been able to discover the child in whom he had reincarnated. I do not think that the steward of the lama's household felt greatly afflicted by that circumstance. He managed the estate and seemed rather prosperous.

Now it happened that in the course of a trading tour, he felt tired and thirsty and entered a farm to rest and drink. While the housewife made tea the *nierpa* (steward) drew a jade snuff-box from his pocket and was about to take a pinch of snuff when a little boy who had been playing in a corner of the room stopped him and putting his small hand on the box asked reproachfully: "Why do you use my snuff-box?"

The steward was thunderstruck. Truly, the precious snuff-box was not his, but belonged to the departed Agnai tsang, and though he had not perhaps exactly intended to steal it, yet he had taken possession of it.

He remained there trembling while the boy looked at him as his face suddenly became grave and stern, with no longer anything childish about it. "Give it back to me at once, it is mine," he said again.

Stung with remorse, and at the same time terrified and bewildered, the superstitious monk could only fall on his knees and prostrate himself before his reincarnated master.

A few days later, I saw the boy coming in state to his mansion. He wore a yellow brocade robe* and rode a beautiful black pony, the *nierpa* holding the bridle. When the procession entered the house the boy remarked: "Why do we turn to the left to reach the second courtyard? The gate is on our right side."

Now, for some reason, the gate on the right side had been walled up after the death of the lama and another one opened instead.

The monks marvelled at this new proof of the authenticity of their lama and all proceeded to his private apartment where tea was to be served. The boy, seated on a pile of large hard cushions, looked at the cup with silver-gilt saucer and jewelled cover placed on the table before him.

*As he had not yet been admitted into the religious order, he was not allowed to wear the ecclesiastic robes.

"Give me the larger china cup," he commanded. And he described one, mentioning the very pattern that decorated it.

Nobody knew about such a cup, not even the steward, and the monks respectfully endeavoured to convince the young master that there was no cup of that kind in the house.

It was at that moment that, taking advantage of an already long acquaintance with the *nierpa*, I entered the room. I had heard the snuff-box story and wished to see for myself, my remarkable little new neighbour. I offered him the customary complimentary scarf and a few presents. These he received with a gracious smile but, apparently following the trend of his thoughts regarding the cup, he said: "Look better, you will find it."

And suddenly, as if a flash of memory had dashed through his mind, he added explanations about a box painted in such a colour, which was in such a place in the store-room.

Less than half an hour later, the set, cup, saucer and cover, was discovered in a casket that was at the bottom of the very box described by the boy. "I did not know of the existence of that cup," the steward told me later on. "The lama himself, or my predecessor, must have put it in that box which did not contain anything else precious and had not been opened for years."

I also witnessed a much more striking and fantastic discovery of a *tulku* in the poor inn of a hamlet, some miles distant from Ansi.

Roads going from Mongolia to Tibet cross, in that region, the long highway which extends from Peking to Russia over a whole continent. So I felt annoyed but not astonished when, reaching the inn at sunset, I found it crowded with visitors from a Mongolian caravan.

The men looked rather excited as if something unusual had just happened. Yet, with their customary courtesy still increased by the sight of the lamaist monastic garments which lama Yongden and I wore, the travelers immediately gave up a room for my party and made room for my beasts in the stable.

As Yongden and I remained in the courtyard, looking at the camels of the Mongolians, the door of one of the rooms opened and a tall hand-some youth, poorly clad in a Tibetan robe, stood on the threshold and asked if we were Tibetans. We answered in the affirmative. Then a well-dressed elderly lama appeared behind the young man and he, also, addressed us in Tibetan.

As usual, we exchanged questions about the country from which we came and where we were going. The lama said that he had intended going to Lhasa by the Suchow winter road, but now, he added, it was no longer necessary to take this journey. The Mongolian servants who were in the courtyard nodded their assent.

I wondered what could have caused these people to change their minds while *en route,* but as the lama retired to his room, I did not deem it polite to follow and ask explanations that were not offered. However, later in the evening, when they had inquired about Yongden and me from our servants, the Mongolians invited us to drink tea with them and I heard the whole story.

The handsome young man was a native of the far distant Ngari province (in South-western Tibet). He seemed to be somewhat of a visionary. At least, most Westerners would have so described him, but we were in Asia.

Since his early youth, Migyur—this was his name—had been restless, haunted by the queer idea that *he was not where he ought to be.* He felt him-self a foreigner in his village, a foreigner in his family. In dreams, he saw landscapes that did not exist in Ngari: sandy solitudes, round felt tents, a monastery on a hillock. And even when awake, the same subjective images appeared to him and superimposed themselves in his material surroundings, veiling them, creating around him a perpetual mirage.

He was only a boy when he ran away, unable to resist the desire of finding the reality of his vision. Since then, Migyur had been a vagrant, working a little here and there on his way, begging most times, wander-ing at random without being able to control his restlessness or settle any-where. Today he had arrived from Aric, tramping aimlessly as usual.

He saw the inn, the encampment of the caravan, the camels in the courtyard. Without knowing why, he crossed the gate, and found himself face to face with the lama and his party. Then, with the rapidity of lightning, past events flashed through his mind. He remembered that very lama as a young man, his disciple, and himself as an already aged lama, both on that very road, returning from a pilgrimage to the holy places of Tibet and going home to the monastery on the hillock.

He reminded the lama of all these things, giving minute details regarding their journey, their lives in the distant monastery and many other particulars.

Now the aim of the Mongolians' journey was precisely to beg advice from the Dalai Lama as to the best way of discovering the *tulku* head of their monastery, whose seat had been unoccupied for more than twenty years, in spite of persevering efforts to find his reincarnation. These superstitious people were ready to believe that the Dalai Lama, through his supernormal power, had detected their intention and out of kindness had caused their meeting with their reincarnated lord.

The Ngari wanderer complied immediately with the usual test, picking out without hesitation or mistake, among a number of similar objects, those that had belonged to the late lama.

No doubt subsisted in the mind of the Mongolians. On the morrow, I saw the caravan retracing its steps, moving away to the slow pace of the big camels and disappearing on the skyline into the Gobi solitude. The new *tulku* was going to meet his fate.

The Gymnastics of the Mystics
(i) Lung-gom-pas: The "Flying Monks" Who Do Not Fly

Under the collective term of *lung-gom* Tibetans include a large number of practices which combine mental concentration with various breathing gymnastics and aim at different results either spiritual or physical.

The term *lung-gom* is especially used for a kind of training which is said to develop uncommon nimbleness and especially enables its adepts to take extraordinarily long tramps with amazing rapidity. Belief in such a training and its efficacy has existed for many years in Tibet, and men who travelled with supernormal rapidity are mentioned in many traditions. We read in Milarepa's biography that at the house of the lama who taught him black magic there lived a *trapa* who was fleeter than a horse. Milarepa boasts of similar powers and says that he once crossed in a few days, a distance which, before his training, had taken him more than a month. He ascribes his gift to the clever control of "internal air."

However, it should be explained that the feat expected from the *lung-gom-pa* is one of wonderful endurance rather than of momentary extreme fleetness. In this case, the performance does not consist in racing full speed over a short distance as is done in our sporting matches, but of tramping at a rapid pace and without stopping during several successive days and nights.

Beside having gathered information about the methods used in training *lung-gom-pas*, I have been lucky enough to catch a glimpse of three adepts. In this I was extremely fortunate as, though a rather large number of monks endeavour to practise some kind of *lung-gom* exercises, there is no doubt that very few acquire the desired result, and in fact true *lung-gom-pas* must be very rare.

I met the first *lung-gom-pa* in the Chang thang* of Northern Tibet. Towards the end of the afternoon, Yongden, our servants and I were riding leisurely across a wide tableland, when I noticed, far away in front of us, a moving black spot which my field-glasses showed to be a man. I felt astonished. Meetings are not frequent in that region, for the last ten days we had not seen a human being. Moreover, men on foot and alone do not, as a rule, wander in these immense solitudes. Who could the strange traveller be?

One of my servants suggested that he might belong to a trader's caravan which had been attacked by robbers and disbanded. Perhaps, having

* An immense wild grassy region at a high level inhabited only by a few tribes of nomad herdsmen living in tents.

fled for life at night or otherwise escaped, he was now lost in the desert. That seemed possible. If such was really the case, I would take the lone man with us to some cowherds encampment or wherever he might wish to go if not far out of our route.

But as I continued to observe him through the glasses, I noticed that the man proceeded at an unusual gait and, especially, with an extraordinary swiftness. Though, with the naked eyes, my men could hardly see anything but a black speck moving over the grassy ground, they too were not long in remarking the quickness of its advance. I handed them the glasses and one of them, having observed the traveller for a while, muttered: *"Lama lung-gom-pa chig da."* (It looks like a lama *lung-gom-pa.)*

These words *"lama lung-gom-pa"* at once awakened my interest. I had heard a great deal about the feats performed by such men and was acquainted with the theory of the training. I had, even, a certain experience of the practice, but I had never seen an adept of *lung-gom* actually accomplishing one of these prodigious tramps which are so much talked about in Tibet. Was I to be lucky enough to witness such a sight?

The man continued to advance towards us and his curious speed became more and more evident. What was to be done if he really was a *lung-gom-pa?* I wanted to observe him at close quarters, I also wished to have a talk with him, to put him some questions, to photograph him . . . I wanted many things. But at the very first words I said about it, the man who had recognized him as a lama *lung-gom-pa* exclaimed:

"Your Reverence will not stop the lama, nor speak to him. This would certainly kill him. These lamas when travelling must not break their meditation. The god who is in them escapes if they cease to repeat the *ngags,* and when thus leaving them before the proper time, he shakes them so hard that they die."

Put in that way, the warning seemed to express pure superstition. Nevertheless it was not to be altogether disregarded. From what I knew of the "technique" of the phenomena, the man walked in a kind of trance. Consequently, a sudden awakening, though I doubt if it could cause death, would certainly painfully disturb the nerves of the runner.

To what extent that shock would harm him I could not guess and I did not want to make the lama the object of a more or less cruel experiment. Other reasons also forbade me to gratify my curiosity. Tibetans had accepted me as a lady-lama. They knew that I was a professed Buddhist and could not guess the difference existing between my philosophic conception of the Buddha's doctrine and lamaist Buddhism. Common Tibetan folk completely ignore the fact that the term Buddhism includes a number of sects and views. So, in order to enjoy the confidence, respect and intimacy which my religious garb brought me, I was compelled to behave in close accordance with Tibetan customs, especially with religious ones. This was a serious hindrance, and often deprived my observations of a great part of their scientific interest, but it was the unavoidable price I had to pay for being admitted on ground still much more jealously guarded than the material territory of Tibet. This time, again, I had to repress my desire for full investigation and remain satisfied with the sight of the uncommon traveller.

By that time he had nearly reached us; I could clearly see his perfectly calm impassive face and wide-open eyes with their gaze fixed on some invisible far-distant object situated somewhere high up in space. The man did not run. He seemed to lift himself from the ground, proceeding by leaps. It looked as if he had been endowed with the elasticity of a ball and rebounded each time his feet touched the ground. His steps had the regularity of a pendulum. He wore the usual monastic robe and toga, both rather ragged. His left hand gripped a fold of the toga and was half hidden under the cloth. The right held a *phurba* (magic dagger). His right arm moved slightly at each step as if leaning on a stick, just as though the *phurba,* whose pointed extremity was far above the ground, had touched it and were actually a support.

My servants dismounted and bowed their heads to the ground as the lama passed before us, but he went his way apparently unaware of our presence. I thought I had done enough to comply with local customs by suppressing my desire to stop the traveller. I already began to vaguely regret it and thought that at any rate I would see some more of the affair.

I ordered the servants to remount their beasts at once and follow the lama. He had already covered a good distance; but without trying to overtake him, we did not let that distance increase and, with the glasses as well as with our naked eyes, my son and I looked continually at the lung-gom-pa.

It was no longer possible to distinguish his face, but we could still see the amazing regularity of his springy steps. We followed him for about two miles and then he left the track, climbed a steep slope and disappeared in the mountain range that edged the steppe. Riders could not follow that way and our observations came to an end. We could only turn back and continue our journey.

I wondered if the lama had, or had not, noticed that we were following him. Of course, though we were a good distance behind him, anyone in a normal state would have been aware of the presence of a troop of six riders. But, as I said, the traveller seemed to be in a trance and I could not therefore tell whether he was only pretending not to have seen us and climbed the hill to escape our inquisitive looks, or if he really did not know that he was being followed, and merely went in that direction because it was his way.

On the morning of the fourth day after we had met the lung-gom-pa, we reached the territory called Thebgyai, where there are a number of scattered dokpas* encampments. I did not fail to relate to the herdsmen how we had approached a lama lung-gom-pa as we joined the track that led to their pasture ground. Now some of the men had seen the traveller when gathering their cattle together at sunset the day before we had met him ourselves. From that information I made a rough reckoning. Taking into account the approximate number of hours we had actually travelled each day at the usual speed of our beasts—leaving out the time spent camping and resting—I came to the conclusion that, in order to reach the place where we met him, the man, after he had passed near the dokpas, must have tramped the whole night and next day, without stopping, at about the same speed as he was going when we saw him.

* Dokpas, literally "men of the solitudes," herdsmen.

To walk for twenty-four hours consecutively cannot be considered as a record by the hillmen of Tibet who are wonderful walkers. Lama Yongden and I, during our journey from China to Lhasa, have sometimes tramped for fully nineteen hours, without stopping or refreshing ourselves in any way. One of these marches included the crossing of the high Deo pass, knee deep in the snow. However, our slow pace could not in any way be compared to that of the leaping *lung-gom-pa,* who seemed as if carried on wings.

Those who aspire to become *lung-gom-pas* undertake a preliminary training. Amongst these exercises the following one enjoys the greatest favour amongst those many Tibetan ascetics who are not of an especially intellectual type.

The student sits cross-legged on a large and thick cushion. He inhales slowly and for a long time, just as if he wanted to fill his body with air. Then, holding his breath, he jumps up with legs crossed, without using his hands and falls back on his cushion, still remaining in the same position. He repeats that exercise a number of times during each period of practice. Some lamas succeed in jumping very high in that way. Some women train themselves in the same manner.

As one can easily believe, the object of this exercise is not acrobatic jumping. According to Tibetans, the body of those who drill themselves for years, by that method, become exceedingly light; nearly without weight. These men, they say, are able to sit on an ear of barley without bending its stalk or to stand on the top of a heap of grain without displacing any of it.

A curious test has been devised, and the student who passes it with success is believed capable of performing the feats here above mentioned or, at least, of approaching proficiency. A pit is dug in the ground, its depth being equal to the height of the candidate. Over the pit is built a kind of cupola whose height from the ground level to its highest point again equals that of the candidate. A small aperture is left at the top of the cupola. Now between the man seated cross-legged at the bottom of the pit and that opening, the distance is twice the height of his body. For instance, if the man's height is 5 feet 5 inches, the top hole will be at 10 feet 10 inches from the pit's bottom.

The test consists in jumping cross-legged, as during the training exercises which I have described, and coming out through the small opening at the top of the cupola. I have heard Khampas declare that this feat has been performed in their country, but I have not myself witnessed anything like it.

It is difficult to understand that a training which compels a man to remain motionless for years can result in the acquisition of peculiar swiftness. However, this is the special training, and in other places we meet with different and apparently more rational methods, including the actual practice of marching. Moreover, it must be understood that the *lung-gom* method does not aim at training the disciple by strengthening his muscles, but by developing in him psychic states that make these extraordinary marches possible.

•   •   •   •

Another meeting with a *lung-gom-pa* happened in Ga, a region of Kham, in Eastern Tibet. I was again travelling with my small caravan. The man appeared under the familiar and commonplace figure of an *arjopa,* that is to say a poor pilgrim carrying his luggage on his back. Thousands of such fellows may be seen on all the tracks of Tibet, so we did not pay much attention to a member of such a large tribe.

These needy, solitary pedestrians have the habit of attaching themselves to any trader's caravan or to any rich traveller whom they happen to meet on their way and following them. According to this custom, the man whom we had met attached himself to our party. We learnt from him that he had been staying at the Pabong monastery in Kham, and was going to the Tsang province. A pretty long journey which, done on foot and begging on the way, would take three or four months. However, such tramps are undertaken by thousands of Tibetan pilgrims.

Our companion had already spent a few days with us when, in consequence of a slight breakdown, it was nearly noon before we started. Thinking that the pack-mules would be late in crossing a ridge that lay ahead of us, I rode on with my son and a servant, to look for water and a grassy place where we could camp before dusk.

The way to the pass was longer than I had suspected, and I soon realized that the pack-mules would not reach the top of the ridge before nightfall. It out of the question to let them attempt going down the other side of the range in the dark, so having reached a grassy spot near a brooklet, I stopped there. We had already drank tea and were collecting dry cowdung to feed the fire* when I saw the *arjopa* climbing the slope at some distance below us, progressing with extraordinary rapidity. As he came nearer, I could see that he was walking with the same peculiar nimble springing gait which I had noticed in the lama *lung-gom-pa* of Thebgyai.

When he reached us, the man stood quite still for a while staring straight before him. He was not at all out of breath, but appeared only half conscious and incapable of speaking or moving. However, the trance gradually subsided and the *arjopa* came back to his normal state. Answering my questions, he told me that he had begun the *lung-gom* training for acquiring fleetness with a *gomchen* who lived near the Pabong monastery. His master having left the country, he intended to go to *Shalu gompa* in Tsang.

He did not tell me any more and looked sad the whole evening. On the morrow, he confessed to Yongden that the trance had come on him involuntarily and had been produced by a most vulgar thought.

As he was walking along with the servants who led my mules, he had begun to feel impatient. They were going so slowly, he thought, and during that time we were, no doubt, grilling on the fire the meat he had seen my servant carry with him. When the three other servants and he himself would have overtaken us they would have to pitch the tents, to look

---

* With the exception of woody regions, the cattle dung is the only fuel used in Tibet. In the parts of the country inhabited by *dokpas*, travellers collect what is left by the animals on the pasture grounds to light their camp fire.

after the beasts, and so there would only be time to drink tea and eat *tsampa* before retiring to sleep.

He visualized our little party. He saw the fire, the meat on the red embers, and sunk in contemplation gradually became unconscious of his surroundings. Then, prompted by the desire of sharing our meal, he accelerated his pace and in so doing mechanically fell into the special gait which he was learning. The habitual association of that peculiar gait with the mystic words his master had taught him, caused the mental recitation of the proper formula. The latter led to the regulation of the breath in the prescribed rhythm, and the trance followed. Nevertheless, the concentration of his thoughts on the grilled meat dominated everything.

The novice regarded himself as a sinner. The mixture of gluttony, holy mystic words and *lung-gom* exercises seemed to him sacrilegious. I felt interested and put different questions to the novice. He was most unwilling to answer, but I managed to obtain some information which confirmed what I knew already. He had been told that sunset and clear nights were favourable conditions for the walker. He had also been advised to train himself by looking fixedly at the starry sky.

I suppose that, like most Tibetan mystics, he had taken an oath not to divulge the teaching imparted by his master and that my questions troubled him.

The third day after his racing performance, when we awoke, at daybreak he was no longer in the tents. He had fled at night, perhaps using his power of *lung-gom* and, this time, for a more worthy purpose than that of sharing a "bonne bouche" (a good mouthful).

(ii) Tumo (or tuomo): The Art of Warming Oneself without Fire

To spend the winter in a cave amidst the snows, at an altitude that varies between 11,000 and 18,000 feet, clad in a thin garment or even naked, and escape freezing, is a somewhat difficult achievement. Yet numbers of

Tibetan hermits go safely each year through this ordeal. Their endurance is ascribed to the power which they have acquired to generate *tumo*.

The word *tumo* signifies heat, warmth, but is not used in the Tibetan language to express ordinary heat or warmth. It is a technical term of mystic terminology, and the effects of that mysterious heat are not confined to warming the anchorites who can produce it.

Only those who are qualified to undertake the training may hope to enjoy its fruit. The most important qualifications required are: to be already skilled in the various practices connected with breathing; to be capable of a perfect concentration of mind, going as far as the trance in which thoughts become visualized, and to have received the proper empowerment from a lama possessed with the power of conferring it.

Tumo initiation is preceded by a long period of probation. Among other objects, I think probation aims at testing the robustness of the candidates. As great as may be my confidence in the *tumo* method, I still doubt whether it could be safely practised by people of weak constitution. It is probable, however, that *tumo's* teachers, wisely, endeavour to avoid failures that might prove harmful to presumptuous disciples and lower their own repute.

I do not know whether, when yielding to my pressing requests and shortening my time of probation, the venerable lama who "empowered" me in *tumo* only wanted to get rid of me or not. He simply told me to go to a lonely spot, to bathe there in an icy mountain stream, and then, without drying my body or putting on my clothes, to spend the night motionless in meditation. Winter had not yet begun, but the level of the place, about 10,000 feet high, made the night rather chilly, and I felt very proud of not catching cold. Later on I took another bath of the same kind, this time involuntarily, when I lost footing as I was fording the Mekong River, near Rakshi in Northern Tibet.

One may easily understand that Tibetans, who are frequently exposed to accidents caused by a hard climate, hold a method that protects them against the cold in high esteem. Once initiated, one must renounce all fur or woollen clothing and never approach the fire to warm oneself.

After a short period, during which he exerts himself under the close supervision of his master, the novice must retire to a very remote, absolutely solitary place situated high up on the hills. In Tibet "high up" means generally an altitude well above 10,000 feet. According to *tumo* teachers and adepts, one must never practise the training exercises inside a house, or near inhabited places. They believe that foul air produced by smoke and smells, together with various occult causes, impede the success of the student and may even harm him. Once conveniently settled, the disciple must see nobody besides his lama, who may visit him occasionally, or to whose hermitage he may repair at long intervals.

The novice must begin his training each day before dawn and finish the special exercise relating to *tumo* before sunrise, because as a rule he has to perform one or another meditation at that time. The practice must be done in the open, and one must be either naked or clothed in a single cotton garment.

A Visualization Exercise to Accompany Tumo

The exercises goes on, through ten stages, but one must understand that there exists no pause between them. The different subjective visions, as well as the sensations which accompany them, succeed each other in a series of gradual modifications. Inhalations, retentions of the breath and exipirations continue rhythmically, and a mystic formula is continually repeated. The mind must remain perfectly concentrated and "one pointed" on the vision of the fire and the sensation of warmth which ensues.

The ten stages may be briefly described as follows:

1. The central artery *uma* is imagined—and subjectively seen—as thin as the thinnest thread or as a hair, yet filled with the ascending flame and crossed by the current of air produced by the breath.

2. The artery has increased in size and become as large as the little finger.

3. It continues to increase and appears to be the size of an arm.

4. The artery fills the whole body, or rather the body has become the *tsa* itself, a kind of tube filled with blazing fire and air.

5. The bodily form ceases to be perceived. Enlarged beyond all measure, the artery engulfs the whole world and the *naljorpa* feels himself to be a storm-beaten flame among the glowing waves of an ocean of fire.

Beginners whose mind has not yet acquired the habit of very protracted meditation go more quickly through these five stages than more advanced disciples, who progress slowly from one to another, sunk in deep contemplation. Yet, even the quickest ones take about an hour to reach the fifth stage.

Now the subjective visions repeat themselves in reverse order.

6. The stormy wind abates, the fiery waves sink lower and are less agitated, the blazing ocean narrows and is absorbed in the body.

7. The artery, which is reduced to the size of an arm, is seen again with the fire enclosed in it.

8. The artery decreases to the size of a little finger.

9. It becomes as thin as a hair.

10. It entirely disappears: the fire ceases utterly to be perceived, as well as all forms, all representations whatsoever. All ideas of any kind of objects vanish likewise. The mind sinks into the great "Emptiness" where the duality of the knower and the object perceived does not exist any longer.

The exercise, either with or without the five last stages, may be repeated during the day or whenever one is suffering from cold. But the training, properly speaking, is done during the early practice before dawn.

It is possible that Milarepa resorted to it when he happened to be unexpectedly surrounded by the snow in a cave of the Lachi Kang (near Mount Everest) and found himself compelled to stay there till the next spring.

I, too, have lived in caves and huts on high altitudes. Though I did not lack provisions, and had fuel enough to light a fire whenever I wished it, I yet know the hardships of that life. But I also remember the perfect silence, the delightful aloofness and the wonderful peace in which my hermitage was bathed, and I do not think that those who spend their days in such wise need to be pitied. I would rather say they are to be envied.

It is difficult for us to get a perfectly correct idea about the extent of the results obtained through *tumo* training, but some of these feats are genuine. Hermits really do live naked, or wearing one single thin garment during the whole winter in the high regions I have mentioned. I am not the only one who has seen some of them. It has been said that some members of the Mount Everest expedition had an occasional glimpse of one of the naked anchorites.

In conclusion I may say that I have myself obtained remarkable results from my small experience of *tumo*.

Is Mental Telepathy Possible?

Tibetan mystics are not talkative; those of them who accept disciples teach them according to methods in which discourses have but little place. The disciples of the contemplative hermits seldom see their master and only at intervals determined by the spiritual attainment and needs of the novice.

A few months or a few years may elapse between these meetings. But in spite of their seeming aloofness, master and disciples—especially advanced disciples—do not lack means of communication when they deem it necessary.

Telepathy is a branch of the Tibetan secret lore and seems, in the

"Land of Snows," to play the part that wireless telegraphy has recently taken in the West. Yet, while apparatus for wireless transmissions are, in Occidental countries, at the public's disposal, the subtler ways of sending messages "on the wind" remain the privilege of a small minority of adepts in that art in Tibet.

Telepathy is not altogether a novelty to Westerners. Psychic research societies have, more than once, called attention to telepathic phenomena. These, however, usually seem to have occurred by chance. The author of the phenomenon was not aware of his part in it. Under some peculiar circumstances, he had sent forth the mysterious waves that had reached, at a greater or lesser distance, a human receiver, but he had not done this knowingly and on purpose. On the other hand, the experiments made to transmit volitional telepathic messages have given doubtful results, for they could not be repeated successfully as often as desired.

Things are different among Tibetans. They assert that telepathy is a science, which can be learnt like any other science, by those who have proper teaching and are fit instruments to put the theory into practice. Various ways are mentioned for the acquisition of telepathic power, though Tibetan adepts of secret lore are unanimous in ascribing the cause of the phenomena to an intense concentration of thought.

One may remark that as far as telepathy has been observed and studied in Western countries its cause has seemed identical with that discovered by Tibetans. Mystic teachers declare that mastery in telepathy requires a perfect command over the mind, in order to produce, at will, the powerful "one-pointedness of thought" on which the phenomenon depends.

The part of conscious "receiver," always ready to vibrate at the subtle shock of the telepathic waves, is considered almost as difficult as that of the sender. To begin with, the intended receiver must have been "tuned" with him from whom he especially expects messages.

Now, volitional perfect concentration of mind on one single object, until every other object vanishes from the field of consciousness, is the basis of the lamaist spiritual training, and this training also includes psychic exercises that aim at developing the power of detecting the various "currents of energy" that are crossing each other in every direction.

Relying on observations which extend over a large number of years, I shall venture to say that Tibet seems to offer peculiarly favourable conditions for telepathy—as well as for psychic phenomena in general. Maybe the very high level of the country is helpful. Perhaps we may, also, take into account the great silence in which the country is bathed, that extraordinary silence of which—if I dared to use so strange an expression—I would say that it is *heard* above the loudest voices of the most furiously roaring torrents.

Again, solitude might be reckoned with: the absence of big crowds whose mental activity creates many whirlpools of psychic energy which trouble the ether. And perhaps the placidity of Tibetans whose minds are not filled, like ours, with cares and cogitations is another of these favourable conditions. Whatever may be the causes at work, telepathic transmissions, either conscious or unconscious, seem to occur rather frequently in Tibet.

Regarding my own experience, I am certain that I did receive on several occasions telepathic messages, from lamas under whom I had practised mental or psychic training. It may even be that the number of these messages has been larger than I suspect. However, I have only retained a few cases in which the lama afterwards inquired if I had understood what he meant to tell at a given time.

Beside communications regarding spiritual matters, which may not be entirely due to telepathy, but to a certain identity in the trend of thoughts between a master and his pupil, I may relate two incidents of an entirely different kind.

One of them happened in the Dainshin River valley, during my journey to Lhasa. Yongden and I had spent the night in the open, sleeping in a ditch dug by the waters during successive rainy seasons, but for the moment dry and hardened by the frost. The lack of fuel had compelled us to start our daily tramp without drinking our usual hot buttered tea. So, hungry and thirsty, we walked till about noon when we saw, seated on his saddle.carpet,* near the road, a lama of respectable appearance who was finishing his midday meal. With him were three young *trapas* of distinguished mien, who looked more like disciples accompanying their master than common servants. Four fettered horses were trying to graze on some dry grass near the group.

The travellers had carried a bundle of wood with them and kindled a fire, a teapot was still steaming on the embers. As befitted our assumed condition of beggarly pilgrims, we respectfully saluted the lama. Most likely, the desire that the sight of the teapot awakened in us could be read in our faces. The lama told us to sit down and bring out our bowls† for tea and *tsampa*.

A *trapa* poured the remaining tea in our bowls, placed a bag of *tsampa* near us and went to help his companions who had begun to saddle the beasts and make ready to start. Then, one of the horses suddenly took fright and ran away. This is a common occurrence, and a man went after the animal with a rope.

The lama was not talkative. He looked at the horse that ran in the direction of a hamlet and said nothing. We continued to eat silently. Then, I noticed an empty wooden pot besmeared with curd and guessed that the lama had got the curd from a farm which I could see at some distance away from the road. The diet of daily *tsampa* without any vegetables proved rather trying for the stomach and I availed myself of all opportunities to get milk food. I whispered in Yongden's ear: "When the lama is gone, you shall go to the farm and ask for a little curd."

Though I had spoken very low and we were not seated very near to the lama, he appeared to have heard my words. Then he turned his head in the direction where the horse had run away. The animal had not gone far, but was apparently in a playful mood and did not permit the *trapa* to

---

* Tibetans ride on a padded saddle with a carpet over it. When a traveller alights to rest on the road, this carpet is often spread on the ground for him to sit on.

† Tibetan travellers always carry a wooden bowl in the breast pocket formed by their dress tied with a belt. Wealthy travelers keep the bowl in a case which is carried by an attendant.

capture it easily. At last it let him throw the rope round its neck and followed him quietly.

The lama remained motionless, gazing fixedly at the man who advanced toward us. Suddenly, the latter stopped, looked around and went to a boulder near by, where he tied his horse. Then he retraced his steps a little way and leaving the road, walked to the farm. After a while I saw him come back to his horse carrying something. When he reached us the "something" turned out to be a wooden pot full of curd. He did not give it to the lama, but held it in his hand, looking interrogatively at his master as if saying "Was that what you wanted? What am I to do with this curd?" To his unspoken question the lama answered by an affirmative nod, and told the *trapa* to give me the curd.

The second incident which I will relate did not occur in Tibet itself, but on the borderland territory that has been annexed to the Chinese provinces of Szetchuan and Kansu.

At the skirt of the immense primeval forest that extends from Tagan to the Kunka pass, six travellers had joined my small party. The region is known as being haunted by daring Tibetan robbers, and those who must cross it look for opportunities of forming as large and as well armed a company as possible. Five of my new companions were Chinese traders, the sixth was a Bonpo *ngagspa,* a tall man whose long hair, wrapped in a piece of red material, formed a voluminous turban.

Anxious to glean anything that I could, regarding the religion of the country, I invited the man to share our meals in order to find an opportunity of chatting with him. I learned that he was going to join his master, a Bonpo magician, who was performing a great *dubthab* [esoteric ritual] on a neighbouring hill. The object of this rite was to coerce a malignant demon who habitually harmed one of the small tribes which live in that region. After diplomatic preambles I expressed my desire of paying a visit to the magician, but his disciple declared the thing utterly impossible. His master must not be disturbed during the full lunar month necessary to perform the rite.

I understood that it was useless to argue with him, but I planned to follow him when he parted with us, after crossing the pass. If I succeeded in coming unexpectedly upon the magician, I might perhaps have a glimpse at him and at his magic circle. Consequently, I ordered my servants to keep good watch on the *ngagspa* so that he could not leave us unnoticed.

Probably they spoke too loudly among themselves about the matter. The *ngagspa* saw through the trick I intended playing upon his guru and told me that it was no use attempting it.

I replied that I did not harbour any evil intention against his master and only wanted to have a talk with him for the sake of enlightenment. I also commanded my servants to keep a still closer watch on our companion. The *ngagspa* could not but be aware that he had become a prisoner. But as he also understood that no harm would be done to him and that he was well fed—a thing to which Tibetans are keenly alive—he took his adventure good humouredly.

"Do not fear that I shall run away," he said to me. "You may bind me with ropes if it pleases you. I need not go ahead to inform my master of your coming. He already knows all about it. *Ngais lung gi teng la len tang tsar*" (I have sent a message on the wind).

Ngagspas are in the habit of boasting of so many and such various miraculous powers that I did not pay any more attention to his words than to those of his colleagues in the black art.

This time, I was wrong.

When we had crossed the pass, we entered a region of pasture land. Robbers were not much to be feared on these wide tablelands. The Chinese traders, who had clung to us day and night while in the forest, recovered their assurance and took leave. I still intended to follow the *ngagspa,* when a troup numbering half a dozen riders emerged from an undulation of the ground. They rode at full speed toward me, then dismounted, saluted, offered "*kha-tags*" (complimentary scarves) and a present of butter. After the polite demonstrations were ended, an elderly man told me, that the great Bonpo *ngagspa* had sent them and begged me to renounce my intention of visiting him, for no one but an initiated disciple ought to approach the place where he had built his secret magic *kyilkhor.*

I had to give up my plan. The *ngagspa*, it seemed, had really informed his master by "sending a message *on the wind.*" To persist would have been useless.

I may add that average Tibetans are much less eager than we are to investigate psychic phenomena. They take them as certainly uncommon, but not altogether extraordinary occurrences. They have no fixed ideas about the laws of Nature or what is possible and impossible, to be disturbed by such phenomena. Educated or ignorant, all implicitly admit that everything is possible to him who knows the way of doing it, and consequently supernormal feats do not, as a rule, awaken any special emotion beyond admiration for the competent wonder worker.

Enlightment in a Lifetime:
A Summary of the Short Path

Padmasambhava is said to have described the stages of the mystic path in the following way.

1. To read a large number of books on the various religions and philosophies. To listen to many learned doctors professing different doctrines. To experiment oneself with a number of methods.
2. To choose a doctrine among the many one has studied and discard the other ones, as the eagle carries off only one sheep from the flock.
3. To remain in a lowly condition, humble in one's demeanor, not seeking to be conspicuous or important in the eyes of the world, but behind apparent insignificance, to let one's mind soar high above all worldly power and glory.
4. To be indifferent to all. Behaving like the dog or the pig that eat what chance brings them. Not making any choice among things which one meets. Abstaining from any effort to acquire

or avoid anything. Accepting with an equal indifference whatever comes: riches or poverty, praise or contempt, giving up the distinction between virtue and vice, honourable and shameful, good and evil. Being neither afflicted, nor repenting whatever one may have done and, on the other hand, never being elated nor proud on account of what one has accomplished.

5.   To consider with perfect equanimity and detachment the conflicting opinions and the various manifestations of the activity of beings. To understand that such is the nature of things, the inevitable mode of action of each entity and to remain always serene. To look at the world as a man standing on the highest mountain of the country looks at the valleys and the lesser summits spread out below him.

6.   It is said that the sixth stage cannot be described in words. It corresponds to the realization of the "Void"* which, in Lamaist terminology, means the Inexpressible reality.

* In a general way, one must understand here, the realization of the non-existence of a permanent *ego*, according to the Tibetan current formula: *"The person is devoid of self; all things are devoid of self."*

Chapter II

. . . .

A Himalayan Guru of the Old Style

Lama Anagarika Govinda

After Alexandra David-Neel, the only other European who traveled in for-
bidden Tibet and investigated its religion was the German Lama
Anagarika Govinda (1898–1985). During the 1930s and 1940s he explored,
safely far from Lhasa, the country's peripheral regions, determined as he
was to preserve through word and image Tibetan Buddhism against the
coming forces of extinction. In the selection below, he describes his guru
more thoroughly than David-Neel ever did hers, and in that description the
mythological puts on the flesh and sinews of actuality.

His involvement with the legendary Geshe Tomo only begins the adven-
tures Govinda records in The Way of the White Clouds *(1966). Once, for*
example, stranded at nightfall in an area of treacherous boulders, he
instinctively did lung-gom *(trance running), his feet practically flying*
from rock to rock, unguided by conscious direction.

Born Ernst Lothar Hoffman, Govinda became a Theravadin Buddhist
monk in Ceylon, but, at a Buddhist conference in northern India, he
encountered the Vajrayana (Tibetan Buddhism). He devoted the rest of
his life to making rational sense of its religious richness, to finding plau-
sible explanations for its world of wonders. About the clairvoyance so
common in old Tibet, he explained it by noting the complete absence—no
radio waves, not even a dentist's drill—to impede concentration and

communication in that pristine environment. His Foundations of Tibetan
Mysticism *(1959), though dry and technical, and now somewhat super-
seded, provided an earlier generation their first detailed manual in English
of how to practice Buddhism, Tibetan-style.*

My Guru before I Met Him

The Lama Ngawang Kalzang had been meditating for twelve years in various caves and retreats in the wilderness of the mountains of Southern
Tibet. Nobody knew him, nobody had heard of him. He was one of the
many thousands of unknown monks who had received his higher education in one of the great monastic universities in the vicinity of Lhasa, and
though he had acquired the title of Géshé (i.e. Doctor of Divinity), he
had come to the conclusion that realisation can only be found in the stillness and solitude of nature, as far away from the noisy crowds of market-
places as from the monkish routine of big monasteries and the
intellectual atmosphere of famous colleges.

The world had forgotten him, and he had forgotten the world. This
was not the outcome of indifference on his part but, on the contrary,
because he had ceased to make a distinction between himself and the
world. What actually he had forgotten was not the world but his own
Self, because the world is something that exists only in contrast to one's
own ego.

Wild animals visited him in his caves and made friends with him, and
his spirit went out in sympathy to all living beings. Thus he never felt
lonely in his solitude, and enjoyed the bliss of emancipation, born out of
exalted visions.

One day a herdsman in search of new grazing grounds had lost his
way in the inaccessible wilderness of rocks high above the valley when he
heard the rhythmic beats of a *damaru* (a small hour-glass–like hand-

drum, used by Lamas and wandering ascetics during their invocations) mingled with the silvery sound of a ritual bell. At first he did not believe his ears, because he could not imagine that any human being could exist in this forbidding place. But then the sound came again and again fear filled him, because if these sounds had no human origin then they could only have some supernatural cause.

Torn between fear and curiosity, he followed the sound, as if drawn by the irresistible force of a magnet, and soon he saw the figure of a hermit, seated before a cave, deeply absorbed in his devotional practice. The hermit's body was lean but not emaciated, and his face serene, lit up with the fire of inspiration and devotion. The herdsman immediately lost all fear, and after the hermit had finished his invocations he confidently approached the Lama and asked for his blessing.

When the hermit's hand touched the crown of his head he felt a stream of bliss flowing through his body, and he was filled with such unspeakable peace and happiness that he forgot all the questions he had wanted to ask, and hurried down into the valley to bring the happy news of his discovery to the people there.

These people at first could hardly believe the news, and when the herdsman led some of them to the hermit's cave they were wonder-struck. How could any human being live in this almost inaccessible mountain fastness? From where did he get his food, since nobody knew of his existence? How could he endure the hardships of winter, when the mountains were covered with snow and ice and even the smallest foot-paths were obliterated, so that neither fuel nor food could be obtained? Certainly only a hermit endowed with superhuman yogic powers could survive under such conditions.

The people threw themselves at the feet of the Hermit-Lama, and when he blessed them they felt as if their whole being was transformed into a vessel of peace and happiness. It gave them a foretaste of what every human being can attain to when he realises the dormant powers of light, which are buried like seeds deep within his soul.

The Hermit-Lama merely made them participate in the bliss of his own achievement, so that they might be encouraged to follow the same path towards liberation.

The rumour of the wondrous hermit spread in the valleys like wild-fire. But, alas, only those who were strong enough could venture to climb up to the hermit's cave, and since there were many who were thirsting for spiritual guidance, the people of the valley implored the Lama to settle among them for the benefit of all who needed his help. The hermit knew that the hour had come for him to return to the world of men, and true to his Bodhisattva-vow he renounced the bliss of solitude for the welfare of the many.

There was a very small and poor monastery in the valley from which the people had come, called the Monastery of the White Conch (Dungkar Gompa). It was situated on a steep hill with a rocky crest in the middle of a fertile wheat-growing valley called Tomo ("To" = wheat). This place was given to the Hermit-Lama, who from now on was known as "Tomo Géshé Rimpoché," "The Learned Jewel of the Wheat Valley."

At Tomo Géshé's Monastery. The Old Attendant There

Whenever I happened to wake up during the night I beheld the benign features of Buddha Maitreya's golden face, which seemed to float high above the shadowy forms that filled the temple in the dim light of the Eternal Lamp. And in the golden, softly radiating face the large deep blue eyes seemed to be filled with supernatural life, and I felt their glance resting upon me with infinite tenderness.

Sometimes in the middle of the night a strange shuffling sound awoke me, accompanied by what appeared to be the sound of heavy breathing. As the nights were very cold and I was well wrapped up, it took me some time before I could make up my mind to raise myself up and to look around. But the knowledge that the temple was closed at night, and that there was no living soul in it except myself, aroused my curiosity.

And then I saw the slowly moving dark figure of an old man in the open space before the altar, raising his joined hands above his head, going down upon his knees and hands, and then stretching himself out upon the floor in his full length, after which he would again get up and repeat the same exercise over and over again, until his breath was heavy with exertions. After that he moved silently along the walls, bowing before each of the images and touching the lower rows of the sacred books and the feet of Maitreya reverently with his forehead. He moved in a clock-wise direction, and when coming back along the right wall towards my corner, I recognized him as the venerable old monk who lived in a small room flanking the porch that formed the entrance of the temple.

It was easy to recognize him because of his slightly bent figure and his long beard, which is comparatively rare among Tibetans. He was the old-est monk in the monastery and hailed from Shigatse. In his younger days he had been one of the personal attendants of the Tashi Lama (or the Panchen Lama, as he is known in Tibet), from whom he still received a small pension which, as I found out later, he mainly used for the improve-ment and beautification of the temple, while he himself lived like the poorest and humblest of monks at the temple door with no other per-sonal possessions than his sitting-mat and his monastic robes. He was bent not so much from age, perhaps, as from sitting for years and years in the posture of meditation, and, in fact, his whole life seemed to be a con-tinuous *sadhana* (religious practice).

But this did not preclude him from playing occasionally with the chil-dren who ran about in the courtyard of the monastery and sometimes invaded the temple in order to tease old Kachenla, who good-naturedly would pretend to chase them among the low benches and the little tea-tables of the temple hall. His friendly little eyes would twinkle in such a way that even his most threatening gestures could not frighten the small-est of the little urchins, who would pull his flapping robes and scream with pleasure when the old man made an attempt to catch them.

In spite of his old age I never saw Kachenla unoccupied: whether he would glide about the temple on two square pieces of felt, in order to

keep the floor polished, or whether he would attend to the hundreds of
butter-lamps, water-bowls, and other altar-vessels, which had to be kept
clean and shining and filled with their various ingredients—ever was he
busy in the service of the temple or in the performance of his spiritual
duties: reading the sacred texts, reciting prayers for the welfare of all living beings, and performing the daily rituals for their protection and well-
being. On special occasions he would be making small clay images of
great beauty, and I was fascinated to see how every phase of the work,
from the mixing and kneading of the clay, the modelling or pressing into
forms, to the drying or baking in the charcoal fire and the subsequent
gilding or painting (or both) of the delicate details, every process was
accompanied by *mantras* and prayers, invoking the blessings of the
Enlightened Ones and the beneficent forces of the universe, present in
earth and air, water and fire, i.e. in all the elements which support our life
and serve us in the accomplishment of our work. Thus even a manual
occupation was turned into a ritual of profound meaning and an act of
devotion and meditation, whose forces would saturate even the material
objects created in this way.

What Kachenla taught me in his humble way was more than I shall
ever be able to convey in words. His devotion and his utter humility prepared my mind for the meeting with my Guru—in fact, he was part and
parcel of the Guru who was ever present in his mind and so inseparably
united with him that the gratitude and veneration which I feel towards
my Guru includes Kachenla.

He looked after my welfare as if I was his own son. He taught me the
first words of Tibetan by pointing at things and pronouncing their
names. In the morning he would bring me warm water—a luxury in
which he himself would not indulge and which none of the other monks
could afford. He would share with me his beloved *so-cha* (Tibetan butter-
tea), which was simmering the whole day long on his little charcoal stove
behind which he had his seat. That I relished this strange concoction of
Chinese tea, slightly "matured" butter, soda, and salt—which few non-
Tibetans seem to be able to stomach—must have been due to Kachenla's

overwhelming kindness. And how important it was to get accustomed to this indispensable and nourishing drink I realised in my later wanderings on the frozen highlands of Tibet.

Before enjoying his morning tea Kachenla would take a pinchful of black seeds, arrange them on the palm of his left hand in the form of a scorpion, and while reciting the *mantra* for protection from all evils, he would drop them into the charcoal fire. On other occasions he would sprinkle some incense upon the charcoal and describe with various beautiful gestures (*mudra*) of his hands a variety of symbolical gifts which he offered to the Buddhas, at the same time pronouncing a formula of dedication for each of them. This was done in such perfect and naturally flowing movements that I could almost see the various objects appearing before my eyes and that I had no doubt of the sincerity with which they were given. There was nothing theatrical or pompous or artificial in these little rituals. They seemed to be the natural expression of the man's inner life, as natural as the breathing of his lungs or the beating of his heart. He moved among the multitude of enlightened beings, as well as among gods and demons, as naturally as among humans and animals, giving to each of them the recognition or attention due to them.

In the evenings Kachenla would generally come into my quiet corner in the temple with a lit butter-lamp, sit down before me on the floor, and motion me to take out paper and pencil; and with infinite patience be would recite and dictate one prayer after another and make me repeat it until I caught the right pronunciation and intonation. It never bothered him that I could not understand a single word in the beginning, though he pointed out the image of the Buddhas and Bodhisattvas concerned, so that I was not left entirely without guidance and could connect the words with a definite mental picture.

He seemed to be confident that he transmitted to me something that was of infinite value, whether I knew it or not; and to say the truth I experienced a similar satisfaction, because I was convinced that a gift given with such infinite love and devotion was valuable through this very fact, and, indeed, I felt that something was streaming over from the old man to me that filled me with happiness, though I could find no reasonable explanation for it. It was the first time that—without knowing it—I experienced the power of *mantra,* of sacred speech, in which the transcendental sound of the spirit that dwells in the human heart is perceived. And because it is the sound of the heart it cannot be heard by the ear or understood by the brain. But this I did not know yet, though I began to experience it.

Later on I was able to understand the contents and the meaning of those prayers, but this knowledge did not surpass the initial benefit I had derived from them, and now I know that more important than the intellectual meaning of the words were the circumstances under which they were transmitted and the spiritual purity and conviction of the transmitter.

I Request to Meet the Guru

I did not know whether the abbot had succeeded in passing on my request, when one day, after returning from my meditation cave at the back of the hill, I found on my place in the temple a huge mango of the most costly and rare variety, growing only in the plains and not yet in season at that time of the year. I could hardly believe my eyes, nor could I understand how it got there, until Kachenla came, beaming with pleasure and pointing up in the direction of the meditation-cubicle (*ts'hang-khang*), and told me it was a gift from the Great Lama. I have never received a more precious gift, because it told me that my wish had been granted, that I had been accepted as a disciple.

Kachenla shared with me my happiness, and no matter how long I would have to wait I knew it was worth waiting even for a lifetime to find a real Guru, i.e. one who not only imparted intellectual knowledge but who could awaken the inner forces of one's own mind by the power of his spiritual achievements and realization.

The term *"guru"* is generally translated as "teacher," but actually it has no equivalent in any Western language, because a Guru is far more than a teacher in the ordinary sense of the word. A teacher gives knowledge, but a Guru gives himself. The real teachings of a Guru are not his words but what remains unspoken, because it goes beyond the power of human speech. The Guru is an *inspirer* in the truest sense of this word, i.e. one who infuses us with his own living spirit.

And consequently the term *"chela"* means more than an ordinary pupil, who goes through a course of instructions, but a disciple who has established a profound spiritual relationship with the Guru, a relationship that is founded on the act of initiation, during which a direct "transference of power" takes place and is embodied in the sacred formula (*mantra*) through which this power can be called up by the Chela at any time and through which a permanent contact with the Guru is maintained.

The "power" of which I speak here is not a force that overwhelms one's mind, but the power that makes one participate in an experience belonging to a higher state of consciousness and realisation, which gives one a foretaste or glimpse of the aim towards which we strive, so that it is no more a vague ideal but an *experienced* reality. Such power can only be created through a life of meditation and becomes intensified with each period of complete seclusion, like the cumulative force of the waters of a dammed-up river.

This became apparent to me on the day when the Great Lama— whose name did not yet mean anything to me at that time, but who was none other than the famous Tomo Géshé Rimpoché—emerged after his many weeks of silent meditation.

From the early morning I noticed an uncommon stir in the monastery, whose population suddenly seemed to have doubled or trebled. I did not know from where all those monks, whom I did not remember to have seen before, suddenly had come, but apparently they belonged to the monastery, though they did not live within its premises. Even those whom I knew seemed to look different, not only because all of them wore their best robes but also because they all looked exceptionally washed and clean.

The long rows of seats in the temple hall were filled to the last place, and some new rows had been added. The huge cauldrons in the adjacent kitchen building were filled with boiling tea and soup, to be served in the intervals during the service in the temple. The temple hall was lit up by more than a thousand butter-lamps, and bundles of incense-sticks wafted clouds of fragrant smoke into the air and wove bluish veils around the golden images high above the congregation.

Suddenly the deep, thundering sound of alp-horn–like tubas, punctuated by the slow rhythm of bass-drums and accompanied by the vibrating voices of oboes, was heard from outside, the doors of the temple swung wide open, and Tomo Géshé Rimpoché, flanked by two Lamas in full ornate and high ceremonial hats, entered the temple. A large orange-coloured silken shawl (representing the upper garment or *civaram* of an orthodox Buddhist monk) was draped around him and a prayer-carpet was spread before his feet. He raised his hands with joined palms above his head in salutation of the Buddhas, knelt down on the carpet, and prostrated himself with his forehead on the ground. This he repeated three times, while the choir of the assembled monks chanted the formulas of refuge in deep melodious voices which formed a rhythmically moving background to the continued blasts of the radongs (the twelve-foot-long bass-horns) outside the temple.

After the Rimpoché had finished his devotions the tall pointed yellow cap, the symbol of his high office, was put upon his head, and then he slowly moved through the middle of the hall and ascended the high throne, opposite that of the Umdze, the leader of the choir and the head of the monastery in his absence. While he moved through the hall a deep silence fell upon the congregation and all sat motionless as if spellbound by the magic presence of this one man, who seemed to fill the whole temple with the accumulated power gained through a long period of concentration and complete absorption. I now began to understand what

Kachenla meant when he said that the Great Lama had become one with the Buddhas.

He Becomes My Guru.
I Become His Chela

Soon my first meeting with the Guru came about. It took place in one of the little shrine-rooms on the upper floor of the Lhabrang (the main residential building of the monastery) which served as his private apartments whenever he stayed at Yi-Gah Cho-Ling, and which even during his absence were regarded as the monastery's innermost sanctuary. Like in the temple, the Great Abbot's seat is a place of special sanctity, as it is here that he performs his daily devotions and spends many hours in meditation, even during the night, which he spends in a cross-legged position in the confined space of his seat, which allows him neither to lie down nor to stretch out. The high back of this boxlike, slightly raised meditation seat bore the emblem of the Lama's high office, the Wheel of the Law, and was surmounted by the traditional canopy with a seven-coloured volant, representing the aura of the Buddha.

The whole room breathed an atmosphere of peace and beauty, the natural outflow of a mind to whom harmony is not merely an aesthetic pleasure but the adequate expression of a life devoted to the realm of the spirit. Exquisite religious paintings, minutely executed and mounted on old Chinese brocades, harmonized with the mellow colours of hand-woven Tibetan rugs which covered the low seats behind lacquer-topped, delicately carved and painted *chogtses*. On the opposite side golden images of the finest workmanship rested in glazed shrines, flanked by dragons and crowned by multi-coloured, carved cornices, and on the narrow ledge before the images stood silver bowls filled with clear water and butter-lamps of chased silver. There was not a single object in the room that was not connected with the symbols and functions of religious life and practice, and nothing that could have been regarded as the Guru's personal possession.* In fact, long after he had left the body of his present incarnation, when, according to the Guru's special instructions, I had the unique privilege to dwell in this hallowed room, I found everything in it as it had been in the Guru's presence—even the silver-mounted jade teacup and the ritual vessels, vajra-sceptre and bell, on the *chogtse* before his seat.

But all these details fused into one general impression of supreme peace and harmony on that first day, when I bowed down before the Guru and his hands lay on my head: hands whose lightest touch sent a stream of bliss through one's whole body, nay, one's whole being, so that all that one had intended to say or to ask, vanished from one's mind like smoke into blue air. Merely to be in this man's presence seemed to be enough to dissolve all problems, to make them non-existent, like darkness in the presence of light.

As he sat on his meditation-seat under the canopy, clad in the simple maroon-coloured robes of a Tibetan monk, I found it difficult to determine his age, though he must have been already about sixty-five years old at that time. His short-cropped hair was still dark and his body looked sturdy and erect. His clean-shaven face showed the features of a strong character, but his friendly eyes and his mouth that was slightly turned up at the corners, as if ready to smile, gave me an immediate feeling of reassurance.

It is a strange fact that nobody ever succeeded in taking a photograph of Tomo Géshé Rimpoché, though many people tried to do so surreptitiously, because they knew that he never allowed anybody to take a picture of him. Those who tried found out that their films had turned into

---

* When moving from one monastery to the other he would take with him only the bare necessities for the journey. To him a cave was as good as a palace, and a palace as good as a cave. As little as he cared for riches and comforts, as little was he afraid of making use of them. He was neither attached to comfort nor to asceticism. He knew that the vanity of asceticism can be as great a hindrance as the vanity of possession. Whatever gifts he received from devotees were either distributed among those who were in need or utilized for the maintenance of temples, monasteries, libraries, or similar purposes.

blanks or were blurred beyond recognition or that something else happened to the films. Whatever happened, the Guru's face was never visible. He detested any kind of hero-worship and did not want his person made into an object of veneration.

On the day on which he formally accepted me as his Chela, he said:

"If you wish me to be your Guru, do not look upon my person as the Guru, because every human personality has its shortcomings, and so long as we are engaged in observing the imperfections of others we deprive ourselves of the opportunities of learning from them. Remember that every being carries within itself the spark of Buddhahood (*bodhicitta*), but as long as we concentrate on other people's faults we deprive ourselves of the light that in various degrees shines out from our fellow-beings.

"When searching for a teacher, we surely should search for one who is worthy of our trust, but once we have found him, we should accept whatever he has to teach us as a gift of the Buddhas, and we should look upon the Guru not as one who speaks with his own voice but as the mouthpiece of the Buddha, to whom alone all honour is due. Therefore, if you bow down before the Guru, it is not the mortal personality of the teacher that you worship, but the Buddha, who is the eternal Guru and who reveals his teaching through the mouth of your human teacher who forms a living link in the chain of initiated teachers and pupils who have transmitted the Dharma in an unbroken line from the times of Sakyamuni. Those who transmit to us the teachings of the Buddha are the vessels of the Dharma, and as far as they master the Dharma and have realized the Dharma within themselves, they are the embodiment of the Dharma.

"However, one should never forget that in every living being *bodhicitta* is present as a potentiality (I, therefore, rather prefer to call it a 'spark' of enlightenment-consciousness than a 'thought' of enlightenment, which only arises when this latent spark becomes fully conscious) and that only our own blindness prevents us from recognising this. The greater our imperfections, the more we are inclined to see the faults of others, while those who have gained deeper insight can see through these faults into their essential nature. Therefore the greatest among men were those who recognized the divine qualifies in their fellow-beings and were always ready to respect even the lowliest among them.

"As long as we regard ourselves superior to others or look down upon the world, we cannot make any real progress. As soon, however, as we understand that we live in exactly that world which we deserve, we shall recognize the faults of others as our own—though they may appear in different form. It is our own karma that we live in this 'imperfect' world, which in the ultimate sense is our own creation. This is the only attitude which can help us to overcome our difficulties, because it replaces fruitless negation by an impulse towards self-perfection, which not only makes us worthy of a better world but partners in its creation."

The Guru then went on to explain some of the preconditions and preliminary exercises of meditation for bringing about this positive and creative attitude: Unselfish love and compassion towards all living beings was, according to him, the first prerequisite of meditation, as it removed all self-created emotional and intellectual limitations; and in order to gain this attitude one should look upon all beings like upon one's own mother or one's own children, since there was not a single being in the universe that in the infinity of time had not been closely related to us in one way or another. In order to be conscious of the preciousness of time one should realise that any moment might be the last of this life and that the opportunity which it offers might not come again easily. Finally he pointed out that what we learned from books about meditation was not comparable to the direct transmission of experience and the spiritual impetus that a living Guru could give us, if we open ourselves to him in all sincerity.

It was my great good luck that I had not only been well prepared by Kachenla's patient teachings but that I had found a friend in a learned Mongolian Lama, who knew English and helped me with my Tibetan studies in exchange for Pali and practice in English. He had studied for about twenty years in one of the great monastic universities near Lhasa, where he acquired the degree of "Géshé," and he had subsequently worked with the well-known scholar von Stael-Holstein in Peking. His name was Thubden Sherab, though he was generally referred to as "Géshéla."

With him as interpreter I was able to converse with the Guru, though—I was to find out soon—I the Guru was in no need of an interpreter, as he was able to read my thoughts like an open book. As he knew that I had devoted the greater part of my adult life to the study of Buddhism, he did not waste time in explaining doctrinal points, but went straight to the practice of meditation, which he regarded as more important than all theoretical knowledge. It was, indeed, also the most important thing to me.

So far I had practised meditation following my own intuition as well as certain instructions which I had found in the sacred texts—especially in the *Satipatthana-Sutta* (which in those days had not yet been popularised in the modern, rather one-sided fashion of the Rangoon School). All the more I felt eager to see the further steps and to be introduced into the traditional methods which could guide one step by step into the deeper realms of meditative experience.

On the day on which Tomo Géshé Rimpoché formally accepted me as his Chela in a special ritual of initiation, in which I received my first *mantra,* I realised one of the most important things that hitherto had been lacking in my religious life: the impetus of a spiritual force that required no philosophical argument or intellectual justification, because it was not based on theoretical knowledge, but on fact and direct experience, and thus gave one the certainty that what one was striving after was not merely an abstract idea, a mere shadow of a thought, but an attainable state of mind, the only "tangible" reality of which we can speak.

And yet the experience through which this "tangible" reality is transmitted is so intangible that to describe the details of an initiation and the essential experiences connected with it would be as inadequate as describing in words the contents or the impact of music. Indeed, any description of factual details would destroy the very basis of the emotional appeal and significance, because "emotion," in the word's truest meaning, is that which *moves* our mind, intensifies and awakens it to a higher life and a wider awareness, which finally turn into Enlightenment, a state of pure Light—which at the same time is pure, unhindered, infinite movement and highest tranquillity. This does not mean that we should give up thinking or conceptual thought—which would be impossible—but that we should not get caught up in it.

Just as a single note in a melody has no meaning in itself but only in relationship to preceding and following notes—i.e. as a moment in a meaningful or organic movement, which cannot be held on to without destroying the melody—in the same way we cannot stop thinking or hold on to a particular concept without destroying its value. The moment we try to analyse, to conceptualise, or to rationalise the details and experiences of initiation, we are dealing only with dead fragments, but not with the living flow of force, which is expressed in the Tibetan word *"dam-ts'hig,"* the inner relationship between Guru and Chela and the spontaneous movement, emotion, and realisation on which this relationship is based.

There is nothing secret in the process of initiation, but everybody has to experience it for himself. By trying to explain what goes beyond words we only succeed in dragging the sacred down to the level of the profane, thus losing our own *dam-ts'hig* without benefiting others. By glibly talking about the mystery, we destroy the purity and spontaneity of our inner attitude and the deep reverence which is the key to the temple of revelations. Just as the mystery of love can only unfold when it is withdrawn from the eyes of the crowd, and as a lover will not discuss the beloved with outsiders, in the same way the mystery of inner transformation can only take place if the secret force of its symbols is hidden from the profane eyes and the idle talk of the world.

Among those personalities I have met Tomo Géshé Rimpoché was undoubtedly the greatest. The inner bond which was created on the day on which I received the *abhiseka,* my first and therefore most important initiation, became a constant source of strength and inspiration. How much the Guru would be able to help me by his presence, even beyond his death, this I guessed as little in those days as I was conscious of the fact that he was one of the most highly revered religious teachers of Tibet and that for millions of people his name was equated with the highest attainments on the Buddha's spiritual path.

My ignorance of his position, however, had the advantage that it enabled me to observe impartially and uninfluenced by others some of the extraordinary faculties of the Guru, which convinced me that he really possessed the yogic powers (*siddhi*) which traditionally were ascribed to the saints of the past. In fact, it all came about quite by chance, when one day my Mongolian friend and I were discussing with the Guru certain aspects of meditation, as we often used to do. Our questions were mostly concerned with problems arising out of practical experience. In the course of this it happened that my friend had some personal questions to ask and since I could not follow the trend of the discussion, I allowed myself to let my thoughts wander in other directions. In the course of this it came to my mind that the day might not be far when the Guru would have to leave in order to return to his main monastery beyond the border, and that years might pass before I had another opportunity to sit at his feet. And in a sudden impulse I formulated in my mind the following request: "Please give me a visible sign of the inner bond that unites me with you, my Guru, something that beyond all words reminds me daily of your kindness and of the ultimate aim: be it a small image of the Buddha blessed by your hands or whatever you might think fit . . ." Hardly had I pronounced these words in my mind when the Guru, suddenly interrupting his talk, turned to me and said: "Before I leave I shall give you a small Buddha-image as remembrance."

I was thunderstuck and hardly able to stutter a few words of thanks— partly from joy and partly from being taken aback at the effect of my thought. At the same time I could not help feeling a little ashamed that I had dared to put the Guru to the test in such a direct way; because as little as I would have dared to interrupt the Guru's talk with audible words, would I have dared to do this even in thoughts, if I had really believed that he could hear them as clearly as if I had uttered them aloud.

That the Guru reacted as he did, even while his attention was absorbed by other things, proved to me that he was able to perceive other people's thoughts not only when his mind was directed towards them or as the result of a conscious effort, but that he possessed the faculty which in the Buddhist Scriptures is described as the "divine ear" or the faculty of clairaudience, which enabled him to hear and to respond to thoughts that were directed to him, as other people would hear spoken words. And, what was more, I had not addressed him in Tibetan but in my own language, which shows that what was audible to the Guru were not the words but their meaning or the impulse that prompted them.

When finally the day of leave-taking came I found myself in a state of great tension. Weeks had passed since that memorable talk, but on no other occasion had the Guru mentioned this subject again, and I naturally had not dared to remind him, knowing full well that he was as conscious of his promise as I myself. Since he knew how much it meant to me, I could only think that perhaps he wanted to test my patience and my faith in him, and that made me all the more determined to remain silent.

But when during the last days of his stay at Yi-Gah Cho-Ling all his time was taken up by people who came to receive his blessings before he would leave, I felt afraid that the Guru might be too occupied to remember my request or that other circumstances had prevented him from carrying out his intention.

How great was therefore my surprise and my joy when during our last meeting—even before I could say a word about this matter—he handed me a small but exquisitely finished terracotta statue of Buddha Sakyamuni and told me that he had kept this image in his hands during his daily meditations.

Now I realised the greatness of his gift and the reason for its delay, and while receiving it from his hands, it was only with the greatest effort that I controlled my tears. I bowed down, unable to speak, and then I felt his hands resting on my head with great tenderness; and again a wave of bliss streamed through my whole being and gave me the certainty that I would never be separated from the Guru, though a thousand miles might lie between us.

The little image has since been my constant companion: it has accompanied me over countless snow-clad passes in and beyond the Himalayas, it has roamed with me the deserted highlands of the Chang-Thang and the fertile valleys of South and Central Tibet. It has saved me in difficult situations in Western Tibet, when the Guru's seal, with which it had been consecrated, gave evidence of the fact that I was not a Chinese agent, but a personal pupil of Tomo Géshé Rimpoché; and in 1948, it pacified the armed tribesmen who surrounded our camp with hostile intentions and left with the Guru's blessings, only to come back with gifts and asking that also their women and children and their flocks might be blessed.

But there is something more to this little image, something that is as important to me as the Guru's seal and benediction: namely the fact that it was not created by some unknown artisan, but by the hands of my Guru's humblest and most devoted disciple Kachenla, whose remembrance is for me inseparable from that of Tomo Géshé Rimpoché. During the years that elapsed before the Guru's return to Yi-Gah Cho-Ling, Kachenla remained my faithful friend and Gurubhai (i.e. one who his become a brother by having been initiated by the same Guru), and whenever I came back to Yi-Gah Cho-Ling—either to stay in or near the monastery—it was Kachenla who would receive me and look after me, especially when later on a younger caretaker was appointed for the main temple, while Kachenla took charge of the Guru's private apartments and their shrines. Thus, when according to the Guru's wishes I made use of the privilege to stay in those hallowed rooms, it was again Kachenla who surrounded me with his love and care and made me feel more than ever that the Guru was with us, as in the days of our first meeting.

Reminders of Géshé Tomo All Along My Subsequent Travels

Tomo Géshé Rimpoché, when emerging from his twelve-year-long period of lonely meditation, had become a healer of such power that the

ribus (pills) which he distributed freely to all those who came for his blessing were sought after all over Tibet and are nowadays more precious than
pearls. When I received three of these *ribus* after my initiation, Géshé
Tubden Sherab, who had assisted me, begged me to share them with him
and related how in the case of a serious illness, when doctors had been
unable to give him relief, he had been cured instantaneously by one of
these *ribus*. Not realising at that time the deeper significance of the
Guru's gift—thinking of it merely in terms of a medical remedy, of
which I did not feel any great need at that time (besides having more faith
in Western medicines)—I gave away two of these precious *ribus;* and
since it never came to my mind to replace them on later occasions, when
I could have asked for them, only one has remained in my possession. It
was only many years later that I realised their value.

The following episode may illustrate the importance attached to these
ribus. When returning from Western Tibet in 1949, together with my
wife Li Gotami, we were surprised to find a small but well-equipped
Tibetan temple containing a full set of the Sacred Scriptures (*Kanjur* and
Tanjur) as well as an enormous prayer-wheel, in Rampur, the capital of
Bashar State, which was ruled by a Hindu Maharaja. Since the population
of Rampur was purely Hindu, we were wondering who could have built
and endowed this sanctuary, until we were informed that it was the
Maharaja himself who had done it, in the fulfilment of a vow.

This is the story we were told: The Maharaja had been childless for
many years, and without an heir his dynasty would have come to an end.
Though he had consulted many learned Brahmins and performed various religious rites to propitiate the gods, he had not been blessed with an
heir. One day a well-known Lama and his retinue passed through
Rampur on a pilgrimage to Mount Kailas, and since his fame had spread
wide and far and thousands of people came to have his *darshan*, the
Maharaja invited him to his palace and, telling him of his predicament,
promised to build a temple for Buddhist pilgrims and to furnish it with a
complete set of Tibetan Sacred Scriptures if through the Lama's blessings
an heir would be born to the throne.

The Lama promised his help, but he made one condition, namely that the Maharaja would provide him with a place where he could retire for meditation, perform the necessary rites, and prepare the consecrated *ribus* for the Maharaja and his consort. The Maharaja, thereupon, had a special pavilion built in the palace grounds and gave strict orders that nobody should be allowed to approach the pavilion or to disturb the Lama during the performance of his religious rites.

However, one of the servants could not master his curiosity, and in the darkness of night he crept to the door of the pavilion in order to peep through the keyhole and to find out what the Lama was doing there all by himself. Apparently he had heard of the "wonderworking" *ribus* and wanted to explore the secrets of their composition, as it was said that they contained many precious substances, obtained from supernatural sources. But when he managed to peep inside the pavilion he beheld the Lama, surrounded by a host of superhuman beings, celestial as well as demonical, so that he fainted with fright. People found him the next morning at the foot of the steps leading to the entrance of the pavilion. When he came to himself he was raving as if in a fever and died within a few hours. After this, nobody dared to approach the pavilion, and for many days and nights the Lama was absorbed in his devotions. Only the sounds of bell and *damaru* and of the Lama's sonorous incantations were heard from time to time.

On the appointed day the Lama emerged from the pavilion, gave his blessings and the consecrated *ribus* to the Maharaja and his consort— and before the year was out an heir was born to them. In gratitude to the saintly Lama, the Maharaja fulfilled his vow and built the promised temple. He sent a special delegation to Tibet to have the Sacred Scriptures printed and to fetch the necessary altar-vessels and whatever else was necessary for the completion of the temple and the perform- ance of religious services.

After having paid a visit to the temple, we were inspecting the beauti- ful Tibetan pavilion in the palace grounds, in which the Lama had lived during his retreat. We asked the caretaker, who showed us around, whether he remembered the name of the Lama. His answer was: "Tomo Géshé Rimpoché."

All along the road from Tibet we heard miraculous stories about the pilgrimage of Tomo Géshé Rimpoché, who had given new faith and hope to thousands of people, and who had healed the sick and encouraged the downtrodden. In the village of Poo, on the Tibetan frontier, a dying girl was brought to him on a stretcher. She had been ill for a long time and her condition was such that her people were afraid to carry her, lest she might die on the way. However, the villagers had such faith in the powers of Tomo Géshé, that they persuaded the girl's parents to take the risk. When they arrived with the stretcher at the Lama's place almost the whole village was assembled there.

Under their very eyes, at the command of Tomo Géshé, the girl opened her eyes, got up from the stretcher, and after having received the blessings of the Lama she walked out of the house as if she had never been ill. The girl was still alive during our stay at Poo, and numerous eyewitnesses vouchsafed for the truth of this event. We had no reason to doubt these reports even if Tomo Géshé had not been our own Guru—because there was hardly a place through which he had passed during that memorable pilgrimage where people did not speak about him with veneration and glowing eyes—though many long years had passed since then—and the Guru himself had given up his body in the meantime.

Though popular imagination may have woven a veil of legends over many of the actual events, the fact of his healing powers and the tremendous impact of his personality upon the people stood out clearly and unmistakably from all the stories that came to our ears. Even during his lifetime he had become a legend, but to all those who had come into actual contact with him it became clear that there is more truth in the legends growing around a saint's life than our critical intellect may suspect, and that even in our times saints are walking the face of the earth just as in the day of Buddha Sakyamuni or Christ, Muhammad or St. Francis of Assisi.

The example of Tomo Géshé Rimpoché shows convincingly that even those who go through the most severe practices of yoga training, living in complete solitude for years on end, do not thereby lose their inner bonds with their fellow-beings, nor their functions and usefulness in human society. Indeed, they played a far greater role and had a deeper influence on the spiritual life of Tibet than those who were exclusively engaged in verbal teaching or literary work.

In Tibet the function of a religious teacher is not so much the proclamation of a doctrine or the elucidation of the commonly accepted teachings of traditional Buddhism but the demonstration that the highest religious aims can be realised and that the ways towards their attainment are practicable. Even a silent hermit may act like a beacon of spiritual light in the darkness of ignorance and illusion. The very fact of his existence, the very fact that he *can* exist in the light of his own inner realisation, is sufficient to give courage and confidence to others.

The Guru Passes Away

Returning from Gangtok, I stayed in Tomo Géshé Rimpoché's private apartments at Yi-Gah Cho-Ling. It was as if time had stood still in the little shrine-room which I inhabited and in which nothing had changed since my first meeting with the Guru. His seat, with his heavy cloak carefully arranged on it in an upright position, looked as if he had just stepped out of it, and on the *chogtse* in front of the seat stood his jade cup filled with tea, together with his ritual implements, such as *vajra*, bell, and rice-vessel. The central butter-lamp before the carved shrine with the golden image of Dolma burned with its steady, timeless flame, which Kachenla, undeterred by age and cheerful as ever, tended with loving care.

To him the Guru was ever present, and daily he would prepare his seat, shake and refold his robe, fill up his teacup (before he would sip his own tea), polish and replenish the water-bowls and butter-lamps, light the incense-sticks, recite the formulas of worship and dedication, and sit in silent meditation before the shrines, thus performing all the duties of a religious life and of a devoted disciple. Serving the Guru was to him the highest form of divine service—it was equal to serving the Buddha.

Not a speck of dust was allowed to settle on the seats and *chogtses* or on the carvings of the shrines and altars. The floor looked like a mirror, and the *thankas* and the lovely brocades, in which they were mounted, had lost none of their softly vibrating colours. The handwoven rugs on the low seats, the wall-hangings above them, the dark brown cloth that was stretched across the ceiling, and the silken canopies above the Guru's seat and the main shrines, edged by rainbow-coloured volants, gave me the feeling of being in the tent or "yurt" of a nomad-patriarch or ruler of old, somewhere in Central Asia—far away from our present world and time. I could feel in this room the traditions of a millennium, intensified and sublimated through the personality that filled this place with its living presence.

A similar feeling had assailed me during our last meeting at Sarnath, when the whole place had been turned into a Tibetan encampment, and at night the camping-ground under the mango-trees was illuminated with countless oil-lamps in honour of Tomo Géshé and his retinue. He himself was staying in a big tent in the centre of the mango-grove, and in the soft light of the oil-lamps and the glow of camp-fires, whose smoke was hanging like transparent veils between the trees and the tents, the grove seemed to me transformed into an oasis far away in the heart of Asia, with a caravan of pilgrims resting after a long desert journey. It was indeed one of the last stages in the Guru's life-journey—a leavetaking from the sacred places of the Buddha's earthly career. It was Tomo Géshé's last pilgrimage to India in 1935–6, accompanied by many of his disciples and received everywhere with great enthusiasm, though he himself shunned all personal honours and public attention.

When passing through Calcutta on his way back to Yi-Gah Cho-Ling and to Tibet, the papers in Calcutta carried the following report: "A famous Lama, who ranks fourth after the Dalai Lama, is staying in

Calcutta at present. The Venerable Géshéy Rim-po-che is on his way to Tibet after completing his pilgrimage to the Buddhist sacred places in North India. Supernatural powers are ascribed to the seventy-one-year-old Lama. He spends the greater part of his time reading the sacred texts, discoursing with his disciples, or being absorbed in meditation. He shuns the public, hardly ever leaves his room, and is said never to sleep. He is accompanied by a retinue of forty Lamas. They visited Sarnath, Gaya, and Rajgir. In Sarnath he and his retinue dwelled in tents."

The idea that Tomo Géshé never slept was caused by the fact that he never used to lie down, but remained in the posture of meditation all through the night, thus never losing control over his body even in sleep, which, according to the highest form of meditational practice, becomes a natural continuation of *sadhana* on a different level of consciousness. Though there is no doubt that Tomo Géshé's spiritual powers were far above those of the ordinary (i.e. untrained) man, he would have protested against the term "supernatural" and still more against giving publicity to such things. In fact, when reporters tried to satisfy their curiosity about magic powers and mystic rituals in Tibetan Buddhism, he broke off the conversation, pointing out that these things would not help them in understanding the essential teachings of the Buddha.

Thus the reporters had to content themselves with the externals of the pilgrimage, which was organised and led by Sardar Bahadur Ladenla, who had served the thirteenth Dalai Lama in various capacities and had been given by him the rank of General. They mentioned that Tomo Géshé and Ladenla had gilded the Buddha-image in the new temple of Sarnath as an act of devotion, and that the Maharaja of Bhutan had sent with them a beautifully worked canopy of silver for the image.

I found this newspaper report in the diaries of Baron von Veltheim-Ostrau, who personally paid a visit to Tomo Géshé Rimpoché during his stay in Calcutta on the 2nd of February 1936. Due to the many visitors who tried to see the Lama, he was not able to talk to him. "In the midst of people's goings and comings he [the Lama] was the only resting pole. He was seated on a rug, smiling and silent. The old man made an extremely dignified impression, ripe with knowledge and wisdom, like one who was already approaching the state of transfiguration."

And this, indeed, was the case, because the ultimate phase in Tomo Géshé's life and his conscious transition into a new one, which took place the following year, was truly a "state of transfiguration," a triumph over death.

Kachenla told me all that had happened during the Guru's last days; and later on, in 1947 during a visit at Dungkar, Tomo Géshé's main monastery in the Tomo Valley of South Tibet, we heard the details about his passing away from those who had been present. The Guru had made it known that he would soon leave his body, which had become a burden to him. "But," he said, "there is no reason for you to feel sad. I do not forsake you, nor my work for the Dharma; but instead of dragging on in an old body, I shall come back in a new one. I promise to return to you. You may look out for me within three or four years."

Not long after this announcement he retired for a longer spell of meditation and gave instructions to be left undisturbed, though he remained in his usual quarters within the monastery. He soon entered a state of deep absorption and remained in it for many days. But when ten days had passed, and the Guru was still sitting motionless on his seat, his attendants began to be worried. One of them held a mirror near to his face, and when it was found that the surface of the mirror remained unclouded they realised that he had stopped breathing: he had left his body during his meditation and had consciously passed over the threshold between life and death—or, more correctly, between one life and another.

He had left his body, before death could snatch it away from him, and directed his consciousness towards a new germ of life, that would carry on the impetus of his will and form itself into a new instrument of the attainment of his ultimate aim and the fulfillment of his Bodhisattva Vow, which might be summarised in these words: "Whatever be the highest perfection of the human mind, may I realise it for the benefit of all living beings. Even though I may have to take upon myself all the sufferings of the world, I will not forsake my aim and my fellow-creatures in order to win salvation for myself only."

Rebirth. The Case for Reincarnation

Tomo Géshé Rimpoché had promised to return to his monastery and to his pupils in due time, and his promise came true. Little, however, did I think that his rebirth would take place in the very house in which I had been staying as a guest during my first trip to Tibet, the very same house which I revisited during my pilgrimage to the Great Hermit: the house of Enche Kazi at Gangtok. It was from his own mouth that I learned the details of Tomo Géshé's rebirth and of his discovery a few years later with the help of the great State Oracle in Lhasa.

Knowing Enche Kazi as a sincere and deeply religious man, I can vouchsafe for the truthfulness of his report. In spite of the fact that he had reason to be proud of being the father of a *Tulku*, his story was tinged with sadness, because he had lost his wife soon after the child was born,* and a few years later, when it became apparent that his son was none other than the rebirth of Tomo Géshé, he had to give up his only child. It was only in the face of overwhelming evidence and for the sake of the boy's happiness, who himself wanted to "return to his monastery," that the father finally gave in and allowed him to be taken to Dungkar Gompa.

The Maharaja himself had pleaded with the father not to interfere with the boy's higher destiny, which was clearly indicated by the findings of the Great Oracle of Nachung and confirmed by the boy's own utterances and behaviour. The latter had always insisted that he was not Sikkimese but Tibetan, and when his father called him *"pu-chung"* (little

---

* It is a common belief in Tibet that a *Tulku's* mother generally dies soon after its birth, and I remember several cases where this was so—the present Dalai Lama being a great exception. Also the mother of Buddha Sakaymuni, Queen Maya, died a few days after she had given birth to the future Buddha.

son) he protested, saying that his name was Jigme (the Fearless One). This was exactly the name which the Oracle at Lhasa had mentioned as the name under which Tomo Géshé would be reborn.

The fact that the State Oracle had been invoked shows how much importance was attached to the finding of Tomo Géshé's rebirth. Apparently the local oracle at Dungkar had not been able to give a clear indication or had advised the authorities to seek further clarification from [the oracle of] Nachung. The latter, indeed, had been most specific by pointing out not only the direction where the child would be found but by giving a detailed description of the town and the locality in which he was born. From all these details it became clear that the town could only be Gangtok. Furthermore, the year in which the boy was born and the exact age of the father and the mother was given, as well as a description of the house in which they lived and of the trees that grew in the garden. Two fruit-trees, which stood in front of the house, were particularly pointed out as a characteristic feature of the place.

Thus, a delegation of monk-officials was sent to Gangtok, and armed with all these details they found the boy, who was then about four years old. As soon as the monks approached the house and entered the garden, the boy called out: "Father, my people have come to take me back to my Gompa!" And he ran to meet them, jumping with joy—rather to the embarrassment of the father, who was not yet prepared to give up his only son. But the latter pleaded with his father to let him go, and when the monks spread out before him various monastic articles, like rosaries, *vajras*, bells, teacups, wooden bowls, *damarus*, and other things which are in daily use in religious rituals, he immediately picked out those objects which had belonged to him in his previous life, rejecting all those which had been deliberately mixed up with them—though some of them looked far more attractive than the genuine articles.

The father, who saw all these proofs and remembered the many signs of the boy's extraordinary intelligence and unusual behaviour which had often surprised him, was finally convinced and—though it was with a heavy heart—he finally gave his consent that the boy should go with the delegation to his monastery in Tibet.

On his journey to Dungkar Gompa the party met the Amchi, the Tibetan doctor who had treated Tomo Géshé during the last years of his life, and the boy, recognising him, called out: "O Amchi, don't you know me? Don't you remember that you treated me when I was sick in my previous body?"

Also in Dungkar he recognised some of the older monks and, what was most remarkable, the little dog who had been his special favourite in the last days of his previous life recognised him immediately and was beside himself with joy at being reunited with his beloved master.

Thus Tomo Géshé had fulfilled his promise, and people again streamed from near and far to Dungkar Gompa to pay their respects to the Guru and to receive his blessings. The little boy impressed everybody with his self-assured and dignified behaviour when he sat on his throne in the great hall of the temple, conducting rituals, presiding over the recitations on festive occasions, or receiving pilgrims and blessing them—while otherwise he was natural and spontaneous like any other boy of his age. But during religious functions it was as if through the innocently pure and transparent features of the child the face of a man, mature in years and wisdom, could be seen. And soon it became clear that he had not forgotten the knowledge which he had acquired in his previous life. His education was nothing but a rehearsal of his former knowledge, and he progressed so quickly that soon there was nothing left that his tutors at Dungkar could teach him. Thus, at the age of seven he was sent to Sera, one of the great monastic universities near Lhasa, for higher studies and for obtaining again his degree of Doctor of Divinity (Géshé).

All this may appear incredible to a Westerner, and I admit that I myself would have found it difficult to believe, but for myself rebirth is neither a theory, nor a belief, but an experience. This experience came to me towards the end of my childhood. I was living at that time on the island of Capri.

One day a friend told me that he and his mother and a few others were holding spiritistic séances, and he invited me to take part in them. As a

Buddhist I did not hold a high opinion about such things—not because I denied the possibility of occult powers, but because I found theories as well as the practices of spiritists crude and unsatisfactory. On the other hand, I welcomed the opportunity to gain some factual knowledge in this matter. So I accepted the invitation and attended one of these séances.

We all sat around a heavy table in a softly lit room, keeping our hands spread out before us on the table, lightly touching its surface in the prescribed manner, and when the table began to move, one of the participants proposed to put questions about the former lives of those present. The answers were, as often in such cases, too vague to be of much interest and besides beyond any possibility of verification. When the questioner enquired about my past the table tapped out a name that was obviously Latin, and nobody among those present had ever heard it. I too was puzzled, though I had a faint remembrance of having casually read the name in a bibliography as being the pseudonym of a comparatively lesser-known author, whose actual name I could not recall. Anyway, I did not take this answer seriously, nor was I impressed by the whole procedure, because it seemed to me unlikely that any intelligent being, whether in the form of a "spirit" or any other conscious entity, should stoop to answer idle questions of this kind and to communicate them in such a primitive and clumsy manner. If they wanted to contact human beings they certainly would be able to discover more adequate means of communication. It seemed to me more likely that the forces invoked by such means were none other than those of the participants' subconsciousness. It therefore seemed to me unlikely that through them anything could be revealed that was not already in them, i.e. in their subconscious or unconscious psyche. I therefore dismissed the matter and gave it no further thought.

Some time later I happened to read to another friend of mine, a young German archaeologist, a story which I had written in my childhood and which I had conceived as part of a mystic novel, in which my religious convictions and inner experiences were symbolically expressed. My friend was a few years older than myself and I greatly valued his knowledge of art and literature and his mature judgment.

After I had been reading for some time he suddenly stopped me and exclaimed: "Where did you get this from? Did you ever read . . ." and there he mentioned the same name that had puzzled me and the other participants of the aforementioned séance.

"Now, this is funny," I said, "this is the second time that I hear this name." And then I told him how it had turned up in that séance.

My friend thereupon explained to me that this author had written a similar novel, but had never finished it, because he died young, suffering from the same ailment that had led me to a sanatorium in the Swiss Tessin, where we first had met. Not only the background of my story and the ideas expressed in it were similar to those of this author, but even the style, the imagery, the symbols, and the use of certain typical phrases.

I was surprised and assured my friend that I had never read a word of this author. And this was no wonder, because, as I learned now, he had died a century ago and was not popular enough to be included in the normal high school curriculum. Greatly impressed by my friend's words, I decided to order the works to which he had referred. But before I could get them (since they were not available in Italian bookshops) another strange thing happened.

One day I was invited to a birthday party, where, as usual in Capri, people of various nationalities were present. Among them was a German scholar who had just arrived on the island for a short stay and whom I had not met before. When entering the room where the party was held I noticed an expression of utter surprise on the face of the newcomer, and even after I had been introduced to him I felt constantly his gaze upon me.

A few days later I met the hostess again and asked her: "Who was the gentleman to whom you introduced me during your party? I wonder why he stared at me all the time. I never met him before and do not remember even his name."

"Oh, you mean Dr. So-and-so! Well, he has left already. But I can tell you what interested him so much in you. He is writing the biography and editing the works of a German mystic writer and poet who died a century or so ago. When you entered he could hardly master his surprise— as he told me later on—because the similarity between you and the only existing portrait of the poet from the time when he was about your age is so striking that it almost gave him a shock."

But a further surprise was in store for me. When the books I had ordered finally were in my hands I recognised not only substantial parts of "my story" but found certain passages *literally identical* with my own childhood writings! And the more I read, the more I began to realise that I read my own innermost thoughts and feelings, expressed in exactly the words and images which I myself was wont to use. But it was not only the world of my imagination which I found mirrored in every detail; there was something even more important, because it related to what I had conceived as my present lifework, the outline of a morphology of human thought and culture, resulting in a magic vision of the universe. I myself had drawn up such a plan with youthful optimism and had started to work on it in various fields (art, archaeology, religion, psychology, philosophy, etc.), hoping to collect and to co-ordinate the necessary material in the course of my life. But soon I found that the frame of the plan was too wide and that even a lifetime would not be sufficient to complete such an encyclopaedic work. Thus I was finally forced to confine myself only to such subjects for which I was best qualified by temperament, training, and inclination. Looking back upon my life, I now know that this was the right thing to do, and that what is left will be continued or accomplished in another life.

It is this certainty which fills me with confidence and peace, and allows me to concentrate unhurriedly on whatever task the present demands. No work of importance, that one's heart is bent upon with single-minded devotion, will remain unfinished.

It is not my ideal to be reborn forever in this world, but neither do I believe that we can abandon it before we have fulfilled our task in it—a task which we may have taken upon ourselves in some remote past, and from which we cannot run away like cowards. This is what Tibet has taught me.

Farewell: Last Village, Last Guru, Last View of Tibet

Poo looked like any other Tibetan village and the people too were the same as on the other side of the Shipki-La, though the political frontier, dividing Tibet and India, was drawn across the pass. This, however, had no meaning to the people on both sides, who spoke the same language, practised the same religion and who moved freely to and fro, while having practically no contact with the population on the Indian side of the main Himalayan Range, which was still five days' journey away from here.

We had hoped to find a post office here, but we were informed that an Indian mail-runner came only once a month, and when we asked when we could expect the next one we were informed: "In spring, when the passes over the Himalayas are open again." "When would this be?" we asked with some trepidation. "Oh, in about three months' time!"

It was then that we realized that it would be four months before we could return to India, because the journey from here to the plains or the first bigger town, i.e. Simla, would take another month. We would not have minded this, if it had not been that both our money and our provisions had come to an end, and we wondered how we would pull through for so many months! However, this was no problem for the good old man who was in charge of the rest-house (which had been provided for the officials of the Public Works Department, in charge of the caravan road across the Shipki-La) and who very kindly gave us the permission to put up there on his own responsibility, since we could not communicate with the authorities. "And if you are short of money," he continued, "I will give you as much as you need. You can return it to me when the mail comes or whenever it is convenient to you."

"But we are complete strangers to you, and we have no means of establishing our bona fides," we countered, whereupon he simply said: "It is my duty to help you and, moreover, I trust you."

His name was Namgyal and though he did not distinguish himself outwardly from the other villagers, wearing the rough, undyed homespuns and little round caps, characteristic of the inhabitants of these Himalayan valleys, he was highly respected in his community as a Nyingma Lama and a man of great religious devotion and knowledge. He treated us as if we were members of his own family, because, as he put it, we all belonged to the Arya-kula, "the noble family of the Buddha." He missed no opportunity of discussing religious subjects with us, and he even brought us some of his religious books, his most valued possessions, so that we could read and study them. Among them were the *Bardo Thodol*, the *Mani Kahbum*, and works dealing with the early history of Buddhism in Tibet and especially with Padmasambhava and the three great kings, Songtsen Gampo, Tisong Detsen, and Ralpachan. He would tell us, besides, many popular stories, of which he had a great repertoire, or he would read to us from one or the other of his books and discuss or explain points of particular interest.

One day Namgyal invited us to his house and showed us his meditation and prayer-room (on the top floor), which contained the house altar with various images and thankas and a proper Lama's seat under a multi-coloured canopy. His wife, an old and shrivelled lady, but with a face that showed strength and character, sang for us religious songs with a voice so beautiful, mellow, and tender, that one forgot her age. They both were ardent devotees of Padmasambhava, who seemed to be always present in their minds. To them Padmasambhava was none other than Sakyamuni Buddha in a new form and appearing to men in different disguises, compassionate as well as fierce, according to their needs. He was the ever-present protector and guide, who would stand by his devotees in danger and inspire them in their meditation. He was the special protector and friend of all animals and might even take their shape. Once, when the landscape was covered in deep snow, we heard the song of a bird. "It is

Him!" Namgyal said with great earnestness. On the tenth day of every Tibetan (lunar) month he was believed to descend among men and his devotees kept themselves ready on that day to receive him in mind and heart and in whatever form he might approach. Innumerable stories about him went from mouth to mouth, and they were all told in such a way as if they had happened quite recently. In fact, nobody thought of Padmasambhava as a figure of the remote past, but as somebody who had just passed through this valley and might return any moment. For the first time we realised the tremendous impact that Padmasambhava had on the Tibetan mind. He certainly was one of the most powerful personalities of Buddhist history. The miracle stories that grew up around him are nothing but the reflection of the unbounded admiration which his contemporaries and disciples felt for him, and if modern historians try to dismiss Padmasambhava as a "sorcerer and a charlatan" or as a "black magician," they only show their complete ignorance of human psychology in general and of religious symbolism in particular.

Would anybody, with any sense of fairness, dare to call Christ a "sorcerer or a charlatan," because he turned water into wine, healed the incurable, roused the dead, exercised evil spirits, defied Satan, resurrected from the grave after having been crucified and ascended to heaven in full view of his disciples? Why, therefore, should one ridicule the story of Padmasambhava's resurrection from the pyre, his victory over demons or whatever other miracles are ascribed to him? In fact, when missionaries came to Poo (many years ago) and told the people that Christ had sacrificed himself on the cross for the sake of humanity and had risen from the dead, they accepted this without hesitation and exclaimed: "It was Him!," thoroughly convinced that Christ and Padmasambhava were actually the same person. Thus the missionaries finally had to give up, not because they were rejected, but because their teachings were readily accepted as a confirmation of those very truths which Sakyamuni and Padmasambhava and many other Buddhist saints had taught.

To us, certainly, Padmasambhava came to life, more than ever before, during our stay in Poo, where his memory was as fresh as if he had been here only a few days ago and might turn up any moment again.

Many great Lamas had passed through this valley on their pilgrimage either from Tibet to the holy places in India or from India to Mount Kailas. One of the most prominent among them was Tomo Géshé Rimpoché, whom Namgyal remembered with special veneration, because it was here that he had restored to life the girl that had been ailing for years and who on his command "took her bed and walked away," to the open-mouthed surprise of those who had carried her on a stretcher and in the presence of the whole village. It was here that he exorcised the man who was possessed by a spirit and showed mercy even to that spirit by asking the villagers to build a small shrine for him as a dwelling-place, so that he would find rest and would no more trouble anyone. Modern people might look upon this as pure superstition; however, the effect proved the soundness of Tomo Géshé's advice: the man was cured and all his sufferings came to an end—whatever their actual cause might have been. A psychologist would probably be able to find a reasonable explanation in modern terminology for such phenomena and he would also admit that Tomo Géshé found the right remedy.

While listening to these and many other strange happenings, we came to hear a lot about the spirits that were supposed to inhabit certain localities. There was a group of old cedar trees not far from the village—the only trees in the otherwise bare landscape—and we were wondering how they could have survived not only the rigours of the climate (at an altitude of almost 9,000 feet), but even more the depredations of man in a place where wood was scarce and people had to roam far and wide to find fuel or wood for building. Namgyal explained that these trees were sacred and nobody would dare to touch them, because they were the abode of gods, and when we asked him how people knew this, he answered that they came and spoke to them and had even sometimes been seen. He said this in a matter-of-fact way, as if it was the most ordinary thing in the world, so that we felt almost guilty of ever having doubted such a possibility. To question such simple facts would have seemed to him the height of ignorance, and so we left it at that, little suspecting that one day we ourselves would witness the presence of these gods.

Tibetans are far more sensitive to psychic influences than most Westerners. They have not yet lost the capacity to communicate with the powers of their depth-consciousness or to understand their language, as revealed through dreams or other phenomena. One day Namgyal came and told us that he had seen in a dream a rainbow over our bungalow and that this could only mean a lucky event, like the arrival of some saintly person. And, indeed, the next day a Lama arrived and put up in a little outhouse belonging to our compound. We only saw him from a distance, while dismounting from his horse; and both the man as well as the horse seemed tired from a long journey. The Lama's robes were old and worn and the horse was limping and half blind. We were told that the Lama had returned from a long pilgrimage and would have to stay here until the passes were open.

Since the weather was cold and cloudy, we had remained in our room, but the following day the Lama himself called on us accompanied by Namgyal. How great was our joy and surprise when we recognised the Lama as our good old Abbot of Phiyang of whom we had taken tender farewells at Tsaparang, not expecting ever to meet him again. We had regretted this all the more, as we felt that here was a man from whom we could learn a great deal, especially in the field of meditational practice, and we felt almost cheated by fate that we should lose this rare opportunity the very moment it came our way.

Whether Phiyang Lama had foreseen that we were destined to meet again or not, one thing is sure: he had read our thoughts at that time, because now, before we could even mention our secret wish, he offered to instruct us in the most advanced methods of Tantric Sadhana and Yoga practices.

As our room was not only bigger but warmer than Phiyang Lama's, since we kept a big fire going the whole day, Phiyang Lama came daily with Namgyal (who thus became our Guru-bhai) to instruct us and discuss our problems. It was a most fruitful time, because never was a teacher more eager to give from the wealth of his own experience than this new Guru of ours, who thus continued the good work of Tomo Géshé and Ajo Rimpoché, for which we shall ever remember him with deep gratitude. And in this gratitude we must include also our Guru-bhai Namgyal, who helped us in so many ways, and our faithful Sherab, who looked after us like a son, so that we could dedicate ourselves completely to our religious studies and practices.

When the news of Phiyang Lama's arrival and continued stay spread among the Poopas, many came to receive his blessings and finally the villagers requested him to perform a Tsewang for the whole community. The ceremony was to take place in the spacious courtyard between Phiyang Lama's quarters and our bungalow. A few days before the great ceremony he retired into his room—much to our regret, as we missed our daily meetings—though we understood that he required some time of solitude and intense concentration in order to prepare himself and to call up those forces which he wanted to communicate to others. But then it seemed to us that another Lama had joined him, probably to assist him during the forthcoming ritual, because we heard another voice much deeper than his own from time to time coming from his room. The long and sonorous recitations of the new voice were sometimes interrupted by Phiyang Lama's voice, but neither he nor the other Lama was ever seen outside. We were greatly intrigued as to who the new Lama could be, but nobody could give us any information. So, one or two days later, while passing Phiyang Lama's door, we heard again the voice of the other Lama, and since the door was wide open, we glanced inside. To our surprise we saw no other person in the room but only Phiyang Lama. He seemed to be oblivious of our presence, and the strange voice came out of him so deep and sonorous, as if another person was speaking through him. We quickly withdrew from the door.

When the great day came, a high throne was erected in the courtyard between our bungalow and the outhouse. The throne stood against a high revetment wall, covered with a decorative cloth curtain, while the courtyard was festively decorated with multicoloured bunting and streamers. Phiyang Lama in the full regalia of an abbot was seated on the throne, his head covered with the tall red cap worn by the Nyingma and Kargyutpa Orders, to which he originally belonged, though being now the head of a Sakya-Gompa. Nobody could have recognized in him the poor old pilgrim, who might have been taken as a mendicant friar on the day of his arrival. The man on the throne had the bearing of a king and the voice of a lion. His face was that of an inspired prophet, and every gesture expressed dignity and power. Whoever was present could feel that here was a man who not merely implored or invoked some unseen power, but one who had *become* that power, by having generated or focalized it within himself in a state of complete and sustained absorption and oneness with a particular aspect of transcendental reality. He had become the very embodiment of Tsépamé (*Tse-dpag-med*), the Buddha of Infinite Life. His vision had become visible and communicable to all who attended the ritual, which held everybody spellbound and in a state of spiritual elation. The rhythm of mantric incantations and mystic gestures was like the weaving of a magic net, in which the audience was drawn together towards an invisible centre. The sense of participation was heightened when everybody received Tsépamé's blessings with a few drops of consecrated water and a small *tsé-ril,* a red consecrated pill of sweetened *tsampa,* representing the Wine and Bread of Life.

It was the most beautiful eucharistic rite we had ever witnessed, because it was performed by a man who had truly given his own blood and flesh, sacrificed his own personality, in order to make it a vessel of divine forces.

Never had I realized more thoroughly the importance of ritual in religion (and especially in community worship) and the folly of replacing it by preaching and sermonizing. Ritual—if performed by those who are qualified by spiritual training and sincerity of purpose—appeals both to the heart and to the mind, and brings people in direct contact with a deeper and richer life than that of the intellect, in which individual opinions and dogmas get the upper hand. Thus Phiyang Lama became the last of our Tibetan gurus.

Towards the end of April news came that the passes were opening and that the caravan road had been dug out from the avalanches which had blocked it during the previous months. The hour of parting came near, and while we were assembling our caravan and preparing for our final return to India, Phiyang Lama set out for his Gompa in the district of Tsaparang. Before our beloved Guru left, he bade us return to Tibet some day and to stay with him at his monastery. He gave us his "Soldeb" (gsol-hdebs), a beautiful prayer composed by him, as a last gift and guidance. Whenever reading it, we would be united with him in spirit.

On the morning of his departure we wanted to accompany him for a few miles, as a mark of respect and gratitude, but he firmly declined to accept this honour and insisted on walking alone. We bowed to his will, prostrated ourselves and received his last blessings. We all had tears in our eyes when we saw him walking along the road, a solitary pilgrim—poorer even than on the day of his arrival, because his horse had died some weeks before. When grazing on the steep hillside, a short distance from our place, it had fallen into a deep ravine, probably due to its one blind eye. The Lama's few belongings had been carried ahead by some of the villagers, who had volunteered for this last labour of love for the Guru who had given so much to the village by his presence and his selfless service.

As soon as the solitary figure had disappeared from our eyes, I turned into the house and began to recite the Soldeb in order to get over the pangs of parting, and lo!—without knowing how it happened—the deep voice of the Guru sounded from my own chest! Li and Sherab came running in wonder and I heard them shouting: "Has the Guru returned?" And then they saw me, and I could only say: "Only his voice has returned!" Since then the voice has come back whenever I remembered the Guru, our beloved Lama of Phiyang.

And so we left the Valley of Happiness, and returned to the world, not knowing that Tibet's hour of fate had struck and that we would never see it again, except in our dreams. But we knew that the Gurus and the treasures of memory that this unforgettable country had bestowed on us would remain with us till the end of our days.

Guru and Chela into the Light

Since it was Tomo Géshé Rimpoché who opened to me the gates of Tibet, it is only fitting that I close this story of my Tibetan pilgrimage with a few words about his new incarnation, the present Tulku, Jigmé Nagawang Kalzang Rimpoché.

By the time we reached India he was again on his way to Sera, where conditions were regarded as safe enough for him to continue his studies. He remained there until 1959, when he passed his final examination as Géshé and was thus confirmed in his former title.

Hardly had he left Sera to take up his residence at Lhasa when the people rose against their Chinese oppressors and saved the Dalai Lama from becoming a prisoner or a tool of the Communists, who had tried to pose as the liberators of the poor—a lie that was once and for ever exploded, when it was exactly the "poor" who, in spite of all inducements offered to then during the first years of Chinese occupation, revolted against their self-styled "liberators."

During these terrible events innumerable people came to Tomo Géshé Rimpoché, who had been all the time in close collaboration with the Dalai Lama's supporters, seeking solace and encouragement. As in his former life, he lavishly distributed his life-giving "ribus" [medicinal pills] to all who asked for his help and his blessings. Many of the Khampas, who had heard of Tomo Géshé's fame and the miraculous powers ascribed to his "ribus," threw themselves fearlessly into the struggle for the liberation of the Dalai Lama and their beloved country.

The Chinese soon began to fear Tomo Géshé's "ribus" as much as the bullets of the Khampas. They arrested him and threw him into prison, where they tried to break his spirit by exposing him to the most inhuman

conditions and humiliations, forced labour for sixteen hours a day on a star-
vation diet, demanding of him the lowest and dirtiest services and alternat-
ing this with the strictest solitary confinement without air and light.

Not long afterwards, people who had fled from Tibet reported that
Tomo Géshé had been killed by the Chinese, who—as we were told—
had poured boiling coal-tar over him, while he was sitting in meditation.
According to their story, he had died without a word of complaint or a
sign of fear.

We were deeply distressed, and the idea that our Guru should have
chosen to return in a human body, only to die a martyr's death, before
even having a chance to fulfil the mission for which he had come back,
seemed to us a particularly cruel and senseless fate.

How great, therefore, was our joy when in 1961 we read a report that
under diplomatic pressure from the Government of India and the personal interference of the Prime Minister, Jawaharala Nehru, the Chinese
had released the Rimpoché and that he had arrived in Gangtok on the
24th of June 1961 after more than two years of imprisonment. The reason for his escape from imprisonment and death was that, being born in
Gangtok (Sikkim), India could claim him as an Indian-protected person.
Now we could see the deeper reason why Tomo Géshé, in spite of his
wish to return to Dungkar Gompa, was not reborn in the Tomo Valley
(as people might have expected), but just a sort distance beyond the frontier of Tibet!

As I was not yet able to undertake the long journey from my present
abode in the Western Himalayas to Ti-Gah Chö-Ling or Kalimpong,
where Tome Géshé lives alternately in his two main monasteries, I
requested the Ven. Sangharakshita Thera, Head of the Triyāna Vardhana
Vihāra, Kalimpong, to ask the Rimpoché whether he remembered me,
his old disciple, and whether he had recognized me at Gyantse. His
answer was plain and simple: "I know him!"

We shall meet again as soon as conditions will make it possible. By
now I have reached the age of my old Guru, while he is now even
younger than I was when I met him in his previous life. But old or young,

the inner relationship between Guru and Chela remains, though the roles may be reversed outwardly. We shall meet again and again, till we both have fulfilled our task—till we both have become one with that ultimate light that is both our origin and our aim, and that unites us through many births and deaths and beyond.

Chapter III

The Lost World of Chinese Buddhism

John Blofeld

*The briefest encounters with Buddhism in England—seeing a motion pic-
ture with Buddhist subject-matter, chancing upon a small statue of
Buddha—convinced the young John Blofeld (1913–1987) to go to China,
where Buddhism still reigned as a living force. His memoirs of his experiences there,* The Wheel of Life, *evoke an exquisite, now-lost way of life,
in which Blofeld serves as a guide to the different kinds of Buddhism. The
Chinese (at least of the upper and middle class) favored a Buddhism of
renunciation and asceticism, he observed, because their daily routines were
aesthetic and epicurean. By contrast the Tibetans compensated for the
harsh, often barren landscapes they came from by creating a sumptuous,
sensual version of the dharma. Unknowingly at the time, Blofeld was
memorializing forms of Buddhism that were in the last years of their long
glory. Shortly before World War II, for example, he participated in a daz-
zling Tibetan festival in western China that gathered in all the fable and
romance of the Middle Ages—a spectacle such as, after Mao's revolution,
the world would never see again.*

*After World War II Blofeld obtained his degree from Cambridge, but,
except for that interval, he never lived in the West again. He settled in
Bangkok, where he taught at the university and headed the editorial services for the United Nations, as he produced translations (of, for example,*

the I Ching) while writing noteworthy books of his own. His Tantric Mysticism of Tibet (1970) was the first overview of Tibetan Buddhism accessible to a general western audience. At the very end of his life, Blofeld expressed hope for the future, for there had sprung up in the West two Tibetan Buddhist centers! Today, a generation later, there are hundreds and hundreds of Buddhist centers throughout Europe and America. Blofeld's career first intimated that such a thriving might come to pass.

Moving to China. Coming Face to Face with a Sage

It was no part of my plan to begin by tying myself down to a regular job. I had arrived [in Hong Kong] almost without funds, but my desire for freedom to travel overrode all considerations of prudence. I lived on what I had brought with me for about a month and discovered that, with the cost of living so low, payment for an article published in a minor British or American periodical was enough to keep me going for weeks. And, when this means failed, a month or two spent in any of the larger cities teaching English to private students could easily provide me with funds for further travels: for I traveled light, did not study comfort, and was content to get about as do the poorer classes of literate Chinese.

To save the expense and discomfort of a hotel, I rented a small ground-floor room giving on to one of those narrow streets falling down the peakside into Caine Road, so steep that even in dry weather a heavy man can scarcely walk down them without clutching at projections of the buildings. For four Hong Kong dollars a month (five shillings) I obtained the services of a sharp little demon called Ah Heng who, though not yet thirteen, could even cook after a fashion.

One evening, I was gripped by a fierce and unaccountable fever. My bones ached, my legs trembled and my head seemed about to burst. I had, just then, no money at all, so it was with reluctance that I sent Ah Heng out in search of a doctor. Obediently, he covered his naked torso with a little jacket of black lacquered silk to match his floppy trousers and walked out barefoot into the lamplit street.

He soon returned, showing no signs of having condescended to hasten, so I was surprised when a doctor arrived almost on his heels. My perceptions were clear again after a short bout of delirium and I gazed at the doctor with growing interest. I saw a slender, scholarly looking man in his middle thirties, dressed in a summer robe of plain white silk and wearing the old-fashioned skull cap topped with a button-sized red bobble which was already as rare in Hong Kong as a top hat in London. His face, with its tightly drawn skin, showed an unhealthy pallor, but the quality of its expression was so striking that I almost forgot my pains and discomforts in the pleasure of watching him. Besides showing concern for a very sick man, the pallid face reflected a deep inner calm, a serenity of mind and good-humoured tolerance which would have made him a good model for the craftsmen who mould the features of the calm, gently smiling Bodhisattvas imaged in wood and stone. I had never before received such an impression of mental alertness and poise, and this impression was heightened by his wholly unstudied grace of gesture and movement.

After some brief courtesies, the doctor stepped close to the camp-bed where I lay and began his "examination." Even before that moment I had begun to wonder how this fragile, inward-centred being could be a man of science; and now I became seriously alarmed. Clearly Ah Heng had been either too thoughtless or just too lazy to go in search of one of the many local doctors trained in Europe or in the Hong Kong University Medical School. Instead, he had summoned a close neighbour, a physician versed in the ancient medical arts of the East. It was all very well for me to admire the great Lao-tsě as a superb philosopher, but I had never envisaged submitting my physical body to the science of the Yin and the Yang. Yet I was soon able to relax. Too ill to deal with the awkward problem of dismissing this doctor and summoning another, I was reassured by the swift, delicate movements of the fingers which drew my hand from beneath the thin sheet.

The feeling of my pulse entailed three consecutive and sustained pressures on each wrist in turn, as though I possessed *six* separate pulses! Meanwhile, a great stillness had fallen upon the doctor; it was as if with his whole being he was absorbing a subtle impression of my condition, perhaps psychic as well as physical. Later, when he asked me about the symptoms of my disease, he spoke with the negligent air of one seeking formal confirmation of something already well-known to him.

After a little while, he seated himself at a cheap rattan table which served me both as a desk and for meals. From somewhere about his person he drew forth a little folder of blue silk containing writing materials. There were a rectangular stick of black ink engraved with squat, solid characters and giving off a faint perfume; a miniature stone ink-slab; two or three thin brushes, and a tablet of very soft paper. Ah Heng, who had been standing by in awed silence, ran into the kitchen-bathroom for water, which the doctor used in grinding his ink with deft, rotary movements of the wrist. I watched the characters of the prescription taking shape beneath a brush which remained uncompromisingly vertical. As with all good calligraphers, the doctor required no support either for wrist or forearm, yet the brush was firmly under his control. When the prescription was ready, Ah Heng was dispatched with it to the Golden Dragon Medical Hall. He ran off holding it reverently as though the brush-strokes had endowed it with sacred properties. He was also clutching two Hong Kong dollar notes which he must loyally have taken from his own pitiful little board. I was so touched that I made up my mind to repay him with 100 per cent interest when I could.

The doctor lingered for a little chat. He enquired my Chinese name, which is P'u Lotao, and informed me that his own "insignificant" name was Tsai Tahai, also that he lived in the next street with his father, a retired physician to the former mandarins of Canton, and that his professional address was in Caine Road, five minutes' walk from my house. Just as he was in the act of rising to take leave, an expression of surprise crossed his face and he arrested his movement.

"Mr. P'u, are you perhaps a Buddhist?"

"So you've noticed my little wall-shrine? Yes, Doctor Tsai, I've been a Buddhist for a few years. And you?"

He nodded vigorously. "Indeed, yes. But this makes me so very happy. I was not aware that the Buddha-Dharma had spread to your honoured country. Now we shall become the best of friends. You will see. Will you not allow me to express my very great delight by making you an insignificant present of my poor medical services? It will give me so much pleasure. You see, I do not charge my friends—ever—and I should like to be allowed to think of you as a friend."

My relief at not having to pay a large bill or to produce ready money was swallowed up in a warmth of affection for the pale, little man—an affection which lasted until his death many years later. I was so moved that I could only smile my thanks.

In a few days, I was sufficiently recovered to return one of his daily visits. As our friendship ripened, I came to spend more and more of my leisure hours in the Caine Road consulting-room. Soon, my camp-bed and rattan furniture were hardly more familiar to me than that lovely room with walls hidden halfway to the ceiling with book-cases, above which were framed laudatory calligraphic inscriptions—presents from grateful patients who had hired the city's finest calligraphers to compose them in his honour. Bookcases and furniture were all of heavy black-wood, its somber magnificence relieved by brilliant spots of colour—the glowing yellow and ruby tints of Ch'ien Lung vases and bowls. I used to sit there for hours at a time, sometimes questioning Tahai about Chinese Buddhism, but more often we would discuss the fast-vanishing traditions to which he clung with gentle and loving determination. In the street outside, twentieth-century traffic roared past. The university-bound buses were often crowded with youngsters self-consciously defying tradition by an elaborate casualness sometimes amounting to downright rudeness and, in some cases, disfigured by nondescript "campus-style" garments inspired by Hollywood. The girls were less brash in blazoning their break with tradition, but not all of them shrank from public flirting so long as no actual contact of hand or body was involved.

The atmosphere of this busy street formed a strange contrast to the quiet of Tahai's study—"consulting-room" seemed a hardly appropriate description of a room in which the sole concessions to medical practice were a three-inch cushion of brocaded satin for use during the feeling of the six pulses, and the volumes of ancient medical treatises confined, in sets of six volumes, in dark blue cloth-bound boxes fastened with ivory clasps. Here the fragrance of a fast-vanishing world still lingered; its essence was compounded of intangibles, while its concrete ingredients were the must of old volumes, the very faint perfume of Chinese ink, the tang of Tahai's Fukien tea, and the scent of ever-present flowering plants which were varied according to season.

Shortly before Chinese New Year came a really cold day. In obedience to some rare whim, on getting up in the morning, I placed a pretty yellow flower in the buttonhole of my warm, English-made suit. That afternoon, I ran all the way to Tahai's place, for a cutting north wind pierced right through my good, warm overcoat. I saw at once that something very unusual was taking place, for which I had come quite unprepared. The large room was densely packed with visitors—all men, and very nearly all in Chinese gowns rather than fashionable suits and overcoats. This small fact told me something about the kind of people they were. Seated upon the couch of honour which, according to ancient tradition, faced the doorway, was an elderly stranger who was clearly a person of great consequence, for I saw at once that he formed the hub of the whole gathering. His drooping 'mandarin' moustache and loose robe of dark purple called to mind the figures in Chinese ancestral portraits. I also noticed with some astonishment that, while everybody else remained standing, three or four of my friends were sitting at the stranger's feet. This was especially odd, for the Chinese, unlike any other Asian race from Egypt to Japan, have used chairs as we use them in the West for as much as eleven hundred years; the floor is considered unclean (even to the naked foot on getting up in the morning); and no self-respecting Chinese dreams of sitting there, even for a moment. One other point I noticed was that, among the few complete strangers present, were three or four whose curiously full gowns were more like robes and were secured by yellow sashes, besides being antique in choice of colour— plum-red or dark ochre. I thought that they might be Mongolians.

While I was hesitating in the doorway, Tahai returned from some- where else in the building and, taking me by the arm, led me straight across to the majestic guest of honour. On the way he embarrassed me by whispering with great emphasis: "Be careful, now. Three full protesta- tions." Then he raised his voice and, using the sing-song inflections of ceremonial speech, called out in his badly pronounced Mandarin:

"Your Reverence. A young friend from the Western Ocean. A Buddhist. Mr. P'u Lotao."

I had long been in the habit of prostrating myself before my shrine morning and evening and, though I had never before done this to a human being, I managed to get through the ceremony with sufficient grace to pass muster, laying hands, elbows and head on the ground from a kneeling position and then standing up, kneeling again, and repeating the movement twice more. While doing this, I noticed that "His Holiness's" robe did not seem to be clerical, despite its old-fashioned cut; nor did he display any clerical adornments, such as a 108-bead rosary. So why the title and why the necessity for such extreme ceremony? It was very puzzling. A deep silence had fallen on everyone, broken only by whispered exclamations of surprise and, I think, of approval. All of them must have known of the normal Englishman's extraordinary aversion to the kowtow, even though he insists on foreigners showing respect to English persons and institutions in the native manner.

The stranger smiled.

"A Buddhist? From *England?* I am glad." I sensed from these few words that he spoke Mandarin fluently, but his diction was so devoid of those tonal inflections necessary to the comprehension of any Chinese dialect that he sounded like a European beginner who has failed to master the tones. Yet he *looked* typically Chinese—northern rather than Cantonese, but certainly like a Chinese of some sort. Or a Mongolian. I could not be sure.

"Yes, Your Reverence, an English Buddhist."

He lightly touched my shoulder, indicating that I should seat myself on the floor where three or four people were already sitting.

"Then, as a foreign Buddhist," the flat voice continued, "perhaps you would care to ask me some questions or discuss some of your special problems with me. We of Tibet are credited with some little knowledge of spiritual matters and especially of meditational methods." He was smiling broadly, either with amusement or with genuine pleasure. Impossible to say which.

"Yes—er—Your Reverence; yes, of course. That is . . ." I felt myself growing confused. *We of Tibet?* Could this be one of the so-called Living Buddhas? But, no, they had not addressed him as *Fuyeh*. I had often read that Tibetan Lamaism is a coarse travesty of Buddhism, thickly encrusted with superstition and black magic, so I had never cared to waste time studying it. On the other hand, this stranger had an unmistakable air of wisdom, kindness and—or so it seemed—of possessing advanced spiritual knowledge; for he made an impression on me like that made by Tahai at our first meeting, though in a different way. This man was more humorous, more laughter-loving, I thought. It had been most impressive to see how he affected the others in the room; I knew them too well to believe that they were mere priest-worshippers or likely to be overawed by a title, however exalted. Just now, Tahai had looked positively like an acolyte before an archbishop. It was all too confusing and, moreover, to add to this confusion, I remembered the stupid flower in my buttonhole. If the stranger was really a man of great spiritual attainment, he would despise me for such silly vanity. My attempt to answer him had long ago tailed off into silence, a silence which had now become embarrassingly prolonged. I felt the narrow, almost lidless eyes examining me with minute attention. At last the calm, uninflected voice spoke again:

"Never mind. A flower is always good."

I felt myself stiffen with shocked astonishment. *Never mind?* Why had he used those words? It was as though he were reading my thoughts like an—well, yes, quite literally like an open book! I waited for what would follow, tense and excited.

"Of course," the voice went on slowly, "flowers symbolize purity. Hence do we offer them to the Precious Ones. Well? You have *no* questions at all?"

I felt he was testing me. By my choice of questions I would reveal the depth or superficiality of my knowledge and spiritual attainment.

"Your Reverence," I stammered. "I—I do not speak much Mandarin. Perhaps I could ask someone to interpret? And, really, I am very ignorant. My questions will make Your Reverence laugh at me."

"You are agitated," he answered soothingly. "There is no need for that. And the matter of language is a trifle, not worth your thought. But I see you are still a little flustered. This happy encounter was too sudden. It means much to me, also. Will you not rest a little and formulate your questions at leisure? I am so very curious to know what they will be."

I seized gratefully at this respite and, getting to my feet, hastened to a far corner of the room, leaving others to crowd forward in my place. For more than an hour, they continued to ply His Reverence with questions or listened while his clear, flat voice stabbed the silence which fell around him when he spoke. Presently, somebody joined me in my corner near the window. This was Ah Lok, a young man wearing a smart brown suit and a tie of pale green who was a distant connection of Tahai's. I had often noticed that it fretted him to have to conform so much to the rigid conventions of his elders, and I had known him speak at once scoffingly and enviously of his relations' preoccupation with Buddhism. He was a likeable youth with a pretty, rather girlish, face, whose beautiful manners seemed more effortless than they were. I was surprised to meet him at such a gathering.

"Hallo, Number Six, what are you doing among all of us would-be Bodhisattvas?" I spoke in English, roughly translating his Chinese nickname which indicated that he was the sixth of several brothers and sisters.

"Don't waste your time on me, John," he answered with a grin. "You should be preparing your *homework* for Teacher. Better think up some high-sounding questions. The Dorjé Lama will not forget, you may be very sure."

"Who exactly is he?" I enquired softly.

"Some sort of Grand Lama from Tibet, returning there from West China. It's easier to come this way and go all the way round by sea to Calcutta. The direct route crosses too many deserts, mountains and jungles—as you should know if you've read the records of the ancient Chinese pilgrims to India."

An older man, a stranger who had been standing within earshot, added some information. His English was less fluent than Six's. "His Reverence, he come from Szechuan Province. He have plenty Chinese disciples there—hundreds, maybe thousands—he stay there twenty-five years, now going back his home, plenty good man, big book-scholar, very holy, have plenty powers. Maybe can fly, but maybe not, or what for he go home by train and ship." The stranger roared at his own joke, yet he obviously held the Lama in high esteem. "His name, Dorjé Chüncheh. Chüncheh is Cantonese for Rimpoché, Tibetan title like D.Litt. in England, but much more higher. When you speak him again, you call him 'Rimpoché,' for make him see you know proper how to do. Let him see English Buddhist is proper Buddhist."

The old fellow, whose manner suggested a small landowner from a remote district or something of the kind, made me a little bow and drew Six away. I was left alone now, more or less hidden behind the backs of a group of visitors who were straining to hear what was being said at the farther end of the room. I was not in the least tempted to make up subtle questions just for the purpose of letting the Rimpoché "see English Buddhist is proper Buddhist." I had come to share the prevailing feeling of respect for the Rimpoché and, besides, thought this a good opportunity to learn something at first hand about Tibetan Buddhism. After some thought, I managed to frame five questions more or less as follows:

1. The Lord Buddha once described ritual as one of the major hinderances to Enlightenment; then why have almost all schools of Buddhism, especially the Tibetan, adopted so much ritual?

2. In Burma and Ceylon, Gautama Buddha alone is offered respect. Do the other Buddhas and gods in the Mahayana system have any reality and importance for us?

3. Do the Bodhisattvas, symbolical of Mercy, Action, Knowledge and the rest, have real power to help us, or are the Burmese right in believing that we must depend solely on ourselves?

4. Which form of meditation or contemplation is best for a beginner like myself?

5. Many Westerners have claimed that the Tibetan form of Buddhism is the least authentic of all, largely on account of the enormous number of deities and demons, and of the horrific portrayals of the forms even of certain Buddhas. How does Your Holiness account for such widespread error?

(I was not then convinced that such writers were in error, but by Asian standards my question was already blunt enough to qualify me for inclusion among those barbarians who delight in combative questions and answers.)

Towards evening, when many of the visitors had already taken leave, I found myself still left alone in my corner, as though everybody was aware that I had been set some special task. At last I began to think that I had been driven from the Rimpoché's head by the spate of questions from other and more learned people. When only four or five people were left in the room, I went across to take leave, carefully masking the mixture of disappointment and relief which I secretly felt. I prostrated myself as before. Just as I rose from the third obeisance the Rimpoché's fingers lightly touched my head and I noticed that he was intoning something in a very low voice. The unintelligible words were followed by some brief sentences in Chinese.

"Come back this evening after your meal. Dr. Tsai expects you, and there will be Mr. Li to interpret from Mandarin into English. I speak no Cantonese and Dr. Tsai tells me that you have but little Mandarin."

"I am grateful, Your Reverence," I answered. "I shall come after dinner."

As I left the room he drew his feet up beneath the purple robe and sat crosslegged on the couch, with eyes half closed, exactly like a painting of an Arahan lost in meditation.

I was taken to dinner in the house of Tahai's aged father, where some eight or nine of the visitors had been bidden. When, an hour or so later, it was time for me to return to Caine Road, I had to go alone, as Tahai was still busy with his guests. I found the Rimpoché seated in the same position as before, as though he had not moved since I had left him. Only one other person was present, a curio merchant from Shantung who had once kept a *bric-à-brac* shop in Bloomsbury. This Mr. Li's English was clear and precise, which made him a good choice for an interpreter, as Mandarin was his native language. We both sat at the Rimpoché's feet and I waited to be asked for the first of my questions.

The expected demand never came. Instead, the Rimpoché began talking, pausing now and then for Mr. Li to interpret whatever I had difficulty in understanding. This was often very necessary, for the toneless delivery was sometimes hard even for Mr. Li to follow. The shock which the words "Never mind" had caused me had been partly forgotten during my efforts to prepare suitable questions, so I was not at all ready for what was about to follow; and it was with fresh astonishment that I stumbled upon a realization of what was happening. The Lama began as follows:

"My young friend, the things that worry you are really much simpler than they appear—that is, simple *in a way*, just as in another way they are among the profoundest things in the world. I so much want you to understand, for you are the first man from the Western Ocean whom I have had the joy of instructing. Because of this joy, I am treating you like one of my most intimate disciples."

I opened my mouth to express my appreciation, but was silenced by a gesture.

"No, please. Listen now, and ask your questions later. Good. Now, touching this problem concerning ritual . . ."

I sucked in my breath. *Ritual?* How could this be a coincidence? Yet surely he could not be dealing with the subject of my very first question, knowing it to be such, at a time when I had given no hint as to what it would be? My astonishment seemed to amuse the Lama, for his face puckered into a smile that was very near laughter. "The Lord Gautama Buddha's condemnation of ritual . . ."

Doubt? How could I doubt? But, equally, how did he know? Telepathy? Magic? Black magic? Or was this power the precious fruit of real Enlightenment—a Buddha's Enlightenment? I would have given much to know, for my disquiet amounted almost to fear. But—great Heavens, I wasn't even listening to what he was saying! Whatever happened, I must not lose another word. Leaning forward, I sought to pick up the thread, determined to "listen with both ears." Fortunately, my withdrawal into myself can have lasted only a few seconds.

". . . is the Buddha's meaning. Empty ritual *unaccompanied by its spiritual counterpart*, repeated by rote and not properly understood by the adept—*that* is meaningless; *that* is what constitutes one of the Four Hindrances! But ritual carefully practised so that every gesture, every use made of the sacred symbols, has a fully understood symbolic meaning, rites which help the adept to focus his mind on some aspect of Truth—how can these be hindrances? These constitute the rope, the axe, the spiked boots with which we assail our Everest in the manner of your Western climbers—our Everest, the Mountain of Wisdom, Mount Sumeru itself. Only when the climber has learnt to fly like a bird can he ascend without these things. Without them, he will lose himself among the snow-drifts of ignorance, or fall headlong into the valleys. I will not conceal from you that there are many in Tibet who mistake the climber's tools for Wisdom's jewels and who seek no further. Western travellers in our country meet such fools and return to their own country ready to laugh at or to condemn us all. Yet I have heard that our sacred texts have been translated into your language. How is it, then, that your people are not familiar with those pure gems of Wisdom and Truth?"

I shook my head. By now I was so much under the spell of the Rimpoché's sincerity that I was past being astonished. Whether, while talking to those others, he had reached his mind out across the room and read my every thought, or whether he was only now reading the questions stored in my memory, or whatever the explanation, it seemed quite unimportant beside the fact of the miracle itself. After a short pause, he continued:

"As for the great pantheon of peaceful and wrathful deities, what are they but emanations from your own minds, corresponding to the noble and evil propensities of your own being? Since Mind alone exists, and since all apparent differentiation between this and that, I and you, is contained within it, where else could the deities (Lha) reside? The mind of every being is as broad and deep as the cosmos itself. It is the entire cosmos, not a part but the whole—call it what you will. If you cannot understand now, be patient until one day when these words will seem to you no more profound than what children are taught by their village teacher. In this world of the senses where I speak to you, good and evil differ as do sunshine and black night, but Mind is above both. Good, evil, lovely, repulsive—all is Mind. The wrathful, blood-drinking deities with their skull-cups and horrid ornaments are as much a part of your mind as the Bodhisattva's compassionate smile."

During this part of his discourse, which was much more detailed than its reproduction here, I was doubly glad of Mr. Li's services as interpreter. Much that the Lama said was hard to grasp; yet there was nothing that seemed hopelessly improbable or contrary to my understanding. He seemed to be expressing on one level things which I had intuitively understood at a lower level.

"That the Bodhisattvas and deities," he continued, "can extend you boundless aid is very sure. Reach out to them and visualize their separate forms, each of which corresponds to something real within yourself. Or, if the method of Southern Buddhism is more to your liking, visualize truth as being symbolized by the Three Gems—so long as you are diligent and faithful, it matters little. As there are many levels of truth, so are there many methods, many means to the one Goal. Once in Kalimpong I met a man from your country dressed all in black, a lama of your people. He quoted to me: 'In my Father's house are many dwellings,' and when he explained these words I perceived that I had been wrong in supposing the people of his faith to be lost in the darkness of ignorance. I would have admired him very much if he had gone so far as to admit that some of those dwellings might be Buddhist dwellings, but he had the defect of narrow-mindedness, like most Christians who come to 'give light to Tibet,' as they call it. Otherwise he was a wise and saintly man. Yes, some of those dwellings *are* Buddhist, and even of Buddhist dwellings there are many and many.

"To use the powers you will gain through meditation, through the inward turning of your mind, you must first gain control of your own 'self' as a wrestler masters his enemy, or as a lover wins and possesses the body of his beloved. For this you will need a Teacher, a guide. I, alas, shall not be with you long; but be assured that when you are ripe for further teaching, a Teacher will appear. Perhaps many. Meditations on the Great Void, on Infinite Mind, visualizations of the deities, contemplation of your own inner being, study of the sutras, the practice and realization of the teachings of the Southern School—all, all are arrows directed to the same target, rays of the same sun, threads of light from the same moon. What does it matter? We of Tibet have long known these things for Truth; yet do not suppose that every monk belted with a yellow or red sash has mastered them. Some there are—simple people—to whom the deities are as *real* as the flower which embarrassed you today. Ignorant, superstitious people. Yet, if they are carried along by the force of their sincerity, they may arrive before you—before me."

The Rimpoché laughed unaffectedly. Then he added words which I shall never forget: "Be tolerant, love, understand. The whole universe is but yourself. When you laugh at me, you are laughing at yourself. When you break the stem of a flower, you break your own leg."

He bent forward to touch my head in dismissal. When I looked up, meaning to express my gratitude, I saw that the old man's eyes were half closed, the broad mouth slightly parted, the knotted fingers joined in the mudra of meditation. His mind might have been a thousand universes away, so withdrawn was his expression. Thanks were not needed. So I performed my prostrations with deep reverence, making each movement a conscious rather than an automatic tribute. Mr. Li, after taking leave with equal reverence, gently pushed me towards the door.

As soon as we reached the passage outside, Tahai and two or three friends appeared from the next room. But I felt a great weariness and disinclination to talk, which Tahai perceived at once. While courteously inviting me to stay awhile, he was actually leading me by the hand towards the front door. I did not even say goodbye; I just smiled my thanks and walked off into the lamplit street, where the noodle-hawkers who come by night were crying their wares.

•   •   •   •

One day, when I had crossed over to Kowloon to teach English to the daughters of a retired general known as "Old Foxy Chan," the Rimpoché, who was very soon to return to Tibet, made an important pronouncement. Later Tahai, who possessed the phenomenal memory of a true Chinese scholar, repeated it to me almost word for word, but in his native Cantonese. The Lama had first spoken of his very real regret at having to leave us so soon, but he was worried about his disciples in Tibet, for his home-monastery could not be reached by post or telegraph in less than several weeks or months. However, he would not leave us without performing a service which we might find to be of lasting value.

"Three years from now," he said, "death will claim me and I should be sorry not to pass my last years at home; so I shall not have the happiness of meeting you again in this life, or of leading you forward step by step as is our custom. Instead I shall bestow upon you a 'Grand Initiation,' which will include the individual initiations normally performed at long intervals for those who have completed the preliminaries to each successive step. You already have enough knowledge and experience to make use of the lower degrees. For the rest, I shall trust you not to pursue any of the higher mysteries until you have faithfully followed out the written and oral instructions which I shall leave with you."

Tahai, fearing that I might be thought too young and too ignorant to be included among those to be initiated, had put in a special plea for me to which the Rimpoché answered that he had already decided to include me, if two of the others would undertake that I would neither practise nor reveal anything of the various methods of inner realization until I had faithfully accomplished the preparatory work. He made this stipulation because, he said, too many foreigners had probed the mysteries either to gain money or fame by writing about them, or else to gratify curiosity, which was sometimes contemptuous and seldom directed at the high ends which those mysteries served. But his own impression, based on slight knowledge of me, was that I was quite sincere. He only feared that, like many young men, I might change later.

A crochety painter from Fukien known as Old Uncle Cheng had at once joined Tahai in pledging my good faith. The old fellow had conceived a curiously grudging affection for me in spite of his intense dislike of Westerners, whose directness of speech he found offensive. This attitude amused the rest of us a good deal, for we all felt that Uncle Cheng was quite often gratuitously rude in a coarse manner that would cause many Westerners to blush. When I returned from teaching 'Foxy Chan's' pretty but subdued and bashful daughters, I received the great news with mixed feelings.

"Of course it *is* a great honour," I said when Tahai told me in Uncle Cheng's presence what had been decided. "All the same, I don't really care for these *mysteries*. Did not the Lord Buddha state that he had kept *nothing* back? Then why should there be any esoteric teaching of Buddhism?"

My reply took Uncle Cheng aback. Very much put out by this fresh example of barbarian bluntness, he glared at me and wagged a forefinger almost in my eyes.

"Surely the Lord Buddha kept nothing back. We all know that, Little Brother. But do you suppose that he taught *all* things to *all* his disciples?

Does any profound scholar, a member of the Hanlin Academy for example, prate to children of the inner meanings of things? To do so would be to sully his jade wisdom, for to the children it would sound like the braying of mules."

Tahai tried to restore peace, but I pressed the argument.

"How do we know," I asked, "that the Mahayana claim to have preserved the highest teachings, some of them esoterically, is valid? Can we be so sure that these 'teachings' were not put into the mouth of the Buddha by later generations of monks?"

Old Uncle Cheng's glare grew fiercer. He exactly resembled an elderly archbishop confronted by a crude, if unintentional, blasphemer. Suddenly he dragged himself to his feet, muttering under his breath, and began limping towards the doorway. Tahai was left to do what he could with this loutish barbarian youth. He smiled a hint I should not take offence and said softly:

"For the present, have faith in your teachers—even in me, a little, if you like. You need age and experience to mellow you, Little Brother. Not that I am so very much your senior, but as you have said yourself, I belong to a race old in wisdom. Did you not say that we Chinese are born white-haired old men, springing thus from the womb like Lao-tsĕ in the legend? If you are wise, you will accept the initiation. Perhaps, years later, you will be glad that you did so."

Silence followed. At last I raised my eyes from the floor where a few red ants were crawling cautiously round my shoe. Then I said:

"All right, Big Brother. I will take your advice. I still have a great hankering to approach the inner world in a simpler way through Zen, or as the Southern Buddhists do. I agree that the Hinayana teaching is more dull and arid than the transcendental soarings of Mahayana, but still think it *may* be nearer the truth. I—I'm just not sure. But don't give me up to my own pride, my confidence in my own judgement. Continue to teach me, and no doubt you'll succeed in the end. By the way, when is the Grand Initiation to take place?"

Pleased with my frankness, Tahai made one of his very rare open gestures of affection. (He had a horror of physical contact with other people.) Taking my hand, he held it during the whole of our short walk to the Tibetans' house, where we went to discuss the arrangements for the initiation.

.   .   .   .

By some mischance, I arrived very late for the rites which were to culminate in the initiation of twenty-six Chinese laymen and myself into the higher mysteries of Tibetan Buddhism. It took place in the large guest-hall of the Tibetans' house. All the usual furniture had been removed and the ground covered with carpets for sitting on. To one side of the room sat the candidates for initiation, crosslegged and upright, but relaxed. They looked grave and even stately in their long ceremonial robes of white cotton. Facing them at a distance was a very low table furnished with various ritual objects. I noticed that the incense-sticks had been laid horizontally upon a bed of ash in an oblong burner, instead of being planted vertically according to the Chinese custom. There were seven miniature silver bowls of pure water mystically symbolizing the treasures of the universe, and a row of finely wrought silver butter-lamps, which gleamed amid the pagoda-shaped *torma* kneaded from buttered flour.

Cross-legged on his cushion behind this altar sat the Rimpoché. He was wearing the "eight-petalled-lotus" hat to symbolize the spiritual forces that would descend through him upon the initiates. His personal followers, now clad like the Rimpoché in the dull red ecclesiastical robes of the Gelugspa (Yellow-Hat) Sect, were ranged two on each side of him. I observed these details from the doorway while I was drawing over my ordinary clothes a long ceremonial robe with butterfly-wing sleeves. I glanced with some interest at the faces of my friends. A few of them were watching with expressions of detachment like observers taking a purely scientific or aesthetic interest in the rites; I saw no indication of the mingled rapture and amaze of people overwrought by revivalist eloquence; nor were there signs of the terrible soul-searing remorse engendered by reminding people of their inherent wickedness, of the grim doctrine of original sin. Equally, I failed to discover any suggestions of self-complacency or of spiritual pride in being thus uniquely honoured by a high dignitary of the Buddhist Church. Rather their faces seemed to have borrowed and intensified Tahai's habitual expressions of outward alertness and inward calm. I recalled, now, that the Rimpoché had promised only to endow them with what he called "seeds" (potentials which must be developed according to precise rules and over a period of years before they would be found spiritually stimulating). This very gradual process of fruition must depend entirely upon the efforts of each individual.

With my gown carefully adjusted, I prostrated myself three times in the direction of the Rimpoché. Then, as unobtrusively as possible, I crawled to a vacant space in the last row of almost motionless, white-gowned figures. The rites, which must have begun an hour or so before my arrival, continued without pause for so long that I lost all sense of time. Chiefly they consisted of sonorous Tibeto-Sanskrit chants intoned by the deep-voiced lamas, impressive but incomprehensible, accompanied by the roll of twirling hand-drums from which clappers depended on silken cords. A profoundly hypnotic effect was produced by the glittering points of flame reflected on burnished silver, the low-pitched hum or growl of the belly-deep chanting, the harsh clack-*clack*-clack-clack-*clack* of the hand-drums, and sometimes by the weaving of the Rimpoché's slender fingers in and out of long, rapid successions of *mudras*. Though, to one ignorant of the words, the ceremony held little variety, I do not think any of us were burdened by a sense of monotony. I, myself, was perfectly happy and at peace until the arrival of cramp-pains in my legs. Surreptitiously I wiggled my feet and raised and lowered my knees beneath the folds of my gown. The nearly motionless calm of all the others filled me with envy.

When it was my turn to go forward, I suddenly recalled my sensations as a child when taking my first communion. Not only was the feeling of awe and trepidation similar, but the Lama gave me the same sort of fleeting smile of encouragement as I had received from the bishop almost ten years before. On this occasion, however, the smile was succeeded by an expression of rather terrifying solemnity, which was all the more disturbing because I had seldom seen the Rimpoché without at least the suggestion of a smile hovering round the corners of his lips or shining from his eyes.

Abruptly, the long invocation came to its end amid a crescendo from the disciples' hand-drums. As before, the Rimpoché raised his hands high in a ritual gesture and this time brought them gently to rest on my head. I had seen this happen almost twenty times to other people, but they had had their backs to me, and I was by no means prepared for what followed. At the touch of those hands, a shock of frightening strength shot through my body, racing down from head to throat and onwards through heart and solar plexus to the base of my spine, and simultaneously shooting out along my arms and legs, penetrating as far as my fingers and toes. My body must have shaken visibly with its violence. The room swam before me and a darkness, shot with fire, rushed upon me. When, after what seemed to have been a long time, I recovered something like normal consciousness, I was very much surprised to find myself still kneeling in the same place and with the Rimpoché's hands only just in the act of rising from my head. I suppose that the 'long time' had occupied no more than a few seconds. Once his hands were withdrawn I felt able to creep back to my place behind most of the others, and in so doing I passed the next candidate. My current sensations were difficult to analyse. In one way, I felt so drained of energy as to be doubtful about my ability to continue sitting upright; in another way, I was conscious of a hidden but enormous reserve of strength which could, I felt, have been summoned into action by the smallest exertion of my will. (This description is admittedly rather nonsense, but it is the nearest I can get to describing that unfamiliar feeling.) The paradox extended further; I could not be sure if my prevailing sensation was one of joy or of fearful disquiet, of almost exquisite pleasure or something very like physical pain.

During the concluding part of the rites, I sat so dazed and shaken—though curiously happy in a way—that half the people with me had got to their feet and were following the lamas out of the room before I was aware of anyone having moved, or that the drumming and chanting had stopped. In trying to get to my feet, I fell twice to the floor, though the others seemed to have risen without difficulty. Several people pushed forward to help me, smiling and joking about my misfortune in having long legs especially subject to leg-cramp. Privately I doubted if my difficulty in getting up had been due to cramp, for I had felt no symptoms of it since returning to my place. Nervous shock might have been the real reason. I did not bother to think it out.

A most surprising aspect of that tremendous experience was the slightness of my later reaction to it. Though it did encourage me to spend more of my time in pondering about spiritual matters and in practising meditation—which I had been more or less neglecting of late—it also led to a certain revulsion from the intricate mystic symbolism of the Tibetan Vajrayana, in favour of what *seemed* to me the nobler simplicity of Zen Buddhism. Very fortunately indeed, this reaction did not set in soon enough to prevent me paying the liveliest attention to the instructions given to me by the Rimpoché on the following day, for which, many years later, I was to be thankful; and when I escorted the Tibetans to their third-class accommodation (chosen on principle and not at all for lack of money) on the Calcutta-bound ship, I was genuinely oppressed with a sense of impending loss. Yet, within a week, the whole episode had come to obtrude very seldom into my mind. This was so disappointing that I had to remind myself that the Rimpoché had promised me no more than a handful of seeds, together with instructions for their proper cultivation; for I had half expected to be permanently uplifted and set free once and for all from desire for purely worldly pursuits. As nothing of the kind had happened to me, I began to tell myself that perhaps I was still too young to see life as a wheel revolving amid an ocean of sorrows; but, at the same time, I realized that until I did see life that way I had no hope of reaching a state of mind capable of yielding the fruits of Nirvana. I was like a schoolboy who well knows that, if he does not soon begin to work for his examination, he will risk failure and perhaps dismissal from the school, but who goes on postponing the task until tomorrow and tomorrow. This state of mind was to continue with brief interruptions for several years to come.

A Journey to the Holy Mountain

Peking, for all its moods of softness, belongs indisputably to the North, where camels and horses take the place of buffaloes. There are times in spring when the sand of the Gobi Desert comes riding in opaque yellow clouds upon the wings of an evil wind, blotting out the sun, seeping through windows and doors, penetrating even into bookcases, and torturing the noses and throats of those who huddle within their houses. In winter, freezing winds bring tears to the eyes which soon form icicles clinging to the lashes. The city's softer aspects are the residue of centuries of imperial rule during which a yearly harvest was reaped of all the manifold forms of beauty which China's far-flung provinces had to offer. So, in pleasant weather, Peking displays southern graces—a gentleness, a languor, a delicacy which offset the grimness of her intimidating gateways set amid ponderous fortifications.

The time came for me to take leave of this voluptuous softness and to journey to Wu T'ai Shan across the great North China plain—in autumn and early spring, yellow and parched as a desert; in winter, a dreary wilderness of snow; in summer, an endless vista of softly waving green or pale yellow. I must enter the lonely mountains lying several hundred miles to the west.

Fortunately it was June, my vacation having begun early owing to a political strike at the university. The little train chugged slowly through the richly cultivated fields which, east and south, stretched to the horizon and far beyond; while, to the north and west, blue and purple hills were already visible. Bare, treeless slopes succeeded the great ocean of rippling green maize and *kaoling;* and, before dusk, we came to Nank'ou, the principal gateway through the Great Wall. Like a monstrous Chinese dragon, the Wall sprawled across the hills, clinging to the ridges in a series of stupendous undulations. A single hundred-yard section of it would be accounted an engineering feat of some magnitude. How was it possible to visualize it rising and falling uninterruptedly from the China Sea almost to the borders of Turkestan? The effort of imagination made me sleepy and, just before sunset, my eyes closed. So I knew nothing more until the train came jerking to a halt at Kalgan, Mongolia's gateway. For the first time I was within bowshot of camel caravanseries; of butter-pomaded Mongols who washed or were washed only thrice in their lives (after birth, before marriage and after death); of crowds of men in bro-caded clothes, their silks glistening beneath the grease accumulations of years; of men who were fit to challenge Cossacks to feats of daring horse-manship—riders who could loose an arrow from the back of a fast-galloping steed and hit the target as unerringly as an army instructor on the regimental shooting-range. But these things I was left to imagine, to reconstruct from my reading and from my knowledge of the Mongols in Peking. Afraid to leave the train, I lay down on the hard, wooden seat, enjoying fitful dreams with a Mongolian background.

At midnight, we reached Tat'ung, having turned southwards back into China Proper. Even after a hot June day, the night air was chilly, so I was glad to find that my room at the inn was provided with a heated k'ang. In fact, it contained very little else. One third of the room-space consisted of a bare brick floor, the rest being taken up by the low brick platform cov-ered with singed straw matting on which I now unrolled my bedding of thinly wadded summer quilts. The only article of furniture was a foot-high table about the size of a large tea-tray placed in the middle of the k'ang for use at meals. A bowl of hot water for washing, a rather grimy perfumed towel and a potful of hot red tea were the only luxuries avail-able that night. Being lunchless and dinnerless, I was hungry, but too tired to care much.

An hour after dawn, a lad in a shabby blue cotton gown appeared bringing a very large bowl of coarse earthenware which contained my breakfast—boiled noodles in mutton broth, flavoured with garlic, onion and pepper. Such food does not make an ideal breakfast, but I found it tasty enough to have the bowl twice replenished. My next visitor was the inn-keeper, a crop-headed, harsh-looking man dressed in jacket and trousers of patched, unwashed white cotton. He asked how long I proposed to stay.

"Just one more night," I answered. "And, if you will find me horses and a guide, I should like to ride over to the Yünkang rock-temples this morning."

This was easily arranged. With my guide mounted on another horse, I rode off through low hills, passing some of the ancient and still primitive coalmines of the region. They were being worked by thin, shabby wretches with packmules. Death by heart-failure overtook men and animals alike with frightening regularity, and they were alike too in being gaunt creatures with hardly any flesh between bone and skin, alike in their lack-lustre expressions, devoid of all joy and hope. I had been told that, in this province of Shansi, after generations of misgovernment, poverty was so great that the farmers scarcely ever tasted the eggs laid by their own fowls, even though they brought in little more than a silver dollar for a hundred and twenty of them—the price of one very good city restaurant meal.

The Yünkang caves, like those of Ajanta, have one thing in common with that very different sort of monument—the Taj Mahal—in that they are among the few places in the world which cannot possibly disappoint even the most extravagant expectations. It is now thought that Buddhism first trickled into China as far back as the second century B.C. By the time these cave temples were hewn from the living rock in the fifth, sixth and seventh centuries A.D., the Indian religion was spreading like a bright flame across the face of Asia. The men who came in contact with it then were inspired with a great upsurge of the spirit comparable to that which led to the building of Europe's loveliest cathedrals. Though Yünkang possesses fewer of those wondrous man-made caves than Ajanta, they are even more stupendous. In each cave, the principal Buddha-image (formed by cutting the rock from around it on three or four sides) is so enormous that, in at least one case, I estimated the nose alone to be twice as long as my six-foot body—perhaps much more than that, for it is diffi-

cult to judge the length of something high above one's head. The image
most often photographed and reproduced in albums is one of the small-
est among the principal images, easy to photograph because the cave has
fallen around it; and even this one is often seen in reproductions with as
many as fifty people standing on the hands and forearms without crowd-
ing. The larger images are impossible to photograph as the space around
them is too confined. At most, the camera can record some detail of face,
limbs or body.

The staggering size of these images strikes the mind with wonder as
soon as the caves are entered; but, before long, this wonder is thrust into
the background by the even more astounding *beauty* of the sculpture,
especially of the thousands of small figures surrounding the giant
images. For centuries, these great statues have sat silently brooding on
human sorrows, their lips touched with the faintest of compassionate
smiles—but not in solitude. In each cave, walls and ceiling are a mass of
intricate carvings. Buddhas, Bodhisattvas, devas, asparas, a host of spiritual beings—thousands upon thousands of them in every cave—stare
down at the puny descendants of their inspired creators. Some reflect the
brooding calm of the central images; others are running, leaping, flying,
dancing, singing, twanging stringed instruments, blowing on horns, waving their arms, flapping their wings, making faces, rocking with laughter
in so lively a manner that it is hard not to believe they are living beings
petrified by a magician's spell.

Begging my guide to leave me to myself, I wandered in and out of the
caves, finding new beauties and fresh marvels each time I re-entered
them. Within three hours, my mind had become so surfeited that I was
glad to emerge into the open air and sit down to contemplate the simple
and familiar sights of hill and sky. During the ride back to Tat'ung, I realized for the first time that an excess of beauty can be as overwhelming
and as wearying as over-indulgence in drink, love-making or laughter.

I was compelled to stay in Tat'ung for several days; the inn-keeper
would not hear of my making the week's journey to Wu T'ai without a
proper caravan or an escort of some kind. At last, a suitable caravan was

assembled, a group of people who, but for the absence of women, could have inspired illustrations for a Chinese translation of the *Canterbury Tales*. Of the thirty or forty members of this caravan, those I recollect most vividly are a mounted Mongol Lama in a splendid robe of purple silk; an elderly and very shabby old Mongol on foot who had spent two years on the journey from his home in Northern Manchuria, begging his food and carrying nothing but the clothes on his back; and my own muleteer, a gay young man from a farm which lay directly on our route, at whose house I was to spend a very comfortable night. Most travelled on foot, using horses and mules as pack-animals, but I preferred to make the journey in primitive luxury. For a small sum I was able to hire a mule-litter—a cross between a sedan-chair and the cabin of a very small boat. The floor consisted of netting on which my luggage had been carefully spread out and topped with my bedding to act as a sort of carpet. The walls and roof comprised a cylindrical tunnel supported on a wooden frame, very much like the cabin of a Cantonese sampan. The whole contraption was firmly anchored to two long shafts which projected before and behind so that it could be slung between two mules walking in single file.

For some reason, I and the muleteer who walked beside me were selected to lead the procession, while the much more important purple-robed Lama rode last of all. In general, holy men and merchants occupied places of honour, front and rear, while the pedlars, illiterate pilgrims and pack-animals formed the centre of the caravan. I found the motion of my wheel-less vehicle so soothing that I passed much of the time stretched flat on my back, dozing or drowsily busy with my thoughts, except now and then when I remembered that this was a pilgrimage and shamed myself into sitting cross-legged for an hour, practising meditation. More genuine pilgrims felt obliged to go on foot; indeed, Mongols often make far longer journeys, crawling on their knees or stopping at every three paces to prostrate themselves. The rough, rock-strewn path may have jarred the feet of the mules, but the litter swung between its poles as gently as a slim boat tossed upon lightly running seas. If I got down to stretch my legs, I had to walk very slowly for fear of losing sight of the caravan plodding ponderously behind.

The Chinese peasants and pilgrims chatted and sang as they toiled along the difficult track, which led steeply uphill nearly all the way. The purple-robed Lama could be seen in the distance, solemnly telling his beads as his horse ambled forward in our wake; while the Mongol beggar-pilgrim whom we came to call "Old Manchuria" would pour forth a stream of pidgin-Chinese to anybody who would listen to him. At nights, we slept in small wayside inns, usually lying in a row on the *k'ang,* about eight of us to a room—except once when my muleteer invited me to pass a night in much greater comfort at his parents' unusually prosperous farmhouse. I learnt that the old couple had never seen a Westerner at close quarters before, but their peasant politeness was so great that they treated me exactly like a Chinese guest, refraining from any questions beyond the normal polite exchange of biographical information.

All the farm-houses and inns were built round wide courtyards, the living-rooms on two sides with cloister-like stables for the animals opposite. The food was dreadfully monotonous, consisting chiefly of potato soup, porridge made from millet, and coarse maize-bread. Eggs were a luxury seldom obtainable. So, whenever we passed through one of the little walled cities or county-towns, I used to treat all the poorer members of the caravan to a mess of boiled pork and good wheat bread, either roasted in a pan with just a touch of oil or steamed in the form of rolls or meat-filled dumplings. I had thought myself poor, but found the cost of feeding so many people almost trifling.

A day's journey was almost exactly ninety *li* (thirty miles), the *li* varying slightly in length according to the hilliness of the road, this unit being based partly on the time it takes to cover a given distance rather than upon distance alone. There were inns at every half-stage. We would get up early enough to be able to set out at dawn, rest for two or three hours in the middle of the day, and arrive just before or just after nightfall. As many of the muleteers were opium-smokers, they insisted on this long midday halt so that they would enjoy at least two hour's placid smoking after their lunch. Naturally, they also smoked in the evenings as soon as their animals had been stabled and fed. Most declared that, without opium, they could not possibly stand up to such a hard life, which may well be the truth.

Once a day, with uncanny regularity, the leader of my pair of mules would throw himself on the ground and attempt to roll over while still in harness! This caused me many bumps and bruises as well as the destruction of all the brittle articles in my luggage. Each time, the ropes would snap, the litter fall into its component parts and my luggage be tossed with me on to the road. Everybody else appeared to think this a perfectly normal hazard of the journey, but on the fourth day I grew vexed and expressed my displeasure to the patient muleteer.

"But, Laoyeh, the animal is sick."

"Then why did you offer me a sick animal?"

"Because I have no other, Laoyeh."

"Then please *do* something about it."

"Yes, Laoyeh."

That evening, he borrowed a savage-looking needle as long as a crochet-hook and, before I could expostulate, jabbed it into the mule's cheek, not far from the eye. I was horrified.

"Old Father Heaven! What have you done, you—you turtle's egg [offspring of adultery]."

"Laoyeh, I am not a turtle's egg. You told me to cure the animal. I am trying."

He seemed astonished and hurt by my outburst, which was the first time I had spoken harshly to him.

"But it was wanton cruelty. The animal can't help being sick. It is abominable to punish a creature for being ill."

"Laoyeh, abuse me if you like. You have the right to do that. Am I not yours till the end of the journey? But you should not have called me a turtle's egg. The women of our village are all virtuous. Look for turtles' eggs among the offspring of city women in Peking or Taiyüan."

"Very well, Lao Wêng; you are *not* a turtle's egg, of course. But you are a cruel master to your animals."

"Cruel, Laoyeh, cruel? Are doctors who cut out kidneys and slice the livers of living men cruel?"

I stalked off to my sleeping quarters outraged by such wanton inhumanity to the wretched mule.

The next day, Wêng watched me climb into the litter without giving me his usual cheery greeting. Obviously I had wounded him as deeply as he had wounded the mule, which I thought served him right. The day passed as usual, but in the evening I noticed that the front mule was stepping out much more cheerfully than before. Neither then nor on any of the three remaining days did he pitch me to the ground or even attempt to roll. It gradually dawned on me that what I had taken for vengeful cruelty had, in fact, been a primitive sort of acupuncture. When I apologized to the muleteer, he told me he had acquired something of this art from a wise old man. He had learnt of twenty-one places on the animal's body, one or more of which must be punctured in accordance with whatever malady attacked it or whatever organ was affected, these places generally having no obvious relationship with the seat of the trouble. It was all very mysterious. The Chinese have long practiced this art successfully on human beings, and, as I have since heard, there are now practitioners of it in Paris and elsewhere in Europe.

On the fifth or sixth day, we came to a deep ford across a wide and swiftly flowing river. Most of the men, who apparently did not share Pekingese prudery, calmly removed all garments below the waist and waded across, pulling their unwilling animals after them. But two or three of the mules were so frightened that no amount of beating would persuade them to cross. They planted their feet squarely on the earth and obstinately refused to budge. Suddenly shabby "Old Manchuria" lost patience (though he had no animal of his own) and shouted:

"Turtles! Turtles! They Chinese not know how proper man do things Mongolia."

Then, dragging off his trousers and tying them round his neck, he rushed ferociously towards the nearest reluctant mule on which he exerted such unexpected strength that the astonished, frightened animal allowed itself to be dragged into the water and goaded over to the other bank. After this loudly applauded success, the indomitable old man plunged back to our side and dragged a second mule into the water. If there were others, they followed of their own accord. Soon the whole caravan was across; but I, ashamed to remove my trousers, had to follow Purple Robe's example in being carried over on the back of the most stalwart muleteer, a man whose sinuous strength amazed me, for he was no more muscular than most other Chinese. He performed the service free of charge, reminding me of the three good meals he had had at my expense. My luggage was sodden and dripping; but, providentially, someone had had the wit to tie the bedding on to the roof of the litter, so that, at least, was dry.

But the next day, the hills had given place to real mountains and, here and there, we passed some of the numerous branches of the Great Wall; or, perhaps, they were short inner walls built to guard certain passes. We were now approaching Wu T'ai itself. Its name means Five Peaks or, more literally, Five Terraces, referring to the five main peaks which rise from around a central plateau where most of the three hundred odd monasteries and temples are situated. The last day of the journey was mostly spent upon the ascent of an approach so steep as to be nearly perpendicular in the worst places. I had to make the tiring climb on foot, as the litter-mules could not have carried me up without hardship as well as danger to themselves and to me. At last, gasping and sweat-sodden, I reached the pass in the company of a few other stragglers. We found ourselves looking down on a sight which might have inspired the original conception of Shangri-La.

The wide, grassy plateau lay only a few hundred feet below the pass. Wild flowers grew in such extraordinary profusion that the old cliché 'carpeted with flowers' seemed the most apt description possible. Here and there, nestling against the surrounding slopes or clinging to overhanging rocks were the monasteries, some large enough to house hundreds of monks, others small temples with only three or four living-rooms attached. To one side of the plateau was a small hill running out like a spur from the surrounding mountain walls. Its slopes were honeycombed with buildings, a monastery even bigger than the Lama Temple in Peking, approached by flights of steps leading from among the clustered roofs of a small town lower down and, at the foot, an exceedingly large *chorten* or Tibetan-style reliquary which resembled a gigantic white bottle. Somebody explained that the town was the residence of the Chinese county magistrate, the chief temporal authority; and that the monastery was the abode of the Kushog appointed by Lhasa as the spiritual ruler of all the thousands of Tibetan and Mongol lamas in the vicinity. Most of Wu T'ai's temples had walls of faded crimson or yellow-ochre surmounted by golden-yellow tiles, once the prerogative of the Imperial Family and of divinities.

Though nearly eight thousand feet above the North China plain, the plateau is so sheltered that the vegetation reminded me of the lush south. Never, even upon the flowery slopes of the Dolomites, had I seen a sight so lovely; nor have I beheld its equal since, unless in some of the high Himalayan valleys.

Our route across one side of the plateau led us past an unusually large Chinese-style monastery, almost the only building in sight to remind me that I was still in China Proper, very far from Tibet and some ten days' walk from Mongolia. The other buildings gave just the reverse impression. We did not stop until we had reached the sloping town just above the giant *chorten* and climbed a flight of steps leading to the gateway of the monastery of P'usa Ting, seat of the Kushog Lama. A merchant in the caravan informed me that, by the terms of a treaty concluded in Manchu times between the Governments of China and Tibet, when the latter was only a nominal dependency, the Lhasa-nominated Kushog was still entitled to exercise control over the monastic population of Tibetans and Mongols. His authority was much like that of a mediaeval cardinal—a Prince of the Church. However, the relatively few black-gowned, bareheaded Chinese monks did not have to submit to the Tibetan Kushog's authority, being responsible to their own abbots and, in case of crime, to the county magistrate. For Republican China recognized no religious authority except, to some extent, that of the religious leaders among their Mongol and Tibetan subjects, who might otherwise have rebelled. Incidentally, I learnt during the last lap of the journey that there was a local Living Buddha who, as an individual, did not command much respect in any quarter. Having been declared an Incarnation, he was forever a Living Buddha; but, as the role did not suit his tastes, he preferred to wear Western clothes; to associate with the local Chinese officials who sarcastically eulogized him as an 'advanced' type of Mongol; and to use his revenue as a Living Buddha for the enjoyment of the usual delights of a rich man in Northern and Central Asia—horses, women, wine, opium, cards and mahjong, together with whatever more eccentric or individual delights happened to please him.

The P'usa Ting Monastery crowning the small hill to which the little township clung was approached by long flights of white steps and built on a series of terraces. To either side of the steps were the shops of the craftsmen, all Chinese, who fashioned all sorts of Tibetan-style ritualistic objects of silk, silver, copper, gold and semi-precious stones, besides painting holy pictures and inscribing banners and charms in one, two or three languages—Chinese, Tibetan and Mongol. Some even added the nearly obsolete Manchu characters, explaining that four gives a more balanced effect to a work of art than three. The enormous monastery was encircled by a blood-red wall, the colour faded, chipped and peeling. On the lower terraces stood the principal halls of ceremony which, inside and out, were so magnificent and in such a glittering state of preservation that I have never, either before or since, seen any magnificence to compare with them. I felt that the sight of them gave me an accurate picture of what the Forbidden City must have looked like in the days of Ch'ien Lung or K'ang Hsi, the greatest of the Manchu Emperors.

The topmost terrace was occupied by the Kushog's own apartments. My quarters were in the principal guest-block just below those of His Holiness. My room was both spacious and richly decorated. The *k'ang*, big enough for eight people, was spread with fine, gaily coloured Tibetan carpets and surrounded on three sides by a frieze depicting in brilliant colours various aspects of Tibetan life, both in this world and some others. The *k'ang* which, though large, occupied only about a quarter of the room, was provided with numerous small tables of carved wood covered with gold and green lacquer. The rest of the room had a red tiled floor and a profusion of Chinese-style furniture decorated in the Tibetan manner.

It was a delicious pleasure to feel that, for a little while, I could enjoy some of the imperial splendour which, elsewhere in China and perhaps everywhere in the Far East except Lhasa, has completely vanished, or else been retained only in the form of palace museums.

I was made welcome by two very elegant lamas, whom I discovered to be illiterate Chinese selected for their efficiency as butlers. Perhaps 'butler' is an unkind word to use. In effect, their duties were somewhere between those of a Reverend Receiver of Guests and of upper servants in charge of the large monastery staff, who might be laymen or monks. Their precise duty towards me was that of deputy hosts, and hosts I shall call them. Both were dressed in splendid dragon-embroidered robes—the first I had ever seen except at the theatre or at fancy-dress parties. I think the senior eunuchs and officials at the Manchu Court used to dress in exactly the same way, apart from the extraordinary lacquer hats worn by my hosts which looked un-Chinese, rather like coloured versions of the stiff hats formerly worn in Korea. Their manners and bearing were faultless, regal enough for them to have passed muster as senior mandarins in the old days, so long as they were not called upon to read or write! Certainly there was nothing ludicrous about them.

When I arrived at P'usa Ting, I told Wang Lama and Ma Lama that I would be able to accept their hospitality for a few weeks at the most. Later, news came from Peking to the effect that the students would not return to work until Chiang Kai-Shek had altered his policy of allowing the Japanese to gobble mouthful after mouthful of Chinese territory without resistance. On hearing this I foresaw that my stay might be extended for several months. Though sick at heart at the thought of China's sufferings, I was delighted at the prospect of staying so long in such surroundings, for I discovered that Wu T'ai was one of those rare places where Asia had remained wholly Asian, being unadulterated by any Western influence whatsoever. It was just the kind of place in which I had always desired to live; and, if my funds had been inexhaustible, I doubt if I could ever have brought myself to turn my back on so much beauty—at least until the invading Japanese came to drag me away by force. As it was, my funds were exhausted long before I began to think of leaving it, so I was forced to borrow from friends who providentially arrived from Tientsin. As to the precious guru-to-chela teaching which I hoped to find there, I received what seemed at the time disappointingly little; but it was probably as much as I was then in a fit condition to receive; and, in any case, Wu T'ai offered me many other gifts, some of them hard to define, yet none the less valuable for their subtlety. At the very least, the spiritual side of my nature, which had long been weakened by Peking's spiritually (as opposed to aesthetically) enervating climate, was daily refreshed by the winds which blew across the plateau carrying the perfume of incense and wood-fires to the nostrils, and singing of the great Central Asian plains beyond, where the world was either very old or very fresh and young. As soon as I had passed the stage of lying about on magnificent carpets and luxuriating in the princely comfort and splendour of my surroundings, which contrasted so strangely with the hardships of the journey, I began exploring the various neighbouring temples.

One of my first visits was to the little Mani Bhadra Monastery which provided lodgings for the poorer sort of Mongol pilgrim. 'Old Manchuria' called specially to take me over there, hinting mysteriously that I should be welcomed by "an old friend." Much intrigued, I gladly accompanied the old fellow whose prowess at the ford had won so much admiration. I loved him for his big heart, his strong limbs, contempt of hardship and body-shaking laugh. The immaculate lamas, Wang and Ma, were shocked by his ragged appearance and had been most unwilling to let him sully the regal splendour of my chamber; but gorgeous priests, wayside brigands, recalcitrant mules, blood-drinking demons and Chinese soldiers were all one to "Old Manchuria." He had just pushed past Their Magnificences and burst into my room roaring with gusty nomad mirth.

The "old friend" awaiting me at Mani Bhadra was, to my immense surprise, no other than the 'shaman' who had performed for me in Peking. He was lodging there during the building of his new temple and far too busy supervising the builders (all of them Mongols working voluntarily for the glory of the Faith rather than men chosen for their skill) to be able to spare any time disclosing some of Wu T'ai's inner mysteries to me. Besides, within a few days he intended to go off on another fund-collecting tour, this time to get money for the gold, silver, lacquer, porcelain and fine woods to be used for the new temple's interior; but meanwhile he seemed very happy indeed to see me.

In his beautifully appointed cell, there was excellent salted tea churned with fresh goat's butter and drunk from porcelain cups with silver filigree lids and turquoise-studded silver saucers. Alas, when I had taken leave from this busy man, "Old Manchuria" insisted on my tasting some of his own hospitality. Again it took the form of salted buttered tea, but this time it had been prepared with hair-impregnated rancid camel's butter, bluish black and doubtless many months old. Still worse, out of deference to my "soft Chinese habits of cleanliness," he took a really filthy old cup and *licked the inside clean with his tongue* before pouring in the smelly tea! Etiquette required that I quaff several cupfuls. I managed it by taking each at a single gulp like nasty medicine, so as not to have to savour it to the full; but this made him suppose that I was thirsty and cupful followed cupful!

Just behind the Mani Bhadra was a cave with a shallow depression in the floor containing water sacred to Samandabhadra Bodhisattva (P'u Hsien, Personification of Divine Action). It was said to have healing powers and to be of mysterious origin. I watched several scores of pilgrims fill their earthen bottles there, yet the water level never decreased, though the pool was very shallow, quite transparent and without any visible means of ingress—apparently there was neither hole nor spring. Eastern places of pilgrimage abound in such small mysteries, some manifestly due to natural phenomena, others much harder to explain, like the Bodhisattva Lights which I was to see later. My Mongol host procured a large, earthen bottle and, filling it at the sacred spring, handed it to me, with many ceremonious marks of esteem, as a remedy against future ills. It was touching to see the delight of these old beggar pilgrims ("Manchuria" and his friends) in being for once the donors of a gift instead of its recipients. In gratitude I assured "Old Manchuria" that I should be very firm with Their Magnificences if ever they should bar his way to my table when he cared to grace it. Shaking with laughter, he cried:

"Good, good. They Chinese-Mongols; they not Mongol-Mongols. Ha-ha-ha-ha-ha. *Chinese*-Mongols! Very funny! Yes, no?"

From this and other incidents, I gathered that the contempt of the warrior nomads for their highly sophisticated but more sedentary neighbours south of the Wall has not changed since the days of Ghengiz Khan.

Another session of buttered tea followed our return from the cave, during which I told 'Old Manchuria' how, on the previous afternoon, two Mongol strangers had walked up to me in the street, demanded a cigarette each, and marched away without a word of thanks. I asked if he thought they were some sort of highwaymen who enjoyed this form of swaggering. The old fellow grinned uncomfortably, but hastened to defend his countrymen in his halting Chinese, by saying:

"Say 'Thank you, thank you'—Chinese way. Give, take—Mongol way. Mongols all brothers. You things me; me things you. You sleep me tent; I eat you bread. 'Thank you, thank you'—not good, not brother-talk. Just give, just take." This explanation reminded me of something the innkeeper at Tat'ung had said contemptuously about Mongols:

"Our Chinese merchants find the Mongols too easy. Tell one of them that a Japanese ashtray is a Han dynasty mirror and he'll believe you. Though he may wonder why he can't see his face in it, he will not doubt your word. On the other hand, if a Mongol (except those accursed horse-dealers) tells you his nag is sound in four legs, why then, so it will prove to be. A stupid people!"

I was beginning to understand why so many Europeans in Peking were such fanatical Mongol-lovers. I saw that Mongols—gay, swaggering, robed in filthy, oily, lice-ridden splendour of silk and satin, straightforward, brave, kind, generous, incredibly "handy"—have many virtues to compensate for the filth of years and the stink of rancid butter oozing from hair, clothes, unwashed bodies and breath. And their virtues are almost exactly complementary to those of the Chinese; so Peking's superlative elegance and refinement sometimes gives birth to a longing for the bluff heartiness of the Steppes.

On my way back to P'usa Ting that afternoon, I stopped among the crowd filling the precincts of the great white *chorten*. Mostly they were Mongol pilgrims, both rich and poor. A stream of them were circumambulating the chorten's base, muttering a never-ending string of invocations, some telling their beads, others with right arms extended so as to preserve the momentum of the great tubular prayer-cylinders encircling it. A richly clad Mongol layman, with an enormous circular fur hat cocked rakishly on one side to display the yellow satin crown, stood languidly staring at me with a half smile upon his lips, as though he would like me to talk to him. When we had chatted for a while, I asked:

"What exactly is the purpose of these prayer-wheels?"

He looked as much taken aback as an English villager would be if questioned as to the *purpose* of church bells!

"Have you not heard, Hsienshêng, that the sacred writings in these wheels are written on one thousand and eighty feet of the finest yellow silk?"

He seemed to think that this was explanation enough.

"Really? Magnificent! But, I mean, are invocations offered in this way efficacious?"

"Indeed, why not? How else could all these illiterates repeat more than a few of them? This way, they offer by turning what they *would* recite if they *could*. Their heart's wish is the same—to honour the Three Precious Ones."

"I see. But I've noticed even learned lamas twisting small hand-wheels in the same way."

"Of course. To each man a single mouth. How else could any of us get through all the recitations we should like to offer in a lifetime?"

"And you, Sir?" Noticing some insignia of nobility on his costume I used a Chinese honorific for minor royalties. For answer, he plunged his hand into the pouch-like fold of his orange silk gown which protruded over a bronze silk sash, and brought out a lovely prayer-wheel of silver and white cloisonné. With the merest flick of his wrist, he set it rotating smoothly like the flywheel of an engine and stood waiting for my reaction with a quizzical smile.

"What a lovely thing!" I exclaimed spontaneously, forgetting all about "You things me; me things you," and so found myself in an embarrassing position. Though he immediately offered me the wheel, he could have had no desire that I should take it, yet I had to be exceedingly careful in refusing it not to give the impression of scorning either the gift or its owner. Somehow or other, I did manage this without causing the bright black eyes to lose their lazy smile.

The circumambulators were not the only active worshippers in sight. Farther away from the *chorten,* nearer the outer wall of the precincts, were numerous devotees, both men and women, each with a broad seven-foot plank extending from just in front of his feet in the direction of the *chorten,* the farther end raised a few inches from the ground. These people apparently possessed unlimited energy, for they were performing the strenuous "grand prostration" several hundred or a thousand times in succession and without a moment's intermission. First the hands were placed palm to palm above the head and brought slowly down to the level of the heart; then the devotee would stoop right down and grasp the two sides of his plank just in front of his feet; after that, the whole body would shoot forwards, the hands running along the edge of the plank from bottom to top, until the devotee was lying flat on his stomach with legs outstretched behind him and hands in front like a swimmer. The final movement consisted of raising the joined palms above the head again while the body remained prone, after which the devotee curled up like a caterpillar, rose to his feet and lifted his joined palms for the next prostration. With each of these separate movements a particular mantra was muttered and, if the mind were properly concentrated as well, then body, speech and mind merged into a single rhythm of pure veneration for the Buddha-Dharma represented by the *chorten*. Whereas a hundred and eight prostrations of this kind would leave me, even in my youthful days, almost too weak to stand, Mongols of both sexes and all ages often perform one thousand and eighty prostrations at a time!

Everybody I met there seemed very willing to talk and to welcome my interest in their affairs. A Chinese craftsman among the bystanders provided me with some facts about the *chorten*.

"As you doubtless know already, Hsienshêng, Wu T'ai is the principal earthly dwelling of Manjusri Bodhisattva (Wên Shu, Personification of Divine Wisdom). We Chinese hold that there are nine sacred mountains, five Taoist and four Buddhist, of which Wu T'ai is one. But to these Mongols and Tibetans, Wu T'ai is a place so sacred that merely to come here and circumambulate the *chorten* one thousand and eighty times ensures rebirth into a state many times nearer *Nirvana* than could otherwise be attained in this life. There is said to be a relic of the Buddha in the *chorten*, but whether the *chorten* was built for the relic or whether the relic was brought here for the *chorten* I do not know. Chiefly, the *chorten* forms a central place of worship where even the most illiterate pilgrims to this mountain may consumate their pilgrimage."

My informant, though a Chinese, was a devout follower of the Vajrayana and loved to lavish his decorative gifts upon the embellishment of the temples. Obligingly he climbed the great steps with me and took me to see some of the work he had helped to complete in the Great Hall of P'usa Ting. The sweeping roof of yellow-glazed tiles, the colonnade of elaborately decorated scarlet pillars and the crimson walls made it almost a replica of one of the halls of state in the Forbidden City, except that it was in a much better state of repair. The fresh lacquer shone like molten bronze still glowing from the furnace; and the appointments of the interior were the richest I have ever seen before or since. The ceiling of carven panels blazed with multi-coloured stylistic designs; the tremendous pillars (formed of tree-trunks carried there from over a thousand miles to the south-west) were wrapped in gorgeous Lhasa carpets, the altar furnishings were of precious metals and fine porcelains; long, silken banners hung from the ceiling, beautifully embroidered with texts in Tibetan, Mongol and Chinese; and the principal statue of the Bodhisattva carrying his Sword of Wisdom was plated with, if not made of, pure gold. It glittered like a network of diamonds, reflecting the tiny points of flame from more than a hundred votive lamps. On a subsidiary altar were receptacles piled with heavy pieces of jewelry, the offerings of Mongol and Tibetan pilgrims—necklaces, bangles, brooches, large ear-ornaments, belt-clasps, buckles, weapon-holders and archery rings, all these being mostly of gold or silver inset with jade, turquoise, coral and other brilliant stones. I wondered how often these receptacles were emptied into the treasury, and I marvelled at the simple sincerity of the Mongols who themselves lived in tents or primitive shacks, keeping for their own use the barest necessities of life. Such generosity may, from one point of view, appear misplaced; but who can fail to be moved by its sublimity?

A Lama explained to me once that the donors of these offerings gain merit in two ways—a little because their gifts help to supply the monasteries with the means required for their upkeep; much on account of the spirit of relinquishment involved, the degree of merit accruing from a gift being proportionate to the relative degree of sacrifice involved— exactly as in the biblical story of the widow's mite. (Incidentally, the belief that the gift itself matters much more than what is done with it accounts for the scarcity of organized charities in Buddhist countries, which now causes some of the younger Asian Buddhists to reflect; yet in Burma and Siam, even today, many more people are willing to devote money to the building of unnecessary temples in places where the temples abound, than to the upkeep of hospitals, schools and clinics.)

In the Second Hall, rites were being performed when we entered but the Chinese craftsman could not explain their significance. The booming of Tibetan horns, ten or fifteen feet long, the wail of flutes, the crash of drums and cymbals accompanied by voices which seemed to come from deep down inside the stomachs of the worshippers, produced an effect at once harsh and magical—harsh in the sense that such music is by no means sweet, magical in that devotees sustained by the powerful wings of those elemental sounds can rise easily into a state of inner tranquillity and arrest the *karma*-forming processes of conceptual thought.

A few days later, I attended the opening ceremony of Wu T'ai's annual Holy Week. Thousands of Mongol pilgrims, with a sprinkling of Central Asians and Tibetans, took part. All men, and all dressed in crimson ceremonial *kasa* [togas], they sat cross-legged in long, evenly spaced rows, facing inwards towards a central lane running east-west across the Great Court [a quadrangle very much larger than Trinity Great Court, Cambridge]. At one end of this lane sat the enthroned Kushog, robed from head to foot in cloth of gold, surrounded by colourful ecclesiastical dignitaries from each of the great monasteries. The rites opened with the same eerie music and chanting as that just described, but with upwards of a thousand people taking part in the chanting and with horns so long that each required six or eight children to hold it in position! This time the wild music reminded me of the more sombre sounds of Nature—the rumbling of thunder or of a distant waterfall, the crash of a gathering avalanche or, perhaps, of cannon shot echoing among embattled heights. When the chanting had drawn to a close, there followed a 'theological' debate. The combatants, who leapt up from among the crowd and ran to the High Lama's dais, swayed their bodies and stamped their feet, striking their left palms with their right hands in what looked like a ritual dance, meanwhile bellowing forth questions and arguments at the tops of their voices. There were elders who trumpeted like bulls and even a few child contestants who had not yet lost their boyish treble. Every speaker received an attentive hearing from the huge assembly which now and then broke silence to roar applause, yelling with joy or laughing their splendid nomad belly-laughs. I wondered if the mediaeval debates at Oxford or Paris had had points in common with this one.

As I knew hardly a word of Mongol, I spent much of the time gazing about me. Crowded against the walls of the Great Court were many ladies, some with a fantastic hair-arrangement imitative of the magnificent horns of a mountain ram. I reflected that, just as the Manchus, who owed an empire to their horses, used to have the sleeves of their official robes cut to resemble horses' hoofs and to wear their hair braided into a "horse's tail," so did these Mongols pay tribute to the flocks which provided them with so much—meat, butter, milk, cheese, garments, skin-tents, blankets, belts, straps, water-skins and many other daily necessities.

Just then, my "shaman" appeared, having apparently delayed his departure for the sake of the festival. He swaggered up to the rostrum and attacked the venerable Master of the Debate so successfully that the audience rolled where they sat in paroxysms of laughter. Even the defeated Master was forced to join in, and from the outer circle of women came peal after peal of shrill mirth. I would have given much to understand! The combination of deep religious feeling with merriment and homely simplicity is always attractive. The Mongols who conduct their religious debates in this way and the Thais who bring picnic lunches to eat upon the floor of the temple seem to me more truly "religious" than the hushed, sanctimonious worshippers I had grown used to during my boyhood. During the days which followed, I began to seek out various Lamas who had been recommended to me for one reason or another, but my ignorance of Tibetan and Mongolian created a barrier which, in most cases, was difficult to overcome. My deepest inspiration came from the simple Mongol pilgrims who inspired me with the belief that learning and scholarship are by no means essential to the truly religious life or to gaining freedom from the Wheel. On this mountain dedicated to Divine Wisdom, I learnt that such Wisdom must be sought for in silence and not at all by discursive thought. As one Lama expressed it, "First purify the temple of your body by expelling all extraneous thought; next, rest in perfect silence with all the doors and windows of that body-temple wide open and, with deep longing in your heart, silently invite the Stream of Wisdom to pour in."

Another Lama to whom I went to pay my respects at about this time asked me if I found Wu T'ai beautiful, which led to my asking him the place of beauty in the process of Enlightenment. "Does not the cultivation of dispassion," I asked, "require that we withdraw from beauty as much as from ugliness, and do not the sutras teach that beauty may be an impediment to Truth?"

"How wrong you are," he answered frankly. "Beauty is an impediment only when we desire its exclusive possession. But the contemplation of natural loveliness—mountains, forests, waterfalls, and the *right* contemplation of works of art do not excite any longings for hampering possessions, or any lusts. Rather they reflect the silent, shining perfection of *Nirvana*. We of the Vajrayana learn to seek *Nirvana* in *Sangsara;* it is the beauty all around us here which makes us so sure that *Nirvana* surrounds us now. When the Third Eye (the eye of the spirit) is opened, you will not seek *Nirvana* elsewhere than in your own heart and own surroundings. The joy of beholding the scarlet and gold of sunrise or the multi-coloured carpet of flowers on this sacred plateau is of the same order as the joy of the Ultimate Oneness, though it be only a reflection of a reflection's reflection. When you go back to the city and find ugliness around you, place flowers or jades in your house to remind you of the beauty which awaits the opening of your spirit's eye."

Of course the ordinary Mongol pilgrims did not understand things thus. To the more simple-minded among them, the Personification of Wisdom had become another god, a process analagous to the deification of Sōphē among certain Byzantine sects—yet even this development deserves more than the scornful shoulder-shrug with which some Western scholars have reacted to it. For Buddhists, Divine Wisdom has nothing to do with factual knowledge or book-learning. *Prajna* is that intuitive knowledge of Reality which lies far above the level of conceptual thought; indeed it is interrupted and blocked out by conceptual thought. It follows that *one-pointed* meditation on *Prajna*, whether conceived of in the abstract or as a deity, is more likely to lead to *Prajna*'s realization than any careful analytical study of the sutras or any amount of discursive meditation to discover whether *Prajna* is a substance, a state, or otherwise. The latter type of "scientific" meditation cuts the mind into many compartments and makes access of Intuitive Wisdom impossible. Thus, there are teachers who claim that direct approach to Truth comes more easily to the illiterate or semi-illiterate than to the scholar, the former having less mental sediment to dispose of.

Scattered on lonely peaks and precipitous slopes, or dotting the fair, sun-warmed plateau were shrines and temples to Manjusri (Wisdom) without number. Generally he was depicted in his benign form as a compassionate being whose smile belied the ferocity of the blue lion he bestrode or the menace of his upraised Sword of Wisdom. Sometimes, he appeared as a lovely youth—symbol of eternal spring; but occasionally he could be seen in wrathful form as the blue-bodied, bull-headed, thousand-armed Yamanataka ringed by a circlet of blue flames and dancing on a bed of corpses. I do not remember the significance of this symbolism. Christian missionaries, on seeing such figures in Buddhist temples, find in them a justification of their belief that the 'heathen' are ruled by fear; but in this they err; for, though in all Buddhist countries terrible monsters, demons and Raksha can be seen in the temples, Buddhists are never taught to fear them. In some cases, they represent the powers of evil which, having been converted to Buddhism, now hold the office of Guardians of the Holy Dharma; in other cases, the beings themselves are held to be divine, but their hideous, ferocious forms symbolize Buddhism's hostility towards the impersonal forces of ignorance and evil (the two are really synonymous) and they are *never* in any single case regarded as hostile to living beings. That would be impossible, for Buddhism teaches that the worst 'sinner' is a poor, sad creature deluded by his ignorance of Truth, and therefore to be pitied rather than hated or despised. In the case of Yamanataka, though I do not remember the significance of the symbolism in detail, I know that the wrathful forms of the various Bodhisattvas in *general* symbolize the perfection of Truth which, lying beyond all duality on the plane of the One Mind, is beyond good and Evil, beauty or ugliness; hence symbolism only in terms of beauty and tranquillity would imply the exaltation of the part at the expense of the whole. The lesson to be learnt from the wrathful and peaceful aspects of the Bodhisattvas is that beauty and ugliness are ultimately one, or rather that both of them vanish when perfection is achieved. This *must* be so, for light is inconceivable without dark; there-fore, if Ultimate Perfection contains the one, it must also contain the other, whereas its own perfection raises it above both.

Before Wu T'ai's innumerable altars, incense and butter-lamps burnt day and night. Some of the pilgrims spent as much as five years on the return journey, travelling on foot from the farthest reaches of Mongolia's deserts and the uttermost confines of Tibet's wilderness of snow to lay their offerings upon these altars. The deep religious satisfaction of the multitudes, twirling their prayer-wheels, clicking their rosaries, bowing themselves to the earth, chanting sutras and intoning invocations before the shrines has probably had no counterpart in the West since mediaeval times. Such boundless sincerity soon put me to shame when I reflected on my own coldly intellectual and sceptical approach to Truth. Wu T'ai taught me that doctrine matters little, that faith, sincerity and a burning desire for Enlightenment provide us with more than nine-tenths of the equipment we need for the journey to *Nirvana*.

One day, the lamas Wang and Ma suggested that I pay a visit to the Venerable Nêng Hai, Abbot of the great Chinese monastery I had passed on my way across the plateau to P'usa Ting—a very Jewel of Wisdom, they called him. I took their advice, but rather unwillingly, as my visits to Wu T'ai's greatest men had previously been disappointing and left me with a strong prejudice in favour of the lesser known Teachers there. For example, my visit to the Kushog Lama (possibly ill-timed) had been a very formal and unproductive affair. Affably, but rather absent-mindedly, accepting a ceremonial scarf from my hands, he had condescended to return it by draping it around my neck with his own illustrious fingers. A good beginning, except that nothing much followed. A few formal words of welcome, a blessing, somebody signalling that it was time to leave—that was all. As for my visit to the Living Buddha, that had been very much worse. A plump youth with a face almost as colourless as his Western-style suit of Shantung silk, he scarcely bothered to look up at me from the photographs he was studying with two Chinese officials from the magistrate's *yamên*. At the moment when I rose to kneeling position from the ritual prostration, he suddenly laughed in my face as though I were a performing ape, thereby providing me with the only instance of discourtesy from a man of high degree which I encountered during seventeen years in China!

"Aha, what have we here? A European Buddhist? Very nice, very nice indeed. May I press you to a glass of Buddha-nectar?" He waved his hand towards a half-empty brandy bottle standing on the table next to the photographs. "No? Aha. Then to what else am I indebted for the honour of your—er—your etcetera, etcetera—you know what I mean?"

The Chinese officials were staring woodenly at the tablecloth, laughter in their eyes, lips firmly compressed lest they, too, be guilty of unmerited discourtesy.

"I came to offer my *respects*," I answered coldly. "Having done so, I ask permission to retire."

"Granted, granted," he cried petulantly, clearly stung by my tone and perhaps afraid that his Chinese companions considered him too boorish. "You may go. We—er—are attending to important affairs. I thank you."

With great deliberation, I repeated the triple prostration as elaborately as I could, forcing myself to concentrate on the teaching: "Bowing to the Robe, you bow to the Buddha, not to the poor, naked wretch it conceals."

With these two episodes in mind, I approached the Chinese monastery scarcely expecting that the Abbot of so grand a place would have much time to spare for me. In general, I had found Mongols and Tibetans more spiritual than the Chinese. Ergo, in a place where the Tibetan Kushog had been briefly courteous but uninterested in me and the Mongolian Living Buddha positively insulting, it seemed unlikely that the leading Chinese Abbot would take me to his bosom merely because I was a co-religionist from the outermost rim of the world. I had yet to learn that the Venerable Nêng Hai fully deserved his reputation as scholar and saint.

Nêng Hai had spent many years in the Tibetan and Mongolian borderlands, chiefly in the Chinese province of Kokonor (Ch'ing Hai, the Blue Sea or Lake) where the three cultures blend. He was now attempting a

compromise between Lamaism and Chinese Buddhism, incorporating
the salient features of both. Symbolically, he wore robes of Lamaistic yellow-ochre cut in the Chinese fashion with butterfly-wing sleeves. His
monastery, Kuangchi Moup'ang, was outwardly like any other important
Chinese monastery, but included a subsidary Great Hall where initiates
practised the higher branches of Vajrayana meditation and rites. My first
meeting with him came near to confirming my worst fears. He was
scarcely more cordial than the Kushog Lama had been, but in this case
the reason was too obvious for me to feel hurt. He had just returned to
his sleeping place after delivering a two-hour sermon and, not being of
strong physique, was naturally tired. Seated cross-legged on his couch, he
accepted my prostrations and offered me a little earthenware plaque of
the Bodhisattva Manjusri which he suspended from my neck by a blue
ribbon. After that I was free to go, partly because he was really tired and
partly, as he told me later, because he took me for one of the countless
pilgrims who used to come to him for no other purpose than to be able
to include him among the 'sights' seen on Wu T'ai. During subsequent
meetings, he became very warm towards me and to this circumstance I
owe much of my knowledge of the Vajrayana.

One day I asked him: "Your Reverence, will you tell me why you,
brought up as a Master of Zen, now prefer to instruct your disciples
through the medium of the Vajrayana? Such cases must be very rare."

"Yes, rare," he replied, "for few of our Chinese monks know enough
of the Vajrayana to appreciate its great value. As for your question, I can
answer it best in symbolic language. Regardless of sect, or even of religion, we must symbolize the Ultimate Perfection as a calm and shining
void, whereas *Sangsara* [Samsara] is a vast whirlpool of shifting forms.
There are, so to speak, various intervening states.

"Now, a Zen adept (and some of other sects, other faiths) seeks to
leap from the muddy whirlpools straight into the pure white, radiant
stillness at the centre. This *can* be done and *has* been done, but it is an
extraordinary feat of which few are capable. Most of us do well to aim
first at a more modest result. The Sages of the Vajrayana have, through

Enlightenment, been able to make a detailed study of the intermediate forces and the Main Transformers nearer the heart of the circle. (With patience, faith and pertinacity, you may discover them for yourself.) They have even learnt to harness these transforming forces and they have handed down to their disciples methods for harnessing the force or forces suited to each one individually. By concentrating upon a force selected by your teacher and harnessing it according to his instructions, you will gain much power—power which all too many adepts foolishly misuse to perform vain 'miracles.' But you must use this power to penetrate more deeply into the circle, to come in contact with the secondary and even with the primary forces; these, being Transformers of tremendous power, will sweep you towards the Centre; in this very life, they will transform your *Sangsaric* surroundings into *Nirvana* itself. Thus will you achieve what you may not be strong enough to achieve by the more direct method of Zen, unless you are one of those for whom Zen is the best way of all.

"As evidence of the truth of all this, consider how many men of different faiths have wrought marvels and achieved sainthood through the power of their God or gods, all attained through fervent prayer and contemplation. What is that God but another name for the Centre, those gods but other names for the Transformers? Names are unimportant. Have you not met Buddhists groping in the outer darkness and Mussulmans or Christians whose faces shine with Truth? Just as many Mongols here regard Manjusri as a god, rather than the personification of Divine Wisdom, so do Christians mistake the Divine Forces for angels, the Centre for God; yet what does it matter? All prayers, rites and methods of concentration which open up the inner man must bring forth the inner Light, whereon their purpose is achieved. I am a Vajrayanist only because I conceive, rightly or wrongly, that the Vajrayana Sages have mapped the road more completely and better understood the methods of harnessing the Transformers than people of most other sects and faiths. I have met Christian missionaries at Kokonor who are laughable in their ignorance; I have also met two missionaries of the Heavenly Lord

(Catholic) Sect who are fully Enlightened Bodhisattvas! Let those Buddhists who are still lost in darkness kneel before them in all humility.

"Truth, as you have known for a long, long time, resides only in the innermost depths of your own being; but there are many layers of truth and many paths to approach Ultimate Truth. The Vajrayana possesses knowledge of more than a thousand of those paths (which are yet the One Path). Other teachers know of one, two or three. So it is to the Vajrayana Sage you must go, if you would learn which of those many paths is exactly suited to you. If you prove worthy, such a teacher will render up to you the keys for unlocking each of the great gates of brass which bar the way to Everlasting Truth."

So saying, he paused and stared at me in silence for what seemed many minutes. Then he asked me certain questions concerning my initiation at the hands of the Dorjé Rimpoché. When I had answered as best I could, he exclaimed with a sigh:

"Such a wonderful opportunity lost! How very sad that you were too young and ignorant to benefit!" Several similarly enigmatic remarks followed, until finally he said:

"Yet the seed once planted cannot die. Water it diligently and it will surely sprout. How could you have been so foolish as to arrive late for that Grand Initiation? In the first part, which you missed, lay something of priceless value to you. Your *karma* is the strangest admixture of good and evil. Ah well, rest tranquil in the knowledge that, when the time comes, the Greenness will be there!"

"Greenness?"

"Yes, the colour of the trees, the colour of the Northern Region."

"I don't understand, Your Reverence."

But he had walked away, leaving me with an enigma not to be resolved for many years.

Staying in Nêng Hai's monastery were a doctor and a banker, two good friends of mine from Tientsin. Though both were wealthy men and likely to bestow large gifts in return for the hospitality they enjoyed, they were entertained in a manner infinitely spartan compared with the luxury I enjoyed at P'usa Ting. The food was strictly vegetarian, the sleeping rooms as simple as could be, the taking of wine, even by visitors, strictly forbidden. The contrast between the two monasteries was significant. Chinese Buddhism, with the partial exception of Zen, places emphasis on the renunciation of the world—this doctrine being a necessary corrective for the Chinese attachment to physical ease and comfort. Tibetan Buddhism, "catering" for the spartan Tibetans and Mongols, teaches the realization of *Nirvana* through *Sangsara* or "seeking Truth *through* life." Though Tibet has its hermits like Milarepa (who cut his trousers into covers for nose and fingers, claiming that if the sexual organ needs concealment, the same must be true of fingers and nose, since one protuberance cannot be more or less vile than another), the Vajrayana on the whole prefers the method of accepting life's glitter, rather than withdrawing from it, since a properly controlled study of baubles is more likely to lead to personal conviction of their worthlessness than the method of turning away from them and *believing* them worthless. This doctrine can be safely practised by the wise anywhere, and even by the majority of people in those countries where material comfort is still far too rare and slight to be overwhelming as it has become in the modern West and, to a lesser extent, in the cities of China. Hence the spartan simplicity of Chinese monastery guest-rooms as compared with the splendour of the richer Tibetan monasteries.

On the day of my first visit to Nêng Hai, my Tientsin friends, Dr. Chang and Mr. Li, walked back to P'usa Ting with me, as they were due to bestow offerings upon the pilgrims assembled for Holy Week. Once more I took my place in the outermost row of the crimson-togaed Mongols seated in the Great Court. The long opening invocation was chanted as usual; I had by this time learnt that it was associated with the offering of a *mandala*—a complicated pattern of precious stones laid upon a mound of rice by the officiating Lama. It represented the whole universe, including sun, moon, earth and stars, together with all precious things therein contained. The words of the invocation include some more or less to this effect. "If the whole universe were mine, with its limitless wealth of beauty, I would offer all of it without exception, as a token of my boundless respect for the Holy Dharma, well knowing that even such an offering is far from worthy of an object thus sublime." In other words, even the glory of sun and moon fades before the brilliance of transcendental Wisdom, Enlightenment, Reality!

My Chinese friends were both dressed in dark silks which formed a striking contrast with the glittering garments of the senior Lamas and the Kushog's robe of cloth-of-gold. After saluting the Kushog and extolling the merits of the assembled pilgrims, who had endured such hardships among burning deserts and dizzy mountains in order to do honour to the Bodhisattva Manjusri upon the sacred mountain, they each handed a sack of silver coins to a gaily dressed attendant. Thereupon, the two attendants moved up and down the long ranks of seated pilgrims, placing five *mou* (half a silver dollar) in the hands of each. Such a gift was at that time equal to the price of four or five simple meals; the total must have amounted to several thousand dollars. Spiritual refreshment followed. More brightly clad attendants appeared, each carrying a tall, silver vessel decked with peacocks' feathers and sacred *kusa* grass. The pilgrims cupped their hands in turn, receiving a few drops of holy water from the spout of the vessel, of which they sipped one part and placed the remainder upon their heads.

"What is this holy water?" I asked an elderly Chinese-speaking Mongol on my left.

"This holy water, first is water. First, people take to temple as offering of purity. Then it symbolized what people give up. Now brought from temple for us, it symbolizes merit come back to us. Two Chinese pilgrims make big merit *by our help.* We receive gifts, so they can get merit. Now we gain merit, for helping them get their merit."

My informant's Chinese was far from good, but I think that this more or less renders his meaning. His words contained an idea quite new to me; namely that, though it may be more blessed to give than to receive, yet he who receives confers a favour upon the giver! The more I thought about it, the more I found this idea acceptable.

After the close of the ceremony, I rejoined my two friends and arranged with them to go upon a tour of the five sacred peaks as soon as Holy Week should be over. Meanwhile, I particularly enjoyed the spectacular events occurring on the last two days of that festival. On the penultimate day, a grand religious dance was held. As with the other public festivals, it took place in the Great Court; but, this time, everybody except the performers was crowded in a densely packed circle, men, women and children all mixed together and forming a kaleidoscopic mass of shifting colours. Close inspection revealed that the silk and satin brocades were covered with grease-stains and every other sort of grimy discolouration, while hair and faces glistened with butter and sweat. From a little distance, the crowd looked elegant enough to grace an imperial reception, so rich-looking their furs, silks and heavy jewelry. Presently the Kushog arrived, accompanied by the usual scintillating throng, together with the Chinese civil authorities in their drab, post-man-like official uniforms, and the Living Buddha, dressed in a suit of sharkskin. His Holiness's boredom was manifest, his smile sardonic and condescending; but to the Mongols he was every inch a Living Buddha, an incarnation of divinity. Though they all knew of this loose manner of living, their veneration for him was unimpaired, unless in the privacy of their own hearts. I imagine that this provides a close analogy with the veneration accorded by mediaeval Europe to the most loose-living of popes.

I am not one of those who dismiss the Tibetan belief in Living Buddhas or Divine Incarnations as mere nonsense. I prefer to think that the Lamas entrusted with the task of discovering such an incarnation from among children born soon after the decease of his predecessor, may sometimes err. In any case, it was quite impossible for me to believe in the divinity of Wu T'ai's Living Buddha, who was very well known for a dissolute mode of life and for scorning his sacred duties quite openly. On the other hand, to a firm believer in the reincarnation of all living crea-

tures, there is nothing incredible in the claim that certain very holy persons can choose where they will be reincarnated and that they can be
identified by their old followers after rebirth. 'Living Buddha' would
seem to be something of a misnomer, except perhaps in two or three
cases. The phrase "Sacred Incarnation" would be less susceptible to mis-
interpretation.

Early in the morning, a magnificent procession set out from P'usa
Ting and followed the traditionally serpentine route to another of the
principal monasteries. According to ancient custom, the Kushog Lama
and all his followers were obliged to pay this visit of state every year.
With the passing of centuries, the procession and attendant rites had
become more and more elaborate. Even the producers of such magnificent spectacles as *Henry V* or *Quo Vadis, The Ten Commandments* and so on
might be excused for goggling at the display I was fortunate enough to
behold that day. The procession equaled a Roman Triumph in scale and
probably surpassed it in the lavishness of equipment and paraphernalia. I
doubt if the most skilful pen could do justice to it and I am very sure that
I can at most give some vague notion of its splendour.

All the morning I stood on a little knoll and watched the two-mile-
long procession approach and recede, winding its way across the flower-
spangled plateau. The gorgeous, scintillating splendour of men and
bedecked animals, their jewels, precious metals, silks and brocades
gleaming in the sun, robbed the wild flowers of their colours, stole the
blue from the sky and the crimson or ochre from the monastery walls.
First came a group of grave, satin-clad beings on white steeds with silver-
chain harness and embroidered saddle-cloths. They were followed by a
rainbow-coloured troupe of musicians, the trumpeters with eight gaily
dressed children marching before each to support their prodigiously long
instruments, which thundered continuously. Immediately after these
musicians came the Bodhisattva's palanquin, its silken curtains parted so
that the golden statue shone like fire in the August sun and lightning
seemed to flash from the blade of the enormous Sword of Wisdom. The

procession of riders and footmen which followed stretched almost two miles to the rear, the great dignitaries and their followers from each of Wu Tai's three hundred monasteries having laid aside their ecclesiastical togas for gay costumes exactly like those worn thirty years before by the mandarins and eunuchs taking part in solemn ceremonies before the Throne of the Son of Heaven. Even the costumes of lamas Wang and Ma (too junior in the hierarchy to take part in the procession) would have seemed drab in such a throng. Almost at the end of the procession came the Kushog on foot, his immediate attendants bearing those ancient symbols of royalty or divinity, a ten-foot gilded pole supporting a golden fan and a many-tiered ceremonial umbrella of white and gold. His face was entirely hidden by a fringe of golden tassels falling forward from his headdress; from a little distance, he looked less like a human being than an animated image entirely covered by plates of gold. So much pomp and splendour was hard to reconcile with the gently austere doctrine of Gautama Buddha; as a spectacle, the procession has never in my experience been equalled.

The traditional route twisted and turned so that the procession would pass through the outer domains of numerous intervening monasteries and enable the various abbots to pay their respects. In each place, a portable altar had been raised, surrounded by dignitaries who lighted incense and candles as the procession drew near. Twice they performed the triple prostration, first to welcome the palanquin of the Bodhisattva and again to pay respects to the Kushog. The latter was preceeded by two resplendent figures bearing long poles to which was attached a horizontal silken banner or curtain, of which the lower edge was only some three feet above the ground, so that the whole formed a moving screen for His Holiness. As he approached, individuals would spring from the ranks of spectators lining both sides of the route, hurl themselves under this screen and then roll hurriedly out of the way of the oncoming Lama. There was a degree of skill in this exercise, for to have touched the banner with one's head would have brought upon one the bystanders' scorn and to have collided with the Kushog would have been so destructive of his majestic dignity as to amount to a kind of sacrilege. Just as I was picturing such an unfortunate collision in my mind, my legs unexpectedly started carrying me forward and, almost as though somebody else had willed it, I found myself flopping to the ground beneath the curtain and then rolling vigorously away as the golden shoes approached. My feelings at that moment were those of a car driver whose vehicle suddenly skids out of control. I have often pondered that curious little event and tried to account for it, but always in vain. I supposed I must have *desired* to do it just for fun and that I was in too much haste for the desire to register properly in my mind, but even this explanation seems very odd.

When the procession had passed, I sat down on the little knoll from which I had witnessed its approach and waited for it to return. Meanwhile I reflected upon my enormous good fortune. Except in Lhasa and perhaps one or two other Tibetan cities, such grandeur cannot be seen in the world today, unless in its synthetic Hollywood form; for pageantry on a vast scale has vanished from the earth. In many countries the totality of all the colourful experiences of a lifetime might not amount to half what I had seen in a space of less than two hours. The days of emperors, kings and princes have gone; their descendants have vanished from the earth or else retain the merest shadow of their forefathers' glory. Even in places where majestic pageantry still exists, as in the Vatican, those taking part seem to be in fancy dress on account of the drab modern clothes of the spectators. Fortunate indeed was I to have beheld during the late thirties of this century a spectacle which perhaps equalled in splendour the progress of the great Ch'ien Lung on his way to sacrifice at the Altar of Heaven, or one of the solemn processions of the mediaeval Church, or the enthronement of some world-conquering monarch such as Alexander. Not only was the procession itself the very acme of gorgeous splendour, but the lovely, flower-decked plateau, the green and purple mountains beyond, the brightly coloured buildings of a score of monasteries and the gay ornaments and costumes of the spectators all combined to provide a harmonious background only somewhat less splendid than the writhing rainbow-hued 'dragon' winding its way across the sacred ground.

Alas, soon after, Wu T'ai was destined to be a battlefield. There, Japanese fought Chinese and Communists fought the Kuomintang Government. How much of her former glories remain?

. . . .

A month or so [later] the day of my departure drew near. The venerable Nêng Hai had a farewell message for me.

"Goodbye, my dear pupil. Prosper. Do not let yourself be led astray. You are too fond of reading all manner of books and seeking out all manner of teachers. Some of them will deny the intellect and the senses. They will say these have no place in the life of one who seeks Enlightenment. They will be wrong. That kind of austerity is not for you. Remember this, a life dedicated to the search for Reality requires the *proper use* of intellect and senses. Intellectual knowledge will help you, if you harness it to the search for Wisdom and do not seek other knowledge as an end in itself. The appreciation of beauty will help you to know what is in store for you, the beauty of Reality being the beauty of a jade bowl or a mountain grove increased to an inconceivable extent. Only, beware of Desire. Take joy in beauty, but never, never desire its manifestations for yourself. Inhale their fragrance and pass on. Goodbye for the present. Remember my words and be sure that we shall meet again in this life."

Then, for the second time since I had come under his instruction, he added something very curious indeed. As I was leaving the room, I heard him mutter as though more to himself than to me: "Meet again, but shall we ever speak again?" These words were so strange that often in the years that followed they would come into my mind. Yet, when we did meet again and the words took on some meaning, they did not so much as enter my head until after we had parted for the last time.

.   .   .   .

A Postscript. (Seventeen years later)

I was sent upon official business to Chengtu, a walled grey-brick city affectionately styled "Little Peking." Its residential lanes bordered by low grey walls pierced with bronze-studded lacquered gates (but black and gold instead of Peking's scarlet) and the charming courtyards lying behind produced a sometimes startling resemblance to the Empress of Cities.

Now it happened that the Omei pilgrimage had brought down wrath upon my head. Some missionaries had written in to the Embassy complaining that the British Cultural Relations Officer had, while visiting Omei, openly worshipped the abominable idols of the heathen, thereby prejudicing their labours in the vineyard and injuring the Embassy's repute. So I had been gently reprimanded and advised to avoid giving further offence in this manner. This kindly meant advice had for me a tragic result which confirmed the veiled prophecy made by the Venerable Nêng Hai many years before.

My visit to Chengtu was undertaken in the company of a not very sympathetic colleague. One day we were standing in a temple courtyard admiring its faded beauty and, incidentally, listening to the hum of a sermon being preached in the building facing us. Presently the flow of sound ceased, benches scraped against a stone floor and the cloth-shod monks could be heard shuffling their feet. Just as we were going to turn away, a chant began, sufficiently melodious to detain us longer. At that moment, an ochre-robed figure came hurrying out of the building and walked straight towards where we stood. It was Nêng Hai.

Seven years before at Wu T'ai, Dr. Chang, Mr. Li and myself had all performed the simple rite whereby we were accepted by Nêng Hai as his personal disciples. This being so, the *only possible* way for me to greet our Teacher after a long separation was to prostrate myself before his feet. But now what was I to do? My Embassy colleague had no idea of my predicament and he was not a man whose discretion I could trust in any matter which seemed to him derogatory to British prestige. My reprimand had been gently worded, but I was intended to obey and, besides, it had come from Sir Eric Teichman, a delightful person whom I should have been sorry to offend and, in fact, more of a 'Teacher' to me than Nêng Hai himself.

My colleague and I were standing right in the path of the oncoming Abbot, whose eyes were raised to our faces and *seemed* to be directed especially at me. My mind in a turmoil, anguish in my heart, I held his gaze for a while and then—impassively stepped aside. The Venerable Nêng Hai walked straight past without turning his head and disappeared into another building. I longed to run after him and throw myself at his feet in the privacy of his room, but just then X (my senior) said: "Hurry up. We're awfully late. Old General Liao has probably never been kept waiting since he and his family took over the province. He fancies himself a sort of king and we had better humour him." Silently I followed him out into the street and ordered rickshaws to take us to the warlord's mansion.

The next day, we left Chengtu at dawn. When, on my next and last visit to that city, I called at the temple, Nêng Hai had gone. Oh, why had I not had the courage to take X into my confidence and hurry after my Teacher, if only to spend five minutes with him? Later on, I thought of several ways in which, had I been less flustered, I could have put the matter right. As it was, I had in a sense been guilty of denying the Lord Buddha as Peter, with much better reason, denied Christ.

I am still unhappy when I recall this incident, so accurately predicted by Nêng Hai himself. Did he, after an interval of seven years, recognize me and, hurt by my discourtesy and ingratitude to one who had spent many precious hours instructing me, pass on in silence? Or did he behold nothing more than two bronzed Englishmen, strangers who were rather slow in moving out of his way? I shall never know. And, assuming that he did recognize me, did he really feel hurt or did he have some intuitive knowledge of the reason for my failure to speak? The latter would have been impossible to explain to him. How could I say to my Teacher: "As I am now a member of His Britannic Majesty's Embassy, it would be regarded as demeaning were I to prostrate myself before you?"

Initiation in Sikkim

During my pilgrimage and subsequent journeyings about India, my thoughts as to the precise nature of the experience awaiting me in the Tibetan border regions had gradually crystallized. Ever since my early twenties when I had been initiated by the Dorjé Rimpoché, I had intermittently practised some of the preliminary meditations and rites open to me, but with small success. Yet my attempts to penetrate deeply into Zen and other forms of Buddhism had always ended in my return to the Vajrayana as being best suited to my attainments and spiritual capacities. Within the Vajrayana, there are literally hundreds of approaches suited to different types of people.

Most unfortunately, or else for obscure karmic reasons, I had allowed something to delay my attendance at the Grand Initiation twenty years before and so missed that part of it which would qualify me for the path I was now determined to follow. In a flash of insight it became abundantly clear to me that the mysterious experience awaiting me in the Himalayas [would repair that omission of twenty years ago].

Now I hesitated no longer. All that remained was to discover where I must go, for no genuine Lama would bestow this initiation upon a stranger just for the asking.

The choice lay among the following places: Ladakh and the other Tibetan border monasteries in or near the province of Kashmir; the semi-independent state of Sikkim ruled by a Tibetan king; Bhutan, a similar state which white men rarely obtain permission to enter; the Indian border towns in the Darjeeling district; and the Tibetan monasteries in the mountains of Nepal. Since the establishment of the Peking Government's suzerainty over Tibet, those places are the only ones left in the world where a Westerner from a non-Communist country may hope to come in contact with Lamas qualified to bestow such initiations. As to which place to choose, a combination of events made it abundantly clear that the longed-for experience awaited me somewhere in Sikkim.

The preliminaries to my journey were soon arranged. Before long, a bus was carrying me up that marvellous road which, winding upwards by the turbulent Tista, leads to Gangtok, Sikkim's capital seven thousand feet above the plain.

I stayed in a small Indian hotel where a traveller can have a bed but not often a room to himself. The balcony overlooked the bazaar with its sprinkling of Indians in white *dhoris,* its crowds of slightly built Nepalis and entire absence of Westerners. Among them strode tall, pink-cheeked Tibetans, the men with scarlet-ribboned queues of thick black hair rolled around their heads, their long gowns hitched high so that they bulged over their waist-sashes and displayed knee-high boots of soft-coloured leather. I had often seen Tibetan men in China, but Tibetan women I now saw for the first time and was astonished by their beauty—pale, smooth-skinned faces with apple-red cheeks, jet black eyebrows and two thick plaits of hair dancing behind them. Their ankle-length, sleeveless robes of darkish wool contrasted with the pale red, orange, yellow or blue silk of their long-sleeved blouses. Many also wore gay, horizontally striped aprons, a few decorated at the upper corners with the brocaded insignia of nobility. None of them in the least resembled the unwashed, butter-smeared, mat-haired creatures whom travellers meet in Tibet's wilder regions. That evening I gained my first inkling of the sophistication of the beauty-loving city-dwellers of Tibet.

The next morning, I hastened to pay my respects to the Chief Minister, a gentle, elderly man with bright eyes and cheeks almost red enough to match the scarlet ribbon entwined in his coiled queue. Except for his red Tibetan sash, he looked exactly like a mandarin who has stepped out from a Chinese ancestral portrait; it seemed incongruous that his English was fluent and correct. We liked each other from the first and he, without appearing too hopeful, promised to help me overcome the chief obstacle lying before me, that of finding a Lama both qualified and willing to bestow the initiation upon a stranger. I was inwardly confident, feeling that events were taking a karmically predestined course of which I knew the end.

"There is," he said, "at least one man in Sikkim perfectly suited to your purpose, the Rimpoché now living at the monastery of Tashiding. But the journey may make you wish you had changed your mind, for the rains have already damaged the paths and may drench you from morning to night. Then, if that doesn't deter you, how will you persuade him to bestow the initiation? Your permit to stay in Sikkim will expire long before you have had time to complete the preliminary course of study and practice which normally takes months, if not years. Another difficulty is that nobody there speaks a word of English and your knowledge of Chinese is useless anywhere in Sikkim. So what will you do?"

Finally he undertook to write a letter to the Tangku Rimpoché explaining that, besides being a Buddhist of many years standing, I had received important initiations at the hands of the Dorjé Rimpoché, also that I undertook to perform on my own all necessary preliminaries to the rites and meditations to be unlocked for me by the initiation.

I stayed in Gangtok several days while preparations for my journey were in hand. The city's chief beauty lies in its splendid panorama of hills; architecturally, the royal temple within the palace precincts is one of the very few buildings of interest. The inner walls are ablaze with murals which, though fine examples of the traditional style, have been executed within the last few years. I pricked up my ears when somebody mentioned that one of the two artists responsible for the work was still living in Gangtok. To him I hastened and commissioned two pictures, including one very important for the meditations I was about to learn. (Mounted on brocaded silk in the royal Buddhist colours and secured to a roller with ends of beaten silver, it now occupies the place of honour in my household shrine, its beauty a constant inspiration). I also bought other objects, chiefly of wrought silver—butter-lamps and various sorts of ritual paraphernalia. To a Buddhist, none of this paraphernalia is essential;

even the most complicated rituals of the Vajrayana can be performed mentally in a bare cave, if necessary; but it is hard to resist the age-old desire to beautify the shrine containing the sacred symbols of a cherished faith, particularly for one like myself who finds properly understood symbolism a great aid to spiritual concentration.

Before leaving, I was invited to my first Tibetan party which took place in a room bright with multi-coloured rugs and carven woodwork painted in colours reminiscent of those used to decorate altar-screens in mediaeval Europe—brilliant but never harsh like the industrially produced paints with which Western manufacturers now flood the more accessible parts of Asia. The entertainment included the constant serving of *ch'ang,* or Tibetan "beer." A very fat bamboo container silver-bound and half filled with fermented grain was set before each guest. It contained a long, thin bamboo to serve as a drinking "straw." On to the grain servants frequently poured hot water, filling the container to the brim, and at each pouring the water immediately changed to a warm, milky coloured "beer," very mild and pleasant to the taste. I tried to be reasonably abstemious, but now and then the ladies of the house would form a circle and dance round me, singing a song which meant something like:

We gladly bid welcome to you.
Alas that your hours here are few.
But, while you are here,
Please drink up your beer
To honour the hosts
Who strive to please you.

Such an invitation is impossible to refuse, so I was relieved to discover that *ch'ang* is the mildest fermented drink I had ever tasted.

The next day, I set out for Tashiding. The first stage was accomplished in torrential rain by bus and jeep along the only motorable road in Sikkim apart from the fine main road running due north and south of the capital. At the end of this short stage stood a Government rest-house and, from its balcony, I was to catch my first view of the glorious snow-peaks beyond. The rain stopped towards evening and, for a few moments, the drifting clouds parted to reveal a jagged line of pure white touched with the first pink of sunset. Almost before I had time to cry out, this tantalizing glimpse of beauty was swallowed up in angry black clouds, as though an elderly Muslim had returned home to find his youngest wife revealing herself at the window to the ravished passers-by. Soon the rain was swishing down more relentlessly than before. All through the night it rattled upon the roof and hissed upon the sodden lawns.

The next day I rose at dawn and, as the rain showed no signs of abating, I put all my trust in my thick waterproof and splendid knee-high Tibetan boots. An hour later, a rain-sodden and dispirited horse, kindly put at my disposal by the local *kazi* (land-owner), was led into the compound by the groom who was to accompany me on foot with a baggage cooly bringing up in the rear. I had not ridden for as much as half an hour when my waterproof belied its name by giving up the battle and allowing the rain to seep in as through a garment of gauze. As for my new boots, their wide tops permitted the water to pour inside and fill all the space between boot and leg.

Knowing that the rain might pour for days, I decided to ride forward at all costs, following a widish path which wound upwards through the dripping jungle. By midday, the top of the slope was behind me. The groom intimated that I should now dismount and walk forward on my own, as the *kazi* did not like his horse to be ridden by a heavy man on a steep downward slope. The cooly had dropped out of sight, probably far behind; so I soon found myself alone in a strange country, unable to communicate with its inhabitants even if any of them should venture out in such weather. Soaked to the skin and increasingly miserable, I trudged forward. The path had narrowed so much that I could almost have touched the streaming branches on either hand. Its centre had become a rushing torrent; I had to drag my heavy, water-logged boots through three feet of water. To either side were slippery banks infested by thousands upon thousands of leeches hungry for good warm human blood. So many of them wormed their way stealthily over the tops of my boots and disappeared deep inside that the water squelching from the boots was soon tinged with the blood flowing from those who, after gorging themselves and increasing their girth tenfold, had been squashed between foot and leather. Once I thought of stopping by a rock to take off my boots and remove the leeches; but I had no sooner sat down than a great host of fresh leeches advanced from all sides, rearing their loathsome bodies up like cobras in excited anticipation of a meal. With a moan of disgust, I leapt up and hurried back to the rushing water in the centre of the path. I guessed that at least fifty of them had found their way into my boots and were busy feasting off my blood. The absence of pain was small comfort, for they filled me with that unspeakable loathing which they inspire in all who see them for the first time. Old-stagers in those jungles find them no more revolting than ants or ladybirds!

My new boots began to chafe my feet, causing increasing pain. I was in a wretched state—soaking wet, hot, sweaty, tired, footsore, hungry, thirsty and ever conscious of the vampire leeches fattening on my blood. Hour after hour went by and still the path bored into uninhabited jungle. I could have wept with vexation and with fear of taking the wrong path and having to spend the night trudging on and on until exhaustion brought me to the ground to become a prey to a whole army of leeches. Then, as from heaven, a warmly comforting thought came to drive away all my woes. Once I had read of a pious Tibetan journeying to seek wisdom from a mountain-dwelling recluse. The hermit, aware of his approach, conjured up terrific snow-storms and fearful landslides all along the route, to test his strength of purpose; yet the traveller never wavered, but pressed forward boldly, for he was determined either to reach his Teacher or perish in the attempt. I do not suppose that my relatively mild sufferings were due to anything more than the normal weather at that season. All the same, I began to regard them in the light of a test of endurance, a mark of heaven's high favour, whereupon my heart lightened and even my horror of the leeches abated somewhat. Thenceforth, I splashed along with renewed energy, singing out the Fourfold Invocation to Guru, Buddha, Dharma and Sangha which I fitted to a lovely old Chinese tune, dwelling on the syllables so that they rose and fell in a cadence of semitones. Had anyone been there to hear, they might not have found it much better than frog-croaking; to me it was inspiring. Not for the first time, I reflected on the immensity of mind's power over matter. This is magnificent, I thought. What I am enduring now will make my pilgrimage a worthy sacrifice. This fiercely driving rain and all my present troubles are omens of success. Formerly the minutes had dragged like hours; now, the last hour of my journey sped by as though I had robbed it of fifty of its minutes. When next I grew weary, the rest-house was perched just a hundred yards above where I was standing. A final spurt of energy and I was beneath its roof.

Within five minutes, a young Nepalese was fanning logs into a blaze in the fireplace; and I, having stripped off all my dripping clothes, was comfortably arrayed in sarong and toga composed of two curtains purloined from the rest-house window. Flinging myself into a chair before the fire, I touched the tails of the leeches clinging to my legs with tobacco unrolled from a cigarette, and had the pleasure of seeing them drop to the floor to be gathered up by the servant and carted out of sight. Next my cooly arrived and proudly displayed my bedding and spare clothes which were not even damp from the rain, so cunningly had he rolled them into his waterproof sheet. On the advice of the Chief Minister, I had brought food with me and was able to enjoy a plateful of curried potato and onion, served with a mound of soft white rice and washed down by my favourite Chinese tea brought all the way from Thailand. At dusk I went to bed and fell into a dreamless sleep.

Dawn the next morning! The first of many glorious, gorgeous Himalayan dawns with the sky-line of monster snow-peaks revealed in all their majesty, their everlasting snows touched with fire by the rising sun. This was the beginning of a seeming miracle. I was now within sight of Tashiding and, for as long as I remained on or in view of that mountain, *no rain fell*. I had come, perforce, at the height of Sikkim's rainy season, when the skies often shed blinding torrents of rain for days on end. Who could have imagined such good fortune? Not until the second day of the return journey did the clouds burst asunder and drench me as before; no spot of rain marred my happiness on Tashiding. Were I one of those people who believe that Heaven will reward the earnest prayer of one individual by withholding the rain, however much the farmers lament its absence, I should surely have claimed a genuine miracle wrought on my behalf.

The final stage had to be covered on foot. When I had engaged a local Nepali as cooly-guide, I walked straight down from the rest-house into a valley some two thousand feet below. The paths were still rushing cataracts, but in that valley no leeches dwell, nor upon the slopes of Tashiding. The valley is shaped like an enormous bowl rimmed with steeply sloping mountains. In the centre is Tashiding, an almost perfect cone rising two thousand feet above a kind of moat formed by two torrents which clash together at its foot, hissing and roaring so loudly as to make conversation in the neighbourhood well-nigh impossible. A fine bridge crosses this turgid "moat" and then the climb begins. Tashiding is cruelly steep, almost precipitous; and the shorter path to the summit is so strewn with rocks and boulders that I often had to use four limbs like a monkey; yet my cooly, half my size and burdened besides with my luggage, leapt upwards like a stag. Later, telling the story of that climb to an English-speaking teacher who arrived after some days, he said: "Poor Englishman. I felt so sad for him. But for his luggage, I should have offered to carry him up on my back." An athletic man unburdened could have covered the distance in less than half the time I took, but my heart pounded so much from the unaccustomed strain that I grew dizzy. A curtain of mist flickering before my eyes and want of breath compelled me to make many pauses.

At last, at last, when the sun was low, I gained a sort of platform near the peak. In front of me was a pile of stones inscribed with the mystic words:

OM MANI PADME HUM

which play so great a part in Tibetan Buddhism—a part so sadly misunderstood in the West that the Lama Govinda has devoted a book of over three hundred pages to expounding the mantra's full significance!* The sight of this inscription galvanized me like the appearance of an oasis in a desert, for it meant that I had arrived, that I already stood within the monastery grounds. I strode forward and found myself gazing at a long street of wooden dwellings running between two sizeable temple buildings.

My cooly had preceded me to give notice of my arrival and to inform the authorities that I was the bearer of a letter from the Chief Minister to their spiritual master, the Tangku Rimpoché. The first person to see me was an old woman who repeatedly raised both hands to her forehead and protruded her tongue in friendly greeting. Hobbling to a nearby hut, she came back with a chair—surely a rarity there and perhaps the only one in that place, for I never saw another. I had scarcely sat down with a sigh of relief, when the sight of a burly monk hastening towards me brought me quickly to my feet. I was amused to find that long acquaintance with Chinese monasteries enabled me, even though this was a Tibetan, to know for certain that he was the Chief Administrator or Head Lama. Not that he wore any insignia of rank; it was just that the seal of authority was engraven upon his face and reflected in the ponderous dignity of his movements. Many Mahayanist temples have two heads—a spiritual and a temporal head, either of whom may be the Abbot. The spiritual head is less easy to distinguish, for there may be several monks as spiritually advanced as himself; or he may belong to a community in which nobody (including himself) has attained to that state. The administrative head is as easy to spot as a mayor among aldermen.

* *Foundations of Tibetan Mysticism*, Lama Anagarika Govinda. Rider & Co.

Dressed in a robe of woollen stuff and dangling a long, black rosary from his left hand, he came striding forward with a smile of welcome. He saw at once that I was very tired, so he cut short the usual courtesies and led me to a little room which had been hurriedly prepared for me. It contained everything essential—a bed, floor-cushions and a desk eighteen inches high. There was also a wall-shrine and a few shelves, some of which had been cleared to receive my scanty possessions. After two days of what to me had seemed great hardship, I thought the room positively luxurious and grinned with pleasure when an old woman appeared with hot buttered tea and some rock-like corn-cakes to be dipped in it until softened.

In China, nobody need carry food with him. Every village has its restaurant and every monastery its provision for guests. The Tibetan custom is different, probably because monks are often poor and food scarce; so I had brought my own tea, rice, curry-powder, onions, potatoes and oil, as well as sugar and coffee. I was just wondering whom I could induce to cook some of this for me, when my truly remarkable cooly carried in a delicious meal he had cooked himself. I had engaged this man at a low figure just to carry my luggage. His assumption of the posts of cook and very efficient body-servant was done entirely from kindness, and from now on he was to look after me as a father looks after a rather feeble-minded son. A member of the blacksmith caste, he was held by Hindus to be a low creature; to me he was a treasure, always smiling and gay, always ready to find means of adding to my comfort, and so highly intelligent that he soon discovered how to converse with me at some length, using my twenty words of Hindi and eking them out with the language of looks and gestures.

Supper was followed by coffee, after which I felt ready to collapse on to the bed and fall into a deep sleep. However, no sooner had I begun to undress than the Head Lama appeared to inform me that the Most Venerable Tangku Lama was awaiting my visit of courtesy.

The Tangku Rimpoché, whose reputation for learning and spiritual attainment has, I believe, made him the most outstanding personality in

Sikkim, is a member of the "Red-Cap" Sect; thus, if any hair remained to him, he would wear it long instead of shaving his head in the orthodox manner. Instead, he wears a wig. Crippled in both legs, he sits all day on a floor-cushion with a rug over the lower part of his body. His plum-colour toga is patched and faded, his absurdly unrealistic wig is worn carelessly askew on his bald head. Almost any other man so dressed would be taken for a clown or for an elderly half-wit, and inevitably become the butt of the local urchins. Not so the Tangku Lama. His expression and above all his eyes demand instant respect and obedience. Were he able to walk and if, in some miraculous manner, he were transported to the centre of a snow-covered village street in England, I can imagine the village urchins rushing towards him with whoops of derision, scooping up balls of snow ready to pelt him. But if, at such a moment, he should turn around and smile straight into their eyes, I surely believe that the raised hands would be lowered and the snowballs fall unheeded to the ground; for the quality of the Lama's expression is such that no reputation for holiness, no knowledge of his exalted position as a Rimpoché, is needed to convince all who see him of his immense power and perfect gentleness of soul.

When I had performed the ritual prostrations and presented him with a ceremonial scarf, he motioned me to a cushion where I sat for perhaps five minutes gazing at him with intense pleasure, while he remained very still, quietly examining me and weighing me up, rather as Tahai had done more than twenty years before. Of course this silence was not according to precedent for such occasions; it was because we had no common language. Except for what was said in the Chief Minister's letter, the Rimpoché's only means of discovering something about me was to scrutinize me while employing that inner vision which no doubt reveals far more to him than his eyes.

A small group of disciples sat in the same room busy with various tasks. I was conscious of their discreet stares and somehow sure that they were friendly. There was no suspicion of arrogance or hostility towards a foreigner. An extraordinary aspect of that first meeting was that, to a small extent, the Lama and I were able to converse. That he should be able to read my thoughts I took for granted as soon as I had seen what sort of person he was; the difficulty was for him to convey his thoughts to me. Somehow, with the aid of my twenty words of Hindi, half a dozen Chinese words he happened to know, the Tibeto-Sanskrit technical terms concerning the matter which had brought me there and which were common to us both, the language of looks, signs and gestures, all aided by our mutual knowledge of the contents of the letter of introduction, the Lama was able to convey to me most of what he wished to tell me.

The following dialogue represents what I am almost sure he would have said in very similar words, if we had had a common language. I suppose it took about half an hour for him to make himself understood by round-about means, employing all the aids I have mentioned.

THE LAMA: "The Initiation you desire cannot be bestowed without careful preparation. When you have learnt and performed all the preliminaries, I shall be happy to perform the necessary rite."

MYSELF: "Rimpoché! I beg you to understand that it is impossible for me to spend more than a few days here—let alone months or years. My permit will expire in two weeks from now and I have to get back to my job by October 1st."

THE LAMA: "We are dealing with deeply sacred matters. Surely you understand that we must act in seemly fashion. What is time? What does your permit matter, or your getting back to your job, when such spiritual benefits are at stake?"

This interview and several of the same kind to follow did not distress me. I knew that initiations are not given away for the asking like apples or a bunch of grapes. I knew that the Lama understood my difficulties very well, but wanted time to observe me, and that his final word had not been spoken. Yet I was so impatient that the following morning I sent my excellent servant back to his village to procure a horse and persuade an elderly English-speaking teacher, who had already refused once to make the journey, to ride back with him to interpret for me. I was afraid the

Lama did not fully appreciate how much of the preliminary ground I had covered already. No doubt it was a foolish or at least a useless action, for the Lama certainly intended to base his decision on what he observed in me rather than on anything I could urge in my favour, but I wished to leave nothing to chance.

During the days while I waited for the interpreter to arrive and for some time after that, I spent most of my time alone. Except for one or two short periods each day when the Tangku Lama sent for me to instruct me in certain Tibeto-Sanskrit verses to be committed to memory, I was left so much to myself that I suspected the Lama had given instructions for me to be allowed solitude in which to prepare myself. If I were right, then clearly he was inclined to grant the initiation. Every morning began with the magical dance of fire upon snow, during and after which I used to sit entranced, entering sometimes into states of consciousness deeper than any I had previously attained. Generally, within an hour or so of dawn, the splendid snow-peaks were swallowed up in cloud; yet, even then, Tashiding enjoyed local sunshine which drew mysterious shadows from the rocks and trees. My morning meditation ended, I would wander about, sometimes going as far afield as some neighbouring heights attached to Tashiding by a narrow spur, thereby just preventing the conical mountain from being an island. All day long, except when I returned to my room for a meal or a rest, I was more or less in a state of meditation. At certain intervals I practised the strenuous concentration which leads directly to the hidden places of the spirit; at other times I let my eyes wander over sky and mountain, feeling keenly alive to each lovely detail but refraining from all discursive thought. This exercise is very difficult to describe. As the eye lingers upon one object or another, the mind registers it in terms of: "Ah, thus it is and thus"; shape, colour and texture are taken into the mind, but not in terms of beautiful or ordinary, nor even in terms of round or long, thick or thin, white or blue. Everything is seen just as it is; no judgement is made, nor any attempt at mental description involving comparisons between black and white, large and small. "It is so, it is so, it is so"—that is all. I believe that contemplating the thusness of rock, tree or hill gave me greater pleasure than can be derived from examining them in the usual interpretive way. As soon as I say: "That hill is blue," I am thinking in terms of opposites—of blue and other-than-blue; but if I just gaze at a hill, taking in all its details without even naming them to myself, without making any comparisons involving differences of colour, shape and texture, I can sense an intimate relationship between the hill and myself; almost I seem to know what it is like to be that hill—or so I like to think. On emerging from this type of contemplation, I used to find my mind wonderfully rested and, better still, the essential doctrine of ultimate Oneness had taken on added meaning, added reality for me.

Another exercise I performed is much easier to describe. I spent some time reasoning discursively about the meaning of life and the place of each individual in the universe according to the understanding I had developed during the last twenty years, particularly my understanding of Buddhist doctrine—but this exercise, though fascinating, is quite unprofitable, as the Lord Buddha was fond of pointing out. Until Enlightenment—intuitive perception of Reality—is achieved, no amount of reason will produce the answers to such questions, and to ponder them is not especially conducive to Enlightenment.

As soon as my servant returned with the reluctant school-teacher, I hastened to visit the Tangku Lama and to reinforce my pleading with the help of an interpreter. The Lama's amused expression told me at once that I had been to quite unnecessary trouble, though I fancy he was a trifle moved by this expression of my urgent longing for his decision. I think that, in any case, I should have received his answer that day or the next. As it was, the old school-teacher had apparent reason to flatter himself that he was entirely responsible for the happy ending to my quest. To him the Tangku Lama addressed these words:

"The day after tomorrow is an auspicious day. Already my disciples are preparing the necessary ritual objects for the rite of initiation. In the afternoon of that day, the English disciple will be summoned. Let him see to it that he is in all ways prepared. Furthermore, let him pay careful heed to this. The initiation is all-important; without it, he could not venture along his chosen path. Yet the rite in itself is worth little without proper instruction. Let him proceed at his convenience to some such city as Darjeeling or Kalimpong and there put himself in the hands of a Lama of high attainment, bringing with him if necessary a Tibetan layman somewhat learned in Buddhism to interpret, and let him study the various stages of the rite and visualization verse by verse, sentence by sentence, word by word, until all is clear as a crystal gem. Then only let him begin to practise. Finally, let him understand that this path, though one among thousands, is in itself sufficient. Let him follow it to the end. Let him cease his leaping from branch to branch and walk straight forward, pausing to breathe when difficulties arise, but never again retreating."

To all of this I joyfully assented. On the eve of the initiation ceremony, I felt not so much excited as wonderfully at peace with myself. Looking back, I saw how I had been advancing step by step by a switchback route towards the peak I was now approaching. My initiation into the Vajrayana more than twenty years before had not immediately borne visible fruit, but it had led me to see in that Vehicle some truths to which my countrymen are often blind. Two decades of intermittent experiment with several schools of Buddhism and many methods had followed and now, at last, I had quite determined to quit shillyshallying and to concentrate my effort along the one Path. Too long I had hesitated through bewilderment at the wide choice of routes. At my age I should have advanced far beyond the stage of wavering between them. Moreover, there had been numerous indications, mostly unheeded at the times when they occurred, pointing steadily in the direction I was now determined to go. My failure to progress in Zen; my frequent fortuitous meetings with learned Lamas, even in South China where Lamas are almost never seen; the veiled prophecy of Nêng Hai; and my curious intuition at Wat Chalerm were only some of the indications driving me not only in the direction of the Vajrayana but towards a particular path within that

Vehicle's wide compass. Further indications of a more subtle and mysterious nature had also occurred. And now the Tangku Rimpoché had promised to unlock the gate and set me firmly upon my way, inspired by all the power he could transmit to me!

At last the day of days dawned. I have already described how it began with the splendid spectacle of the gods dancing, followed by the evocation of vivid recollections from the long-forgotten past, as though this too were part of the Lama's plan for me. All was prepared just as I had so earnestly desired; and yet, when I entered the Tangku Lama's room where the rite was to be performed, I was nearly overcome with trepidation.

Of the initiation itself it is not proper to say much. During its course, I was conducted to the two Great Halls to pay my respects before the Lord Buddha and Guru Rimpoché (Padma Sambhava), the founder of the Vajrayana in Tibet. After that I was led back to the little room where the rites continued for many hours. Their climax came when the sacred symbol of my chosen Path was laid upon my head. During the few seconds it remained there, I experienced physical sensations similar to those which, so many years before, had accompanied the Dorjé Rimpoché's laying on of hands; except that, whether because my perceptions had coarsened with the years or for some other reason, the feeling of shock was less intense and I felt no fear. On the other hand, the immediately following sensation of spiritual elation was beyond anything in my experience.

At the very end of the rite, I felt a spontaneous desire to lay my head against the Lama's crippled and carefully covered limbs. He smiled at this and I felt his hands rest upon my head in calm benediction. Now at last I had my heart's desire. This *could* be the turning point of my life. Except for certain instructions to follow, all that others could do for me had been done. Henceforth, my fate rested, not in other hands, but in my own.

To celebrate the conclusion of a long and arduous rite, which had proceeded for eighteen hours in all, some large meat dumplings were served to all who had taken part. During this meal I sat cross-legged next to the Lama who, with true Tibetan hospitality, pressed more and more dumplings upon me. I do not think I have ever in my life seen a lovelier sight than the smile on the face of the Rimpoché when he pressed the thirteenth and last of my lion's share of the dumplings into my mouth. It was a smile of sheer happiness and boundless affection for those who shared his meal.

Chapter IV

· · · · · · · · · · ·

Taoism
and/or
Buddhism?

Peter Goullart

The Russian Revolution hurled Peter Goullart (1902–1978) into exile across half the globe, depositing him finally in a rough-and-tumble existence in Shanghai. Goullart found solace for his initially hard lot there by exploring China's religions of Taoism and Buddhism. His books, especially The Monastery of Jade Mountain *(1961), evoke those two faiths as they were lived on a daily basis and, almost unintentionally, preserve in charming, picturesque recollection China as it was between the two world wars.*

Westerners contrast Buddhism and Taoism, but the Chinese priests and monks that Goullart encountered insisted the two faiths were complementary. Goullart, a devotee of both, explores how a religion based on nature (Taoism) is related to one that is based on "spirit" (Buddhism). In Forgotten Kingdom *(1955), Goullart's depiction of Buddhist society on the southwestern Sino-Tibetan borderlands paints an unlikely near-utopia on earth.*

By the late 1940s, this Russian expatriate had lived the majority of his life in China and had become both a Chinese citizen and a Chinese official. Then a second Marxist revolution, Mao's, uprooted Goullart from his adopted country and cast him once more into the unknown. His religious studies had taught him that "if one sincerely desires a thing, one will get it; if one door is closing, another will be opened." Exiled from his second motherland, Goullart spent productive years, establishing cooperatives and working for the United Nations in Hong Kong, Singapore, Malaysia, India, Pakistan, and Sarawak. His books about his experience (only a couple of which have been published in the United States) serve as monuments to forgotten kingdoms and markers of lost religions.

Background: Heaven and Hell

The days of my childhood and youth were happy, with a loving and prudent mother to guide me, who, at the same time, was able to win and hold my confidence as my intimate friend and adviser. Many people, brought up in the lap of nature, take for granted the beauty and freedom of forests, hills and rivers, and the glory of wild flowers and fragrant air; and their appreciation of these blessings comes to them only a long time afterwards, in retrospect, or as an afterthought when they have become tired drudges in a big town. My mother in her wisdom taught me to enjoy them to the full while they lasted, and not to wait for some hypothetical future joys. Even now I have twinges of cold horror when I reflect that I might have been born and brought up in the slums of a great city with the foetid air of small gloomy rooms, potted geraniums for flowers, and some distant dusty park to play in.

As I grew older, I was sometimes seized with an inchoate presentiment that this happiness could not continue for ever. This feeling, as I see it now, was perhaps natural to me, my mother being very sensitive and credited with clairvoyant powers. It seems I have inherited this mysterious faculty, which is now fashionably called *Psi*, and it has helped me on a number of occasions to extricate myself from situations of considerable danger. My forebodings were realized when World War I had been declared. The first blow was to my further education. My mother had arranged for my entrance to a special lyceum where youths were trained for the diplomatic service. Now it was all off, the school having been temporarily suspended. The Revolution brought chaos in its wake, when the Bolshevists had concluded the Brest-Litovsk treaty. Millions of soldiers rushed home wrecking all transport. Deprived of flour and other necessities from the Ukraine, a terrible famine seized central Russia. We were starving for weeks, an experience I shall never forget. So acute were the pangs of hunger that even a morsel of bread, made of old buckwheat with sawdust and straw to add to its bulk, appeared a wonderful delicacy. Ever since those frightful days I have a profound respect for food; its waste distresses me and whenever I see a piece of bread carelessly thrown on to the pavement I always pick it up to tuck away somewhere for a hungry dog or bird rather than see it trodden under foot. At the same time I dislike persons who make a fuss over their food. They would eat anything, were they really hungry.

The world continued to crumble about us. It seemed that all reality had disappeared and that we were emerging from a pleasant dream into a monstrous nightmare. Where there was order and honour seemingly only yesterday, now there was chaos, brutality and sheer barbarity. My mother and I could not stand it, neither could we fit into the new bestial set-up. We packed in a hurry all we could and, with enormous difficulties and dangers, made our way to Turkestan hoping to escape to India. Horrible adventures awaited us in Samarkand and Bokhara, and the road through Afghanistan was blocked by bloodthirsty bands of robbers. It took us many weeks to retrace our steps until we found ourselves in a train for Vladivostok, only to be blocked again by the Czech uprising in Siberia. It was a terrifying journey but we survived and, when Vladivostock was about to fall to the Reds again, we sailed for Shanghai.

Shortly after arrival I was fortunate to find an accounting job with a Greek cigarette factory. The salary was small, but we were given a spacious and comfortable apartment in the factory owner's house. I liked China at once and I soon picked up the rudiments of the Chinese language. A few years later I improved it by staying for some time at a Chinese school in Soochow. My mother, however, never fully recovered from the sufferings we had undergone and from the realization that we had lost everything. Now and then she was seized with fits of despondency and nostalgia. Her depression was made worse by her isolation from people, as she did not know English and was too old to learn it.

It was with a sense of utter helplessness that I watched my mother slipping into melancholia. I earned barely enough for our ordinary living, and there was nothing left to provide her with little luxuries or distractions. I wanted to take her on trips to beautiful places like Soochow or Hangchow, or buy her interesting Russian books or other things. Alas! our budget did not permit it. She lived entirely in the past, the strange and fascinating oriental life around her leaving her cold. Only cinemas seemed to hold her interest, and we went to one almost every evening.

The beginning of the end came in a macabre manner. Almost every week we had séances with an ouija-board, merely for pleasure and not for any necromantic purpose. We always had responses from a certain spirit called Omar, who amused us by spinning all sorts of interesting stories about an old Roman treasure buried on an island somewhere off the Philippines or Celebes. One evening Mother asked him how long she was going to live. The ouija-board spun madly for awhile and then clear, firmly written words were produced: "A year from now you will be dead." After this shock we discontinued the séances. I do not like to pronounce any judgment on this prophecy, but the fact is that in a week or so my mother was suddenly convulsed with terrible pains at night and had to be rushed to hospital for an operation. The operation was not a complete success—the surgeon frankly told me to expect her death within a day. With my heart in my mouth I rushed out to buy three quarts of Mumm champagne and let her sip it whenever her heart began to palpitate. She rallied, to the doctor's astonishment and relief, but never completely recovered. At last, after Christmas she was moved to a hospital only to be permitted after ten days or so to come back home to die.

The poignancy of my grief, when I realized that she was leaving me, can only be imagined, but it was the manner of her dying that inflicted a lasting wound on my mind through the sheer terror that I experienced. The last night she slept peacefully, all her pains having left her. In the morning she looked more fragile and her face was luminous and peaceful, as if she had realized that her losing struggle for survival was at last over. She beckoned me to her side and pointed out to the far corner of the room whispering that a group of her dead parents and relatives was standing there waiting for her. She said they did not speak but made signs that it was her last day on earth. Through my tears I smiled and bowed in the direction indicated, and Mother said that I was recognized and the relatives smiled in return. Then she firmly told me to stop sniveling, as we did not have much time left and she wanted to give me her last advice and admonition. In the evening she began sinking, and about ten o'clock she drifted into a coma. I thought she was already dead. Then suddenly, without the least warning, she sat bolt upright in her bed, her arms extended in front of her and her hands twitching in the manner of claws. A sort of animal growl issued from her throat and she croaked, "Where are you, wretch? Where are you?" Her eyes, apparently unseeing, were bulging and her mouth became square like a mask of Greek tragedy. Terrified out of my wits, I shouted for a Russian lad I had engaged to assist me in these harrowing days and he rushed into the room, still dazed with sleep. We both tried to make her lie down again, but her strength was enormous and the hands like steel. She gashed him deeply in the arm, croaking again "Just let me find you! I will tear you apart limb from limb!" With a scream of terror he bolted from the room, leaving me alone with the monster. In my horror I sank by the bed unable to move. Then, just as suddenly, she fell back on her pillows and soon opened her eyes, smiling gently. She was my poor, dear mother again.

"Where was I?" she whispered. "I do not seem to remember what happened to me." Then she uttered her last blessing and farewell, promising to come back to me and let me know if indeed there was no final extinction of her personality. Then she said she felt very, very drowsy, closed her eyes, and in a few minutes the ordeal was over. I was a wreck, utterly crushed by my sorrow and by the brief demoniac possession so clearly manifested. I was left alone in the world, without parents, relatives or friends. I felt as if I had stepped into a void.

Spring came, yet I still could not shake off my despondency. Seeing little improvement in my condition, my employer suggested a holiday in
Hangchow. It was a lovely place on the West Lake, he told me, and a holy
one. It was to the Chinese what Jerusalem was to the Christians. I
accepted his offer gratefully.

Taoism and Buddhism: Nature and Spirit

It was a dull winter day; the clouds hung heavily over the Jade Emperor's
Mountain and snowflakes gently fluttered down among the pines like
tiny white moths. The courtyard of the monastery was crowded with
Buddhist monks and nuns. Some were old and wizened, some in the
prime of life and some still young. In their thin, grey robes, they all felt
the cold and shivered visibly. They milled about stamping their feet and
rubbing their benumbed hands. Many of them wore thick, knitted black
caps or padded cowls which protected their necks from the biting wind.
Almost all looked underfed and some emaciated but their manner was
animated and joyful, and their eyes shone with pleasurable anticipation
as long tables and low benches were set out and arranged in neat rows by
the monastic servants. Clusters of steaming bowls were placed on each
table and heavy tubs of rice in the centre. The clashing of cymbals and
the tinkling of bells in the main temple had stopped and the abbot
emerged out of the gate accompanied by Chungan and other priests.
They were respectfully and even affectionately greeted by the assembled
Buddhists. Abbot Lee invited them to be seated and begin their meal.
Then, walking from table to table, he and Chungan handed to each guest
a small *hungpao*, a ceremonial red packet containing a gift of money.

Afterwards Chungan came up to me and explained that it was a yearly
festival arranged by the monastery for their Buddhist brethren, especially
the poor ones. The monastery demonstrated its sympathy and solidarity
with other religions through providing a hot meal during the seasonable
cold weather and monetary assistance to these impecunious monks. As

the monastery was one of the wealthiest in China, he felt it was their bounden duty to help the less fortunate religious of whatever faith they might be. They would treat in the same manner, he assured me, any Christian monk or priest if he came to them in need.

"Alas," he remarked to me with a sigh, "many Christian missionaries come here to visit our temple. We always discern in their outwardly polite attitude more of a snickering contempt and disapproval of our 'idolatry' than the desire for genuine brotherhood with us. They have their own material symbols of the Divine so why do they condemn ours? Both are mere physical objects and both serve only as signposts to indicate the road to spiritual reality."

As we were talking, the meal had come to an end, and a tall Buddhist monk rose from the table and advanced towards us. I seemed to remember him. Chungan stepped forward drawing him to me.

"This is Abbot Mingzing," he said warmly as we bowed to each other with the palms of our hands joined together, murmuring *"Nanmu Amithaba."* Before my eyes suddenly floated the picture of a delightful little hermitage with vermilion walls.

"Yes, of course!" I exclaimed brightly. "From the Monastery of the Purple Bamboo Grove." Abbot Mingzing was delighted that I remembered my previous visit to the Monastery and clasped my hands.

"You must come! You must come and stay with us for a few days," he insisted. With my powers of perception already considerably accentuated during my long sojourn on the Jade Mountain, I felt at once that the invitation came from the depths of his heart.

"I will come tomorrow," I said impulsively, and he went down the path with a smile, accompanied by one of his novices.

The sun shone brightly the following morning as I set out from my monastery, and the dazzlingly white blanket of fresh snow covered everything. There was snow on the grey rocks, on the pines and on the feathery bamboos, which bent slightly under its weight. All the mountains around were white and the lake appeared as green as an emerald. The pillars of monasteries and temples glowed like polished cinnabar. Weeping willows along the causeways sparkled with myriads of brilliants, dipping their snow-burdened branches into the placid waters of the lake. There was joy and exhilaration in the keen air, and the sound of farmers playing on their *huching* violins sitting outside their wattle huts.

A rickety bus brought me to the Monastery of the Spirit's Retreat. As I was walking past the magnificent Hall of the Maitreya, the boom of a great bronze bell rent the air and a cornice of sparkling snow, dislodged from the roof, slid down in a white cascade almost on my head. The deep sound, concentrated in that narrow valley, reverberated to and fro, now loud and sonorous and now a mere whisper. I turned right into a narrow passage and, reaching the end of a cul-de-sac, knocked at a small gate in the vermilion wall. It was opened by a young novice and I stepped into a small courtyard adorned by creeper plants, chrysanthemums in stone and pottery vases and a picturesque clump of bamboos with purple stems in the corner. It was this rare kind of bamboo that gave the monastery its unusual name.

Abbot Mingzing rose from a seat by the round stone table in the centre and led me to a chair of honour, while a little monk brought a pot of tea and cups. After some polite conversation and a few cups of tea he got up and showed me round his monastery. Although it was a small establishment it was well known for the reception hall contained many photographs of prominent Buddhist prelates and wealthy businessmen from Shanghai, Singapore and Penang, who had visited the hermitage and were evidently so pleased with its spiritual comforts that they had put it on their permanent contribution list. The prayer hall was of modest size with a statue of Buddha in the middle and a few *arhats* along the walls. The remaining rooms were intended for visitors and each had a wide bed with a coarse mosquito net, a small oblong table, a chair or two and a washstand. One of the best rooms was immediately allocated for my use. Then the abbot and his assistants disappeared and shortly afterwards I heard the sounds of sizzling and frying from the near-by kitchen.

The meal was served at noon on the round stone table in the little garden. It was not so elaborate as the wonderful food to which I had become accustomed at my Taoist monastery, but quite appetizing and whole-some. Abbot Mingzing's novices were as unsophisticated as they looked, and had not tried to imitate roast duck, fried chicken or ham in their cooking. There was a small pewter jug of steaming hot rice wine and this the abbot took in both hands and poured me out a drink into a porcelain cup. It was an act of exquisite courtesy as, not drinking alcohol himself, he wanted to please his guest. He apologized profusely saying how poor monastic fare was and, of course, just as vehemently, I praised his monks' culinary attainments.

Actually I felt happy and at peace at this small retreat, with the sun playing on the purple bamboos and flowers, and on my friend's ascetic face. He was a tall and handsome man of thirty-four, as he himself had told me. He had a thin, refined face with a short, straggling beard, and large expressive eyes. He had indeed an atmosphere of saintliness about him—a sort of Chinese Jesus in appearance, if I may put it this way. He spoke in a subdued voice, calmly and gently, as if loath to offend me with some unexpectedly harsh tone or expression. I sat quietly sipping my wine and watching his long sensitive fingers as he wrote a character or two to illustrate his meaning. I told him about the pleasant time I was having on Jade Mountain. His eyes sparkled.

"Wonderful men! What good friends they are!" He commented enthusiastically, "Especially Chungan who is like a brother to me." He sighed. "The Lungmen Taoists live with one foot in the fullness of this terrestrial life and with another in the kingdom of the spirit." He became silent again regarding me kindly with his great earnest eyes. This was the ideal time for confidences and I plunged boldly.

"I have studied Buddhism for some years, and now my visits to Jade Mountain have given me a glimpse of the graces of real Taoism. Please tell me whether the gulf between your religion and theirs is very wide." And I looked at him expectantly. My candid query pleased him and his face became animated with a touch of colour on his hollow cheeks.

"We do not look for gulfs when we compare religions, rather we try to find similarities and unity. This is the essential difference between the

Chinese and Western view points. We firmly believe in the truism that all faiths are the paths leading towards the Ultimate Reality, just as the spokes of the wheel converge to its axis. When the people are too immersed in the dogmas and rituals of their chosen religion, it appears to them to be the only one worth following and they defend their own particular faith. However, when they have acquired enough wisdom, charity and discernment, they too are bound to perceive that the road to Heaven is nobody's monopoly and that the divine laws apply equally to all. It is the dogmas, ritual and the mode of worship that divide the faiths and not the basic essence of their beliefs.

"But I am not in favour of conversion from one faith to another, neither do I believe in the fusion of all religions into one. The Ultimate Truth is one, but it has an infinite number of aspects and what is more beautiful than that each faith should reflect only one facet of the Divine, all of them together creating a shining gem of beauty. Would the world be more beautiful if all the flowers on earth had been blended into one uniform colour or all mountains razed to make the globe monotonously flat? Each religion offers something glorious, peculiarly its own, to point out the road to the Ultimate Reality. What man or group of men would be able to prescribe a single form of religion that would satisfy all and everybody? That would be an attempt to give a finite concept of the Infinite and, of course, it would fail.

"Taoism and Buddhism are very close to each other, so close indeed that we have borrowed a number of their saints and deities, not to speak of the monastic architecture and, in turn, they venerate many of our symbols of the Divine. But it would be wrong to imply that we had fused together or that we are more or less the same.

"Taoism is a purely Chinese philosophy which developed into a religion. It is practised nowadays in all its purity by the Lungmen Taoists, i.e. our friends on Jade Mountain and their allied monasteries. There are also Chengyi and Changtienssu Taoists, but they are very different as you will learn later and cannot be regarded as true Taoists. China has been an ideal country to produce and develop such a sublime teaching. It was always tranquil and fertile, and populated with a particularly reasonable and intelligent people—law-abiding, practical and devoted to peaceful agricultural pursuits. In the West the knowledge of God has been imparted amidst the flashes of lightning and peals of thunder on Mt. Sinai against the long and painful background of war, struggle, treachery and misery. In the China of those ages the calamities of war, on the scale waged by the Assyrians, Babylonians and Egyptians, were unknown, and spiritual awakening came in the paradisical atmosphere of green hills, lush fields, clear streams and the uncomplicated labours of simple and happy farmers and soul-satisfying discussions with congenial friends over a bowl of rice wine and pigs' trotters at a village tavern. Thoughtful and intelligent men had time to observe nature and her slow and wise work and correlate it with human activities. They pondered upon what they had seen and meditated in the quiet seclusion of their mountain caves until, at last, a revelation of the Reality underlying the world had been vouchsafed them. Then the great Teacher Loatze succinctly wrote down the doctrine of the Divine Tao and the new religion made its appearance. It teaches that, if man merges himself into Tao, his peace and happiness are assured here and now and shall remain with his spirit when his physical body has been dissolved.

"Our Buddhist faith also originated in the peace and calm of rural India but, unlike Taoism, it did not grow up spontaneously out of the meditation about nature and the guiding wisdom behind it. India already possessed at that time a very ancient and profound religion with its well-established dogmas of Karma and Reincarnation. Prince Gautama never questioned the validity of this ancient teaching. In his meditations he sought the way out of the appalling misery and suffering which afflicted humanity from birth to death. A flash of Divine Wisdom during his Illumination revealed to him the path to Nirvana—the Ultimate Salvation and Bliss. He realized that man's real self was a spirit, a spark of the Divine Flame, a drop of the Boundless, Shining Ocean, imprisoned in the illusory world of Being. Attached to existence, bound by his senses and desires and dragged from life to life by his evil Karma, man wallowed in Ignorance like a pig in mud. Prince Gautama found the liberation for himself and became Buddha, the Enlightened One, and, full of compassion, showed the Way to his fellow man so that the 'drop' could slide back into the Shining Ocean and be free for ever from the Wheel of Life.

"To us Buddhists it is a sorrowful world as men are born, sin, suffer and die to be reborn again and again to expiate the evil deeds committed by them in previous lives. Nothing can be done for them, for Karma is an Immutable Law and each man must reap what he has sown before he achieves his Liberation.

"We monks can only advise and exhort, and show Lord Buddha's Way by the example of our own monastic life. Alas, few people in this modern world of ours care to undergo the rigours of sacred vows or lead the life of poverty and austerity. And thus the Wheel of Life goes on revolving and sweeping with it all humanity—a king in this life and, perhaps, a beggar in the next—all and each according to his deserts—without pity, without mercy and without grace.

"Our friends, the Taoists, also believe that the process of Being or to put it another way this world with its many planes of existence, has issued from the Void, i.e. the Infinite Spirit corresponding to our Adi Buddha, The Primordial Buddha, The God-head. This Divine Mind, objectified as Tao, became relative to Itself as Yang and Yin and began to flow in series and numbers which produced The Ten Thousand Things. Naturally the phenomenal world of forms and appearances is illusory to the Taoists too, but they do not regard it as a place of sorrows and suffering. They argue that as the world is the creation of Tao it cannot be evil in its essence. To make the world live and move, the interplay of the Duality Principle, Yang and Yin, is a prerequisite—light and shadow, warmth and cold, sadness and joy; otherwise the Universe would become static and, if everyone was uniformly happy and content, all human progress and initiative would cease.

"The Taoists do not believe in the Wheel of Life to which all living beings are chained. Instead, the existence is visualized by them as a glorious, ever-ascending Spiral of Evolution. The whole Universe, they teach, is a marvellous, vibrant Unity wherein everything, visible and invisible, pulses with life and consciousness. As consciousness develops through the experience of existence, its vessels—man and other sentient beings— are swept onwards and upwards by the mighty stream of the Eternal Tao to higher forms of expression and activity. Man does not die; he merely extends into new fields of expanded consciousness. Nothing is lost and nothing is dead in the Divine economy and no being is left in unhappiness and suffering for ever by the Infinite Love. Like us Buddhists, the Taoists teach that the end of man is his return to the Ultimate Reality— our Nirvana and the Moksha of the Hindus. Like a happy traveller after a very long voyage, he shall come back home and lay on the altar of the All-Highest the rich spiritual gifts he has acquired."

It was a long and exhilarating talk and the sun was setting as Abbot Mingzing rose and went to supervise an early evening meal. We ate in silence watching the evening shadows creep into the little garden. It became damp and cold, and I shivered as I sipped cup after cup of steaming rice wine to warm myself up. After dinner the abbot excused himself and I was left alone in my room. Soon I heard the sounds of subdued chanting and afterwards the monotonous drone of my friend's voice reciting the Diamond Sutra to the rhythmic tinkling of a small bell. Then there was utter stillness. I knew that it was his time of meditation and I forbore to disturb him much as I wanted to talk to him again. Instead, I unlatched the gate and stepped into the gloom of the passage leading to the great Lingyin temple.

A side door was open and I entered the great hall and sat down on a bench by the counter on which piles of incense sticks lay ready for the pilgrims in the morning. An old monk glided, like a shadow, out of the corner and poured me a cup of tea out of a large porcelain pot kept warm by a bamboo cosy. I looked at the colossal golden images of the Trikaya— the Trinity representing the Primordial Buddha, the Buddha of Heavenly Spheres and the Buddha of this Illusory World. A huge oil-lamp of purple glass, burning in front of them, barely lit the outlines of their faces making them seem more mysterious, majestic and beautiful. I slowly lapsed into meditation, Mahayana-style, concentrating on all known attributes of their Divinity.

How clever Chinese artists were in making these statues in the likeness of the human body and yet, at the same time, so majestically divine. It was right, I meditated, to imagine the Deity in human form for is He not the source of all forms? In all ages and in all sacred scriptures we read that gods and archangels appeared to man also in human guise. How else could the Infinite Love manifest Itself without inspiring terror in man? Surely not in the form of geometrical symbols or some mythical animals. Man cannot conceive spirit without a form; neither can he connect intelligence, understanding and love with some cold, remote and impersonal source. I am sure that as long as humanity exists, man will always long for a vision of an effulgent and transcendentally beautiful Person to whom he can direct his love, adoration and prayer.

As I sat there reflecting on these things, the golden radiance on the great faces seemed to deepen as warmth and well-being began to flow into me. Their inverted gaze beckoned to me to look into my own heart and the enigmatic smile promised great understanding through peace and repose. This was the prayer and the response, and I felt strangely comforted and exhilarated. Wonderfully relaxed and inspired, I made my way back to my room.

Next morning I related my experience to Abbot Mingzing and he was very pleased with my spiritual progress. He told me that, as I was still in the world, meditation should be practised by me only infrequently and sparingly, as sublime refreshment for the soul. Too much of it would prematurely detach me from my ordinary existence—a step very unwise to take without due preparation, both spiritual and material. To devote myself to meditation at all times I must either enter a monastery, which takes care of the monk's bodily needs or I must have sufficient means to dispense with all other activities and devote myself to holy life and meditation. Since I was not inclined to be a Buddhist monk and at the same time was poor, he advised me to stick to my Taoists where spiritual development was a woof to the warp of mundane life.

An Exorcism

Since the reader is undoubtedly more familiar with Buddhism, it might be more useful to give a savor of Taoism, here in the strange rite of exorcism.

Next morning, as an anticlimax to the festival, there was to be an exorcism ceremony at ten o'clock, Abbot Lichun informed us. As it was only eight and we had already finished our breakfast, he made a sign to us to follow him. Again we walked up and down dark stairways and along dimly-lit galleries. I noticed that the windows did not have glass panes in them but, instead, each leaf of the window consisted of numerous latticed squares with a translucent oyster shell cunningly inserted. Now and then I caught a glimpse of a bamboo grove or a pine tree in a tiny garden concealed between the twists of a corridor and some hidden apartment.

We entered a large hall, furnished with long chairs and carved teatables. Lichun invited us to sit down and ordered a novice to bring tea. I looked around with curiosity and my gaze was arrested by a long row of large photographs running the whole circumference of the hall. Each represented a young Taoist priest, formally dressed in a black silk robe, with a square cap adorned with a plaque of white jade. None of them could be more than thirty-five years of age, some were younger and many were good-looking with large penetrating eyes. In the centre was an outsize portrait of a very old man with a long beard. He was attired in ritual vestments and wore a small lotus-shaped crown on his bald head. His obesity was phenomenal and he sat there in the picture like a monstrous mountain of flesh, but his eyes were gimlet-like and had a tremendous power in them. I looked at Lichun questioningly.

"Are these the monks of the monastery?" I inquired. Lichun nodded his head and his eyes became clouded.

"They were. These are the pictures of the departed abbots," he said with a note of sadness and reverence.

"Do you mean to say that they all died so young?" I exclaimed looking incredulously at the photographs and then at Lichun.

"They all died in the prime of their life," murmured Lichun lowering his head. "They were sectional abbots and they sacrificed their life just as the living ones are sacrificing theirs." He straightened up, sipping tea, and looked at me wistfully. "Most of the senior monks here are doomed men and must die in the flower of their manhood." I put down my cup mechanically, gazing at him in silent horror.

"Lichun," I stammered. "What . . . who . . . kills them so young?" He looked at me calmly but his eyes were half-closed.

"They dedicated themselves to exorcizing evil spirits; this is their work of love and their chosen path to the Throne of the Almighty." He spoke in an even tone not looking at me. "But for every energumen, cleansed by them of his terrible possessors, a number of years is deducted from their earthly lives." He paused and sipped tea again. "The more successful exorcisms an abbot has to his credit, the sooner his own end comes." Still in the grip of horror, I looked at him uncomprehendingly.

"But this can't be!" I cried vehemently. "It is impossible. Science says there are no possessions; it is only some mental disease from which people suffer. Why don't they send their patients to mental hospitals, to good psychiatrists in Shanghai?" I stopped and looked at him, my indignation had made the blood rush to my face. Lichun was silent, contemplating me placidly with his half-closed eyes; he was thinking. At last he spoke quietly and in a soft voice, carefully choosing his sentences:

"We have great respect for Western science but, compared to our esoteric tradition, it is still new and its main preoccupation is with materialistic phenomena. Ever since the birth of Christianity your churches arrogated to themselves the privilege of dealing with and interpreting all spirit manifestations, prosecuting and severely punishing those engaged in metaphysical research. We Chinese have never been handicapped in this respect and there were periods in our long history when the Imperial Government itself saw fit to encourage our efforts to learn more about the denizens of the unseen world. In the meantime, for centuries, your

Western world had to rely on the scraps of illicit information gleaned here and there by alchemists, black magicians, fortune-tellers and other charlatans. Only now have your scientists taken the right direction with their delving into the powers of the mind, but your science is still too young and immature to comprehend the mysterious workings of the spirit universe, which has its own laws and its own mode of being." He rose from his chair and stopped in front of me.

"You should not think that all our work in monasteries is founded on superstition and we are not so naïve or stupid as to deceive ourselves with hocus-pocus or lull ourselves into false security with sham doctrines. We also seek illumination through research and prayers and there is a basis for our actions and faith." He looked at me strangely. I was impressed by his sincerity.

After this we went out into a long gallery and turning a corner Lichun opened a door into a small apartment simply but comfortably furnished. It was a small study with a blackwood desk and an altar on which from a brass incense burner issued a thin wisp of fragrant smoke. A curtained door led into an adjoining room. We seated ourselves on the chairs by the door. The curtain, hiding the doorway into the next room, was pulled aside and a youngish Taoist monk entered the room greeting us warmly. Lichun introduced him to us as the friend with whom he used to stay. I looked at him with interest. He was about the same age as Lichun and was almost as tall, but his body was much more fragile. He was pale and his skin had a strange luminosity. His eyes were unnaturally brilliant as if he had a touch of fever. His lips were very red, their colour deepened by the pallor of his face. He appeared to be pleased with our visit and his manner towards us was deferential. We exchanged the usual pleasantries and then Lichun murmured something into his friend's ear; he nodded in assent. Lichun then turned to me.

"My friend is going to conclude an exorcism service this morning and, if you are really so interested, he hopes you can come and witness it." He paused uncertainly. "But I must warn you that it is not a pretty sight. Really it is most unpleasant, disgusting and revolting. . . ." He paused again. "It is to some extent dangerous, but it depends on the potency of the demon who is in possession of the energumen." My curiosity was too great to back out and I promised, with great enthusiasm, to attend as we bade good-bye to Lichun's friend.

Abbot Lichun called for us after ten o'clock to take us to the exorcism ceremony. He said it had been going on for two days but today would see the final effort, made by his abbot friend, to dislodge the recalcitrant spirit or spirits who had taken possession of a young farmer a year ago. He enjoined us not to be afraid and, above all, not to upset the ceremony by talking aloud or asking too many questions or by screams of fright.

We arrived at a medium-sized stone courtyard, half-way up the hill, situated in front of a temple. There was a small group of onlookers standing in corners in the shadow of the walls, among them a distracted couple who, Lichun pointed out, were the energumen's parents. The energumen himself, a rather emaciated man of about twenty-five, clad in white jacket and trousers, lay on an iron bedstead on a rush mat. He was very pale and there was a wild, roving look in his fevered eyes. The priest, Lichun's friend, was attired in full ritual robes and stood before a portable altar on which was an incense burner, the small image of a god, a vase with holy water, a ritual sword and other articles and a book from which he was reading. Two monks were assisting him, whilst four muscular men watched the prostrate demoniac.

The abbot was reading the scriptures in a monotonous, droning voice, repeating *mantras* over and over again with a great deal of concentration. Then he stopped and, taking an elongated ivory tablet, the symbol of wisdom and authority, he held it ceremonially in both hands in front of his chest and approached the bed slowly. There was a visible transformation on the energumen's face. His eyes were filled with malice as he watched the priest's measured advance with a sly cunning and hatred. Suddenly he gave a bestial whoop and jumped up in his bed, the four attendants rushing to hold him.

"No! No! You cannot drive us out! We were two against one. Our power is greater than yours." The sentences poured out of the energumen's distorted mouth in a strange shrill voice, which sounded mechanical, inhuman—as if pronounced by a parrot. The priest looked at the victim intensely, gathering all his inner strength; beads of perspiration appeared on his thin face.

"Come out! Come out! I command you to come out!" He was repeating in a strong metallic voice with great force. "I am using the power of the One compared to whom you are nothing. In His name I command you to come out." Immobile, he continued to focus his powers on the energumen's face. The man was struggling in the bed with incredible strength against the four men who held him. Animal growls and howls issued from time to time from his mouth which became square, his teeth gleaming like the fangs of a dog. Now his face became purple, now white, like paper, or covered with red blotches which appeared and disappeared with bewildering rapidity. I had the impression that a pack of wild animals was fighting inside his body. For a moment the struggling ceased and the energumen turned his baleful eyes on the monk with such a look of unearthly hatred that involuntarily I shrank into the shadows. Terrible threats poured out of the contorted mouth, now fringed in white foam, and interspersed with such incredible obscenities that women had to plug their ears with their fingers; they did not dare to look at the priest or the people around them. But the uncontrollable curiosity and desire to see this dreadful and macabre business to the end kept them rooted to the ground.

Again the abbot cried his command to the unseen adversaries to leave the prostrate man. There was a burst of horrible laughter from the victim's throat and suddenly with a mighty heave of his supernaturally strengthened arms he threw off the men who held him and jumped at the priest's throat like a mad bloodhound. But he was overpowered again. This time they bound him with ropes and fastened the ends to the bedposts. The energumen, evidently exhausted, closed his eyes and there was a deathly silence. The abbot, still immobile, continued his conjurations in a metallic voice, his eyes never leaving the body. With unutterable horror, we saw that it began to swell visibly. On and on the dreadful process continued until he became a grotesque balloon of a man.

"Leave him! Leave him!" cried the monk concentrating still harder. A novice handed him the book and he began to read again in a strange, unintelligible jargon, the words of power and release. Convulsion shook the monstrous, swollen body, and the things that followed were disgusting and revolting in the extreme. It seemed that all the apertures of the body were opened by the unseen powers hiding in it and streams of malodorous excreta and effluvia flowed on to the ground in incredible profusion. Not only I but also Lichun and Koueifo and others were overcome by the stench and sight of these loathsome proceedings and became nauseated. For an hour this continued and then the energumen, resuming his normal size, seemed to come to rest, with his eyes watching the unmoved priest who was still reading. The attendants untied the demoniac and, forming a screen with bed-sheets, hurriedly washed him, changed him into another suit of coarse pants and a jacket and cleaned up the mess.

It was already long past lunch-time but none of us could even think of food. The priest stopped reading; with sweat pouring down his face, he backed down to the altar, laid down the tablet and took up the ritual sword. Threateningly and commandingly he stood again over the energumen.

"The struggle is useless!" he cried. "Leave him! Leave him in the name of the Supreme Power who never meant you to steal this man's body!" Another scene of horror evolved itself before our dazed eyes. The man on the bed became rigid and his muscles seemed to contract turning him into a figure of stone. Slowly, very slowly, the iron bedstead, as if impelled by an enormous weight, caved in, its middle touching the ground. The attendants seized the inert man by his feet and arms. The weight was such that none of them could lift him up and they asked for assistance from the onlookers. Seven men could hardly lift him for he was heavy as a cast-iron statue. Suddenly he became light again and they put him on a wooden bed which had been brought in. A long time passed with the abbot reading and commanding interminably. At last he sprinkled the inert man with holy water and advanced to him again with a sword. His concentration was so deep that he did not seem to see anybody. He was utterly exhausted and swayed slightly. Two novices came up to support him.

"I have won!" he cried triumphantly in a strange voice. "Get out! Get out!" The energumen stirred and fell into dreadful convulsions. His eyes rolled up and only the whites were visible. His breathing was stertorous and he clawed his body until he was covered with blood. Foam was issuing from his mouth and a loud gurgling sound. He wanted to shout something but could not control his vocal cords. The abbot raised his sword threateningly, making mystic signs with it.

"Damn you! Damn you!" came a wild scream from the foaming lips. "We are going but you shall pay for it with your life." There was a terrific struggle on the bed, the poor man twisting and rolling like a mortally-wounded snake and his colour changing all the time. Suddenly he fell flat on his back and was still. His eyes opened. His gaze was normal and he saw his parents who now came forward.

"My parents!" he cried weakly. "Where am I?" He was very feeble and they carried him out in a specially ordered sedan chair. The abbot himself was in a terrible state of prostration and was half-carried and half-dragged away by his novices and Abbot Lichun. Koueifo and I, shaken, scared and very sick could hardly walk back to our apartment.

·   ·   ·   ·

Although we were expecting Abbot Lichun early next morning, he appeared only during lunch and joined us in our simple meal. He looked worried and sad and Koueifo could not resist asking him what was the matter.

"My friend is utterly exhausted after yesterday's seance and cannot get up," Lichun explained. "I have been staying with him the whole morning. He can hardly eat anything." After the meal we insisted on going together with Lichun to visit his sick friend. We found the young abbot in bed sitting propped against the pillows. He smiled when we entered and made an attempt to get up but I restrained him.

"I shall be all right in a day or two," he said confidently, but he looked much weaker than when we first saw him. I really wondered how long a man could last after such superhuman exertions. There was no doubt that he had evicted the demons but at great sacrifice of his own vital forces, and I now implicitly believed Abbot Lichun about the killing effect of exorcisms.

Among the Lamas

My favorite lamasery was Yuenfoungsze or Shring Moupo gompa. It was the largest and most active lamasery in Likiang district. The Tibetans believe that the gods reside alternately on particular peaks of western and eastern Tibet. High lamas keep a strict record of the cycles of these divine migrations and name the year and month during which the gods move from the one to the other. When the gods have reached Shanri Moupo and the Chicken Foot Mountain across the lake from Tali, which is also honored, then it is time for the Tibetan pilgrims to run their steps toward Likiang and Tali, to pay respect to those holy thrones of the gods, and to acquire merit by offering service or donations to the nearby monasteries and shrines.

The Shangri Moupo lamasery was some eight miles from the city, along a narrow road which, passing fields and villages and crossing deep streams, led in a steep climb through the forest of pines and rhododendrons. The forest belonged to the lamasery, and was therefore a sanctuary for animals; so that the climb, though arduous, was like a progress to paradise. Birds sang from tall, shady trees; crystal streams rushed down in orchestrated cascades; rare flowers pushed up from under bushes, and the air was heavy with the fragrance of blossoms. After the first mani pile, with the stones and slabs engraved with the eternal "Aum mani padme hum!" the road wove through a dense spruce forest. Then, suddenly the lamasery was there, lying in a hollow of the mountains like a huge bowl, with a green meadow in front and very old trees dotted around. There was a huge circular fish-pond, fed by mountain streams, and a flight of stone steps leading to an imposing gate, beyond which sat four giant grinning avatars, representing the four manifestations of power or energy; and across a vast courtyard was the great prayer hall itself, reached by two stone stairways. The courtyard was profusely decorated with flowers in pots and stone vases and there were rose bushes and old cassia-trees in the stone-lined tubs.

To the right of the courtyard there was a passage which led to a spacious dining-room decorated with huge mirrors. In front of it was another large courtyard, paved with cobblestones, at the end of which were stables for the horses and the mules and a huge kitchen. Connected by a veranda to the dining-room was a two-storey wing, in which my good lama friend, the manager or bursar, lived below his clerical staff. He was a convivial fellow, with bright intelligent eyes and a great forehead, and was quite bald. He came from a village not far from ours and, people said, he was happily married and had children. I asked him about it one day and he laughed heartily.

"Well," he said, "if nobody gets married, where are the little lamas to come from?"

I had met him at Madame Lee's bar, where he always went when in town as he was very fond of a cheering cup. He was most hospitable, and often invited me for week-ends. I always brought with me my medical kit and some flowers and vegetable seeds for the lama himself, for, like the other lamas, he was very fond of gardening.

My arrival was usually on a Saturday afternoon. After a drink of the special white wine made by the lamas themselves, the bursar disappeared on business, and I made excursions into the surrounding woods, searching for flowers, particularly the kounpanyas, which are little purple orchids. On my return to the lamasery I called on a few other lamas I knew and offered any medical help that I could give. There was usually an inflamed eye, a touch of a skin disease, a bout of malaria or an attack of indigestion, and they were very grateful for these little tokens of attention. Then the evening came, with the cold of an altitude of about

11,000 feet, and we sat by the brazier awaiting the gong for dinner.

I was always placed at the large round table at which the senior lamas sat. They were very dignified elders, some with white beards, clad in their red togas. All victuals were produced at the lamasery and the meals were very good. There was beef, pork and mutton, *sauerkraut,* rich potato soup, and everything was helped down with cups of wine. Rice was seldom served, but instead we ate the *babas*—thick wheat pancakes with butter and ham shavings. Young trapas served at the table and before and after the meals grace was said by the oldest lama.

Afterwards I lay on rich rugs in my lama friend's cell, with butter lamps flickering before the golden Buddhas on an altar. Outside there was the hooting of owls and screeching of wild animals, and now and then the sound of a bell from some distant shrine. Before dawn there was the noise of a drum, then the mysterious, hollow call of a conch shell. Then there was the dawn service with its murmur of recited sutras, punctuated by bells, conch-shell blasts and the wailing of trumpets. I got up at about six or seven and at nine there was breakfast of butter tea, sauerkraut, hard-boiled eggs and fried pork, accompanied by the inevitable *babas.* At about ten there was again a call to prayer and I went to the main hall. The lamas entered in a stately procession, each wearing a tall curving yellow hat with fringes. They seated themselves, cross-legged, on low benches and began to recite sutras spread on low tables in front of them, while the blare of trumpets, conch shells, bells and drums punctuated certain passages. Two trapas with long-spouted pots passed from lama to lama filling little white cups with wine. This was always done in rainy or wintry days to protect them from chills and to keep up their strength during long services.

Behind the main hall and dining-room there lay a miniature city sprawling over the hillside. It consisted of one-storey houses with small gardens, all walled in. These were the residences of the high-ranking lamas. Each compound was occupied by one or two lamas and their attendants. Their old parents or male relatives could also stay with them; and a room could always be found for a guest for a few days.

I and my friend Changtehkuan, a Chinese from the Duchy of Bongdzera, often stayed with a close relative of his mother's, who was a Tibetan. This venerable lama, who was in charge of the sacred music, was not really very old but he had a magnificent long beard, which is a rarity among the Tibetans, of which he was inordinately proud. He shared his apartments with another lama and had his old father staying with him. His house had two wings; one was their living quarters and the other contained a shrine of his favourite deity. The old man loved flowers and in his jewel of a little garden he tended his pots of crooked plum- and cherry-trees: his miniature bamboo grove and his cluster of roses.

Rich merchants and officials from Likiang came to stay with their lama friends for a week or two. I always avoided them as their ideas of relaxation were diametrically opposed to mine, and they either smoked opium all day long or played mahjong. They could never understand my desire to climb the mountains or visit the tribal villages.

Quite high above the lamasery, on a precipitous spur of the mountain, there was a curious shrine, always padlocked and sealed. I climbed to it several times but saw nobody. At last a friend explained to me that this was a hermitage where some thirty-five young lamas had been shut up for meditation and study for a period of three years, three months, three weeks, three days, three hours and three minutes. Guided by a guru, usually an old, saintly and learned lama, these young men chose a sacred word or text to meditate upon. The favourite word, I was informed, was "*Aum*," whose mystic meaning could seldom, if ever, be properly understood, but which contained power and enlightenment. Between meditations a regular course of Tantric theology was pursued. On the expiration of the seclusion each man became a lama in his own right and, if he chose, he could go to Lhasa to undergo further training and take examinations for higher initiations. I was told that two years more would be needed before the hermitage could be unsealed in a brilliant ceremony and the young lamas released. In the meantime, they stayed there strictly incommunicado with food passed through a small window by an old caretaker.

I had almost forgotten about the young lamas when later, to my surprise, I was invited by my lama friends to go to the lamasery for the great day of the opening of the hermitage. The news spread quickly and the whole town talked of nothing but the forthcoming event.

I started with my friend Changtehkuan on the eve of the ceremony. The road to the lamasery was crowded with groups of people in their best dress: old gentlemen, in formal Chinese garb, proceeded on horseback, escorted by their sons or attendants: women, in black mitres and silk tunics, carried in their baskets the *houkous* and all sorts of dainties. *Pangchinmei*, also with baskets, walked in droves with the local beaux in the rear. The lawn in front of the lamasery was covered with picnicking families sitting on rugs. The overflow of people was such that few expected to find shelter at night within the lamasery or in the lamas' apartments. We put up with our long-bearded lama, but his house too was crowded and we had to sleep three in one bed. All night long there was singing and dancing outside the lamasery. The invited dignitaries and merchants played mahjong or smoked opium in adjoining houses.

Next day, early in the morning, the service started in the main hall. All the grand lamas, attired in yellow silk jackets and new red tunics, were there chanting the *sutras*; but, advised by our lama friend to hurry, we started on our way to the hermitage. Had we tarried, we should not have reached it at all so great was the press of the milling multitude.

From the terrace of the hermitage the view was breathtaking in the early morning sunshine. Clouds of incense issued from the lamasery, and the sound of great trumpets, the throb of a huge drum, the wail of conch shells and the tinkling of bells reverberated in the narrow valley. At last the great procession to the hermitage started. Senior lamas walked first, gold chalices in their hands sparkling like flames, followed by richly attired dignitaries and a vast crowd. The scene was indescribable in its splendour and beauty, with Mt. Satseto sparkling in the background, deep blue sky and green pines and rhododendrons in bloom forming a vast stage setting for the glittering conclave. There was a short service before the sealed gate. Then the Grand Lama sprinkled it with holy water, dipping a bunch of the sacred kusa grass into the gold *kumba* (chalice). In the presence of the Pacification Commissioner and elders of the city, a gold key was inserted into the padlock, seals removed and the gate was flung open.

I thought the hermitage would be a mean, crowded place with a row of cells, like cages, along a narrow corridor, without light or air. It was nothing of the kind. Instead, I saw a vast oblong courtyard with age-old shady trees and masses of flowers. In the centre there was a tall and spacious prayer hall with a brightly polished floor. It was here that the lectures were delivered to the neophytes. All around the courtyard there were single-storey buildings divided into light and comfortable rooms. These were the students' private apartments. In front of each room, in the courtyard, there stood a small kiosk with a golden Buddha and dozens of brightly burning butter lamps. A stall in front of each kiosk was heaped with sweet meats and there was a row of small cups filled with wine. Each graduate stood by his kiosk welcoming friends and acquaintances with a bow. Expecting a group of ascetic and emaciated young men worn down by lack of food and the severity of their mystic exercises, I was confronted with bright-eyed, well-fed men in resplendent vestments who laughed and chatted and pressed us to eat and to drink, while themselves setting a good example.

Tables were produced in no time, and food, brought by the parents and relatives, was spread. The houkous, in the centre of each table, spewed smoke and flames like miniature volcanoes and a joyous feast was soon in progress. I was led to a terrace where several tables were prepared for the dignitaries, and was seated with the jovial Pacification Commissioner and the high lamas. The food was superb and the wine still better, and by the time we got up it was late afternoon.

The meadow in front of the lamasery was crowded with richly caparisoned mules and crowds of relatives in preparation for the triumphal send-off of the newly made lamas. Each young lama was affectionately assisted into the saddle and led off with infinite care by his admiring folk, some of whom cried unashamedly with joy and unutterable happiness. It was the culmination of a cherished ambition, and an unparalleled honour not only to the family concerned but to the whole district from which the young lama came. Not all the graduates came from the Likiang district. Some were from Tongwa and Hsiangchen, from Bongdzera and Lotien and other little-known regions. They were Tibetans and Nakhi and members of other tribes who had adopted Lamaism, and were now to be the torches of the light of truth, going to dispel the darkness of *avidya* (ignorance) in their barbaric lands and to be the shining, priceless jewel of faith.

Nature itself smiled on the men during this felicitous day. The air was warm and scented, the sky so cloudless and blue; the Snow Mountain waved a long white plume, as if in greeting, from the glittering crown of its summit. The city was en fete and there were delirious celebrations in many houses that evening before the departure of holy caravans on the morrow.

It will be several years before this glorious festival is repeated. It takes a long time to find and prepare a group of serious-minded and ardent neo-phytes willing to endure such a long seclusion for the sake of faith and spiritual glory. Perseverance in studies and intellectual honesty are required. The full implication of solitude, obedience to guru, renuncia-tion of worldy desires and tastes is not easy to inculcate and still harder to practise. The wise High Lamas have to exercise an infinite care not to include in the group any undesirable person. Any debauchery, or the scandal of escaping inmates, would destroy for ever the high repute of this holy and famed hermitage. The comparative comfort of existence, similar to some Taoistic hermitages in China, presents greater tempta-tions than the life in certain Tibetan and Christian retreats, where the emphasis is on the mortification of the flesh. The problem of man was understood better at this hermitage. Man is not only a spirit: he has his physical nature as well. It is not with the destruction of one aspect of his being by the other that he fulfils his existence. It is by a harmony of the two that he becomes perfect. Jesus, Gautama and Gandhi emphasized this balance between the two extremes and it was for this reason that they were able to render their great services to humanity. Mortification, carried to excess, is no good either to man himself or to humanity. The greater victories come to the man who does not concentrate on murdering his body but utilizes its strength and energy in developing his spiritual gifts. A withered tree bears no fruit.

Chapter V

. . . .

Reality
in a Zen
Monastery

Janwillem van de Wetering

When Janwillem van de Wetering (b. 1931) knocked on the door of a Zen monastery in Kyoto in 1958, he knew no one who had been to such a monastery, and he had no idea what was in store for him. Speaking no Japanese, van de Wetering pointed to his suitcase, to indicate he wanted to stay at the monastery. Witnessing European life at a critical impasse had prompted him to make this journey in the dark. During World War II, the bombs had rained continuously down near his childhood home in the Netherlands, and of his classmates (most of whom were Jewish) not one survived the war.

After the war van de Wetering became part of a new, restless genera- tion, eventually moving to ten countries, while being truly at home in none of them. In London, he studied philosophy in order to discern the purpose of life. The philosopher A. J. Ayer informed him that philosophy did not teach anything remotely like that, and suggested that Buddhism might address the basic questions troubling him. For two years at the Kyoto monastery, at the bargain price of two English pounds per month for room and board, van de Wetering lived the routines of a (lay) Buddhist monk. As related in The Empty Mirror (1973), he found meditating in the lotus position as excruciating as sitting on a mound of ants, but gradually his body—and not only his body—limbered up: mentally he gained an insight into the mind that was neither philosophy nor psychology.

Following his sojourn in Japan, van de Wetering studied with Chögyam Trungpa in New England and joined a Buddhist monastery there, which supplied the material for A Glimpse of Nothingness *(1975). As a writer, van de Wetering is best known for his "Amsterdam Cop" mystery novels, but his other works include* Little Owl *(1979), a book for children about the Buddhist Eightfold Path, and an English translation of Alexandra David-Neel's novel* The Power of Nothingness *(1982). Van de Wetering never became officially a Buddhist, finding organized Buddhism marred by the same compromises and corruptions that he saw in other religions. But what he learned at the Zen monastery pervades even his mystery novels and offsets the horrors he witnessed when young and keeps him, he says, "postponing his suicide."*

I Enter a Zen Monastery

The idea of my going into a monastery had been inspired by an English philosophy professor in London, some years before I came to Japan. He had made me read some twenty books, and during a short conversation, when I ran into him accidentally in one of the corridors of the university, I had told him that none of the books he had advised me to read and none of his lectures had brought me any closer to the truth.

"But what are you looking for?" the professor asked and stood still abruptly, forcing me to stop as well.

"Well," I said, "you know. Truth. Why it has all started, and what's the good of it," and I gestured vaguely about me.

"Absolute truth," the professor lectured patiently, "does not emerge from the study of philosophy. Philosophy is a science, and science means approaching truth. By engaging in experiments, by thinking logically, we try to get nearer to truth by determining probabilities. Then we draw conclusions. We say that this is more probable than that, because of this or that reason. But to really know something, to be quite sure of something, no."

"Then I am on the wrong road," I said, "because I want to be quite sure. I want to be absolutely certain that life on earth serves a purpose, because as long as I am not certain I am not content and that's putting it mildly. I sometimes get so depressed, and everything around and in me becomes so utterly hopeless, that there's nothing I can do, except lie down and feel cramps in my stomach."

"Yes," the professor said kindly. "Depression. A well-known phenomenon. Can lead to suicide. Most unpleasant."

"But how do I get rid of depression? Do you know?"

"Yes," the professor said and filled his pipe. "Manual therapy may help and psychoanalysis, of course, but if you ask me, most of it is useless for treating your sort of affliction. What you have is what all mystics have had, and the only way of solving your problem is to join a mystic training. Go to a monastery, find a master, an adept who has finished his training, and he'll cure you or you'll cure yourself."

    •   •   •   •

The gate of a monastery in Kyoto, the mystical capital of Japan. Tokyo is the worldly capital, but Kyoto is a holy city, so holy that it was saved by the American bombers in exchange for the Japanese promise that there would be no antiaircraft guns. Kyoto contains eight thousand temples, mostly Buddhist. I was facing one of these temples, a Zen monastery. I was alone, twenty-six years old, neatly dressed, washed and shaved, for I was applying for a job as a monk, or lay brother. It was a hot morning in the summer of 1958. I had put down my suitcase, which contained only some clothes, books and toilet gear. The taxi which had taken me there had driven off. Around me I saw grey-white plastered walls, about six feet high, topped with tiles made of grey baked clay. Behind the walls were beautifully shaped pine trees, cut and guided by trained and careful hands; behind these rose the temple roof: flat-topped, with sides that sloped down and then turned upwards abruptly at the ends.

I read enough about Zen masters to know that they do not like long stories and prefer methods without words. According to the books Zen masters will shout suddenly, trip you up while out for a quiet walk, beat you on the head or say something which, apparently, doesn't make sense at all. It seemed to me that it would be better to make my statements as short and concise as possible.

"I am here," I said carefully, "to get to know the purpose of life. Buddhism knows that purpose, the purpose which I am trying to find, and Buddhism knows the way which leads to enlightenment." While I tried to explain my intentions in this way I already felt ridiculous. I felt that life *must* have a purpose, and it seemed very stupid to have to admit that I didn't know the purpose of the creation of what is around us and also what is within us. But I didn't know what else to say. To my surprise the master answered immediately. I had thought that he would be silent. When the Buddha was asked if life has, or does not have, a purpose, if there is, or isn't, a life after death, if the universe has, or does not have, an end, if we can speak of a first cause or not, he did not answer, but maintained a "noble silence." He would have done that to indicate that these questions about life were not expressed in the right way. Our brains are given to us as instruments, capable of a specific, a limited task. When trying to understand the real mysteries, the brain stops short. The brain can contain neither the questions themselves, nor the answers. To come to real understanding, to enlightenment, quite another instrument has to be used. Intuitive insight has to be developed by following the eightfold path, the Buddhist method. What Buddha wanted was that his disciples should use the method which he had found and perfected. Buddha was a practical, a pragmatic man.

But the Zen master, in his simple grey gown, an old man, well into his seventies, but with clear glittering eyes, did not maintain a noble silence.

"That's fine," he said. "Life has a purpose, but a strange purpose.

When you come to the end of the road and find perfect insight you will see that enlightenment is a joke." "A joke," said the American translator, "and stared seriously at me. "Life is a joke; you'll learn to understand that sometime—not now, but it will come."

I asked if I could be accepted as a disciple. The teacher nodded. His consent surprised me. Obviously the books which I had read about Zen were faulty, written by inexperienced writers. Zen masters, I had been assured, do not readily accept disciples. Admission is always apparently blocked by obstacles. The disciple is told that the master is too old, or too ill, or too busy, to accept new disciples. Or the disciple hears that he hasn't developed himself sufficiently to become a disciple but that he can be admitted, temporarily, as a woodcutter or farm laborer.

But no, I could be accepted. If (there was a condition) I was prepared to stay for eight months; during a shorter period I wouldn't be able to learn anything. "I can stay three years," I said. "That isn't necessary," said the master. "Three years is a long time in a man's life. You do not have to commit yourself, or promise anything, but you should stay eight months. That period you'll have to fix in your mind—you should get used to the thought that you have to be here for eight months. It isn't easy here. We get up at three o'clock in the morning and we do not go to bed before eleven at night. We meditate a lot, there is work in the garden, there's a lot of tension, and you'll have the extra problem of being in a very strange environment. Everything will be different for you, the language, the way we sit, the food. You can't make use of anything you have learned. But that is good."

The master spoke for a long time. "I could answer your questions but I won't try because you wouldn't understand the answer. Now listen. Imagine that I am holding a pot of tea, and you are thirsty. You want me to give you tea. I can pour tea but you'll have to produce a cup. I can't pour the tea on your hands or you'll get burnt. If I pour it on the floor I shall spoil the floormats. You have to have a cup. That cup you will form in yourself by the training you will receive here."

•   •   •   •

The first meditation is forever etched into my memory. After a few minutes the first pains started. My thighs began to tremble like violin strings. The sides of my feet became burning pieces of wood. My back, kept straight with difficulty, seemed to creak and to shake involuntarily. Time passed inconceivably slowly. There was no concentration at all. I hadn't been given anything to concentrate on anyway, so I just sat and waited for the bell to ring, the bell which would finish the period of agony.

Later I was able to study other beginners, westerners and Japanese. I never saw anyone who was as stiff as I was when I started. Mostly they could find some way of sitting in balance but I had to spend three months on top of an anthill before I stopped wobbling, and could get one foot up. The worst was over then, although I didn't stop suffering at once. There are many kinds of suffering.

I believe that meditation is difficult for everybody. Our personality forces us to be active, we walk up and down, we gesticulate, we tell stories, we crack jokes, to prove to ourselves and to others that we exist, that our individuality is important.

We are frightened of silence, of our own thoughts. We want to play some music or see a film. We like to be distracted. We want to put things together, light cigarettes, have a drink, look out of the window. All of these occupations fall away during meditation.

The first day in the monastery passed quietly. After the early morning meditation I wasn't admitted to the master's room, but sent to my own room. Someone came to fetch me for breakfast. We sat on the floor at low tables, in the lotus position of course, although I was allowed to kneel. This was easier but also painful after awhile, for the dining room had a hard wooden floor. Before eating the monks sang a *sutra*, one of the Buddha's sermons, in classical Chinese, while the cook hit a wooden drum to keep time. It was a hypnotic sound, that singing, short and staccato, the monks cutting the words into syllables and droning them with sharp, abrupt endings. After that we were given small bowls filled with rice and hot water and another bowl containing pickled vegetables; these didn't taste too bad. We were also served *takuan,* an orange radish, pickled and sliced. I put a few slices in my mouth but they were very sharp and I grimaced, sucking my cheeks in and looking about desperately, as I felt sweat prickle under my hair. One wasn't supposed to speak at table but everyone giggled, even the severe head monk, when they saw my reaction to the delicacy. Later, when I got used to the taste, I even began to like *takuan* and used to help myself secretly when I passed through the kitchen.

After breakfast we worked. I was given a mop and taken to a very long corridor. There were other corridors to be cleaned when I had finished the first. Eventually someone rang a bell and we had an hour off. I went to my room and fell asleep; it was 6 A.M., still very early.

At seven, I followed the others to the vegetable garden to harvest cucumbers. The monks wore overalls, and they laughed and talked, pushing and tackling each other. Most of them were young, between seventeen and twenty-one. A few were older, but I only got to know the young ones; the older monks kept to themselves.

The head monk had his own room. Because he was the practical leader of the monastery and because he was a priest, and therefore higher in rank than the others, he was treated with respect. He received guests, took care of the administration of the monastery, paid the bills, collected gifts, wrote letters. My monthly payment was arranged with him—about £2 a month for board and lodging, the lowest rate I ever paid in my life.

Another older monk worked as cook. The daily menu was simple: vegetables, rice, barley gruel, no meat at all, sometimes fried noodles of a dish which resembles the Chinese *tjap tjoy,* a vegetable stew which the cook could make very tasty. We also had feasts from time to time and then the cook had three or four assistants and prepared complicated dishes. But mostly the fare was very simple and not very nourishing, a diet which didn't do much for me. Within a few weeks I began to feel ill and weak. The monks called a doctor and he prescribed better food, so I was given permission to get a meal from outside once a day (if it was possible to go out, for sometimes the monastery cut itself off from the outside world and closed its gates for a week) and I found a small restaurant close by where I could get fried rice and meat salads.

In the afternoon the meditation started again: four periods, two hours in all. Dinner was early, at 4 P.M., and was the last meal of the day. In the evening we meditated from seven till ten. Meditation times differ in a Zen monastery. In winter there is more sitting than in summer, but I found even this light summer training of six hours a day far more than I could really put up with. Even so, I got through it. I had to of course—my pride wouldn't let me back out of it.

While I was in the monastery I was continually referred back to the daily routine, the simple everyday life. If I wanted to expound some clever theory I was either ignored or ridiculed or curtly told not to talk nonsense. What mattered was "here and now," whatever I happened to be doing, whether I was peeling potatoes in the kitchen, washing rice, pulling out weeds, learning Japanese, drinking tea, or meditating. I had to solve my *koan,* the subject of my meditation, and I shouldn't fuss.

Each disciple starts off with one of the "big" *koans.* He may get the Mu *koan,* an extraordinary story about a monk who asks his teacher whether a puppy dog, who happens to be around, has the Buddha nature as well: a senseless question to any Buddhist, because Buddha said that everything has Buddha nature, so the puppy cannot be an exception. The teacher answers by saying "Mu." Mu means no, nothing, emptiness, denial of everything. The monk doesn't understand and is told to meditate on the word Mu. His training has started. Another "big" *koan* is: Everybody knows the sound of two clapping hands. Now what is the sound of one hand clapping? A third *koan* is: Show me the face you had before your parents were born. Show me your original face.

All *koans* are illogical and go beyond the reasoning mind. The monk may try to give a sensible answer, but if he doesn't it will be just the same: the master will ring his bell and the monk has to leave the room.

The answers which, after many years of hard work, despair and near insanity, may be accepted, will be diverse. Perhaps the monk will make a nonsensical remark; maybe he laughs, or looks at the teacher in a peculiar way or does something, like knocking on the floor or waving. If the master nods, the next *koan* will follow, to deepen the monk's insight. There are rows of *koans,* and the monk who solves them all has to leave the monastery to practise his insight in the world, perhaps as a teacher, perhaps as an inconspicuous civilian. Only very few disciples come to the end of the road, which doesn't matter, for the monastery is not a school intended to produce nothing but masters. Everybody is required to do what he can, and the teacher helps, quietly, often passively, sometimes by force. If you do anything at all, do it well. Don't look at the result. The result is important to you, did you say? Don't talk nonsense.

•   •   •   •

"In Hinduism there is a lot of talk about the Atman, the divine self which never changes," the head monk explained. "It lives many lives and comes closer to its Godlike core with every new existence on earth so far that, after many purifications, it will live its final life on earth before it finds Nirvana, the only real heaven, the sphere of God himself. But Buddhism doesn't attach itself to any theory, not even to the doctrine of Godlike self. A neurotic boy becoming a balanced man is an interesting process to watch, but without significance. That a man lives many lives, and that all lives are connected and flow into each other, is nice to know. But we, in this monastery, are not engaged in psychiatric treatment, and neither are we a school of philosophy. If you are interested in eastern philosophy and religion, if you want to study reincarnation and karma, you can go through the gate, turn left twice and right three times and you will find yourself in the university of Kyoto. There are professors over there who will be able to answer all your questions, but when you analyse the answers, they will be questions again. The intellect is a beautiful instrument and has a purpose, but here you will discover a different instrument. When you solve *koans* you will have answers which are no longer questions."

"Yes," I said, "that's what I want. Insight."

Rohatsu, Week of Weeks

Sesshins, the meditation weeks of a Zen monastery, fill the first seven days of six months of the year. A week has seven days; I had forgotten that fact. I was still thinking that a week had five days of regularly repeated obligations, followed by two days of another order altogether, two days in which to forget the five days.

But a week in a Zen monastery has seven days and not one minute is given away. Every meditation period lasts exactly twenty-five minutes, and the pause between two periods lasts five minutes. At 11 P.M. the last stroke on the large copper bell ebbs away slowly and only then is there sleep. Some *sesshins* contain more meditation hours than others: in summer, when there is a lot of work in the ornamental and vegetable gardens, seven to nine hours a day; in winter eleven hours a day.

But it could be much worse, as I heard from the monks, although I didn't believe them at first. The first week of December is Rohatsu. Rohatsu is the *sesshin* which rules all *sesshins*. Fifteen hours of meditation per day: from 2 A.M. to 4 A.M.; from 5 A.M. to 11 A.M.; from 1 P.M. to 5 P.M.; from 7 P.M. to midnight. That is seventeen hours altogether, but the visits to the master take time and are deducted from the meditation time.

I couldn't believe it. It had to be an impossible exercise, even if there were regular beating up and shouting. No human being can sit still for fifteen hours a day, and under stress as well, with an unanswerable question tucked away in his belly. I would faint or go raving mad. Certainly, Buddha had meditated for weeks on end, under a tree, on a rock. But that was 2,500 years ago. A holy man, shrouded in the haze of antiquity. Christ had meditated in the desert for forty days on end. That was 2,000 years ago. But I was a westerner of today—a restless, nervous, noisy seeker without insight, without power. With some sense of humor and a somewhat indifferent outlook on daily life one cannot sit still for fifteen hours a day. All right, I had managed to sit still for eleven hours a day, but with a lot of wobbling about and secret glances at others and at my watch, and with rest periods of an hour or more so that I could sleep or sit on a gravestone and smoke cigarettes and dream.

I tried not to think about this coming horror, just as in the past I had pushed away the image of an approaching visit to the dentist or an examination, drawing nearer and nearer. But this was something quite different. Dentists and examiners had been pushed on me by strong powers around me, powers outside myself, grim and overbearing powers against which I couldn't defend myself. But what had forced me to undergo a training which asked me to perform an absolutely impossible feat?

•   •   •   •

I sat on the little staircase leading down into the garden from my room, smoked and looked about and saw the ornamental fir trees, cut and guided into enchanting shapes, now lightly covered by a thin layer of snow: a miraculous and beautiful view. I had said something about it to the head monk who happened to pass by and he had stopped for a moment, looked politely at the indicated trees, and had admitted dryly that they were beautiful. "Just like a picture!"

His remark annoyed me. "Just like a picture." What an inane thing to say. Limited, bourgeois. And this was supposed to be an enlightened man in whom *satori*, the lightning of sudden real insight, should have taken place at least several times, for he had finished his *koan* study.

A Zen *koan* exists which asks why Bodhidharma, the first Zen master, went to China: a symbolic question, an essential question, a question in the order of "What is the essence of Buddhism?" The answer which one Zen master accepted was: "The fir tree in the temple garden." Just a tree, like the tree standing here in front of me. Because a tree shows the perfect beauty in which everything else is expressed, and especially the essence of Buddhism and the reason of Bodhidharma's long wanderings through a strange country. I could feel that quite well. In any case, I liked trees. But if I were to say to the master that the truth of everything, the purpose of life, is expressed in a tree, he would pick up his bell and ring me out of the room or he would grunt and shake his head.

And that was why I had come, to visit an old Japanese gentleman who ridiculed everything I said or could say, and to sit still for fifteen hours a day on a mat, for seven days on end, while the monks whacked me on the back with a four-foot long lath made of strong wood.

I cursed softly. What on earth was wrong with me? Why couldn't I live normally and do my best, like my brothers and sisters, like my father had always done? My grandmother, whom I never knew, would have said that one mustn't break one's head about questions which cannot be answered. My mother had asked her what exists outside the universe. "If you come to the end of the universe," my grandmother said, "you will see that everything has been pasted over with newspapers." An intelligent answer, which had satisfied my mother. Why couldn't I be content with an end-less wall, built of wooden lathe work and pasted over with the *New Rotterdam Herald?*

But while I mumbled to myself, and lit my fourth cigarette that morn-ing, Rohatsu was coming closer and I knew that I wouldn't run away from it. Han-san and Ka-san, and whatever the other sans might be called, the young monks would all have to get through it.

Country lads, given by their fathers to the monastery. If they could do it, couldn't I do it? I can't do it, I thought. These country lads were Japanese, easterners, quiet and patient boys with a large reserve of inher-ited tolerance. And I knew that some of them had already solved *koans.* Perhaps Japanese are privileged beings who have a special talent for attaining insight into the mysteries.

Perhaps I'll be able to do it next year, I thought. If I train myself for another year I shall be able to sit comfortably in half-lotus. I'll ask for dis-pensation; the head monk will surely realize that I can't get through this week of terror. He may be tough and severe but for me, a westerner with

exceptionally stiff legs, he will make an exception. I cursed again for I
remembered that I had called him, a few days ago, to the meditation hall
to show him that I was sitting much better. My thigh muscles had grown
a little for I could, with a little extra exertion, get my right foot on the
instep of my left foot, and if I pushed and strained and pulled, even on
the calf of my left leg. With an extra pillow under my bottom I could
gain a reasonable balance. He had smiled and patted me on the shoulder.
Why couldn't I have restrained myself, why did I always have to show off
and endeavor to show any so-called progress to the world?

That day I was called to see the head monk and two of his colleagues.
They spoke to me at length, but I didn't understand them very well. After
several repetitions I nodded. I had understood that they weren't very
happy with my progress and that this Rohatsu would be a final test. If I
managed to get through the week all right I could stay in the monastery,
and the master would continue to receive me. But if I gave up halfway
through Rohatsu I should have to leave the monastery. They even gave me
the name of a small hotel in the neighborhood where I could go and stay.

I bowed and returned to my room. Very well. What has to be done has
to be done. I swore that I would get through the week even if my legs
were so stiffened with cramp that they would never be usable again, and
even if my mind gave way. Even if I went insane I would sit it out, if need
be as an idiot, dribbling at the mouth, but I wouldn't enable them to
chase me out of the monastery. I had another two days to prepare myself.
I bought chocolate slabs and ordered a large bag of the peanut and raisin
mixture via Gerald. I bought an extra heavy jersey and six undershirts; I
would wear three at a time so as to keep the stick off my skin. I even
bought the heating apparatus which most of the monks were using. It
looked like a spectacle case but instead of spectacles contained smolder-
ing sticks of charcoal. A monk had told me that these cases, if worn next
to the stomach, gave a splendid heat which spread right through the
body. The stomach is nearest the plexus solaris, the most important nerve
knot of the human body. Once it gets warm everything becomes warm. I
had heard a lot about the plexus solaris. The master always pointed to his

belly. That's where the real feeling is, the real center of observation. Music shouldn't be listened to but felt, here in your belly. Other people should be felt. The *koan* should be tucked into the belly. Don't think with your brain but concentrate here, in your belly.

During the meditation exercises I had learned to regulate my breathing: first take a short breath, then press out the belly and "push the breath into the belly," and then keep it there. The master was quite a small man but he had such strength in his belly muscles that he could push my fist, and the weight of my body behind it, back by merely extending his stomach.

When Rohatsu began the head monk locked my room. During that week we wouldn't just meditate in the hall but sleep there as well, if sleep it could be called, for we were only given two hours a day, from midnight to 2 A.M. I came into the hall with my sleeping bag under my arm. A small cupboard would hold my chocolate, nuts and raisins, toothbrush, soap and small towel. The clothes I was wearing would have to last all week. I sat down, moved into the most comfortable position I could find and the head monk struck his bell. Two o'clock in the morning. I had all my jerseys on and my three undershirts. The spectacle case glowed away, wrapped in a thin piece of cloth, against my stomach. It was freezing in the meditation hall but I didn't feel the cold. The first period of the first day. I would count them all carefully, one by one.

The head monk delivered a small lecture.

"This is going to be heavy going. Use this week well. Think of nothing, become one with your *koan*. Forget your friends, forget the meditation hall, forget yourself, forget time. Don't think of your body. Don't think of food or cigarettes or sleep."

And don't move. The young monks shouldn't move either. Neither should the newcomers move. Nor the westerners. There were only two westerners, Gerald and myself, and Gerald never moved. I did, but I wouldn't be able to do it now. He had meant me and he would pay special attention to me, and shout: "Jan-san, sit still. You are disturbing the others." I didn't want him to shout at me. I wanted to draw attention to myself because I was doing something well, not because I was always doing everything the wrong way. Not to be able to do things well was getting to be a bit of a bore.

The head monk was also becoming bit of a bore lately. I would show him that I could handle him for a change, that he didn't have to pour his will all over me all the time.

And when the spectacle case became too hot for comfort I didn't move.

My belly was getting strangely warm. I didn't understand it, couldn't I manage this either? All the monks had these cases and I saw them sitting all around me, apparently at peace and quietly happy in their concentration. Why did I have this glowing belly? The feeling of warmth was slowly changing into pain. I had the unmistakable feeling that my skin was getting scorched. But I didn't move; another ten minutes and the bell would be struck. For the first time I felt no pain in my legs. It seemed as if I didn't have any legs. But I *did* have a belly, and my belly was on fire.

When the bell was struck I jumped off my seat and rushed out and pulled all my shirts out of my trousers. I had a burn of several square inches. Gerald, who came to see what ailed me this time, shook his head and looked puzzled.

"Did you just wrap the case in that thin piece of cloth?"

"Yes," I said; "shouldn't I have?"

"No, you shouldn't have. You should have wrapped it in a towel and then have stuck the whole bundle in a belly-wrap. You can buy them in any store." He started to laugh but controlled himself. "That's a nasty burn. It should be treated."

He went back to the hall to speak to the head monk and we were both excused for the next period. The cook, the only monk who didn't take part in the meditation as he had to cook for thirty people, spread some ointment on the wound and bandaged it neatly. He tried to behave in a compassionate manner but finally broke down and began to laugh as well.

"These cases are really prohibited," the cook said, "just like the padded vests and waistcoats the monks wear."

"Yes," Gerald agreed. "And you don't need a case at all if you concentrate properly, you can sit in the snow stark naked. You could sit in a fire as well." He addressed the cook: "True or not?"

"Yes," the monk said. "With concentration you can do anything. But you are in my way, both of you. Go back to the hall. The head monk is waiting for you."

The first day passed. The second day passed as well. The third day wasn't too bad. The fourth day was one long interminable hell of pain and boredom and frustrated restlessness. That day I was being hit regularly and I hated the monks. I had to use all my strength to keep myself from jumping off my seat to attack them. Gerald, who wanted to say something to me during one of the short breaks, stepped back when he saw the murderous expression on my face and found another spot to lean against a wall and relax for a few minutes. The head monk snapped some command at me and I snarled and ground my teeth in response. I had to light three cigarettes one after another, the first two had become powder in my hands.

The fourth day is the worst, the others confirmed later. Six laymen from the neighborhood had come to join us that week: a medical doctor, the local baker and four men I didn't know. During the fourth day they all disappeared. Even their cushions had gone. Their disappearance wasn't discussed by the monks. Japanese are polite, if something goes wrong; the fact is recognized and greeted in silence. But Gerald and I were rough foreigners, barbarians from the west, and we grinned at each other.

Gerald's face had become hollow, his cheekbones jutted right out, and his eyelids were red and seemed inflamed. Our hands were thick and puffy from lying in our laps, hour after hour. We stumbled as we walked. The master seemed very changed as well. For the first time I saw him in the meditation hall and he was with us continuously, except when he was away in his little house to receive us. His eyes had sunk well back into their sockets, and his shrunken face bristled with the beginning of a sparse beard and moustache. Instead of his usually gleaming skull I now saw a fringe of grey down.

But his fatigue was only on the outside; he was the same hard pusher and puller I knew from the former *sesshins*. His little room trembled with power, and more than ever before I had the feeling that I was crushing myself against a thick wall but that the wall, in some mysterious way, was trying to help me—that there was an opening, and that I could find that opening. The sixth day the pain became so bad that I began to groan and the head monk sent me out of the hall. I had to walk up and down on a slightly elevated stone-tiled path, and on both sides, some three feet below me, were low shrubs. I must have closed my eyes and suddenly I found I was lying in the brushwood, not knowing who I was or where I was. I hadn't fainted, I had fallen asleep. The head monk heard the thump of my fall, then some rustling of leaves, then nothing. He came, exceptionally, for he hadn't left the hall except for meals in the main temple, to see what was wrong, and he woke me up and pulled me back onto the path where he brushed the leaves off my clothes and hit me softly in the face.

"Wake up, it won't be long now." In his eyes I saw warm friendship, an emotion which I hadn't recognized in his face before.

The seventh day passed reasonably quickly, I fell asleep, hit the monks, was beaten up in return, visited the master five times a day, and was marched to the dining room and taken back to the hall under escort of the head monk and Ke-san, his assistant. Nothing irritated me any more. The last day. At midnight the exercise would be over, the end was in sight, nothing worse than what I had already experienced could happen now.

I counted the minutes of the last period. Another twenty-four minutes. Another twenty-three minutes. The bell was struck. I expected a general relaxing and joy, laughter, sudden talking, but the quiet tense atmosphere in the hall did not change. I looked at Gerald, who was studying his watch. I hissed at him and he shrugged his shoulders.

I went outside, washed my face with cold water and waited for the others to come out, but to my surprise the bell was struck again. The meditation continued and I was late. I ran back, bowed to the head monk to excuse myself and he pointed at my seat. When he saw that his order bewildered me he whispered that it would go on for another two hours. I was told later that he had only told *me* this; he had wanted to add another exercise by giving us the impression that he was going on for another complete day, but he probably thought that I had suffered enough and defined the duration of the added practice.

I got through the two hours, slumped in my seat and dulled into a half sleep. The hall was not patrolled at this time, and I could wobble if I wanted to. I felt no pain, only a soft buzzing in my legs, and the burn on my belly ached a little. All I had to do was fight the sleep which threatened to engulf me. I wasn't sufficiently in balance to be safe when asleep. If I toppled over I would make a spectacle of myself and might crack my skull on the stone floor below me as well. At 2 A.M. the head monk struck his bell with force, and its clear sound sang through the hall. Gi-san jumped down, rushed outside and attacked the temple drum, and the two youngest monks began to strike the six-feet high, massive bell in the clock tower. We streamed out of the hall, after a last formal bow in the direction of the altar. I lit a cigarette and laughed at Gerald, who embraced me and mumbled something which I didn't catch. The head monk shook me by the hand.

"The bath is ready. I'll wash your back. It's tradition. The last will be the first. You jump in first!"

I saw steam rise from the bathhouse: the cook had taken care of everything, he had done all the chores by himself all the week and was, if possible, even more exhausted than the others. His soft wide face was split by a tremendous smile.

My clothes were caked to my body and I didn't know how quickly I could strip them off. I kept on pouring bowls of hot water down my back and front while the head monk, naked and tiny, massaged my back with his strong hands. In a corner sat Gerald flat on the floor with his legs stretched wide apart, brushing his teeth till his beard was white with foam. The young monks splashed contentedly and talked softly to each other. The story of the case which had burned my skin was repeated many times and everybody squealed with pleasure, even the head monk, even the master who came to see how we were doing and who had put on a clean bathrobe. We spent more than an hour in the bathhouse and I shaved my stubby beard hair by hair.

When the head monk told me again how pleased he was with my effort I said that I didn't understand him. Hadn't he told me that I would *have* to get through Rohatsu? That I would be sent down if I dropped out?

"What?" he asked. "What is this nonsense?"

Gerald was asked to join in the conversation and I finally realized that I had misunderstood the instructions which the head monk and his two colleagues had given me. They had tried to explain to me that they didn't expect me to be able to get through the complete exercise. But I could, they had repeated at least three times, give up. Only, they couldn't have me wandering about the monastery while the others were trying to get though Rohatsu. That's why they had given me the name and address of a hotel close by. It took a little time before it all got through me. Gerald explained it again.

"Never mind," the head monk said. "I am glad you didn't understand me. Because whatever your reasons were, you pulled through. That's very good."

Gerald sat down and laughed till he had tears in his eyes, I had to throw cold water over him to make him shut up. "You," Gerald said, "are such a nitwit that you'll enter Nirvana by mistake."

After the Monastery

After eight months in the monastery, Janwillem moved to a house nearby, which he shared with his fellow practitioner Pete. Zen remained the center of his life in Kyoto and he still spent most of his days at the monastery. The following episodes show what it is like when a Zen adept (i) rides a motorcycle and (ii) tries out a little meditative magic on the train.

(i)

That scooter was a source of joy. Every morning I rode her to the monastery, through a quiet fast-asleep city in which only policemen, baker's assistants, newspaper boys and late merrymakers were alive. The first time I was stopped by two constables who asked for my papers. I didn't have them on me, but when I told them I was a disciple of the Zen master they both bowed simultaneously and apologized. I met them, or their colleagues, regularly afterwards, and was always greeted by military-style salutes which I would acknowledge by bowing mildly in their direction.

The scooter disturbed the head monk.

"*Koan* study," he said, "leads to understanding that all things are connected. All beings are bound to each other by strong invisible threads. Anyone who has realized this truth will be careful, will try to be aware of what he is doing. You aren't."

"No?" I asked politely.

"No," the head monk said and looked at me discontentedly. "I saw you turn a corner the other day and you didn't hold out your hand. Because of your carelessness a truck driver, who happened to be driving behind you, got into trouble and had to drive his truck on the sidewalk where a lady pushing her tram hit a director of a large trading company. The man, who was in a bad mood already, fired an employee that day who might have stayed on. That employee got drunk that night and killed a young man who could have become a Zen master."

"Come off it," I said.

"Perhaps it will be better if you hold out your hand in future when you turn a corner," the head monk said.

(ii)

The head monk allowed me to break my promised eight months' continuous stay in the monastery and gave me an entire day off, and I took the tram to the station. I had put on a new nylon shirt which wouldn't let perspiration through and it was a warm day. I looked at freedom through the open windows of the bumping and shaking tram and realized that I had lived for almost five months in seclusion. I had been through the gate every now and then but never further than, at the most, half a mile. I saw crowds of people, enormous advertisements for films, showing half naked women and aggressive men handling firearms, shop windows full of puppets dressed in new clothes, and grey heavy buildings housing banks and trading companies. I felt relieved but also irritated. I hadn't chosen the monastic life but rather accepted it, as a means to an end, but now that I was free of the pressure of the monastery, I longed for the silence of the garden with its lovely grey and green shades and the monotonous robes of the monks. Here there was too much bustle; it was too full, too exaggerated. The screaming colors of the advertisements weren't necessary, the shouting and laughing were annoying. Perhaps it would be a good idea to force everybody to meditate regularly, in halls which would be built in all the cities of the world. Every evening from seven to nine, compulsory silence, and every morning at 3:30, an unavoidable visit to a master. A master to every street.

The need to find out whether the training was having any effect had long been an obsession, as if *satori*, enlightenment, reaching the holy goal, were bound to a certain place and I should be getting closer to that particular spot. "Have I got anywhere or not? Am I understanding more? Am I getting lighter, more loose?" I kept on asking myself, although the master often warned me against the folly of such measuring.

In the train I found myself pressed against several people, one of them a woman, some twenty years old perhaps. I had already looked at her and noticed that she was beautiful, with a rather sensuous body, large slanting eyes and thick black hair. Attracting the attention of women I don't know has always been below my sense of dignity, or perhaps I am too shy for that sort of thing; anyway I didn't try it that time either, although I was enjoying the contact with her body. I thought of the concentration exercise I had been doing for months. It could be tried. Before I knew it I began to breathe deeply and very slowly and fixed the image of the woman, as I remembered it from one short glance, in my thoughts. I tried to think of nothing else and when I knew that I had gained a certain measure of concentration I ordered her to press herself against me. And miracle of miracles, she obeyed. I felt how she rubbed herself, softly and furtively at first, but gradually more firmly, against me and I heard her breathing becoming deep and heavy. And while she rubbed herself against the side of my body she trembled.

"What now?" I thought, for the contact made my blood surge. "Shall I talk to her? Shall I ask her to get off at the next station? We can go to a hotel room—I have enough money on me. And I can go to Kobe this afternoon. The consul has time to spare."

But my excitement broke my concentration, the woman was released and moved away a little. She looked up at me and I saw a troubled look in her eyes. The train happened to pull up at the station and she got out. My skin was prickly under the nylon shirt and sweat was running down my face. "Black magic isn't all it's cracked up to be," I thought. "A lot of trouble and waste of energy."

To Be or Not to Be
(a Buddhist)?

I had now spent a year and a half in Japan. But I had never become a Buddhist. When I paid my monthly 2000 yen (£2) to the head monk I told him that I would like to become a Buddhist, to enter the religion officially.

The head monk put the money into his drawer, drew some artistic characters in his ledger and noted on a strip of paper: "Jan-san, 2000 yen," and the date. The strip of paper was glued to the wall of the corridor, where it became the last miniature paper flag at the end of a row of thousands of strips. When the corridor was full he would tear them all down and begin again.

"Well," he said, "it can be done, of course. But it's up to the master really. He is the high priest and he decides about an important matter like this. I'll mention your request and you'll hear from us."

About a week later Han-san came to tell me that the master was expecting me. The master was having dinner when I came and I waited, kneeling on the floormat, till he had finished. He never had his meals with us but was served, three times a day, a tray with covered bowls: a bowl of rice, a bowl of vegetables and a bowl of soup; and a pot of green tea. The distance from the kitchen to the master's little house was about a quarter of a mile and his food, especially during winter, must have been cold many times. I pitied him; it would have been better if he had shared our meals. We could always have second helpings by folding our hands and staring at the cook while he was serving—we weren't allowed to point but we could indicate the required dish by looking at it and shaking our heads if he got it wrong. The master had to satisfy himself with whatever was brought to him.

I knew he had two ways of relaxing: he would watch baseball on TV and when an important match was on he would lock his house and nobody could see him. He would also go to the cinema sometimes, but only when he could see a picture connected in some way with Africa; he liked animals and the jungle—lush, tropical vegetation. I had even witnessed a difference of opinion between master and head monk. The master wanted to go to the cinema and asked the head monk for money. The master never had any money, because the monastery's funds were in the hands of the head monk. The head monk refused.

"You have been ill. You are supposed to stay in and sleep in the afternoons. You have a weak heart."

"Maybe," the master said, "but I want to go to the cinema now. It's the last day this picture is on, I looked it up in the newspaper. Who knows if and when the picture will come on again. There's an elephant hunt in it and I must see it."

In the end, the monk gave in, on condition that the master took a taxi and Han-san went with him in case he became unwell.

The master had finished his meal and looked at me.

"I hear you want to become a Buddhist."

"Yes," I said. "I have been your disciple for some time now, but I have never entered the faith, or the church, or whatever I should call it. I should like to do so now."

"It can be done," the master said. "We have a special ceremony for this purpose. Quite an impressive ceremony really. All our monks, and also all priests connected with the monastery in one way or another, will come. They will all dress in their best robes. I'll wear the garb which you'll have seen me in before, at New Year for instance; the robe is uncomfortable because brocade is heavy, but it looks well. *Sutras* will be chanted and you'll have to come forward and kneel down and I'll ask you some questions to which you'll have to answer 'yes.' You'll have to declare that you are seeking refuge in Buddha, in the Teaching, and in the Brotherhood of Buddhists. You'll also have to confirm that you will refuse to enter Nirvana till all living beings are ready to become part of the ultimate reality.

"Then I'll wave my horsehair brush and the *sutra* chanting will begin again and Gi-san will play his drum and the head monk and Ke-san will strike their gong and after that there will be a feast for monks and guests. It can be organized. I'll have to ask the head monk to find a suitable date for the ceremony."

He looked at me. I didn't know what to say. It seemed a very acceptable proposition. But it seemed that the master was expecting something.

"All right then," I said in the end. "Many thanks for your trouble."

He nodded and I thought the interview had ended, bowed and got up. When I was near the door the master called me back.

"There's something I wanted to ask. Why do you want this ceremony to take place? Do you think it will do something for you?"

I had to admit that I didn't think so.

"Do you think that, by becoming a Buddhist, you'll get closer to solving your *koan*?"

No, I didn't think so.

"Hmm," the master said and turned away. The interview was now really at an end and I left the room.

In the garden I looked for Han-san and found him loading cucumbers into a wheelbarrow.

"Are you a Buddhist?" I asked.

Han-san might be a simple country lad but he was quick on the uptake.

"I?" he asked innocently. "I study Zen Buddhism" (literally translated he said "I do Zen Buddhism study").

"Yes," I said impatiently, "I know. But are you a Buddhist?"

"You know," Han-san said, "that 'I' don't exist. I change all the time. Every moment I am different. I exist in the way a cloud exists. A cloud is a Buddhist, too. You call me 'Han-san' and pretend that I was yesterday what I shall be today. But that's your business. In reality there is no Han-san. And how can an unreal Han-san be a Buddhist?"

"Don't be so intricate," I said. "All I ask you is whether or not you are a member of the Buddhist brotherhood."

"Is a cloud a member of the sky?" Han-san asked.

I gave up. The ceremony was never mentioned again.

Whatever Ends Begins

After Janwillem had endured a year and a half of hard, diligent endeavor, he became depressed, thinking he was no nearer the truth than when he started. He fantasized briefly about suicide; he planned definitively to return to Europe (where he would keep up his Zen meditation). At the very end of his stay in Japan, however, he perhaps had his brief moment of satori after all.

I had broken my program to go out on a trip. Kyoto is surrounded by mountains and I had ridden off without looking at the map. After half an hour I saw no more people. I was riding on a mountain path meant for mountaineers. I saw bits of forest, alpine meadows, and sometimes a glint of Lake Biwa, far below me. Near the precipice I thought that I could, by twisting the handlebars a little, solve a lot of problems very easily. A crumpled scooter and a broken body, and the world, the universe, would cease to exist.

But how about my soul? Buddha had always refused to answer the question. Soul or no soul, life after death or no life after, an empty question. Walk the eightfold path and the question will drop away by itself, later, now, it doesn't matter. But I was sitting on a rock with my legs stuck to nothing. If I entered Nothing altogether, what would be left over? And suppose something were left, where would it go? Heaven or Hell? The hell of suicides, a sad sphere filled with sad shuffling shapes, complaining transparent shadows? I pulled in my legs, walked back to the scooter and was back within an hour. On the way I hardly looked at the landscape and the busy farmers and their women folk, working in their picturesque kimonos. I tried to come to the end of my line of thought. What had I learned, after a year and a half of falling over and getting up? That I had to do my best, that I had to try to do everything as well as possible. But I could have learned that in Rotterdam. Dutchmen, and the inhabitants of Rotterdam in particular, do their best; it's a national custom. All I would have to do is imitate my environment, which should be the easiest exercise in the world; it is much easier to join one's examples than to go against them.

But they managed to teach me something else here. Not only has one to do one's best, one must, while doing one's best, remain detached from whatever one is trying to achieve.

Peter tried to comfort me but I was now so depressed that nothing he said made any impression. The whole Buddhist adventure now seemed one huge failure, and I wanted to leave. There was no longer any reason to stay in Japan. I didn't know what I wanted to do. There was enough money left for a boat-trip to Europe and some six months' modest living. I assumed that I would be able to find a job within that half year, a simple manual job if need be. I could find a room in Paris or Amsterdam and continue my meditation during the evenings.

• • • •

Three days before the ship sailed I rode to Kyoto to say goodbye to the master. The head monk gave me tea, didn't show any disappointment, and took me to the master's house. The master received me in his living room. He gave me a cigarette and sent the head monk to the meditation hall to fetch a stick, the sort of stick which the monks use to hit each other. He drew some characters on it with his brush, blew on the ink, waved the stick about, and gave it to me.

"The characters mean something which is of importance to you. I wrote down an old Chinese proverb, a saying taken from the Zen tradition. 'A sword which is well forged never loses its golden color.' You don't know it, or you think you don't know it, but you have been forged in this monastery. The forging of swords isn't limited to monasteries. This whole planet is a forge. By leaving here nothing is broken. Your training continues. The world is a school where the sleeping are woken up. You are now a little awake, so awake that you can never fall asleep again."

The head monk looked at me kindly and the master smiled. The heavy gloomy feeling which hadn't left me fell away from me. I bowed and left the house.

Part II

. . . .

The Era of
You and Me

Introduction

A few readers of David-Neel, Blofeld, and Govinda came to the last page, shut those volumes, and started packing their bags. Inspired, those readers determined to become more than readers: they would duplicate their hero's voyage. But today the world map hides even fewer "white spaces" than it did then: the under-known areas those earlier travelers explored are now overdeveloped and/or blotted from the globe entirely. David-Neel's, Goullart's, even van de Wetering's strange Buddhist countries of beckoning otherness have all disappeared, either politically extinguished (Tibet, Mahayana areas of China) or streamlined into a familiar modernity (Japan, South Korea). Yet, as if in compensation, the tiny bypath that those earlier pilgrim-souls hacked out, by sweat and risk, has turned into a modern highway, one which sometimes still leads to Asia, it's true, but equally can pass by one's little house back home. Before the twentieth century Buddhism loomed forbiddingly "other" and faraway; a century later it had become so familiar that Americans or Europeans may just as well stay put and let Asia, or Buddhism, come to them.

Anthropologists once studied pygmies in Africa or headhunters in South America, but, with the globe's geo-cultural differences dwindling, contemporary field-students of anthropology analyze Philadelphia street gangs or Seventh Day Adventists. So likewise the more recent contributors to this anthology do not live in caves or mountain monasteries but integrate their Buddhist practice with contemporary issues nearer at hand—feminism, say, or the frustrations of the workplace. Even the decision to become a Buddhist can now require no more resolve—probably less—than a midlife career change does, when an accountant returns to school and becomes a doctor.

The life frustrations that once propelled David-Neel to India or van de Wetering to Japan now send their spiritual descendants, more modestly, on weekend retreats to the next state or just across town to the local Buddhist center. On those retreats and at these centers Buddhism becomes a country of the psyche and meditation its own subcontinent. For all their familiar everyday flavor, the later writers in these pages— Tsultrim Allione and Jan Willis, Sharon Salzberg and Michael Roach— reveal something as important, as key, as their great explorer-predecessors earlier did. They demonstrate how an age-old Buddhism gets integrated into individual make-do existences today, without communal or family support, regardless of job and personal obstacles that get in the way. They show how one practices Buddhism in one's own backyard or, if there is no backyard, then in a studio apartment, or in the corridors of the office.

Theirs is the latest adventure, and the quietest: what their predecessors achieved by trekking the Himalayas or banging on strange monastery doors, they are recreating, in miniature, with limited funds, limited opportunities, limited movement. Michael Roach and Tsultrim Allione explore the uninhabited places of their own interior beings, a contemporary landscape whose borders shift with the decisions they make and the actions they take. They and Jan Willis and Sharon Salzberg say in a fresh way what a previous generation of Buddhist pilgrim expressed: *Look away, then look homeward, restless traveler: the mind is its own problem; the mind is its own solution.* The Diamond, the Heart, and the other sutras are full of such high and wise precepts, but it is these American Buddhists who tell what happens when those precepts fast-forward into the modes of twentieth- and twenty-first-century lives.

Chapter VI

· · · · · · · · · ·

An African-American Woman's Journey into Buddhism

Jan Willis

It was a long way from Docena, Alabama, to the astrologer's house outside Kathmandu. As a young black girl in rural Alabama, Jan Willis (b. 1948) watched the Ku Klux Klan burn crosses in her front yard. The threats to her were not only external. Willis broke an unspoken taboo by being conspicuously intelligent at a time when intelligence was considered unseemly in a southern white girl and unforgivable in a black one. She internalized the disapproval from her elders until they became divisions within her own psyche: she was simultaneously and contradictorily proud and self-hating, timid and defiant. She marched with Martin Luther King, Jr., in Birmingham and was ready to become a Black Panther when a junior year abroad in India led her onto a different course. On a trip to Nepal she met Lama Yeshe (he lived in the former royal astrologer's house), perhaps the most beloved of the Tibetan teachers living in exile. As Willis relates in Dreaming Me *(2001), Lama Yeshe understood her better than she did herself; at every turn in her development he was there waiting for her and encouraging her. During her fifteen years as his student, her deep psychological and cultural wounds dating from her childhood slowly healed.*

If people are "made to feel confident in their own abilities to think for themselves, that can change their lives," Willis writes. Teaching, along with medicine, was considered one of the two noblest occupations in Tibet,

*and she became a teacher, "to pass the gift [she received from Lama Yeshe]
along." Today the once armed and embittered Black Student Alliance member at Cornell is herself a popular professor of Buddhist and Indo-Tibetan
Studies at Wesleyan University in Connecticut.*

Meeting Lama Yeshe

I should have told him the truth when he'd first asked; should have
blurted out that I suffered; that I was often frustrated and angry; that slavery and its legacy of racism had taken their tolls on me; that I had come
seeking help in coping with feelings of inadequacy, unworthiness, and
shame. I should have told him that I felt a certain kinship with the
Tibetans because they, too, had suffered a great historical trauma and yet
seemed able to cope very well and, indeed, even to be quite joyful. And I
should have told him that I also felt a special and unique kinship with him
in particular, though we had only just met, because from the very first
moment I had heard his name, I had somehow known that he was to be
my teacher. But at our first meeting, I said none of this. When Lama
Yeshe asked us why we had come, I had responded with a textbook
answer, saying with superficial glibness, "Because *samsara* is suffering."

As Randy, Rob, and I made our way down the switchbacks from
Kopan [Lama Yeshe's primitive home outside Kathmandu, soon to
become a retreat center] that evening after our first meeting with Lama
Yeshe, these were the thoughts that troubled me. I felt like a complete
jackass; and I could only hope that I hadn't forever missed a most important opportunity, perhaps *the* most important opportunity of my life.

Everything before our meeting had gone just as those two strange fellows who'd come to visit in Banaras had predicted. With half my attention focused on the ruts in the makeshift road from Kopan back to

Bodhanath, the other half vividly replayed that evening in Banaras.

Cletus, Randy, and Rob had gone out to a nearby cinema to see an Indian movie. I stayed in. About an hour after they left, I heard a knock on Cletus's door. When I opened it, there stood two quite odd-looking Americans. One was a long-haired man dressed in pants and a Western-style shirt with an Indian *jola*, or bag, draped over his shoulder. The other was a giant of a man dressed completely in Indian-style clothing with long matted hair and facial makeup like that of a Hindu *sadhu*, or holy man. Both men also appeared to be quite stoned, a fact that was no accident in a place where state-run shops sold marijuana and hashish by the gram. I tried not to appear too nervous, but my expression must have given me away. The shorter man explained, "Hi. We're friends of Cletus. Is he around?" I told them about the movie and then invited them in for tea.

During our ensuing conversation, I learned that both these men had been on the India circuit for quite some time. The tall one—who stood more than six feet five inches, caused a stir wherever he went, not only because he dwarfed most Indians in size but because he dressed like a Siva devotee, right down to wearing a *dothi* and a sacred thread across his chest. He was actually a Sanskrit language student at the Sanskrit University in Varanasi. The shorter of the two men spent his time mainly studying with Tibetans in Sarnath and Dharamsala. They asked what I and my two friends were planning for our subsequent travels. When I explained that we were headed for Nepal, that I had an invitation to stay at the Gelukpa Monastery in Bodhanath, and that the three of us had hopes of somehow hooking up with a Tibetan Buddhist teacher there, the smaller, soft-spoken man became quite deliberate in his speech, and I craned closer to listen.

"Well, there are two really good teachers who live just a few miles out-side of Kathmandu," he said. "Actually, they live in small *gompas* just outside of Bodhanath. There's a road that winds behind the main *stupa* there; anyone can point it out. The road travels up past a place called Kopan. At that place, there is a lama called Thubten Yeshe." As he contin-ued to talk, I began to experience a strange, though pleasant, sensation. It was unlike any sensation I had ever experienced before: a sort of warm tingling feeling that began at the nape of my neck and then radiated downward and outward to encircle my whole body. Then, as though I had suddenly stepped into an invisible field of static electricity, I noticed that the hairs on my skin stood up erect. As the warm tingling continued, I tuned back in to the stranger's advice. ". . . I don't know this Yeshe fellow, but I hear he's guarded by a woman named Zina who is famous for discouraging visitors." At that remark, the two men looked at each other and shared a wink. Presumably, this woman was the brunt of some joke. But again, at the sound of "Yeshe," all the hairs on my skin gently stood erect. He went on to describe a second teacher, but I only vaguely heard his words. Something had subtly happened to me, and I was by then thoroughly intrigued by the thought of meeting the first lama he'd mentioned, this Lama Yeshe. I thanked the man, and the two visitors left before Cletus and Rand and Rob returned.

During the next few weeks, leaving Cletus to study for his exams, my two buddies and I made our circuit around India, traveling by train. Yet during all of our travels, I couldn't get the thought of that lama out of my mind. We returned to Banaras, said our good-byes to Cletus, and caught a flight on Royal Nepalese Airlines to Kathmandu. We were heading for the sacred valley rimmed by the wondrous snow-clad Himalayas, the green valley where we might actually make contact with our teacher.

By the time we had been in Kathmandu for a week, I was installed in a room at the monastery in Bodhanath, and Rand and Rob were still enjoying the pleasures of hippie life in Kathmandu. When I'd asked my new monk-friend Sonam about the high lamas in the area, he'd taken me out back of the *stupa* and, pointing to a distant hill, said, "Up there is Kopan. Lama Yeshe lives there. He is a very good, a very high lama." I felt the tingling sensation again. So I hurried into town, picked up Rand and Rob from their hotel, and returned in a taxi with them. Then the three of us set out walking up to Kopan to meet Lama Yeshe.

The walk began fairly pleasantly. It felt nice to be away from the bustling of crowds. But the sandy and mica-sprinkled road gradually became ever more steep. By the time we hit the base of Kopan hill, we were all pretty winded, and the steeper switchbacks were yet to come. When at last we reached the top of the hill and turned into the compound of the Nepalese Mahayana Gompa, we were relieved. We walked down a grassy path to a gate and opened it. On our left was a small building containing perhaps two rooms. Farther in and up some stone steps to our right was a fairly large brick house. All was quiet. We saw no one. Then, from the larger house, preceded by the tiny yelps of two Lhasa apsos, a tall Western woman in robes appeared. She greeted us and introduced herself as Zina. When we explained that we'd come in hopes of meeting Lama Yeshe, her smiling countenance immediately changed and, while waving her hands for emphasis, she said, "Oh, no! That will be quite impossible! The lamas—both Lama Yeshe and Lama Zopa, are very tired, you see. They are resting now and cannot be disturbed. You cannot meet them today. Sorry, but you simply cannot."

We were crestfallen. Then, with pity in her eyes, Zina added: "Well, you've walked a long way. You must at least stay for lunch before going down. Go there and sit in the shade." Tired, hot, and dejected, in silence we did as she bade us. Seeing our compliance, Zina turned away from us with a regal flourish, clapped her hands, and called, "Machela!" A small, skinny Tibetan man in dark pants and a white shirt appeared. She gave him some directions. The man disappeared in a flash and just as quickly returned with a large straw mat. It became a picnic tablecloth, and before too long, Zina and the three of us were dining in the shade and cool breezes of Kopan. We had seen no one else; no lamas were visible.

Zina became animated. She was in her element, entertaining guests and happily narrating the story of how she came to be living here with Lama Yeshe and his chief disciple, Lama Zopa. After breaking up with her former husband, Conrad Rooks—the director of the movie *Siddhartha* and others—she had met the two lamas in Darjeeling. She had pleaded with them to become her teachers, took ordination at their suggestion, purchased this compound (a former Astrologer's House), and brought the lamas here to be her private tutors. They had some plans to turn the place into a monastery for teaching Westerners, but those were plans for the future and there were, at present, no other people in residence. It was clear that she enjoyed her status as the "mommy" of this fledgling monastery.

Zina talked while we ate and listened. A couple of hours went by. Then, rather abruptly, she announced that it was probably time that we started back down to Bodhanath; we would want to make the walk while there was still daylight. When we inquired about a future date to meet the lamas, she told us she had no idea. She would ask them but she couldn't give us a time to return. We thanked her for her hospitality and gathered ourselves for the trek back. Zina turned away and quickly mounted the steps to the large house. With no further fanfare, she disappeared back into its darkened hallway.

Slowly, the three of us headed for the gate. But then, just as we reached the farthest corner of the smaller house, now to our right side, its door creaked open and a hand both shushed us and beckoned us inside. The hand was attached to a broadly smiling, shaven-headed Tibetan man in robes with large dimples and a gap between his teeth. Quickly we glanced around. The coast was clear. We silently slipped inside. In makeshift English he said, "Hello! I am Lama Yeshe and I am so glad that you have come." We could hardly believe what was happening. Zina was somewhere in her house, hardly twenty feet away, and here we were, actually meeting Lama Yeshe in spite of her efforts to dissuade us. Speechless, we simply grinned and bubbled in our good fortune. "Was your meal well?" he asked. "Yes, very well, ah, very good, thank you!" we finally managed, still awestruck. There was a radiant youthfulness about Lama Yeshe. He seemed both calm and playful, alert, present, and genuinely happy to see us. We engaged in brief introductions, and then our conversation just began to flow. At a certain point, he asked, "Now, please tell me, why have you come?" It was then that I gave that dumb textbook response. Lama Yeshe only smiled and said, "Yes. That is true. Hm-hum." He told us a bit more about how he and Lama Zopa had come to be there with Zina, and about the few other Westerners whom he had met since coming to Kopan. He added, "Zina . . . Mommy . . . is sometimes . . . how you say? . . . too much protective, but she is becoming a good nun. Well, I hope you will come again." Grinning from ear to ear, we stood and prepared to sneak out. Then, Lama Yeshe said something that completely bowled us over. In the course of our conversation, none of us had made any mention of our accident in France. Yet standing in his tiny little room, our mouths dropped open in unison when, leaning over and looking deeply into our eyes, he said, "Lama is so happy that you three have come, especially after . . . you know . . . that bad thing in France." When our dumbfoundedness subsided, we told him that we would, most certainly, return.

The Test

One morning after spending the night at Rand and Rob's, I sat perched upon the grassy knoll just above the little house that served as Lama Yeshe and Lama Zopa's abode. Lama Yeshe pushed open his door, toothbrush in hand and towel draped across his arm, heading for the bathroom on the other side of the house. For a brief moment he paused, looked up at me piercingly, and before continuing his journey, said, "Living with pride and humility in equal proportion is very difficult, isn't it? Very difficult!"

In that moment, it seemed to me, he had put his finger on one of the deepest issues confronting not only me but all African Americans. There is a great existential difficulty in attempting to count oneself a human being equal with all others after having suffered through the experience of centuries of slavery. Our very humanity was challenged and degraded at every turn and yet, through it all, we have maintained the desire to stand tall, with dignity and love of self. Only two decades before Lama Yeshe's remark, throughout the civil-rights marches in the southern United States, African Americans had carried signs that poignantly proclaimed, "I am a man!" and "I am somebody."

It is the trauma of slavery that haunts African Americans in the deepest recesses of our souls. This is the chief issue for us, the issue that must be dealt with head-on—not denied, not forgotten, not suppressed. Indeed, its suppression and denial only hurt us more deeply by causing us to accept a limiting, disparaging, and at times even repugnant view of ourselves. We as a people cannot move forward until we have grappled in a serious way with all the negative effects of this trauma. With just a glance that morning, Lama Yeshe had captured my heart's dilemma: How to stand dignified, yet humbly, in the world?

I was soon to discover that Tibetan tantric Buddhism offers tools to help with this dilemma, for it provides methods that show both how to get at those deep inner wounds and how to heal them. One method, for example, employs the meditative notion of divine pride. According to this theory, we are all inherently pure, or divine, at our cores. Our task is but to realize this truth. There is, of course, a very fine line between confidence and arrogance. Belief in one's own innate purity and power can easily be confused with an all-too-human pridefulness. The consequence of misunderstanding this crucial distinction, and of thereby going astray, is the creation of more suffering rather than the elimination of it. Hence the great need for a true and authentic guide on this most important journey of discovery. This fact was brought home to me personally and powerfully in the ensuing weeks.

* * * *

For Randy and Robbie, Lama Yeshe was everything they could have imagined in a teacher: his face glowed, his eyes twinkled, his smile radiated loving compassion and gentleness. He was well educated and seemed genuinely happy to teach us. In my heart of hearts, I was greatly attracted to Lama Yeshe as well and had strangely felt drawn to him even before we actually met. Now that I had had my own experiences with his warmth and wise counsel, I felt all the more fortunate.

But I was still cautious and tentative. I held back, wishing not to seem so easily won-over. I saw humility as a virtue and I wanted to be humble—like Lama Yeshe. Yet I also wanted to be strong and not to feel as helpless, weak, and vulnerable as I had so often in the past. These two opposing forces seemed to be doing constant battle inside of me. Given all the disappointments, demeaning instances, and frustrations I had suffered since early childhood, it was, quite simply, difficult for me to trust anyone. I said to the two of them, "Yes, he is compassionate, but so are lots of Tibetans. I want to learn something about wisdom." Lama Yeshe, for his part, was patient and loving toward me, even when I was not so nice to him.

One day as we were finishing up a session with him, Lama Yeshe surprised me by saying, "I think you should go and study with my teacher, Geshe Rabten. He is a great teacher and is especially skilled in teaching about Buddhist wisdom. He is living in India, in Dharamsala, but since you know Hindi, traveling there will be no problem for you." I felt both proud, that he recognized my academic intellectual side, and a bit rejected, since he made it clear that Randy and Rob were to stay there with him at Kopan. I told myself that this arrangement would be better. I would finally get to be with the wisdom-being, the master teacher I wanted and deserved. Surely, pride goeth before the fall.

On the way to Dharamsala, I stopped off in Banaras to visit Cletus. I stayed there for two or three days, going to movies, relaxing, and just playing around before I headed up to the former British hill-station of Dharamsala. Finally arriving there, I found my way to Geshe Rabten's place. He was actually in retreat, living in an old mud-caked hut out in the woods. Serving him there were only a monk-cook and a young incarnate lama-charge of his, named Gonsar Rinpoche, who stood in as his translator.

I waited a moment outside the hut while Gonsar introduced me. When he motioned me inside, I touched my hands together in *anjali* and began to bow to Geshe Rabten. These were the normal forms of greeting. But suddenly, Geshe Rabten abruptly cut me off, delivering a long and seemingly angry tirade in Tibetan. He pointed his finger at me and went on and on in a raised voice. Clearly I had done something wrong. After a while, Gonsar Rinpoche translated: "Geshe-la wants to know why you have arrived late," he said.

"I beg your pardon?" I began, but a longer outburst from Geshe Rabten followed. I couldn't understand how he *knew* that I could have arrived any sooner. Lama Yeshe had given me a letter of introduction, and since I was myself carrying that letter, how could Geshe Rabten know that I had stopped off in Banaras? Still, his lengthy and animated declaration left little doubt that he did know and that he was chewing me out for my tardiness.

He didn't want to hear any excuses. He asked nothing about my background or personal history and didn't care who I was or where I had come from. He was a teacher, I had been sent by one of his disciples, and he would teach me. That was all. I was told to take a seat. He began right away, that very day. After getting over the shock of that first meeting, I felt like I was in paradise.

I lived in Dharamsala for six weeks, taking lessons each day from Geshe Rabten. They were lessons about how creating and then clinging to false images of ourselves only serve to create more suffering for us, about the impermanence of such self-projections and the need to lessen our attachments to them, about the pitfalls and burdens of swapping one pretense for another, and about how, ultimately, since we create our own suffering, only we can put an end to it by living life authentically. Eventually the time came when I had to return to Nepal. Six weeks was the arrangement I had made with Lama Yeshe, and my Indian visa was up. Geshe Rabten had been inordinately kind to me. I gave little thought to the fact that he was trying to do a meditative retreat of his own. I told myself I was learning a lot from this master teacher about lessening self-grasping, but in fact I was self-centered, elated at my good fortune, and completely oblivious to anyone else's needs. I was also proud and more than a little arrogant. I thought I deserved to study with a teacher of Geshe Rabten's stature because *I* was such an intelligent student.

As I returned to the compound at Kopan near dusk late one evening, I glimpsed Lama Yeshe in the distance coming down the stairs on his way to his room. He seemed to see me, too. But rather than that warm smile he always gave, he turned his head sharply away and continued his steps.

He seemed to make a point of ignoring me. Returning after so long, I felt immediately rejected again. After all, I was coming back from studying with his guru. I walked toward Lama's room and noticed Randy and Rob's shoes outside his door. Apparently, he had begun giving them extra lessons. Again, I was the outsider.

I tapped gently on the door and slowly entered. Lama Yeshe was quietly talking with them. Then, suddenly, he looked up at me with what seemed a completely different look in his eyes, almost like anger. Before any of us knew what was happening, Lama Yeshe pointed his finger at me and began yelling in Tibetan. The string of words that issued from his mouth sounded *exactly* like those Geshe Rabten had used at our first meeting. Lama Yeshe had never spoken to any of us like this before. Rand and Rob, like me, were completely stunned.

Then, in a flash of insight, I knew what Lama was doing. It was a teaching directed solely at me, and it was perfect. Lama Yeshe knew a great deal about me. He knew that I had been judging between him and some other type of teacher. He knew that I prized wisdom over compassion, not seeing that both qualities were essential requisites in any true teacher. He knew that my seeming arrogance was only the flip side of my low self-esteem, and that low self-esteem was my deepest and oldest wound. He also knew that I was intelligent and determined. He had sent me on that journey to Geshe Rabten's so that I would come to see all these things about myself; and so that once they were clearly recognized and claimed, he and I could begin to work on the delicate balancing act needed to heal them. I realized then how difficult it must have been for this kind teacher to feign anger toward me, or toward any living creature for that matter.

I fell forward on the tiny floor, bowing to Lama Yeshe, and sobbing full-force. I asked for his forgiveness. He had seen into my heart and soul. It struck me that such wisdom and compassion are truly inconceivable. And I knew—from that moment—that I could trust Lama Yeshe to be my teacher and my guide.

When I first met Lama Yeshe, I arrived carrying a lifetime's worth of self-pity and low self-esteem. I knew that I worked hard and was determined; I kept plugging away, in spite of often feeling beaten down. I also knew some of the causes for my particular state of being. But I usually saw these as having to do with external conditions or persons. Lord knows, I had my reasons, and many of these were true. But peace was what I was after, some way to still the constant frustrations I experienced and to feel comfortable living in my own skin. Whether our suffering takes the guise of self-pity or self-absorption, its source is the same: holding too tightly to our projected images of ourselves. We know, for example, that when we are depressed, our minds turn about one point: me. Poor me. Why me? How could this have happened to me? The nub is always me, me, me. Though it may be more difficult to see how self-absorption causes pain, here, too, attachment to self-image wreaks havoc with any contentment. Always there is the desire for more. More attention, more applause. More recognition of *me.*

Lama Yeshe saw my wounds, correctly diagnosed my chief illness, and like a skilled doctor, over the course of the next fifteen years, worked with me to help me heal.

Joy of the Dharma

I had been taking myself pretty seriously up to this point. It was only by facing my self-esteem issues and getting out from under the self-pity I'd been carrying around for so long that I could begin to develop a healthy sense of who I was—and a healthy sense of humor. In Buddhism, as in most of the world's religious traditions, gaining a new name is part and parcel of the ritual one undergoes when one *commits* oneself to the faith or to a particular path of practice. Though I very seldom use my Tibetan name, it is quite special to me.

The truest marker of any Buddhist is that she or he takes refuge, or places full trust in, the "Three Jewels," namely: the Buddha, the Dharma, and the Sangha, or, again, in the founder of the Buddhist tradition, in his teachings, and in the community of his followers. But there is also, for each Buddhist, a ceremony that is performed—usually early in life but at least at the beginning of a specific path of practice—that marks her or his official entrance into the community. This is how I came to earn my Tibetan name.

Lama Yeshe had already given me a new name shortly after I began studies with him. He had dubbed me "Lobsang," a name that echoed the monastic name of Tsongkhapa who had founded the specific order in which Lama practiced. "Lobsang" means "of keen intelligence." I liked it. But when Lama Yeshe sent Randy, Robbie, and me together to study with his teacher, Geshe Rabten, he had advised us to ask *him* to perform the ritual initiation for making us official lay Buddhist practitioners. In Dharamsala, we made our request.

Geshe Rabten graciously agreed to perform the initiation just for the three of us. We were so proud. We entered his tiny retreat hut carrying flowers and incense offerings. Gonsar Rinpoche translated as Geshe Rabten explained the ceremony to us in detail. He told us that the ritual required that we plead for the vows of an *upasaka,* or lay follower. This meant that we should make our requests with folded hands, down on our right knees. "Of course, you don't have to stay like that because the ceremony goes on for some time. You should start out in that position, as a symbol of requesting the vows, but when it becomes uncomfortable, please sit down comfortably." I heard those words, but being stubborn, I determined that I would do the ceremony from beginning to end on my right knee.

So the three of us got down on our right knees and the ceremony began. After some time, I saw Rand and Rob sit back. I thought, "Hah! Not me! I will see the initiation through till its end like this." Well, two and a half-hours later, I was still on one knee on the cold and damp mud floor of Geshe Rabten's hut when the ceremony ended and we each had new names. Rand was now "Light of the Dharma," Robbie "Dharma's Accomplishment," and I "Joy of the Dharma." My friends stood up, beaming. But I, of course, could not move. I was completely frozen in place. My right leg had been numb for more than an hour and a half. So, Rand and Rob had to help me up. Each had me under the arms as I stood—on my left leg—trembling, between them.

Suddenly, Geshe Rabten began calling to his monk-cook to come and see the spectacle. When the cook arrived, he told him what had just transpired, and the cook doubled over with laughter. Gonsar translated for us, "Geshe Rabten is delighted. He says, 'What a perfectly great name you have been given, Joy of the Dharma. Just look at all the joy you are causing!'"

In my youth, I had been dragged—kicking and screaming—to be baptized. In spite of all my protests then, I had found the immediate aftermath of that experience to be quite wonderful, for it was as though, for the first time, I was lovingly enveloped in the arms of a community. Now, as an adult, I had entered into this Buddhist naming ceremony freely and of my own choice. Even so, my old stubbornness—about following the rules, about being a good Buddhist—was still there. If anyone could use a little lightheartedness in her life, I figured it was me. The monks' laughter was spontaneous, joyous, and nonjudgmental. I could see that, though painful, my stern antics had actually been quite comical. I liked this warm and welcoming community; and I looked forward to the time when my new name might actually be an accurate description of my inner being. Here, in the midst of these Buddhists, I felt the hard shell of my rigid self beginning to soften. And, joining in with them, I burst out laughing.

Flesh and Bones Buddha

After we had been given our new names by Geshe Rabten, Randy, Rob, and I stayed in Dharamsala for another six weeks. The weather was cold and rainy. We had arrived totally unprepared for it, or the harsh conditions, but being hippies we made the best of it. The floor of our little room in what was called "Naro-jee Villa" was concrete. At the one street market of Dharamsala, we bought straw mats upon which to lay our woefully inadequate sleeping bags. So when we were not having a session with Geshe Rabten, or clambering up and down the steep trail to the market, or preparing a meal on our borrowed kerosene stove, we each sat in meditative posture, facing a wall of our room, trying to bring to mind a sharp, crisp image of a Buddha, our teeth chattering. Life was challenging but good.

Being in Dharamsala meant that we were in the place where His Holiness the Dalai Lama actually lived. In subsequent years, it became much more difficult to arrange for a private audience with the Dalai Lama, but in those days, it was a simple and quite informal matter. His Holiness's private secretary, though soft-spoken and refined, counted himself a simple monk. In the late afternoons he often strolled the one street of Dharamsala's marketplace. As our time of training with Geshe Rabten drew near a close, one evening we approached Tenzin and told him of our desire to meet with His Holiness. He reached into his robes and took out a small datebook. Looking it over, he raised his head and asked, "Would tomorrow at three o'clock be all right with you?"

"Why, yes! Yes, it would. We will be there. Thank you so much." That was all it took.

The next day we prepared by taking good though frigid baths, dressing in our cleanest clothes, and getting our best *kattas,* or greeting scarves, folded neatly and ready to offer to His Holiness. When we arrived at the residence just behind the Namgyal Monastery, we were ushered into a simple but eloquent foyer. Tenzin inconspicuously ducked into a room and then came out to tell us that His Holiness would see us.

The thing I remember most about that first meeting, for there have been many since then, was that His Holiness seemed much taller than I had thought him to be. His voice, too, was quite incredible, deep and rippling and, at times, seeming to come from other parts of the room. Like the student-hippies we were, just after entering the room we had begun doing prostrations. His Holiness quickly put an end to this formal ritual by coming over to us and saying as he gestured with his hand, "All right, stop that. None of that is necessary. Please, come and sit down." We found ourselves completely at ease.

He was charming and energetic. His very being exemplified the ideals of Mahayana, that form of Buddhism in which all spiritual practice aims at, and is perfected through, compassion and service to others. He was the true *bodhisattva,* a being whose sole intention is to make himself into a proper tool to serve and fulfill the needs of all beings; who compassionately strives to do whatever is necessary so that others can be helped and not harmed.

After graciously commending us for studying with Geshe Rabten and for being students of Lama Yeshe, he wasted no time in engaging us in a discussion about student protest in the United States. His Holiness wanted to know everything about recent demonstrations and unrest. We talked for some time about the shootings at Kent State. He made it clear that he wanted to know how we, as students, saw what was happening and why. He listened with eyes set firmly upon us and with a kindness and compassionate understanding that made our own words flow smoothly.

I was supposed to be following the same path that helped the Dalai Lama become as kind and great as he is, so I asked, "Given that we have taken *bodhisattva* vows, Your Holiness, what are we to do if, once back in the States, we find ourselves in a position where we too are facing policemen or National Guardsmen who want to shoot us?" Talking with the Dalai Lama brought up again for me my old dilemma about violence versus peace. Back at Cornell and on my subsequent trip to California, perhaps to join the Black Panthers, I had had my own near brushes with violence, and I had thought a lot about the possible consequences of armed confrontation. Though I had chosen to turn away from violence, I was still concerned about becoming too passive. I knew that the Dalai Lama himself had had to face similar issues when his own country was violently invaded by the Chinese. His Holiness became intensely reflective. Then with deliberate and attentive clarity, he advised us as follows:

"You have now entered upon the Mahayana path. That is very good. Very good, indeed. The Mahayanist, the *bodhisattva,* as you know, works for the benefit of beings. He or she wishes to aid beings wherever they are in need. You should know that your first duty, now that you are on this path, is to practice *patience.* You are meditating to gain clarity. You must have clarity in order to act appropriately. With patience and clarity, you know with certainty whether you can or cannot help a given situation. If, after looking at the situation with clarity, you determine that you cannot help, then it is better not to worry. Worry accomplishes nothing. But if you are clear and you can help, then you will know what to do and how to do it. So, patience and clarity are essential."

"Yes, Your Holiness," my impatience made me push, "but what if you think you have looked at all the alternatives—with clarity—and you find that your only course of action is to be on that line along with others, facing those policemen or those guardsmen, then what?"

"Again," he said, "patience is most important. But if you are certain that there is no other alternative, if you are clear and certain about this, then what you must do is this: First, you must think lovingly and with compassion about the policeman. If you think or call him a pig, then you must let him shoot you! But if you can wish him well, and pray for his future happy rebirth, then of course, you stop him from harming the others. You stop him by any means necessary." We were relieved and amazed.

He continued, "When I came out of Tibet, many Khampas with guns accompanied me. They were concerned about me. They wanted my safety. I could not say to them, 'You are wrong to have guns.' Many monks too in Tibet took up guns to fight the Chinese. But when they came here, I made them monks again. You should not believe that the Mahayana asks you to think of beings' welfare only in some future time. You should try as much as possible to help in the here and now. Still, patience and clarity are most important, most important."

Lama Yeshe had made a similar point several weeks before we came to Dharamsala. He had been talking with another student and was telling him that one should actually do whatever is necessary to help beings and not cause them harm, even if that sometimes meant breaking one's vows. He had said, "Sometimes, compassionately helping someone requires what a purist might view as breaking one's vows. For example, suppose a woman runs by you screaming that a man is after her and wants to kill her. In a few moments, you see a man brandishing a big knife who asks you, 'Where did that woman go?' Now, your vows tell you that you should not tell a lie. But if you tell the truth, the man will probably kill the woman. So you choose to tell a lie here in order to protect the woman from harm. Doing so also protects the man from creating negative actions. The vows are not so much proscriptions as they are guidelines. You must use your intelligence, your wisdom and clarity, as well as your compassion to be of service to others."

Talking with the Dalai Lama brought this truth home again. Buddhism was a process; one did not need to delude oneself or to pretend to be other than oneself, and one did not have to become completely passive in order to embrace the notion of peace. Choosing peace did not mean rolling over and becoming a doormat. Pacifism did not mean passivism. Still, patience and clarity were essential. My heart basked in the glow of his words.

Before we knew it, almost two hours had gone by. His Holiness had been so open and so frank with us that he seemed to me to be like an old friend and wise counselor rolled into one, a true flesh-and-bones Buddha.

A Spot of Blonde

My appearance at birth, which caused so much trouble, would come back to haunt me with the Tibetans in a totally unexpected way. Everywhere I turned with them, my confidence and self-image couldn't help but improve. When I was born, my head was covered with curly blonde hair. As I grew older, the overall color became darker as the blonde hair contracted inward, leaving a blonde spot of hair about two inches in circumference at the center and top of my head just slightly to the back. This spot of blonde has remained to this day; it adorns my Afro, almost like a tiny, flat crown.

Just before I was to leave the country on my very first journey to India, my blonde spot came to the attention of a black woman who frightened me to no end when she literally began to dance with joy upon seeing it.

Miss Dolly Green ran a beauty shop in Urbana, Illinois. I was there doing summer studies in preparation for the Wisconsin program trip. Just days before our departure, I decided I would go to get my hair done. This was a pretty futile effort, as I was going away for at least nine months. Since I didn't have a perm, my hair, once straightened with hot combs, would not last very long without turning back to its natural state. But neither did I, as yet, wear an Afro. So one day during our last week in Urbana I asked someone about beauty salons and was directed to Dolly Green's place.

A small bell above the door jingled as I entered her shop. Miss Green, motioning me over to a chair, told me she'd be with me soon. She was a dark-skinned woman, short in stature but sturdy. She wore a flowered print cotton dress over which she'd tied a clear plastic apron that was stained with smudges of hair tints and dyes. I hated going to beauty shops. It was as much a big social thing as a service for making women feel better, that is, prettier. I always felt ill at ease in such places: "A college student with nappy hair!" "Oughtta have more respect for oneself!" I told myself to calm down. After all, I didn't know anyone here.

One might be able to imagine then how thoroughly surprised I was when Miss Green suddenly grabbed my arm, spun me around in the chair, and started dancing as she shouted: "Praise the Lord! Chile, now I know why the Lord put me here in Urbana! I's seen eleven of you now. Blessed saints. Praise be to God!"

"Ma'am? What, ma'am? I beg your pardon?"

Miss Green was doing her dance. I'd seen it before. It was the dance holy rollers did, a kind of praise-step where one dances without lifting the feet completely off the ground. If either foot actually left the floor, the dance became secular, and the work of the devil. I knew then that Miss Green was sanctified. I, on the other hand, was simply scared to death.

I had been reading Dick Farina's latest novel that summer. In the novel, when things got scary, Dick's main character intoned the phrase, "Monkey-demon week." That phrase now reverberated in my frightened mind. What had I done to cause this woman's outburst? And was it, I hoped, only temporary?

I wanted to race to the door and get away from there. Forget the hairdo! But Miss Green blocked the door. She was happy and she wanted to tell me, and the two other ladies who sat there waiting their turns, exactly why.

"Yes, Lord. Now I know why He sent me here. Praise the Lord! Jesus done showed me eleven of you. The Bible says he anointed fifty in heaven 'fore sending them here. You sho' are one, chile! Now I can rest easy. I done seen eleven of you."

"Monkey-demon week" echoed louder in my mind.

I don't remember whether Dolly Green ever calmed down enough to do my hair that day. I don't remember if I ever calmed down enough to have her do it. Anointed? Me? In the midst of my brewing anger at the rest of the world, I found it highly unlikely.

•   •   •   •

Over the years, many of my students at Wesleyan have asked me how, or why, I came to be so involved with Tibetan Buddhism. Given my background and appearance, the question strikes me as a fair one. But honestly *I don't have a clue.* Of course, I know the general contour of how my interest unfolded, but as to why a black American woman in the late sixties came to be so enamored of and so readily accepted by Tibetan Buddhist refugees living in India and Nepal, that question is deep and perhaps ultimately unfathomable. Now, what is interesting and also true is that Tibetans seem to have no problem with the question at all. Without ever asking them, they have eagerly, and often reverentially, explained to me that in a former life, I was a Tibetan. And more than that, I was instrumental in helping to establish Buddhism in Tibet.

The first time I heard this explanation was in 1970. That year in Nepal, I had become friends with a teenaged Tibetan girl named Tenzin. She had continually pleaded for me to visit her and her mother at their home. One day, I went into town with her to do so.

Her family—she, her mother, and other siblings—all lived together in two tiny rooms in a larger house owned by a Sherpa. I remember being struck by how old her mother looked. Too old, I thought at the time, to be Tenzin's mother. Her brow had numerous deep grooves, and though she still maintained a head of long, well-greased dark hair, her body seemed leathery and weather-worn. She smiled and I saw that her mouth was almost completely toothless. She did sewing of various kinds, making and embroidering pillowcases and other things that she hoped would be bought by tourists.

I bowed to her respectfully and then noticed that she became very animated. After she'd told Tenzin to make tea for us, she put her sewing tools to the side and launched into an excited narrative. My spoken Tibetan was not very good then. Consequently, I was relieved when Tenzin set three cups down before us so that she could interpret.

As it turned out, Tenzin's mother's excited tale was all about me. Not exactly about the "me" of this present life, rather, it was about who I once had been, and who I now simply reincarnated. It seems that when the first Buddhist monastery had been built in Tibet, back in the late eighth century A.D., whoever I was back then had helped to build it. The mother called me one of the earliest Buddhists of Tibet. I was flattered but I didn't pay much attention. We sat in silence, had our tea, and smiled at each other.

I would probably not have remembered this particular story were it not for the fact that some days after that visit, back up at Kopan, Lama Yeshe had suddenly summoned me to the second-floor balcony of the monastery. He was standing next to a Western woman who had arrived at Kopan earlier in the day. "Arrived" is not the most appropriate word, since her coming had been heralded long before we actually saw her. Great plumes of dust were raised up the winding hillside, and the grunts and spurts of the rickety taxi—of all things!—she had somehow bribed and cajoled into driving her up had preceded her appearance. This woman was clearly a foreigner and unlike any of us who normally lived at Kopan. We knew that cars never attempted to drive up to Kopan owing to the simple fact that there was no road leading there. Everyone— Tibetans, Western hippies, and the Nepalese whose hill it was—walked; and walked fairly slowly at that!

The woman with Lama Yeshe had come for the day only. She was quite a sight, in her sequined high heels and heavy makeup. After lunch and a conversation with Lama, she wanted to meet with Tulsig Rinpoche, a renowned lama of the Nyingmapa lineage who was residing in Bodhanath. Lama Yeshe told me to take the woman to meet him. I wasn't thrilled to serve as the woman's chaperon, but I was delighted by the prospect of actually meeting Tulsig Rinpoche. This renowned teacher rarely came down from his mountain monastery. The chance to see him was a real opportunity, a gift, worthy of even the bumpiest and scariest taxi ride.

At the house in Bodhanath where Tulsig Rinpoche was staying, Tibetans moved in and out of rooms silently as if floating just above the floors. Messages were being passed in hushed tones. A line of guests were waiting their turn to visit this grand teacher. I spoke to the monk who seemed to be in charge, and taking his hand gesture to mean that we should wait there, I stood feeling a bit awkward next to the woman in her white suit and sequined shoes. After a few minutes, we were both called in.

I motioned for the lady to go in ahead of me. When I reached just inside the door, I glanced at Tulsig Rinpoche and began to perform my prostrations to this most holy lama. Suddenly, he stopped me and beckoned me forward. I moved trembling toward him, head bowed. He cut a lovely figure in monk's robes, large in size, powerful though gentle. His smile was captivating. With his right hand, he tenderly raised my head. Then everything took on an air of magic.

As his fingers lightly held my chin, he began a discussion with the other monks flanking him. When I gave a puzzled look, one of the monks began to interpret.

"Rinpoche says that you should not bow to him. He says that he should make prostrations to you, since you are one of the people who built the first Buddhist monastery in Tibet." I forgot completely the woman I was supposed to be accompanying. The monk continued.

"Rinpoche asks if you know the name of that first monastery."

"Yes. Its name was Samyas Monastery," I replied, still trembling. "The name means 'Inconceivable.' Legend has it that the monastery was constructed by ordinary beings during the day, and during the night by the gods." The other monks approved of my response.

"Rinpoche says that when the great Samyas Monastery was completed, the king of Tibet, King Trisong Detsen, had all those workers, all those who built the monastery, line up and pass before him. When they did, King Trisong Detsen sprinkled *tsampa* (barley flour) in their hair. Rinpoche says that the light spot of hair on your head comes from this sprinkling. He says *he* is fortunate to meet *you!*" Tulsig Rinpoche, still gently holding my head, then beamed a broad smile right into my eyes.

After that, I was motioned over to a cushion, given tea, and the conversation turned to the business of the woman I had brought.

It was only a spot of color I happened to have in my hair. Yet Tulsig Rinpoche's explanation of it made me feel really special. Like a proud father, his appreciation gave me the sense of being a worthy human being. A part of me was deeply touched because it was one of the first times anyone had actually looked up to me, let alone anyone of Tulsig Rinpoche's stature. Part of me felt those old wounds begin to resurface from all the times I had been told, or made to feel, just the opposite. Part of me smiled in disbelief since I had never accepted the notion of reincarnation. And part of me just wanted to put the whole idea far away because I couldn't imagine that I might have anything positive to contribute to this world—whether now or in the past. I wanted to believe him, wanted desperately to believe Rinpoche and Dolly Green and

Tenzin's mother. It was only right. It had to be true. All people were special, each and every one of us. But truly feeling this would take some
time. Finally, I managed to let go of all these conflicting emotions. And I
sat there, basking in the warmth of Rinpoche's presence.

My Great Seal Retreat

He did not mean the sea mammal of that name. Lama Yeshe was offering
me the chance to try out the advanced system of tantric meditation perfected by Tibetan yogic masters who had quickly attained enlightenment
by using it. It was the early summer of 1981. I had been living in Nepal
for a year and a half. I had gone there on a National Endowment for the
Humanities fellowship to work primarily on collecting the oral histories
of certain living Tibetans. But first Lama Yeshe had asked me to translate
the lives of some of the early Gelukpa saints who had gained full enlightenment very quickly. These particular practitioners had followed the
meditative instructions developed by Tsongkhapa, the founder of the
Gelukpa school. His system was known either as the Ganden Oral
Tradition or the Gelukpa Mahamudra, though the great yogi Milarepa
had first brought prominence to the method. *Mahamudra* means "Great
Seal" or "Great Gesture," referring both to the subtle shift, or gesture, of
the mind, which ushers in enlightenment, and to the badge or "seal" of
this attainment. For more than a year I had worked on the translations
Lama wanted, which became the basis of my book *Enlightened Beings*.
Now, I planned to get on with my oral history work.

Though the translation work had been challenging, as well as inspiring, it had never crossed my mind to try out the grueling methods of the
Great Seal tradition. For example, one of its practitioners, a sage named
Jampel Gyatso, had chosen to sustain himself while he meditated for
almost three years by eating only tiny pills fashioned from crushed
juniper berries mixed with mud. Another, Gyelwa Ensapa, had continued
his strenuous practices even while his body was being ravished by small-

pox. Even though by 1981 I had been doing some meditations for about twelve years, the commitment required to tackle Great Seal practices seemed to me almost superhuman.

Lama Yeshe was preparing to leave Nepal for a tour abroad that would begin in Australia and keep him away from Nepal for the remainder of my stay there. One day he asked me, in quite a serious tone, "Don't you want to know what the system these people practiced was like? I mean, don't you want to *try it yourself?*"

One part of me was flattered. The other part of me was scared. Immediately I thought, "Right. Does he really think that *I* could actually sample anything so lofty as the practices that had ensured these men enlightenment?" I had meditated a bit during the years I'd known Lama—had even had some pretty good results—but this was serious stuff and a big commitment. I didn't think I was ready or brave enough to undertake it. My response to Lama Yeshe's offer came out of my mouth with far too little reflection. It was a cowardly and knee-jerk response. I said, "No. Thank you, Lama, but *no way!*" He looked a bit stunned.

"Why, daughter, wouldn't you want to try something so wonderful?" I said, with emphasis, "Thank you, Lama. I am happy you'd consider introducing me to such mysteries, but I don't think I'm ready." Probably sensing my fear, his response then was compassionate and gentle: "Well, think about it, dear. Think about it." When he turned toward other activities, I left the monastery and literally ran down the hill away from Kopan.

All the way home, his offer stayed with me. I had been translating the lives of these saints for a year. I had studied other *nam-thar,* or "liberation life stories," for many years before. These were exceptional practitioners. Devout from the beginning, committed to the Dharma until the end. I didn't think I could practice like they had. I didn't have the will, the determination. I was chicken, right down to my toes.

Moreover, those Great Seal practitioners had felt the great Mahayana wish to liberate all beings from suffering from the time they had issued from their mothers' wombs. I wasn't sure I wanted to save all sentient beings. I surprised myself with that thought. In a flood of emotions, all the hesitations and doubts I had previously only thought about regarding Buddhist renunciation, about giving up everything in order to help others, came rising up. One thing seemed certain: I did not possess it. Could it actually be that I liked suffering too much? And then, I didn't know what to expect from the practice. I was afraid I might end up in some strange place, like Castaneda's Itxalan, catatonic and alone. I was afraid that I might actually *succeed,* and thereby *lose* myself. These fears surfaced all together and at once. I was a wreck by the time I reached home.

I tried, with no success, to have a restful afternoon. In spite of my fears, there was something so tantalizing about Lama Yeshe's offer. I knew it would be stupid to let it slip away. "Be brave," a stray thought encouraged me. "Be a Buddhist, girl! Here's a chance to really practice. Put your actions where all your study and thinking has been. Answer Lama with your heart."

Almost without full awareness, I called Lakshman, my young, eversmiling yardman, and gave him a scribbled note to carry back up to Lama Yeshe. The note said simply, "I would be happy to try the practice. Thank you so much. Your Daughter."

Lakshman had recently purchased a new bicycle with the ample rupees I was paying him and he liked nothing better than a mission such as this. I had asked him to please hurry back, but several hours passed before his return. When he did enter the front gate, ringing the bell loudly, I raced out to the porch to meet him. I could see that he was grinning from ear to ear. In fact, his face was luminous, as though Lama Yeshe had performed some special magic just for him. Which, of course, he had.

"Ma'am *sahib!* Ma'am *sahib!*" Lakshman blurted out through gleaming white teeth. "Your Lama has sent you a special present!" From his *jola* bag Lakshman pulled out an object wrapped in layers of rice paper. Cook Kanchi joined us in the living room as Lakshman excitedly narrated the details of his splendid adventure. After reading my note, Lama Yeshe had been very pleased. He had ordered a very fine meal for Lakshman, with tea and dessert. Lakshman had eaten on the top patio of the monastery while Lama Yeshe rushed back and forth preparing the statue that was contained in the rice paper.

"That statue, ma'am *sahib,* is very precious. Your guru, Lama Yeshe, told me so. And he has *filled* it, ma'am *sahib,* with many precious things!"

In their presence, I carefully unwrapped the gift Lama had sent me. It was a Nepalese terra-cotta Buddha about eight inches in height. My first impression was that the little image was rather gaudy, painted in thick and overly bright colors. I had seen lots of statues much more subtly executed. Perhaps, I thought, Lama Yeshe's student Lama Zopa had painted this one; he loved doing such work. But perhaps Lama Yeshe had done this one himself. I was not taken by the statue's attractiveness. It was clear, however, as Lakshman had reported, that the statue had been very recently sealed up at the bottom; rice paper was freshly glued around its lotus base. The idea of Lama Yeshe's having stuffed the statue with many precious things made me smile. I knew that lamas did this when statues were ritually consecrated, stuffing every available nook and cranny with everything from soil from sacred Buddhist sites to hairs from famed teachers to gemstones and minutely written mantras. Lama Yeshe had consecrated this Buddha image just for me and my practice. It was a gift from him. And it seemed to carry along with it his joy that I was willing to undertake the practice. I touched it to my head in reverence and I treasured it.

The next day I walked up to the monastery at Kopan to meet with Lama and discuss the details of my upcoming retreat. He met me with a broad smile and said, "I am happy, dear, that you will do this practice. And I am sure—one-hundred-percent sure—that you will be able to taste the great Mahamudra bliss. Don't worry, dear. You will."

I apologized for having at first turned down his offer, to which he responded, "All right, dear. Now you will do it. That is very good." He then reminded me that I was extremely fortunate at this time to possess all the external necessities for doing such a retreat, namely, a nice, sturdy, and quiet house; a cook to prepare my meals; a yardman to handle any needed shopping; and a fireplace in which to conduct nightly fire-offer-ings. The external conditions, in fact, could not have been better. The retreat would last six weeks. It would be a *silent* retreat. I could walk inside my house's compound but could not go farther than the yard. I could not read or enjoy any form of entertainment. Nor could I receive visitors. I balked a bit at the silence part but, upon reflection, thought that it might be a relief. So far so good. I was still willing to give it a try.

Next, Lama told me that we would discuss the specific details of the practice at a later time but that for the time being there were certain req-uisites that I needed to begin assembling. First, I would need to have another statue made, one of Dorje Sampa, whose Sanskrit name is Vajrasattva. The Buddhist deity used primarily for purification, his medi-tative practice is a necessary requisite to all advanced tantric meditation. I had been doing a practice that focused on this deity since 1969. The statue required now would need to be a special one, one that I had myself commissioned, made to certain specified standards. *And* it would need to be specially consecrated by a group of monks. Lama suggested that I request someone at Samteling Monastery, my earliest monastic home, to handle the consecration for me. I should also begin collecting the neces-sary grains and various other offering materials to be used in the fire ritu-als I would have to perform each evening during the retreat.

The preparations for my retreat took a full two weeks. As it turned out, I was fortunate to get everything done by then because Lama Yeshe was leaving on his trip just a day or two later. I had Lakshman shop for most of the grains I needed. He had to purchase big bags of rice and black sesame seeds, enough to last for six weeks. Some of the offering materials, like *kusha* grass, I had to shop for myself.

To have a statue made just for me required several trips out to Patan, the little town that had once served as a capital of Nepal. Many artisan families lived in Patan, descendants of people who had been supplying monasteries in Tibet with their statuaries for centuries. Visiting a number of stores that sold such statues. I finally found my way to a respected and trustworthy clan of artisans. Before a deal was actually struck, I was guided through numerous back alleys and up and around several darkened stairways. Finally, I stood in a room, lit only by the light from a tiny window. The chief bronzecaster offered me a wooden stool and then reached under a low thatched Nepali bed. Pulling out a tray, there suddenly appeared twenty or so bronze molds of statues, lying on their backs. They were each about ten inches tall, half-bodied and still rough, but somehow wondrously lifelike.

The bronzecaster asked me to choose the statue I liked most. Surveying them, one in particular caught my eye. Even in this early stage of production, its limbs were graceful and its face sublime. Watching me, the bronzecaster gently lifted out that particular form and, holding it up, said to me, "This is your Dorje Sampa." I smiled.

I saw my Dorje Sampa statue twice more in differing stages of completion. I decided at the next meeting that the statue should have its exposed limbs gilded and, on the subsequent viewing, that its face should be delicately painted with gold. When, after ten days, the statue was finally presented to me, it was magnificent. In fact, it was the most beautiful Dorje Sampa I had ever seen.

Still, I had to have the statue filled and consecrated. Lama Yeshe's suggestion proved right about who would be best to handle this part. I took the statue to my friend Lama Thubten Palden, a respected monk at Samteling who was also the monastery's ritual specialist. Lama Palden listened attentively as I explained that I needed the statue in order to do a six-week Mahamudra retreat under Lama Yeshe's guidance. Moreover, he seemed unruffled when I added that I needed the consecration done in just a few days. I learned later that Lama Palden had begun work on the statue as soon as I left him. He himself had made trips around Kathmandu Valley gathering various materials with which to fill the image. He had traveled up to Swayambhunath to get certain substances from teachers living there: dust from Bodhgaya, diamond chips and rubies from other lamas, hairs from revered lamas of the past. Back at Samteling, he had filled the statue with these items, dressed it, and then recruited three other lamas to help him perform the consecration rituals.

The four monks conducted special ceremonies that lasted two complete days and nights. When next I saw my statue, it was as if it had become alive. It was draped in a tiny brocade robe and wore a necklace of coral and turquoise, and it evinced a living spiritual presence. As the traditional Buddhist saying goes, "Its eyes had been opened." I thanked the lamas and Lama Palden and made them a small offering. The preparations for my Great Seal retreat were done.

During that week, Lama Yeshe had sent me a note asking me to come to Kopan to receive final instructions for the retreat. When I arrived, I found the *gompa* in a buzz. Lama was leaving the next day. He motioned me over to his own small room.

A huge suitcase was flopped open on his bed. Various articles were scattered all over the tiny room. Lama searched through his stack of *pejas,* Tibetan woodblock-printed texts, wrapped in various colors, until he found the one he wanted. He turned to me, licking his fingers and flipping through the long pages, as he said, "As you know, dear, you are about to undertake the great Mahamudra retreat, the retreat taken by so many precious Gelukpa saints, and that brought them to the experience of actually *tasting* the Dharma's power and richness. This great meditation involves both deity-yoga and voidness-yoga, both generation-stage and completion-stage practice. Its central deity during the deity-yoga stage is Dorje Sampa."

Suddenly he paused, as if having an afterthought, and asked me, "How many Dorje Sampa mantras have you already completed, dear?"

"Well, now. Let's see. . . . I did the practice for two hours each night while I lived in Ithaca," I said as I began trying frantically to tally the specific number of sessions I'd completed, then counting 100 mantras for each session and multiplying. Fortunately, at that point a nun came in holding up for Lama's inspection a sleeveless yellow shirt worn by Geluk monks under their robes.

"This one, Lama?" she asked. Lama Yeshe gave his quick assent, "Yes, all right, dear. That one will be okay." The interruption gave me a chance to complete my tally.

"I'd say roughly thirty-five thousand Dorje Sampa mantras, Lama." He looked at me with a startled expression on his face. *"That's all?"* he asked in disbelief.

"Well, yes. I think so. Maybe a few more, but not many more than that." No need to lie to your guru at this point, I thought. He began flipping through the *peja* again, perhaps, I thought, to find a watered-down version of the practice, one more suitable for a lazy practitioner like me.

Another nun entered the room carrying a monk's shawl. "This *dzen*, Lama?"

"No, dear, I have enough *dzens* already. Thank you."

I was thinking, "What a way to get such a powerful initiation!" Yet amid all the busyness of Lama Yeshe's packing and all the things he'd no doubt have to attend to later in the evening, he kept instructing me. Things began to calm down. Lama Yeshe was now reading aloud from instructions on the retreat. He began to speak slowly, intently, and directly.

"This retreat requires some strict, that is, some rigid meditation, and some relaxation meditation. It is important that you do the relaxation part fully as well." I took out the small notebook I'd brought up and began to scribble notes.

"You are to practice in six sessions for a total of eight hours each day," he said, "and to perform a two-hour fire-offering *puja* every evening. The schedule should be like this: Wake at five-thirty A.M. Take tea. Begin your first session at six, six to seven. From seven to seven-thirty, attend to your altar. From seven-thirty to eight-thirty, second session. Break nine to ten, third session. Ten A.M.–one P.M., break and lunch. One to two, fourth session. Two to four, break. Four to five, fifth session. Five to six, break. Six to eight, Fire-*puja*. Eight to nine-thirty, dinner. Nine-thirty to ten-thirty, sixth session. Then, sleep!"

I asked Lama questions about the overall practice, and he cleared them up quickly and easily. He checked that I knew how to correctly perform the fire-*puja*. I did. He stressed to me again that *relaxation* was very important to the success of this retreat. No visitors. No talking. No reading, even. It was to be a completely silent, completely relaxed retreat experience.

Satisfied that I'd grasped the details of the retreat, Lama Yeshe closed the *peja,* hurriedly rewrapped it, and sat it back upon his stack. Looking kindly at me and almost shyly, he then said, "Now, I have to do this little thing, and tell you this." He made a quick gesture of pointing up to the sky, while he leaned forward and said to me, "Mind is like the sky."

I felt something quite simple and quite extraordinary at the same time; something akin to grace. A vast, blissful calmness. A stillness that was, in its immensity, all of a piece and all peace-filled. I had glimpsed such peacefulness only once in my life, as I emerged from the baptismal waters outside our little church in Docena. Then, the touch of hands reaching down for me had kept my mind from completely spacing out. Lama Yeshe never actually touched me, but, I am absolutely convinced, his blessings allowed me to touch, and to taste the richness of, that vast infinity of peace. Years later, I would read Buddhist texts that described that special moment of instruction as the "deep pointing out."

"Okay, dear," Lama was saying. "That's all. Have a good retreat. Lama will be praying for you."

I don't know how long I sat there. When I came back to myself, a nun was walking out of the room carrying some other item of clothing. I thanked Lama Yeshe. He told me again that he would pray for me and that I should remember to relax!

Of course, relaxation was the farthest thing from my mind. I was, after all, a Pisces, determined to *do* anything that I could. Now, with this jewel of a practice, I wanted nothing more than to throw myself completely and wholeheartedly into it. Lama Yeshe flew out of Kathmandu the next day.

At my cozy house in Maharaj-ganj, everything for my Great Seal retreat was in order. Kanchi understood that I could speak to her only sparingly, to give assent or not to meals. She agreed to keep Lakshman busy, making sure that fire-*puja* materials were sufficient and that a fire was prepared at the appropriate time each evening. Under ideal conditions, my retreat began.

Each evening, my retreat practice required that I perform a two-hour fire-offering. To my amazement, Lakshman proved totally inadequate as a firemaker. Perhaps it was the modern fireplace. The first couple of days I demonstrated for him, in silence. Still, it took him a few days to catch on. The practice itself was simple but powerful: I sat on a raised seat before the fire. Within the flames of the fire, I envisioned a squatting, dwarflike deity called Dorje Khandro, with an upturned face and gaping mouth. I made mental offerings to this deity, who is viewed as the great destroyer of negativities.

Next, I thought about all the suffering beings throughout the realms of existence. Thereafter, I visualized taking into myself all those beings' various sufferings in the form of smoky streams that I inhaled, letting them come to rest at my heart-center. After some minutes of such inhalations, I breathed out several times into the mixture of grains and butter that had been prepared beforehand. It was this mixture that I then offered, in ladlefuls, to the gaping mouth of Dorje Khandro, visualized inside the fire. The crackling sounds of the mixture's being consumed by the fire brought the day of meditation to its completion and assured me that countless negativities and situations—whether of harmful emotions or physical ailments, mine as well as those of all other sentient beings— were being purified. It was a very satisfying way to end each day.

Keeping silent has an uncanny way of sharpening one's other senses. During the early days of my meditations, especially during break times, I found my sense of vision in particular to be greatly enhanced. I began to take special notice of the birds that came each day to rest on the wall of my house's compound. Indeed, the wall seemed to be a favorite spot of these tiny blackbirds with bright yellow beaks. One particular morning, early on in my retreat, I noticed that each bird, though of the same species, had its own distinctive face, body, and idiosyncracies. I noticed. I took notice. I was astounded: each was different. I began to take special delight in watching the birds, *seeing* whole families, *seeing* individuals and mates, seeing what they talked about. Lama Yeshe had continually reminded me to relax. I found that relaxing with the birds was a joy

beyond measure. Wasn't this the same bliss the Christian mystics had
spoken of? For the first time, I felt I had some understanding of the great
joy and peace that St. Francis enjoyed with God's creatures. This kind of
peacefulness was not limited to Buddhism.

Then one day during one of my breaks, after I'd been practicing hard
for about two weeks, quite unexpectedly a most tantalizingly blissful
awareness occurred. I was sitting on my bed, looking out of the window.
Thinking about nothing in particular, I noticed that I could see myself
standing on the roof of a house some distance away. I had the strange
sensation that I was not only standing there but that I could also look
back toward the house I was actually in and see myself sitting there. My
mind and body felt completely free and unhindered. My normal seeing
orientation just suddenly, and subtly, shifted. It was no longer anchored
to my physical eyes. I could see myself anywhere I chose, and I could see
anywhere. It felt as though my mind suddenly became immeasurably
vast. It encompassed everything, the very universe, itself. There was no
longer any separation between me and everything else in the universe.
The duality of "subject" and "object" simply dropped away and disappeared. The birds and I were of one essence. I was completely convinced
that I had tasted that ineffable knowledge about which only the saints can
speak. I felt happy, light, ecstatic, completely blissful.

My meditation sessions thereafter became seamless with the rest of
the day. There was no distinction between my meditation periods and my
nonmeditation periods. My awareness was consistently lucid, vast, and
fully attuned to life. Nothing was a distraction any longer because everything was part and parcel of the great encompassment I had directly
experienced. This new way of seeing, and the state of utter bliss it engendered, lasted for several days. Kanchi must have thought I was nuts. I
moved around, silently, with a permanent grin on my face.

Then the bottom dropped out. It was not that the luminous state of
mind departed. Rather, it was that my physical body began to fail me. I
began to notice a sort of dizziness. Later this state turned to one of slight
nausea. My head started to droop and fall forward. I could not look down

or to the side without almost falling over. Things began to spin. Because this was a tantric retreat, it followed the guidelines of earlier Indian practices wherein tantric practitioners, in reversal of traditional religious norms, imbibed forbidden substances: alcohol, meat, fish, and some others. Consequently, for the practice, I was required to sip a tablespoon of *rakshi*, Nepali liquor, at the beginning of each session. Always watchful, Kanchi began to worry. She suggested that perhaps the *rakshi* that I was taking was bad. *"Rakshi karaab, ma'am sahib!"* She strongly encouraged me to discontinue taking it. But I was as stubborn as ever. Taking a sip of *rakshi* was part of the requirements of this retreat, and even though I suspected she might be right, I didn't want to leave off following any of the directions I had been given. Why it didn't occur to me to have Lakshman search out another brand of *rakshi* I don't know. The sickness got progressively worse.

I began to do my meditations propped against the wall. During break times, I literally had to hold my head up with my hands. Kanchi was beside herself with worry. "Please, ma'am *sahib*. Stop this meditating. Your Lama would not want you to suffer so!" But I tried to keep at it.

Sometime, after I'd been suffering like this for a few days, two Tibetans came to the door. I was on break and had decided to sit in a chair downstairs in my living room. Visitors were off-limits, but no one had told these Tibetans that. I recognized one of the men. I had met him in California some years before. He had come to Nepal to visit friends while on his way to Tibet. Not knowing about my retreat but knowing where I lived, he and the other monk had decided to visit me. Kanchi gladly let them in; she wanted me to get help.

I, too, decided that, given my physical condition, I needed to talk to someone, and these teachers were certainly capable of offering me advice. After listening to me and seeing the shape I was in, the two monks counseled with each other. Then one gently spoke: "It seems that you are experiencing what we call '*tsok-loong*,' a type of inner-wind disorder. Because of your strenuous efforts with this Mahamudra practice, your winds have become crossed and entangled. It is a condition that often happens when performing such retreats. Even in Tibet, monks used to make several attempts at this practice before succeeding with it. Also, it can be life-threatening. We suggest that you consult with your guru right away and that, for the time being, you take things very slowly."

I felt like crying. I did cry. Lama Yeshe was far away. I didn't know if I could reach him. But I thought until I could reach him, and until he advised me, I shouldn't break off doing the meditations. Lama had said over and over again that I should relax. I blamed myself. Because of my ambition, my overzealousness, I was suffering. I told myself to just try and take things easier.

Wisely, and weakly, I did manage to scribble a note to Lama Yeshe and asked Lakshman to send it as a telegram to the center in Australia where I hoped Lama would be. I described my symptoms and told him what the two lamas had said. I ended the message with the straightforward, and urgent, question: "What should I do?"

A couple of days after the lamas left, I could not get out of bed. Everything was spinning all the time. I could no longer walk on my own. Even Lakshman had become concerned. When Kanchi arrived, I called her upstairs. "Have Lakshman go for the American doctor, Kanchi. Ask him to come right away." I could see the relief in Kanchi's face as she ran from the room screaming, "Lakshman! Ho, Lakshman!"

Hours went by. Miserable, I lay helpless on my bed. I heard the ring of Lakshman's bicycle bell. Then Kanchi's angry rejoinders. Lakshman had not found the doctor in. He had waited, but he'd never returned. But Lakshman had not left a note or message for the doctor. Kanchi was furious. When she came up to report Lakshman's incompetence, I found myself trying to soothe her: "Tomorrow," I told her, "I'll send Lakshman with a note and forbid him to return without the doctor. If he's not at his office, Lakshman should go to his house." The American doctor lived somewhere in Maharaj-ganj; it could not be too far from my house. I made it through one more night.

The next day around noon, Chad, the doctor taking care of American AID people and other American officials in Nepal, came to my house. When he observed my condition and listened to my symptoms, he made two recommendations. The first was to stop doing the retreat. I told him I didn't think so. The second was to begin taking that most dreadful stuff, Flagyl, for amoebic dysentery.

"But I don't have dysentery!" I whined. "I just can't hold my head up."

"Nevertheless," he said, it was still indicated.

I took the Flagyl, and for the next day and a half literally crawled into my bathroom and threw up globs of red stuff that looked like stewed tomatoes. The dizziness and weakness continued.

I stopped trying to sit. Chad began dropping by in the evenings on his way home. In spite of the Flagyl misprescription, we became friends. He didn't have a clue about what was happening to me, but I enjoyed his company.

I was a little more than halfway through my Great Seal retreat. I had had incredible experiences and had gained actual insights in a really short time. Perhaps if my desire for success had not been so all-consuming, I might have done better.

One day, feeling slightly better when I woke up, I determined to move from my bedroom into the adjoining room where I'd set up my altar and where I meditated. I would stay here permanently. I would meditate when I could. A part of me resigned myself to the idea that I might very well die here, as well. This Joy of the Dharma, I mused, was anything but joyous now. A little while later, Kanchi came running upstairs with a telegram. It was from Lama Yeshe. Trembling and weak, I took out the typed note from its envelope. Its message read: "Health most important. Stop retreat!"

Seeing those words, I finally really broke down. Perhaps the retreat had been too much of a strain. At any rate, my sickness certainly pushed it over the edge. Stopping the sessions altogether, slowly, slowly I regained some steadiness. I still could not walk well on my own. And I found Chad's advice not to move very fast—"No bicycles or taxi rides!"—to be, in fact, very helpful.

Years after my Great Seal retreat, I discovered that I am allergic to the sulfates in liquor. Taking a tablespoon of *rakshi* six times a day had been slowly but surely poisoning me. Yet I believe the diagnosis offered by my two Tibetan visitors was more on the mark. Tibetan Buddhist medical theory says that the root of all sickness, whether of body or mind, is holding too rigidly to the self. The mental poisons that arise from this grasping are the harmful emotions of ignorance, hatred, and desire. The physical ones are closely related and are, therefore, also classified into three main divisions: a disharmony of bile is said to be caused by hatred; of phlegm, by ignorance; and a disharmony of wind energy is caused by desire. During that retreat, desire was clearly my problem. Though Lama Yeshe had constantly encouraged me to take it easy, I had gone after the goal of the practice with greediness and with a vengeance. Telling myself it was a tantric and, therefore, speedy practice, I went for overnight results. It was like getting my Buddhist name—stubbornly, on one knee—all over again. How many times had I heard Lama say, "Be gentle with yourself, with your mind and your body. If you are gentle with yourself, then you can be truly gentle with others"? How many times, as we meditated together, had he counseled, "Let go, dear. Just let go"? The point was to let the drives and the worries go, to let the ambitions go.

Tantric Buddhism offers methods for transformation, but change doesn't happen overnight. It is a gradual process. When I look back at myself, at the timid and insecure self that first arrived before Lama Yeshe, I can clearly see how I have changed, how I have become less fearful and more confident and capable. These changes occurred in small increments and over some time. The point is to allow them to happen, without grasping and attachment; to have faith that positive change will come and, in the meantime, to try to be gentle with yourself. It was like this for all the Buddhas throughout the ages. They were each, at the beginning of their journeys, beings just like us: tossed and pummeled by ordinary fears, worries, and insecurities. And yet, with steady and patient practice, they each became Awakened Ones. They have given us a model of moderation to follow. If we practice as they did, who knows? We might just become the next Buddhas.

One Woman's Liberation

When I reflect upon the fifteen years during which Lama Yeshe was my teacher, it seems clear that his personal mission with respect to me was to build my confidence. He wanted me to realize and understand that, like everyone, in my innermost core I was pure, intelligent, compassionate, and powerful. He sought to help me manifest that understanding. Lama Yeshe often said that low self-esteem and lack of confidence were the main traits he observed among the hundreds of Western students that flocked to him. I was not only one of Lama's earliest students; I was one of the ones that fit that bill perfectly. Some of the reasons are clearly cultural and racial: being a black American, a woman, from the South, and an African American woman interested in Buddhism. There are lots of reasons why, when I first met Lama Yeshe at the age of twenty-one, I was a less-than-confident human being in the world. Throughout the course of my relationship with him, I see his primary efforts as having been directed toward having me manifest the qualities of confidence, pride, strength, and capability that he knew I possessed.

Lama Yeshe used to tell me that I should not hide so much. He'd say, "You should be *beautiful* in the world, and *strong!*" I vividly recall taking him to hear a lecture by [the radical black activist] Angela Davis once when he was visiting California. She was speaking at the University of California, Santa Cruz, in the outdoor amphitheater on campus. Lama Yeshe was visibly excited to see and to listen to Davis speak. Several times during her talk, with clenched fists, he said aloud, "This is how one ought to be: strong and confident, like this lady!" He absolutely loved her. And for a number of weeks after that, he would say to me—never as a put-down but just as a *reminder*—"You should be strong, like this woman! You should show *your* beauty and *your* strength to the world!"

Lam called me daughter. I assumed that he called any number of other single women daughter as well. But I know that he thought of me, in some way, as being special. His mission was to make me feel that specialness, too, and to teach me to trust my own power.

There is a vast gulf between "different" and "special." My mother had seen me as being different; Lama Yeshe saw me as being special. And special means loved for one's self alone, for one's core, which is ultimately pure, wise, compassionate, and powerful. Lama Yeshe knew this about me, as he knew it about *all* beings. And this is what genuine teachers do: they love us without reservation because they truly see us as precious, each in our own right—as nothing less than Buddhas. The wonder is that if someone whom you trust and admire views you in this way, even *you* begin to feel that way; and with continued reminders, you begin to see *yourself* in this way.

In my case, several reminders were necessary. Sometimes they came in the form of embarrassing public episodes; other times, they came in private moments of validation that touched me deeply.

When I was in Nepal in 1980—now as Professor Jan Willis—Lama Yeshe asked me to give a lecture one evening to a group of Westerners gathered at Kopan for the annual monthlong retreat course there. I gave a talk on the life and philosophical views of Asanga, the fourth-century A.D. founder of the Yogacara school of Mahayana Buddhism. In the course of my remarks, I mentioned that some texts say that Asanga's mother had been cursed to be born a woman. Immediately following my talk, a group of women attending the retreat bombarded me. One said, "We *heard* that—that she was cursed to be a woman! And we hear that there are some other Buddhist texts that say we can't attain enlightenment in a woman's form. What do you say about all of this?" I responded, "Oh, come on, now. Just look at Lama Yeshe; look at your own experience. Have you ever experienced that?" But the rumblings I'd stirred up must have continued.

Some days after that, Lama Yeshe and I were having lunch together and having a discussion about the set of life stories I was then translating. At some point we walked out together onto the upper deck of the monastery. From that vantage point, we were looking down onto the front courtyard, where we could see the entrance to the *gompa* as well as Kopan's library and the mailroom down below. There were a number of Western students milling about in the courtyard, on a break from the day's activities. Suddenly, Lama Yeshe grabbed my arm and began calling out to all of them below. In a booming voice, he called, "Look, all of you! Look! Look! You want to see women's liberation? *This* is"—pointing at me and patting me on the shoulders—"this *is* women's liberation! *This is* women's liberation!"

Now, for me, this was both a very wonderful moment and a very awkward and humbling one. I was bending down and trying to get away from everyone's gaze and from Lama Yeshe as he held me there, patting me on the shoulder and telling all of them that I was women's liberation. As he was bellowing my accomplishments, I was saying, "No, no, Lama, please no, don't say this; please don't say this!" And he was smiling the whole time. Even though that particular occasion was embarrassing to me, it seemed to cause Lama Yeshe a good deal of happiness; and it also seemed to make everyone else feel good.

While Lama's claim about me was pure hyperbole, his pride in me was genuine. Thus, his showing me off was completely unlike those moments I'd experienced when I'd been paraded in front of and made to perform before white superintendents at my all-black elementary school, occasions that left me only with feelings of anger and resentment. As a child, I had been shown off because I was smart; but when Lama Yeshe showed me off it was a loving way of helping me to heal a long list of old wounds: my mother calling me evil, the white superintendents' amazement at a black child's intelligence, the sense of the dire mistake I'd committed by solving my sister's math problem, the humiliation I'd later suffered because I couldn't spell, going to college amid Klan threats, and the bogus idea that universities were lowering their standards in order to let in black students.

It was as if Lama Yeshe were saying, "Let the old wounds go, daughter. Let them all go." Standing there with him, for the first time in my life I began to feel that I could let them go; let them all go and embrace my true self, which was, like the true selves of all other beings, clean, clear, capable, loving, and lovable. At that moment, confidence arose strongly in me, and I knew that everyone ought to feel this way.

From the very beginning, Lama Yeshe had pointed out and celebrated my intelligence. During that first year when Randy, Rob, and I lived and studied with him at Kopan, he would sometimes say to me, "You see. I tell you one thing, and immediately you make five!" Unsure of his meaning initially, I asked, "Is that bad, Lama Yeshe?" "Of course not!" he responded. "It is very *good*! It means that your mind is quick! That is very good, dear." After that, to make the same point, he would hold up his hand and spread his fingers for emphasis. Because I so admired Lama Yeshe's own intelligence and because when I'd first met him I already considered myself to be quite a serious student of Buddhism, this kind of validation was especially important to me. Lama Yeshe continually encouraged me that it was okay to be smart. In fact, over the course of the fifteen years that I was his student, he treated me more like a colleague.

Two years before I gave that talk at Kopan, Lama had privately given me his seal of approval in a way that was so powerful it still moves me today. I had been offered a visiting appointment at Wesleyan for the academic year of 1977–78. Lama Yeshe and I had been discussing this when he mentioned to me that he would himself like to try out the university experience. Though the University of California, Santa Cruz, where I had been teaching had never had an enrobed lama on its faculty, as it turned out, it was a fairly simple matter to have them hire Lama Yeshe to replace me for a quarter's term. He would teach only one of my courses, and it was, appropriately, "Tibetan Buddhism." So, during the academic year of 1977–78 I taught at Wesleyan while Lama Yeshe taught at UCSC during the spring quarter. Now, the academic year at Wesleyan ended before the spring quarter at UCSC, so Lama Yeshe invited me to come out and to give a guest lecture in *his* class during the last week of the term. Though I had given lots of guest lectures in numerous settings, that particular occasion will forever stand out in my mind.

Lama Yeshe briefly introduced me to the class, then took a seat among the students. I gave a lecture that compared the sacred life stories (called *nam-thar* in Tibetan) of two of the most famous Buddhist yogis, Naropa and Milarepa. I began by first writing the term *nam-thar* on the blackboard in Tibetan. The students seemed impressed by the beauty of the script as well as by my general remarks concerning how such spiritual biographies work to impart, in narrative and aesthetic form, the essence of practice. I proceeded to narrate each of the yogis' lives—with all the facial, hand, and body gestures that I am famous for—and then to compare and contrast certain details of the stories. The time flew by; I was in my element. When I finished, the hundred or so students gave me a standing ovation. Just before the class's question-and-answer period, Lama Yeshe beckoned me over to him. He was beaming like a proud father. When I leaned near to him I could see that tears were streaming down his cheeks. Lifting his robe to partially cover his face, he whispered to me, "Lama is *so very proud* of you!" I thought my heart would burst wide open. It seemed at that moment that *this* was the assurance I had been waiting for all my life.

Another story that stands out in my mind is Lama Yeshe's asking me to teach him Western philosophy. Sister Max, an African American woman who took nun's ordination in the 1970s and became his special aide, called me early in 1983 and said that Lama wanted me to arrange a brief course for him. When I asked, "Why me?" Max said, "Because Lama knows you've studied Western philosophy as well as Buddhism and he knows you're a great teacher!" I was flattered no end. It was decided that we would have to conduct the private tutorial in the summer after Lama had completed teaching the monthlong retreat course at Vajrapani Institute in California.

That particular trip turned out to be Lama's last teaching tour in the States; he died early in March of the next year. What happened during our mini-summer course together was absolutely remarkable. Lama

Yeshe set aside one month in which just he and I met each day for three hours—from 9:00 A.M. till noon—six days a week, and I led him through a course in Western philosophy.

He had asked me to prepare a short anthology of selections for him. He wanted to learn about key Western philosophers and their major ideas by actually reading their works directly and then discussing them. In keeping with his request, I prepared a little booklet that contained important arguments from the giants of Western thought, selections of roughly four to five pages in length, all in English. I called the booklet "From the Pre-Socratics to Wittgenstein."

I had done my best to design a good, short survey course for Lama. But once we actually started, *he* did most of the work. He carefully read each of the selections and then responded to them with a mind that was so quick and so incisive I simply marveled.

For example, I would have provided Lama Yeshe with a passage from Plato that discussed his notion of ideal forms. For the *next* day, there would be a piece by Aristotle, wherein Aristotle refuted Plato's claim. Most Westerners know about this famous philosophical debate. Namely, Plato made a claim for ideal forms, what we later came to call "universals." But Aristotle subsequently pointed out, in rebuttal to Plato, that universals did not exist in the world but could only be demonstrated in, and through, particulars. Therefore, Plato's concept of ideal forms was, logically speaking, erroneous; universality is only an ideal construct that lacks logical proof; only particulars manifest in the world. Now, *before* ever having read Aristotle's response, in our morning discussion of Plato, Lama Yeshe began right away by saying that he strongly objected to the argument. And in explaining his reasons for doing so, he argued *precisely* in the way that Aristotle did. As soon as he had understood what these philosophers were saying, he could immediately see the faults in their arguments. And I got to witness a demonstration of his incisive philosophical acumen day after day after day. The fact that Lama Yeshe wanted to spend hours studying Western philosophy—at a time when his health was so rapidly failing—was amazing in its own right. He believed that if he understood the philosophical underpinnings of Western thought, then he'd understand where his students were coming from and could better communicate with and teach them.

That summer was also great because, for a solid month, there was just Lama Yeshe and me working together—one to one—every morning. Afterward, we would be joined by Aye, Lama's Danish personal attendant, for lunch. After our three hours of discussing philosophy, Lama Yeshe would go out to his garden—he always gardened wherever he was—and pick some chives, onions, or other vegetables and then come in and cook lunch. It was a time of incredible closeness.

As our monthlong tutorial neared its end, one extremely touching moment occurred which I alone witnessed. One morning when I arrived for our class, Lama was lying on the couch. He appeared totally exhausted. Aye was off that particular day. When I entered, Lama raised his arm with effort and held out a set of keys. By this time, his heart condition was getting a great deal worse. Though none of us knew it then, he would be with us only a few months more. He said to me, "A lady stopped by earlier this morning, a generous older student. She has a house on the ocean down south. Please take me there."

He had already packed a tiny knapsack. When I helped him to his feet, he handed me a scribbled map to the house.

We drove south for fifteen or twenty minutes before turning right onto a dirt road that headed off directly toward the ocean. We found the woman's house and with her keys entered it. The house was gorgeous, a two-storied structure covered in bougainvillea, tucked away behind palm and Japanese coastal trees, private, quiet, and serene. It stood just above the cliffs overlooking the blue ocean. Her living room walls, on two sides, were constructed completely of glass. The view was breathtaking. It appeared that Lama Yeshe had been here before. He told me that he was going upstairs, to "his room," to lie down and that I should call him at lunchtime.

After a couple of hours went by, I pulled together a meager lunch with the vegetables and fruits I found at the house. Then I tiptoed up the outside steps that led to the room Lama Yeshe had entered. I really didn't want to wake him; I hoped that he was getting some rest. But I thought he might also need some food. I tapped lightly on his door. No answer. Then I began to wonder whether he might be meditating or, worse, really sick. I tapped again. No answer. I pushed open the door.

What I witnessed then was at the same time a great relief and a searingly poignant moment. Lama Yeshe hadn't heard me knock because he was already up and in the bathroom washing up for lunch. That was a relief! Then I noticed the room. In the foreground was Lama's bed, which was set against another wall of glass overlooking the ocean. On it was his tiny knapsack, opened; and on one of the pillows of the bed was the little philosophy booklet I had prepared for him. It was turned to the selection on Feuerbach that we would be discussing the next day. Lama had been reading and underlining key passages with a yellow marker.

I have been fortunate indeed to have had such a close relationship with Lama Yeshe for almost fifteen years, to have received incredibly profound teachings from him and, near the end of his life, to have enjoyed such a special time with him. He was a true master of *empowerment,* not just of the formalized rituals lamas perform, but of genuine empowerment. Though we all possess innate purity, clarity, strength, and potential to be infinitely wise and compassionate beings, still we need *someone* to encourage us and to show us how to manifest those qualities. Lama Yeshe directly helped me to do this in ways great and small.

I have also been fortunate in other ways. Though my own family was poor, my parents, my sister, and I were close-knit and loving. In spite of that memorable and damaging remark, I know that my mother loved me without bounds, as most parents love their children. My father still refers to me as "daughter," with pride. In my case, however, it took a gentle Tibetan lama who also called me "daughter"—and who lived thousands of miles away from Docena, Alabama—to help me to understand and appreciate the preciousness of familial love. Both Lama Yeshe and my mother have now passed away. Yet because of their love, I now know that spiritual liberation is a true possibility.

Perhaps a Buddhist After All

It was the kind of slow-motion thing that you see in movies. My car was skidding, swerving out of control on the slush and ice of a highway recently plowed—but not recently enough. I was returning from Boston, trying to get back home to Middletown before the big snow-and-ice storm forecasted for later that afternoon arrived. Now I knew that I should have taken my hosts' advice and stayed in Boston.

The storm had been the delight of weather forecasters for days, and I did not want to be caught in those treacherous driving conditions that had been their theme all week. Leaving Boston on the Mass Pike around 7:00 A.M., things had seemed all right. I put on some music and applauded myself for making the right decision. After driving for about an hour, the flurries began. It was a beautiful thing, snow; and I'd soon be home. By the time I turned off onto I–84, the roads were getting bad. Attempting to calm myself, I determined that if I slowed down, keeping ample space between my car and the ones in front of me, I'd still make it okay.

Then suddenly I saw things from the perspective of an observer. The car was spinning out. It turned almost sideways then, suddenly, righted itself. Then it began to slide toward the center guardrails. I silently mused, "So, this is how it is. Just like that, one's last moments." Images of my father and sister flashed by. No time to say anything to them. I saw the guardrails rushing toward me. The car would hit them in the next second and that would be it.

A booming *OM MANI PADME HUM!* woke me up. I was screaming the mantra at the top of my lungs. I saw myself leaning forward, clutching the steering wheel so tightly that my knuckles were white. My car had moved back into the tracks of the middle lane. I don't know how it got there. In less than a split-second, it had simply jumped back into the tracks of the lane, as if some giant invisible hand had snapped it up and placed it down again.

I looked to my rearview mirror. Behind me, cars were braking and swerving. They had been attempting to stop as they saw me careening into the guardrail. I said another few *OM MANI*s for them while I held tightly to my steering wheel.

As I continued on, now moving very slowly, I thought more about that near brush with death—how quickly our treasured selves can be extinguished; how fragile life really is. And I thought about how surprisingly that booming *OM MANI* had come out of me, in what I thought was my last moment of this life. It is the mantra of Avalokitesvara, the Buddha of Compassion. I regularly intoned it whenever I passed a dead animal on the highway, to wish it peace and blessings. Perhaps in those compressed seconds I saw myself as a dead animal. The best I can figure, however, is that it was the shortest prayer I knew. What went along with it, I think, was the wish not to be separated from Lama Yeshe in whatever future rebirth. Perhaps I was a Buddhist after all.

Chapter VII

. . . .

In Search of
Women's Wisdom

Tsultrim Allione

Coming from a family legacy of strong women, Tsultrim Allione (b. 1948) had the confidence to venture in directions that few girls of her age dreamed of. Her grandmother gave the fifteen-year-old Allione a book of Zen poetry, which awakened her interest in Buddhism. At the age of nineteen, on a trip to India, Allione encountered Tibetan Buddhism, then in the first stage of its disapora. Venerated lamas were available to instruct her personally, as they would not have been before (or later). In 1970 she was ordained a Buddhist nun, and in the simple and peaceful rhythms of a nun's life she could, she felt, conquer emotional poisons like jealousy and anger. A few years later she returned her nun's robes because she wanted to have a family, which turned out to be a humbling experience. The emotional turmoil reemerged as she tried to practice amid the circus of daily distractions (carpools, mortgages, a suburban house in need of repair) and, with four small children, never having a full night's sleep. She understood what the poet Milton meant when he said that he could not approve a "cloistered virtue": It was during this period that her practice "deepened into reality."

The list of Allione's teachers reads like a roll-call of the legends of contemporary Tibetan Buddhism: the Dalai Lama, the Sixteenth Karmapa, Dudjom Rinpoche, Dilgo Khyentse, Khamptrul Rinpoche, Lama Yeshe,

Chögyam Trungpa, and Namkhai Norbu. But Allione wanted something they could not teach her: the hidden, submerged stream of feminism in Buddhism. Eventually she wrote Women of Wisdom *(1984), recounting the lives of six female Tibetan mystics, to provide exemplars who could inspire women of her generation. Although the "sacred feminine principle"—or just the feminine principle—may be difficult to describe, Allione observes that it was blatantly absent from the 9/11 terrorist attacks on the World Trade Center or, for that matter, from the Bush administration's response to them.*

In India Allione had idly daydreamed about finding some place in her own country where Americans could practice as profoundly as the old Tibetans once did. In 1993, she acquired five hundred acres in southwest Colorado, which she renamed Tara Mandala and established as a retreat center. In 2001, with her children grown, Allione was able to go on a year-long, solitary retreat. She was quite sick at the time, but after a few months in retreat she felt the plants were speaking to her—not in words, of course—and she intuited which plants would (and in fact did) heal her. If among the leaders of western Buddhism women are now as numerous as men, Tsultrim Allione is one of the pioneering figures who helped usher in this development.

I

In June 1967, when I was nineteen, my friend from the University of Colorado and spiritual sister, Victress Hitchcock, and I flew from San Francisco to Hong Kong to join her parents, who were in the diplomatic corps in Calcutta. We traveled by boat from Hong Kong to Bombay, and there we were taken ashore by small boats, which left us at the bottom of a long flight of wide stone steps. As I walked up these steps I felt that I had finally arrived in a place where I could find true wisdom.

We stayed with Victress's parents in Calcutta for the monsoon. Her father was the Consul General in Calcutta, and his wife, Maxine, arranged for us to work as volunteers at Mother Teresa's "Orphanage and Home for Unwed Mothers." They hoped that this kind of work would get the fantasies of the "Mystic East" out of our heads and set us on a more acceptable path, but then they sent us to Kathmandu to work with Tibetan refugees.

One day, as we were exploring the upper stories of a house in Kathmandu, we went out onto a balcony, and in the distance I saw a small hill at the top of which was a white dome topped by a golden spire. It looked like something from a fairy tale, glittering invitingly in the bright sunlight. We were told that this was called "The Monkey Temple" as it was inhabited by wild monkeys; but its real name was Swayambhu, which means "self-sprung." This small hill topped with a cluster of temples and a huge Tibetan stupa is sacred to both the Nepalese and the Tibetans. We were told that during the summer there were predawn processions from Kathmandu to Swayambhu and we decided to try to get up early enough to join one of these.

We rose the next day long before dawn and, when we stumbled bleary-eyed into the streets, we joined in a very bizarre parade consisting of Nepalese of all ages screaming songs and making noise with anything they had on hand from battered trumpets to tin drums. We were told that all this noise was to wake up the gods so that they would not forget to make the rice grow. We walked through the narrow stone and dirt streets of the city over a bridge and then up to the base of the hill, where we began a steep ascent.

We staggered up the hundreds of stone steps hardly aware of the ancient stone Buddhas, prayer flags and wild monkeys that surrounded us. It was beginning to get hot even at that hour. We were breathless and sweating as we stumbled up the last steep steps and practically fell upon the biggest vajra (thunderbolt scepter) that I have ever seen. Behind this vajra was the vast, round, white dome of the stupa, like a full solid skirt, at the top of which were two giant Buddha eyes wisely looking out over the peaceful valley which was just beginning to come alive. We wandered around this stupa amidst the singing, banging Nepalese and the humming Tibetans who were circumambulating the stupa spinning the prayer wheels which line the lower portion of the round dome.

We were just catching our breath when several six-foot-long horns emerged from the adjacent Tibetan monastery and started to make an unbelievable sound. It is a long, deep, whirring, haunting wail that takes you out somewhere beyond the highest Himalayan peaks and at the same time back into your mother's womb.

I was so moved by this place that I took a small hut on the neighboring hill, Kimdol, and began to rise very early in the morning and make the rounds of the Tibetan monasteries on Swayambhu hill as they were chanting their morning rituals and having their first cups of Tibetan tea. There was one monastery which attracted me particularly. It was the one right near the stupa, and I used to linger there, sitting in an out-of-the-way corner at the back of the temple. One day I arrived early in the morning as usual and found they had left a little carpet there for me to sit on and a cup of the morning tea. From that day onward the little carpet was always waiting for me, and one of the monks, Gyalwa, who became my friend, always made sure I had tea.

It was as if the monks understood my bond with the place and the irresistible pull I felt from the stupa. As I sat there I felt as though part of myself, which had up until then remained empty, was being filled. A joyful sense of being in the blessings which were almost tangibly present began to steal over me. Although I had no intellectual reference points for this experience, later, after years of formal training in meditation, I realized that this was "beginner's mind,"* and that the direct connection with the "bliss waves"† sent forth by great lamas held the secret of my search.

*"Beginner's mind" is a term used by Shunryu Suzuki in his book *Zen Mind, Beginner's Mind*.
† The Tibetan word for these splendor waves or waves of divine grace is *jin lab* (*byin labs*); the Sanskrit is *adhishtana*. They are a very important part of the transmission received from one's guru and lineage.

One cannot force or grasp a spiritual experience, because it is as delicate as the whisper of the wind. But one can purify one's motivation, one's body, and train oneself to cultivate it. Because we come from a culture which teaches us that there is always something external to be obtained which will lead us to fulfillment, we lose contact with our innate wisdom. As the Indian Tantric Buddhist saint Saraha says in one of his *dohas* (poems expressing the essence of his understanding):

> Though the house-lamps have been lit,
> The blind live on in the dark.
> Though spontaneity is all-encompassing
> And close, to the deluded it remains
> Always far away.

Beyond the profound impressions of the land and the sacred power places I visited, I also met several significant people who made profound impressions on me. After moving to Kimdol I met a Japanese traveler, Sawamura, who had been living with the Tibetans. He was traveling to northwestern India to see the Dalai Lama and invited me to go with him. So we traveled third class without tickets and hitch-hiked all the way across northern India, stopping at various Tibetan refugee camps or staying with hospitable Indians on our way.

When we arrived in Dharamsala, the Dalai Lama's headquarters, he went to stay in a monastery with two lamas, Geshe Rabten and Gonsar Tulku. I, as a woman, had to stay down in the town. I had almost no money, so I stayed in a room made out of flattened kerosene tins papered with old newspapers. I had no sleeping bag, and since it was November it was already freezing at night in the mountains. I bought a blanket and a piece of cloth of equal size, sewed them together and stuffed the middle with newspapers. But the wind still whistled through the walls, and the rats who shared my room chose to move around at night, so I began to get up at four in the morning to circumambulate the Dalai Lama's residence with the devoted Tibetans who did this before beginning their work day. I had never been happier in my life.

After several weeks, Sawamura came and told me that there was a fasting ceremony beginning the next day which we could attend. I decided to do this, not realizing that we would not only fast, eating only once in two days, but we would also be doing thousands of prostrations on the freezing floor every few hours and hardly sleeping at all.

After five days I was called for an appointment with a high lama whom I had requested to see about studying mandala painting. He told me it would take at least a year to learn one mandala, and then at the end of my interview he said to me that the time I spent doing spiritual practice was the only time which would have any lasting value. This now seems obvious to me, but as I had no understanding of the path at that time, this statement struck me and I thought about it for a long time. Someone else said to me during this period: "Cut off your hair, hang it on the wall and contemplate impermanence." As I was only nineteen and had lived all of my life in America, I had never thought much about death, but had rather lived as though I were immortal. These two statements planted the seeds for what was to follow and I contemplated them when I returned to the West.

With the Tibetans I found a living esoteric tradition that had been carefully transmitted from teacher to disciple, without interruption, for centuries. The Tibetans also had an intelligence and a sense of joy and humor that I had never encountered before. After six months in India we returned to Nepal, and as my parents had sent me a ticket I decided to return to the West. When I was on my way to the airport, Gyalwa, my friend from the Swayambhu monastery, appeared at a crossroads in Kathmandu. He pressed a string of mantra beads made of bodhi seeds and a picture of Swayambhu hill into my hands. It was as if he knew that these would help to bring me back to what I had discovered there.

When I was back in the United States I recited the mantras I had learned from the Tibetans using this string of beads. This helped me to keep in contact with the blessings of the Tibetan lamas, but I was still homesick for "my mountain." Though I tried to fulfill my parents' wishes and go back to school, I was miserable.

After a year I managed to get to a Tibetan meditation center called Samye Ling in Scotland. The day I arrived, I heard that the abbot of the place, Chōgyam Trungpa Rinpoche,* was to return from the hospital where he had been recovering from a car accident. I had imagined he would be a wise-looking old man, so when I saw him I was shocked to see a youthful, handsome Tibetan, who was still badly paralyzed from his accident.

I did not have any contact with Trungpa Rinpoche for several months, because he was still too weak to receive people and he was surrounded by a group of very possessive disciples. When I finally did meet him, it was quite funny and wonderful.

I was scheduled for an official "interview," which was something I had never experienced before. I told the people organizing the interviews that I had no idea what to say to him, but they assured me that I need not worry, for he would start the conversation. So I went into the room and sat timidly on the floor in front of his chair and looked at him. He did not say anything; nor did I. We stayed like that for about forty-five minutes.

Now I realize that what happened was some kind of mind-to-mind transmission, but at the time I only knew that I had experienced something that was completely beyond words and form. It reminded me of some of the experiences I had had sitting near the stupa at Swayambhu. It was an experience of space that extended outward without any reference back. This space was luminous and bliss-provoking, a release, similar to, but beyond, sexual orgasm. When I emerged everyone was eager to know what he had said and I had to respond, "Nothing!"

Trungpa Rinpoche was still not teaching formally, nor was Akong Rinpoche, the other lama there, so, when I heard of a Volkswagen bus which would be taking passengers from London to Kathmandu for a minimal fee, I leapt at the chance. Before I left, Trungpa Rinpoche gave me permission to take a copy of "The Sadhana of All the Siddhis," a

* Rinpoche is a title for a Tibetan teacher. It means "precious jewel."

Tantric practice he had written in Bhutan in 1968 while in retreat in the
cave of Tatsang. This *sadhana** was the most evocative and poetic piece of
writing I had ever read. Part of it was an invocation to various incarnations of the great Karmapa, the leader of the Kagyu sect of Tibetan
Buddhism.

I read this sadhana as often as possible during my overland journey
from London to Kathmandu. The trip was tortuous. In Afghanistan there
were days and days of dirt roads so dusty that even when we closed all
the windows and wrapped clothes around our faces, the dust penetrated.
There were eight people of five different nationalities in the bus, which
during the trip had two completely new engines, numerous repairs, and
had to be towed two hundred miles at night over icy roads in the mountains of Turkey. We pulled into Kathmandu just before Christmas in
1969, after six weeks of continuous travel.

I went to Swayambhu and immediately noticed a hubbub of activity
and an incredible assortment of monks, yogis with long matted hair, and
Tibetans in an assortment of regional costumes. I learned that this was
because His holiness the Karmapa had come to Kathmandu for the first
time in thirteen years. He was staying at the monastery near the stupa
which I had visited every morning during my first visit to Nepal. I was a
bit put off by all the pomp and pageantry and the pushy Tibetan crowds,
but then something inexplicable started to happen to me. I started to feel
very agitated and was unable to eat or sleep much. I knew I had to make
a connection with someone there. Of course the obvious person was the
Karmapa, but perversely I was sure it was someone else. I went around
for several days looking for signs, becoming more and more agitated.
Then one day I was reading through the sadhana Trungpa Rinpoche had
given me and noticed the continual references to Karmapa. Suddenly it
dawned on me that it was obviously an auspicious coincidence that I had
arrived in Kathmandu at the same time as his visit and that he was there
in "my monastery." At the same time I came across a line in the sadhana

* A *sadhana* is a complete Tantric practice involving the invocation of and visualization of a particular Tantric deity or deities, the recitation of a mantra, etc.

which said: "The only offering I can make is to follow your example." Since he was a monk it was clear to me that I should follow his example and take the robes.

I went directly to the monastery on Swayambhu and, disregarding all the usual prostrations and formalities, walked in, offered him some flowers and indicated that I wanted to cut off my hair.* He laughed and then gave me a look I shall never forget. It was as though he was seeing everything: the past, the present and the future. Then he nodded his head and asked me to sit down. Through a primitive translation it was decided that I was to be ordained a week later in Bodhgaya, where the Buddha had reached full illumination under the bodhi tree.

I was given my ordination on the day of the full moon in January 1970, by the Karmapa in the presence of the four major *tulkus* in the Kagyu lineage. I was told by the Karmapa's translator that before I had come to him in Kathmandu he had seen me in a crowd and had said that I would become a nun and that I had been his disciple in a previous lifetime. He had therefore waived the usual preliminary stages and had given me ordination immediately. It was at this time that I was given the name Karma Tsultrim Chodron, which means "Discipline Torch of Dharma in the Lineage of Karmapa." I began to be called this by the Tibetans, and when I eventually returned to the West, although I could have changed back to my Western name, I decided to carry on using my Tibetan name. I wanted to be continually reminded of the change that had taken place in my life and to be connected to the blessings of the Karmapa. Now, fourteen years later, my previous name, Joan Rousmaniere Ewing, sounds foreign to me, and I feel more comfortable with the name Tsultrim, even though it sounds a bit odd to Western ears and I often have to explain it.

After my ordination I returned to Kathmandu. There I discovered that I had a serious case of hepatitis and had to go to bed immediately. Two American friends, Pamela Crawford and John Travis, took me in to their

---

* The shaving of one's hair is symbolic of the renunciation of wordly life and becoming a monk or nun. When the Buddha left his princely life he shaved his head to symbolize this renunciation.

house, and as I was lying there very light-headed from the fever, my Tibetan friend Gyalwa appeared and gave me some Tibetan medicine which made me feel better almost immediately. A few days later an American woman, Zeina Rachevsky, who had taken the robes from His Holiness the Dalai Lama, arrived and insisted that I go to stay in her house on Kopan hill, near the Baudha Stupa. I stayed there for six months and was helped and supported by Lama Thupten Yeshe and the young Sherpa Lama Thupten Zopa. At that time there were only three Westerners and these lamas at Kopan. Since that time it has become an international meditation center and these lamas teach all over the world.

When I was strong enough I went up into the mountains with them and spent six weeks near Lama Zopa's cave, from which we had a view of Mount Everest. We were actually living in the clouds at 16,000 feet. We used to dig out little U-shaped places in which to meditate in the side of the mountain and pass our days there.

When I returned to Kathmandu I decided to move to Swayambhu and to begin to study Tibetan. Gyalwa found me a room right next to the stupa which was so small that I could sit in the middle and touch all the walls. Here I cooked, studied, slept and meditated. My lessons started at 6:30 A.M. I was taught by two other nuns, who had a rigorous meditation schedule and had only this time to teach me.

My room was like a little tree house. The windows opened onto some huge old trees. Living so near the stupa I came to know its life, day and night and through the seasons. What happened around the stupa was a condensation of the magical religious life and festivals of both the Nepalese and the Tibetans.

After a year in Nepal I went to India and went to see Karmapa in Sikkim. He said he had been watching me, and I felt so close to him that when it came time to leave I cried for a whole day. I had never felt this kind of grief before and I was inconsolable. But when I did leave and went to Bodhgaya, and to Sarnath where the Buddha first turned the wheel of the Dharma, and then onto Tashi Jong and Manali, I felt his presence constantly.

In Manali I decided to enter a long retreat in order to complete the *ngondro* (preliminary practices) and began formal training under the guidance of the great married yogi Abo Rinpoche. Previously I had been relating to my meditation in a rather unorthodox way. I had had several initiations and had done these practices, but mostly I had been reading *The Song of Mahamudra* by Tilopa and trying to practice in this way:

Do nought with the body but relax,
Shut firm the mouth and silent remain,
Empty your mind and think of nought.
Like a hollow bamboo
Rest at ease your body.
Giving not nor taking.
Put your mind at rest.
Mahamudra is like a mind that clings to nought.
Thus practicing, in time you will reach Buddhahood.

While I was doing this practice I met another Western nun, and when she asked me what practices I did, I said mostly Mahamudra. She was horrified as this is supposed to be a very advanced practice, and she told me I must do all the preliminaries first. I was swayed by her and I began with the preliminary practices and then continued with various tantric visualization practices with mantra recitation and so on for the next eight years. Up until then I had had my own personal way of approaching the teachings, and at this point I entered into "the system," so to speak. Previously I had had direct contacts with Karmapa in dreams and visions in which he gave me specific teachings and initiations. After this it became harder and more forced, and my dreams and visions became fewer and fewer over the years; but I acquired a better knowledge of Buddhism and went through some rigorous mind training.

My favorite thing to study was the biographies of the great teachers of Tibetan Buddhism. Since I was trying to follow the same path I found the stories of their struggles and the ensuing realizations that they gained tremendously helpful and inspiring. I found tidbits of stories of women here and there and I reread them many times, but there was nothing very substantial. Now it is obvious to me why I longed for stories of women and amazing that I did not consciously wonder about the lack of women's biographies. I guess it was part of my conditioning to accept that all the important saints were men.

After two and a half years in India I decided to return to the United States to see my family, and also Trungpa Rinpoche who had moved there from Scotland. I stayed in the United States for a year, studying with Trungpa Rinpoche, but found that wearing the robes there became more of a hindrance than a blessing. I think I was the only Tibetan Buddhist nun in America at that time. To me the point of the robes was to simplify one's external appearance so that one could concentrate on one's inner development. The novelty of the Tibetan robes in America seemed to have the opposite effect. I felt that I wanted to live in America as staying in India had been very draining on my health; but I was in a quandary as to whether I should continue as a nun or give back my vows.

Trungpa Rinpoche suggested that I return to India to see Karmapa and invite him to the States, and to make my decision there. When I got to India there was a war in Sikkim and I could not go to see Karmapa. I had to send him the invitation, and I went to Tashi Jong where Dilgo Khyentse Rinpoche was giving a series of initiations which could last up to three months. Here I met again my meditation teacher from Manali, Abo Rinpoche, who had come from Manali to take these initiations. I also met a man I had known in Holland four and a half years before, with whom I had been corresponding.

Abo Rinpoche had four children and a wonderful wife, and he had a great sense of humor. When I told him I was having repeated dreams about a baby he laughed so hard he almost fell off his seat, and then he said: "All nuns should have babies." I didn't know quite how he meant this, and I continued to struggle with my decision until one day I told him I was having a lot of sexual thoughts and feelings and that I really felt I could not continue as a nun. I asked him when he thought I should give back my vows. He said: "It depends how much longer you can wait!" Then he laughed so hard that tears were running down his face. I also saw the absurdity of the situation and that I was holding on to something that wasn't appropriate anymore. He also assured me I would be able to continue my meditation practice as a lay person.

I returned my vows the next day to Khamtrul Rinpoche, who was a monk. Rather than making me feel guilty, he just quietly said that I should dedicate the merit I had gained by being a nun for the benefit of all sentient beings, do some purification practices and continue on the path.

I now see the time I spent as a nun as an invaluable experience. I think it is important for women to have the experience of living a "virgin" existence. I mean virgin in its true sense: a maiden alone, complete in herself, belonging to no man.

This time gave me a chance to develop myself without the inevitable drain that comes with relationships. As I was only twenty-two at the time of my ordination, I was not formed enough myself to resist being swept away whenever I fell in love. The robes and the celibacy that went with the ordination served as a protective shell in which I could grow and find myself. But once this process had been established, holding on to this form would have become repressive for me. One of the most important things to realize is that during this time, although I had my vows, I was not obligated to ask permission from anyone to travel or study where I wished. I lived alone, but usually near a lama who could teach me, and I was free and independent. Some Tibetan nuns choose to live within a monastic situation where one has obligations, but others live and travel freely as I did.

Shortly after I disrobed I married the Dutchman, Paul Kloppenburg, with whom I had been corresponding and whom I met again in Tashi Jong. He had been studying with the Tibetans for four years also. Within a year I went from being a solitary nun to being a mother.

The internal changes and adjustments were enormous. I realized that the physical demands of pregnancy and nursing a baby were going to make it impossible to continue my meditation practice with the same intensity as before. I had made a decision which could never be reversed and I was suddenly under the power of forces from within my body that were stronger than I had ever experienced before. We got married in India and then moved to Vashon Island in the Puget Sound near Seattle where we made a small meditation center. I became pregnant again with Aloka, my second daughter, nine months after the birth of Sherab, my oldest daughter. We lived very simply, growing our food and living in one room with a separate meditation room and retreat hut. We would take turns with the babies so we could meditate. During this time, I appreciated sharing information with other women in similar situations. When I was in my second pregnancy a group of island women decided to meet and discuss their babies and breast-feeding problems. After one meeting we decided we did not want to talk about our babies but we wanted to explore our own interior lives and to hear each other's stories. Through these meetings I began to be aware of the female experience and to cherish the company of women.

Though my first husband was kind and helpful, after three years I felt constrained by the relationship and wanted to move out on my own for a while. We moved to Boulder with the children in 1976. I began teaching at Naropa Institute and within the Buddhist community in Boulder, and lived separately from my husband. I also did some lecture tours around the States during the following three years.

Although I enjoyed living in a Buddhist community, after several years I felt unhappy with the patriarchal, hierarchical, structured organization there. I also felt I was often parroting the words of Trungpa Rinpoche and losing touch with my own experience. I was becoming an expert rather than a beginner.

As I was experiencing this crisis I met my second husband, Costanzo Allione. He came to Naropa Institute to film the poets. Allen Ginsberg, who was the co-director of the Naropa poetry project, introduced us at a party. Allen and I had been friends since I had been in the States as a nun and had traveled around the western part of the States together with Ram Dass (Richard Alpert) raising money for a retreat center. When I came back to Boulder, Allen had asked me to act as his meditation instructor, so it was in this capacity that I was introduced to Constanzo. After a year of traveling back and forth from Italy, we got married in Boulder and moved to Rome.

Within a few months I was pregnant again, and almost immediately the doctor began to question the date of conception. When I was six months pregnant we discovered I was having twins.

This period was my own personal "descent" experience. I had left all my friends and my work behind. I had been teaching and lecturing around the States and had many good friends with whom I could share my spiritual path and who understood the world within the context of the Buddhist teachings.

Suddenly I realized that I had left more than I thought. My husband was gone most of the time, working in Rome or traveling. Our villa, which was an hour from Rome, was isolated and very cold. I was practically immobilized by the pregnancy and depression. I had nothing except my two small daughters and my giant womb. I had gone from being very independent, to feeling extremely dependent and powerless. It was as though my whole path had been diverted into a whirlpool of emptiness. I felt alienated from everything and everyone and could not motivate myself to meditate. I was uncomfortable standing up and lying down. The last two months I had to stay in bed so that the twins would not be born too early. I could foresee nothing except years of babies, fatigue, and loneliness.

The birth experience was traumatic. I had had my daughters at home with the assistance of a home-birth clinic from Seattle, but there were no such facilities in Italy, and since I was having twins I had to go to the hospital anyway.

Italy is very behind the times in terms of childbirth and postpartum care. The worst thing was that after the twins (a boy, Costanzo Kunzang, and a girl, Chiara Osel) were born, they put them into incubators and would not allow me to touch them for two weeks. Even though they both weighed over five pounds, I could only see them from a distance of twelve feet through two glass walls that were usually fogged over. Once I sneaked in to get a look at them and was harshly reprimanded by the nurse. I only saw their weight chart, which was going down every day. The pediatrician kept assuring me this was normal and could not understand my floods of tears. I knew that they needed me as much as I needed them, and that they had almost as much need to feel the loving body of their mother as they needed food. I felt they needed to be touched or they would not survive.

Finally, through an American friend, I got in touch with an American pediatrician, Dr. Renzulli, who asked me why I wasn't nursing my babies. When I told him the hospital would not let me try, he said I must try and if they could nurse I should get them out as soon as possible. He really helped me and compromised his reputation by going against the advice of the hospital. I shall be forever grateful for his intercession at a point when I was too weak to assert myself.

When I did finally get to nurse the twins they sucked strongly and each took in a very substantial amount. We took them out the following day, against the hospital's recommendation. Although the following weeks were exhausting and my eyes were always red and burning, I was so happy I did not mind.

Everything was going well and they were passing their pediatric checkups with flying colors until, at two and a half months, the little girl died of Sudden Infant Death Syndrome. I found her dead in her little bed one morning.

This death proved to be a turning point for me. It was the bottom of my descent, and having hit the bottom I had a springboard to push myself back to the surface. Namkhai Norbu Rinpoche, a Tibetan lama who lives in Italy, came to do the funeral. When I asked him why this had happened, ready to believe the worst of myself and my karma in my guilt-ridden state, he just said very softly: "It was for her own reasons." Then I told him I had lost faith in everything and he just looked at me and did not say anything. He quietly set about making a protection bracelet for the remaining twin and gave me a special practice for my own protection and for the rest of the family. I felt that he was releasing us from a strange curse.

Since I had left Boulder and all that it represented to me, I had been in a state of inner turmoil and depression. This state left me open to negative forces, and the weaker I became the more oppressed I felt by strange negativities. We were living in a huge spooky old villa, and from the moment we had arrived there things had become worse and worse. The furnace did not function, most of the time. There were hurricanes and earthquakes and many disturbances. When the baby died we decided to leave immediately, but Norbu's visit already alleviated a lot of the strange feelings I had been experiencing. Then, when we went to the hospital where Chiara's body was, he did something which made me begin to understand that he is a very great lama, even though he is not surrounded by an entourage and dresses and acts like an ordinary person.

I had called him as soon as I had found her dead and he had performed the transference of consciousness (powa) from a distance. A few days later he and a group of his students came to do a funeral practice at our villa, and afterwards we went to the hospital morgue. He put a paper mandala on Chiara's navel and some sacred sand on the crown of her head. Then we went outside and I went to him and threw my arms around his neck and started to weep uncontrollably. Instead of hugging me and comforting me, he just stood there very relaxed. I do not know if it was my surprise at his lack of reaction or what, but I suddenly felt the pain draining out of my tight body and my mind fell into a state of vastness, like a broad, peaceful lake. I simultaneously realized that I was charging myself up and making it worse by clinging to her. I realized that thousands of babies die every day and that I had just been protected from this reality by living in an affluent country.

Since the death of Chiara everything has been uphill. I have been re-emerging from my descent. This has not been easy. I have had to reassess every aspect of myself. The death of the baby put my relationship with my husband, which was already strained, into a crisis. Many people think that this kind of tragedy brings couples closer together, but actually, ninety percent of the time it works the other way. We had to work with our relationship in many different ways. My contact with Norbu Rinpoche helped me to find my way back to the spiritual path. As he is a *Dzog Chen* teacher and works with each individual, the direct transmission of energy he connected me to brought me back to the "beginner's mind" I had experienced in my first year in Nepal.

In a way I have traveled a full circle on my spiritual path, but I also realize that through all the various disciplines and life experiences I have changed and am now integrating these experiences with what I am beginning to understand as women's spirituality and Dzog Chen. I do not feel my search for my path as a woman conflicts with practices I have done before but, rather, it is bringing forth other kinds of awareness.

I realize now that, for me, spirituality is connected to a delicate, playful, spacious part of myself which closes up in militantly regimented situations. The more I try to limit my mind in outward forms, the more this subtle energy escapes like a shy young girl. It is as if I need to trust the vastness of my mind and let go, let my shoulders drop, not try to control situations, and yet not follow rampant discursive thoughts or hold on when my mind gets fixated.

I think that this luminous, subtle spiritual energy is what is meant by the *dakini* principle. She is the key, the gate opener, and the guardian of the unconditioned primordial state which is innate in everyone. If I am not willing to play with her, or if I try to force her, or if I do not invoke her, the gate remains closed and I remain in darkness and ignorance.

II

Gradually, however, as I emerged from the initial shock of the change from being a nun to being a mother in less than a year, followed by the birth of Aloka seventeen months later, the twins four years after that, and then Chiara's death, I began to see mothering as a great practice opportunity.

My children were my training, and what a powerful and underestimated path this is. This was a real place where selfishness—"self-cling-ing"—was revealed. Although I might have been tired or wanted to read or practice, I was constantly interrupted. Through my challenges I saw that had I stayed in the comfort of solitude, I would not have been tested and trained in these ways.

As a child, you focus everything on yourself, everything is about "me." When you become a parent, just by the force of what you have to do and your love for your baby, the focus turns away from your own happiness to the happiness of someone else. This turning away from self-cherishing is the key to all Buddhist practice. The focus shifts from "me, me, me" to "Oh! There's a world out there, there's somebody else besides me." This internal revolution is the essence of practicing Dharma. This is a recognition of the web.

Had I not gone through sufferings like the death of Chiara and my marriage, I might have become superficial in relating the Dharma to others, like a man who spoke to me three days after Chiara's death.

As I sat silently, tears streaming down my face, a bearded, middle-aged man holding a little Tibetan dog approached me and said, "You should not be so attached to this baby: everything is impermanent."

I asked him, "Do you have children?"

He said, "No." I walked away unable to say more, wondering if a few years before as a nun I might have been capable of such insensitive advice. Because of the depth of connection I felt toward my children, I could no longer dismiss these ties so easily. Was this attachment or relatedness?

As I cooked in the cauldron of motherhood, the incredible love I felt for my children opened my heart and brought me a much greater understanding of universal love. It made me understand the suffering of the world much more deeply. This has been an important thread for me, both as a practitioner and as a human being.

I realized that since I was nineteen and fell in love with the Tibetans, I had been parented by the lamas and filled by their authority. My whole life had been guided by them. Certainly I had greatly benefited from and been enriched by my teachers, but after the death of Chiara, I had to begin to find my own authority. I had to meet the dark goddess, I needed the healing to come from a revaluing of the feminine and through the work with the mandala of the fierce goddess.

There are several factors that brought my return to the world of light after being in the pain and dissolution of the underworld. One of the most significant elements was my practical understanding of a practice known as Chöd. Chöd took on a more personal meaning for me during my divorce. It is a practice for severing attachment to ego and involves offering one's body to all beings related to one's life.

In 1985, as the divorce proceedings were under way, I wanted to move back to America with my children. We had moved to Italy with the understanding that we would only stay five months, and seven years had elapsed with one excuse after another from my husband Costanzo Senior for why we couldn't move back. The issue that he and I struggled with was not whether or not I could go, but whether I could take my son with me if I left Italy. Legally, I could not leave Italy with my son without my husband's permission.

One night during this struggle, I decided to do Chöd. During the practice I offered my husband everything he needed. I offered my body as nectar giving him the love, security, and warmth he longed for. I also gave form to the fear within me and fed it. My "fear demon" took form as a blue being with a terrible grimace, spiky hair, and suction-cup hands like an octopus. By nourishing my husband and this demon with complete acceptance and compassion I was no longer split in conflict.

During this practice I ceased the "me against you" struggle and offered the "enemy" everything I had been holding back. Afterwards I felt a relaxation I hadn't felt for months. By feeding the "demons" of my husband and also my demon of fear, something shifted.

I didn't expect the practice to have any outward results, and so was surprised the next day when my husband came to my apartment and sat down in the living room physically shaking. I asked him why he was trembling. He said that he had decided to allow us to leave. In a complete reversal of his previous stance, he said that he understood my need to return to my country of origin and that it wasn't right to keep me in Italy against my will.

When I got over my shock, I assured him that I would do anything I could to facilitate his relationship with our son. So I left Italy, and since that time we have grown to be friends and collaborated in raising our son who has grown up with a warm, loving relationship with each of us. Since our divorce, Costanzo Senior met his demons and transformed them.

It is important to point out that Chöd is not done to "get what you want." The point of Chöd is really the opposite, to let go of what you cling to. In the section of the Chöd practice called the "black feast," we give form to "disease bearing beings, obstacle-makers, and debt-holders" and offer them our body, letting go of all attachment. Often, as a result of this offering, healing and freedom are experienced. Traditionally Chöd also was known to end epidemics, as well as cure diseases, possession, or obsession.

Since all of our suffering comes from our self-clinging minds, the freeing of that struggle may have actual effects, such as my husband's change. But that is not the point. The point is to let go of our self-cherishing. I saw that my "demon" husband was not an external force, but rather a projection of my own mind that had manifested outwardly. From this experience I learned to give form to my fears, illnesses, and attachments and feed them to their complete satisfaction.

My approach to practice in general was profoundly affected by this. I understood that the "demons" to be fed in the Chöd were not some sort of Tibetan-looking gargoyles, but my own dispossessed and ignored projections, aspects of myself projected onto the people in my environment with whom I was struggling.

●　　●　　●　　●

In 1991, I took a group on a pilgrimage to the feminine power places of central Tibet. As a practitioner of Tibetan Buddhism for more than twenty years and a former Tibetan Buddhist nun, I was excited to visit the places that I had only read about.

A life of pilgrimage was common among Buddhist practitioners in Tibet. With a staff, a tent, and minimal religious materials such as texts, a drum and bell, they would take off for years at a time, meditating in various places for days, months, or even years before moving on. Often a teacher would send a disciple off on a pilgrimage route that would last his or her whole life, as Marpa did with Milarepa.

Because many of us were Chöd practitioners, one of the most important places for us to reach was the cave of Machig Lapdron, founder of the Chöd practice, at Sangri Khamar, "The Red Citadel on the Copper Mountain." This is where Machig settles at the age of thirty-seven after she had had her children and had re-ordained as a nun. To reach Sangri Khamar we had to cross the Tsangpo River, the "Great Purifier." There had been very heavy rains, and the day before we got there the ferry was closed. The river was muddy and roaring angrily through the narrows. Thirty-two people had drowned in the river the year before.

As we sat next to the river, many members of the group used their own methods to see whether we could go or not. Some people had already decided not to go. One person insisted Machig had appeared to her and said playfully, "Come on over! Most things in life that are truly worthwhile involve risk or danger."

This was a very interesting moment in the pilgrimage, because the practice of Chöd is all about attachment and the demons of hope and fear. Here we were on the bank of this river, close to Machig's place and thus full of hope, yet the rushing water told us death was a real possibility if we tried to cross.

I decided to relax completely and allow Machig to help us, and if that meant staying at camp, that was okay. I saw that faith is a form of relaxation, and this turned out to be one of the most powerful realizations of the pilgrimage for me. Faith is taking things one step at a time, relaxing, trusting. It is moment-to-moment opening to the wisdom beings. I saw that in a pilgrimage, the path is the fruit in the sense that the challenges in the pilgrimage are the teaching. It's not supposed to be easy. The challenges test and hone inner development. The obstacles that arise symbolize our inner obstacles to union with our wisdom nature.

As we sat on the edge of the angry river, two local men with tobacco stained teeth and Chinese hats started talking about an alternative place to cross the river. The day before, we had been told there were no alternatives. But they said there was a ferry crossing one hour's drive up the river. This sounded hopeful, but there still remained the problem of how we would get to Sangri Khamar once we had crossed. Just then a truck arrived at the opposite side full of Tibetans wanting to cross. Our guide called and asked the driver to meet us up the river where the other ferry crossed. He agreed. If the truck hadn't arrived at that moment, we would have given up.

So we drove up the river singing the invocation to Machig Lapdron from the Chöd. When we got there we found the river wide and calm, and climbed into the small ferry and crossed easily. Then the truck took us on a wild ride along fields and through villages. The day was warm and sunny, and holding onto the sides of the truck as it lurched through sand was fun. Our exhilaration became edged with fear as the valley narrowed and the road often broke down the cliff side into the river below. We passed the first ferry and waved to those whose inner guidance had told them not to go. Then we swung around the corner and saw the beautiful copper-colored mountain we had longed to visit approaching at breathtaking speed.

As we jumped off the truck and went up the hill, the monk in the rebuilt *gompa* invited us to do Chöd in the *gompa*. We settled onto the long, low mats and the monk brought out all the extra cushions. The small hall was filled with the song of the Wisdom Mother, and rows of smiling faces filled the door.

Then we went down below, into Machig's cave, overlooking the river. The cave contains a new statue of Machig and in the corner is a hole that the monk said leads to 108 charnel ground cemeteries. He then put what looked like a stone in the shape of a foot, which he said was Machig's foot, on our heads, throats, and hearts and anywhere we had pain. When we did Chöd in the cave, most of us had strong experiences of Machig, who taught each person in a different way. Her presence at Sangri is truly tangible.

The next day I awoke feeling very different than before. I no longer feared death. I had a renewed sense of clarity about my own life. This experience has informed and influenced my life ever since then. Knowing both worlds makes it easier to be here.

Chapter VIII

· · · · · · · · · · ·

Suffering and Its
Partial Cure

Sharon Salzberg

Sharon Salzberg's childhood unfolded, she writes, "through terrifying, uprooting turns and incomprehensible losses." First her mother died; then the grandfather with whom she lived died; next her father had to be permanently mentally hospitalized. Salzberg (b. 1952) dealt with these sorrows by pretending indifference, yet inwardly her misery seemed to enter a plea of guilty about the person she was.

What, Salzberg wondered, was she to do about her problem—about the damaged, unhappy person she was? In college a course on Buddhism provided some solace, and she decided to go to India, to learn more about the religion. In the early 1970s Buddhism and meditation had yet to become faddish, and initially Salzberg had trouble finding anyone to instruct her in meditation. Hardly a promising beginning for someone who eventually was to have half the luminaries in both the Tibetan and Theravadan traditions as her teachers.

Salzberg returned to America in 1974, and she taught a meditation course at Chögyam Trungpa's fledgling Naropa Institute. For the next two years she traveled here, there, anywhere an individual or small group asked her to teach meditation. In 1976 she, along with Jack Kornfield and Joseph Goldstein, founded the Insight Meditation Society in Barre, Massachusetts, so there could be a permanent and "sacred" place for teaching and learning meditation in the United States. Two decades later, approximately twenty thousand people have taken courses at their center in Massachusetts.

In instructing Americans in meditation, Salzberg realized that she must first teach them confidence—confidence in themselves, confidence that they can do the practices. In traveling around the country she had discovered a widespread discouragement, particularly during the Bush administration, with many people feeling that they are living in a destructive time and that there is nothing they can do about it. Salzberg's mission is to encourage them—to heal old wounds and become whole persons and exert a positive influence on the common welfare. Her latest book, Faith (2002), could as easily have been titled Enlightened Confidence.

Disorder, Early Sorrows,
and a Plane to India

I told myself for years that I didn't deserve to be happy. Throughout my childhood, I believed that something must be intrinsically wrong with me because things never seemed to change for the better. My father, whom I adored, disappeared when I was four, and my mother and I moved in with my aunt and uncle. One night when I was nine years old, my mother and I were home alone. She had recently undergone surgery and seemed to be recovering well. In celebration of her return, I was wearing my ballerina Halloween costume. We were sitting close together on the couch, watching her favorite singer, Nat King Cole, on television, when suddenly she began bleeding violently. I ran out into the hallway to get someone to help us, but couldn't find anyone. My mother managed to tell me to call an ambulance immediately and then to call my grandmother, whom I hardly knew, to come get me. Shaking uncontrollably, I complied. After that evening, I never saw her again. About two weeks later she died in the hospital. After that, I lived with my father's parents and rarely heard mention of my mother again.

My childhood continued to unfold through terrifying, uprooting turns and incomprehensible losses. When I was eleven my grandfather died, and one day my father returned. The handsome prince I'd secretly imagined had been replaced by a disheveled, hard-bitten, troubled stranger. A few days after he arrived, my entire body broke out in hives. When I got back from the doctor's office, my father told me, "You have to be tough to be able to survive life." Six weeks later he took an overdose of sleeping pills. I stood outside in the cold, holding my grandmother's hand among a crowd of gawking neighbors as he was carried out on a stretcher. I watched as the flashing red lights receded and the sirens faded. Now both of my parents had been spun away from me in the back of an ambulance. That night my father entered the mental health system. He was never able to function outside of it again.

One of the hardest parts of all the loss and dislocation was that it was surrounded by an ambient, opaque silence about what was happening. Because no one spoke openly or even acknowledged all the changes as loss, my immense grief, anger, and confusion remained held inside. Whenever the cover slipped, I scrambled to hide the feelings, or distort them, so no one would really know, especially not myself. When John Kennedy was assassinated, I couldn't stop crying. My grandmother asked me why, and I replied, simply, "Because his children have lost their father."

The story I was telling myself was that what I felt didn't matter anyway. It seems as if I spent most of my childhood, and even my teenage years, curled up in bed, lost in a separate shadowed existence built of sadness. I repeatedly invented scenarios of having parents just like anybody else. The dream of answering, just like anybody else, the schoolteacher's question, "What does your father do for a living?" was the kindling that fed the fire of many of my secret fantasies. I'd summon images of my mother coming back, as though from a long trip, like anyone else's mother might. But I wasn't at all like anybody else seemed to be. Of course, none of them were like they seemed either, but I didn't know that then. Feeling so different, I liked playing it safe more than anything, seeing life from a distance, never really engaging, preferring to lose myself in the seductive play of listlessness.

While silent dreams and desires played out within me, in most situations I'd insist with bravado, "I didn't want that anyway." When I lived with my grandparents, color television was just becoming the rage. I longed for one, but they couldn't afford it. To compensate, my grandmother, who cared a lot about me, bought a special plastic sheet to place over the black-and-white screen to create a faint illusion of color. This rainbow aura bore no relationship to the figures and settings of the stories depicted in the programs. I wanted to rip off that bizarre front and plead for the real thing; instead I silently tolerated the charade, not betraying my desire. I didn't care about anything, or so I hoped it seemed. I came to know very well the protection of distance, of a narrowed, compressed world. Though it was my own act of pulling back, I felt forsaken. I told myself a story that there was no way out of the world that turned me in upon myself.

My resistance to participating more fully in life came to feel like the most alive, vibrant thing about me. I often found myself, in many endeavors, not really trying because I was secretly sure that I'd fail. I'd learned well to hold life in abeyance. For years, I hardly spoke. I barely allowed myself a full-blown emotion—no anger, no joy. My whole life was an effort to balance on the edge of what felt like an eroding cliff where I was stranded. I was waiting, suspended. Though it mimics death, waiting isn't necessarily death's prelude, but might rather be the life-force conserving itself. When I was a child my favorite animal was a caterpillar, never a dog or a cat, and somehow never a butterfly. Like the body being cooled down before surgery to slow its vital functions, my very life depended on stepping out of time and expectation, depended on waiting for . . . *something*.

At sixteen I entered the State University of New York at Buffalo, feeling as lost and afraid as ever. By this time the smooth, monochromatic shelter of abeyance, which had once saved me, was now engulfing me. I was slowly being forced to wake up out of my slumber. Having to choose an academic major confronted me with defining what I wanted out of life. Just that one choice provoked the uncertainty and risk of discovering what it might mean to be alive. Sometimes I thought of majoring in history, sometimes in philosophy. I heard that the Asian studies department offered a philosophy class on Buddhism, and I enrolled.

In my second year of college, although my life was slowly opening up, the only time I really came alive was for an hour and a half on Tuesdays and Thursdays, in my Asian philosophy class. I found myself beginning to wonder if I might one day be truly happy. Maybe I didn't have to be lonely and afraid forever. Maybe I didn't have to be so pressed down by my circumstances forever. While the repeated disintegration of my family had kept me frightened, this glimmer of possibility kept me alive.

Like a subliminal message being played under the predominant music, a sense of possibility, no matter how faint, drives a wedge between the suffering we may wake up with each day and the hopelessness that can try to move in with us on a permanent basis. It inspires us to envision a better life for ourselves. It is this glimmer of possibility that is the beginning of faith.

When I learned about the school's junior-year-abroad program, I felt strongly attracted. Despite the fact that the only time in my life I had even left New York State was for a short trip to Florida, I felt ready to leave everything I had known and travel to a place about which I knew nothing. I could no longer simply endure, could no longer be half-alive and willing merely to get by. I yearned for embodiment, for a sense of belonging; I yearned to transform the waiting into finally coming alive. I wanted to take up my place in the world.

When I tell people I decided to go to India when I was only eighteen, they often think I knew what I was doing. Once someone remarked, "You must have been such a clear thinker," and I had to reply, in all honesty, "No, in fact I only had one clear thought," which was that I could solve the "problem" that was me if I learned how to meditate. That one clear thought was enough. It would set me on a journey that would remake my life.

My First Meditation Retreat

I arrived at the New Delhi train station, having traveled overland from Europe through Afghanistan and Pakistan. The moment I stepped off the train I was assaulted by the intensity of India. Insistent young men surrounded me, demanding to carry my bags. Vendors pushed close and loudly hawked their wares. Gaunt women carrying infants came over to me, begging for money, as did old men with broken bodies. I saw a *sadhu* for the first time, a half-naked mendicant smeared with ashes to signify the inevitability of death. All around him children chased one another, laughing loudly. Throngs of people and animals pressed in on me. I had never seen life displayed so openly before, had never felt it pulsing so fiercely, with joy and suffering all jumbled together. Nothing seemed hidden, and there was nowhere for me to hide. In the sultry air, diesel fumes, antiseptic, and dust mingled with layers of jasmine and frangipani. Standing in the midst of it, even though it was so new, so intense, I was glad I'd come.

A few days later I traveled north by train and then jeep to Dharamsala, home of the Dalai Lama and a great portion of the Tibetan Buddhist refugee community. Dharamsala is poised on a spur of the snowcapped Dhauladhar Mountains, the foothills of the Himalayas. Over the next couple of months I attended various classes taught by Tibetans I had heard about from other Westerners. I began to realize that the tradition prevalent there emphasized study of religious texts before beginning meditation practice. Though I loved what I did learn of the teachings, I grew impatient to learn meditation, to see if it would give me what I was looking for.

To my relief, I finally heard about a teacher who offered practical meditation instruction. The following morning I walked along the mountain trails to the scheduled class only to find that it had been canceled because the teacher was sick. The next time I went, the teacher had recovered but the translator was away, so once again the class was called off. Frustrated,

I waited a week for the next class, trudging up the trail only to find that both teacher and translator had gone off on a trip of unknown length. I began to wonder if I'd ever get any meditation instruction at all. It was growing harder to trust life enough to live by the "pretence of accident"—to trust that opportunity were always there.

Then one day, while sitting in a local restaurant, I overheard an American woman casually mention an international yoga conference about to take place in New Delhi. Thinking that I might find a meditation teacher there, I left Dharamsala and made my way back to New Delhi. At the conference, I encountered swamis and yogis galore, but no one I felt drawn to accept as a teacher.

That old familiar sinking feeling started to return. For months I had been grappling with how to find someone to teach me meditation while also trying to find something I could safely eat, remembering to look for cows before crossing the street, avoiding the monkeys who would bite when intentionally or unintentionally provoked, and figuring out how to live with only what I could carry. I was beginning to wear down.

One day the conference hit a low point when several of the presenters started shoving each other to grab the microphone and be the first to speak. I felt horribly dispirited. I had come all the way to India to find a holy person. Now I wondered if that was even possible.

I thought of leaving New Delhi, but I didn't know where to turn in intense, tumultuous India. I was sorely tempted to withdraw, to declare that searching for a guide was stupid and futile, and that I didn't care at all anyway. But each morning I found myself getting up and returning to the yoga conference, not sure of what I'd find, but spurred on by a flickering faith that just wouldn't let me give up.

On the final day of the conference, I heard a paper read by Daniel Goleman, an American who decades later wrote the best-seller *Emotional Intelligence*. At that time he was a graduate student in psychology, doing research in India. At the end of his talk he mentioned a Buddhist meditation retreat he was about to attend in Bodhgaya, along with Ram Dass, a spiritual leader I had heard speak back in Buffalo. I had found Ram Dass's lecture there inspiring, and I was eager to meet him. Immediately I decided to join the group formed of several people who had attended the talk, and go with them to Bodhgaya.

My new story was about to begin. It would be one that explores what happens when, in the face of any circumstance, whether joyful or painful, we choose to have faith in generosity, kindness, and clear seeing. It would be the story of learning to have faith in our own innate goodness and capacity to love. It would be the story of seeing past the apparent randomness of "sheer happenings" to uncover layers and layers of connection. It would be the story of knowing, even in the midst of great suffering, that we can still belong to life, that we're not cast out and alone. This new story was the Buddha's story. I would work to make it my own.

.   .   .   .

I arrived in Bodhgaya in late December 1970 and fell in love. I fell in love with the meditation teachers I found there, and with the community of students who gathered around them. I fell in love with the Buddha's teachings. I fell in love with the place. Even discomfort and uncertainty didn't tarnish the romance. Getting to Bodhgaya involved a seventeen-hour ride from New Delhi in a train so crowded that people were hanging out the windows. This was followed by a wild hour in a bicycle rickshaw with the driver pedaling furiously to outrun any lurking bandits.

Arriving so late meant that finding a place to sleep would be difficult. Finally my companions from the New Delhi yoga conference and I were allowed to put our sleeping bags down on the dining room floor of a tourist hotel. I woke to roosters crowing, dogs barking, women chatting at the water pump outside, and prayers being broadcast over loudspeakers. Blaring Hindi film music drowned out everything else. It was the dawning of a hot, dry, dusty day, and the beginning of my new life.

I stepped out into the golden light of Bodhgaya. Warm and pervasive, it wrapped itself around the vibrant colors of roadside spice stands, the curling smoke of charcoal and wood blazes, the rainbow-hued women's saris, the saffron, and the ocher and burgundy robes of Buddhist monks and nuns. In that glow, boundaries blurred and softened.

The half-mile walk to the center of town from my hotel presented an array of new sights. I passed a Thai pagoda and a Chinese temple; teams of water buffalo plowed the patchwork of rice fields between them. At the edge of the marketplace there was a Tibetan restaurant, housed in a large, dingy tent, and surrounded by tea stalls made of wooden boards tacked together at odd angles. Peanut vendors, roasting nuts on hot ashes, called out the excellence of their product, and old men proffered huge baskets of tiny bananas, deep lavender eggplants, bright green chilis, oranges, and pomegranates. A blind beggar held out his hand for alms, and scrawny dogs hunted for scraps of food. A couple of cars made their way through this scene, honking incessantly, and two men prodded an elephant down the road. I fell in love with this teeming wonder of life.

Just past the market is the center of Bodhgaya, and the center of the Buddhist universe—the bodhi tree under which the Buddha sat while he achieved enlightenment. A direct descendant of the original tree grows at the same spot now, a highly venerated shrine.

Covered with shiny, dark green heart-shaped leaves, the bodhi tree rises majestically, its arms spread wide, as if holding the sky. In Buddhist legend, it is said that after his enlightenment the Buddha stood for a full week gazing in gratitude at the tree that had sheltered him. Now I was beholding the tree, absorbing the feel of it, yearning for the protection of its immense arms. My heart leaped. For the first time in my life, I understood the sacredness of a place, how it could possess a transporting power and open the door to a new way of looking at the world. Tibetan Buddhists had strung prayer flags between the bodhi tree's lower branches, so that the wind could carry prayers for all beings around the entire globe. As I watched them flapping, I realized that perhaps as a child I had been less alone than I had thought.

Next to the bodhi tree stands the Mahabodhi temple, commemorating the wondrous freedom of mind the Buddha attained there. Gathered around it were devotees ringing bells in ancient ritualized rhythms, pilgrims burning incense, and clusters of monks and nuns whispering prayers or singing them aloud in a cacophony of languages. A young man in saffron robes was being ordained into monastic life, and dozens of Tibetan practitioners performed full-length prostrations to convey their respect to the Buddha and to purify their minds.

Despite all the mantras and prayers, movement and activity, I experienced a profound quiet. It was as though an echo of the Buddha's awakening, 2,500 years earlier, still lingered in the air. Centuries of people honoring the place and what it represented about human possibility had only added to the calm. I felt the stillness as a force field, penetrating my own jumbled mind, widening and enlarging the space within until my thoughts were less like hammers striking an anvil and more like ripples on a quiet sea. My body and mind felt at peace with the world.

As I circled the bodhi tree, I came upon a ragged elderly man in the burgundy robes of a Tibetan monastic. His lips moved silently in prayer as he counted the beads of his *mala,* similar to a rosary. He looked up at me, smiled, and offered me a seed from the bodhi tree, motioning to me to eat it. I popped it into my mouth, not stopping to think of any symbolic significance to his gesture, or of the transfiguration we might have just celebrated. Then the monk indicated that I should sit next to him. I later found out that this simple, kind, and unassuming man was a renowned scholar and practitioner, Khunu Rinpoche, whose many students included the Dalai Lama.

Khunu Rinpoche served as my welcoming committee to a world different from any I had known, a world that offered release from the dominion of suffering. In my Buddhism class at college I had read about the Third Noble Truth—liberation from suffering—but didn't yet know how that might apply to the intensity of my own pain. Here I recognized the possibility in the feeling of the air, in the kindness of Khunu Rinpoche's eyes, in the murmurs of Buddhist texts being recited out loud, in the compassion symbolized by the prayer flags. They were the promise of the Third Noble Truth come alive.

As I sat next to Khunu Rinpoche, I sensed deep within me the possibility of rising above the circumstances of my childhood, of defining myself by something other than my family's painful struggles and its hardened tone of defeat. I recalled the resignation in my father's eyes at the constraints that governed his life. The boundary of his autonomy was the decision about where to have lunch if someone took him out of the hospital on a pass. With a surge of conviction, I thought, *But I am* here, *and I can learn to be truly free.* I felt as if nothing and no one could take away the joy of that prospect.

This state of love-filled delight in possibilities and eager joy at the prospect of actualizing them is known in Buddhism as bright faith. Bright faith goes beyond merely claiming that possibility for oneself to immersing oneself in it. With bright faith we feel exalted as we are lifted out of our normal sense of insignificance, thrilled as we no longer feel lost and alone. The enthusiasm, energy, and courage we need in order to leave the safe path, to stop aligning ourselves with the familiar or the convenient, arises with bright faith. It enables us to step out, step away, and see what we can make of our lives. With bright faith we act on our potential to transform our suffering and live in a different way.

Some Instances in the Life of an American Buddhist

I was involved in a car accident in the late seventies. Some friends and I were on our way out to dinner when a drunk driver, who had fallen asleep at the wheel, collided with us head-on. The rearview mirror tore off and hit me in the face as I was flung out of the passenger seat and into the dashboard. The next thing I knew, I was coming to as people were pulling me from the car and laying me down on the grass. Enveloped by the gray veil of a concussion, I watched as the people around me, the trees, the buildings and cars, began to float, dreamlike.

In the hospital, a nurse asked over and over, "What is your name?" I reached for it but it just wouldn't come. The world, already attenuated, faded even more. As I watched her face change, the random thought that she was worried about me passed through my mind, but I couldn't figure out why she would be.

Lying on the X-ray table, I felt my consciousness leave my body. I was flying down a tunnel, moving at an incredible speed, thousands of discordant and chaotic images clamoring for my attention. I was terrified. As the intensity and speed accelerated, I grew more and more agitated. Suddenly I heard a gentle voice saying, "Watch your breath."

I had little idea of what anything around me meant, let alone "Watch your breath." I had been practicing meditation for more than eight years by that time, and had watched many a breath, but in the chaos of my mind there was no recollection of anything related to the practice. Yet the voice came again, insistent, "Watch your breath."

Even though I did not have a clue as to why I would do that or how it might help, I struggled to focus on the in-breath and the out-breath. As I breathed, the images began to slow down and the world around me grew more coherent, more compelling than the tunnel. Each time I lost focus and began to "fly out" again, the voice would come back. Each time I watched my breath, I would calm down.

As I was lying there, an image arose in my mind of a friend who was in Burma, living as a monk. I saw him clearly wearing a monk's robe and standing outside an Asian-style building speaking to an older Burmese monk. *That's Alan,* I thought hazily. *Who's he with?* The vision calmed me, and made me feel strangely happy.

I continued to watch my breath, and the vision faded as I felt my consciousness return fully to my body. Slowly I began to recognize the elements of a familiar world. I knew who I was, and that I'd be all right.

Five years later in Massachusetts, I saw Sayadaw U Pandita for the first time. Even though I hadn't seen photographs of him, he somehow looked familiar. In the middle of an afternoon meditation the whole experience came flooding back—the shock of the car crash, the ambulance ride in the night, the tunnel where things moved faster and faster, my terror, watching my breath, and that vision. The older monk in that scene was Sayadaw U Pandita. And Alan had in fact been with him in Burma at the time of the accident.

Some might say that this apparent connection was merely my imagination, a burst of fantasy dictated by my growing regard for U Pandita, and I can't deny that it might have been just that. The story defies logic—but then, so does science these days. Several years later I read about a scientific experiment that provided me with a language that felt linked to my experience.

In the sixties, the physicist John Stewart Bell theorized that particles that were once connected will, when separated, behave as if still connected, regardless of the distance between them. Some years later a French physicist, Alain Aspect, conducted experiments offering physical proof of Bell's theorem. In Aspect's setup, which used lasers to excite calcium atoms, a single photon was passed through a special crystal that split it into two "daughter" photons. The two daughter photons were allowed to travel off in opposite directions. Each was randomly directed to one of two devices that determined the direction of its polarization or "spin." Aspect's results showed that no matter how far apart the photons were, when the spin of one was measured, its partner simultaneously showed the opposite, or complementary, spin. The correlation was instantaneous: It happened faster than the speed of light.

Theoretically, according to Aspect, the distance of the whole universe can separate these two particles, and when one spins "up," the other spins "down." If one spins "right" the other will spin "left." The inescapable conclusion is that two particles that were once connected will continue to behave in relationship to each other, even when separated by vast stretches of time and limitless space. Einstein called this kind of thing "Spooky" action at a distance.

To me this characteristic of elementary particles seems connected to the spooky experience I had of Sayadaw U Pandita while lying on the X-ray table. It is as though we had been spinning through lifetimes, apart yet related, and in a critical moment our link had been made conscious again. According to the Buddhist cosmology, we have all died and been reborn countless times, in the course of which we have been one another's mothers and children and students and teachers and friends and enemies. We have loved one another and hurt one another, laughed together endlessly, and cried an infinite number of tears in one another's arms. And we have reminded one another to breathe.

Either viewed through the dharma or through science, the fundamental condition of reality is wholeness, interrelatedness. This immense, interlinked, commonly hidden world is the realm where our actions play out. Knowing we are intimately connected to this bigger reality upholds our faith as we take action in the world.

*   *   *   *

Many years ago, when I was living in India and practicing meditation in Bodhgaya, I had gone with a friend to spend a few days in Calcutta. When it was time to leave, we found we were running late to catch our train back. The only way we could get to the train station on time was to take a rickshaw. In many other places in India, rickshaws are pulled by people on bicycles or motorbikes, but in Calcutta they are actually pulled by people running on foot. So, even though we hated the thought of being carried by another human being in this way, we caught a rickshaw to the station.

The rickshaw man took us by shortcuts, through dark streets and down back alleys. At one point, suddenly out of nowhere, an extremely big man approached the rickshaw driver and stopped him. Then he looked at me, grabbed me, and tried to pull me off the rickshaw. I looked around the streets for help. There were a lot of people everywhere, as there often are in India, but I did not see a single friendly face.

I thought, "Oh my God, this guy is going to drag me off and rape me.

Then he's going to kill me, and nobody is going to help me!" My friend who was sitting with me in the rickshaw managed to push the drunken man away and urged the rickshaw driver to go on. So we escaped and got to the station.

I was very shaken and upset when we arrived in Bodhgaya. I told Munindra, one of my meditation teachers, what had happened. He looked at me and said, "Oh, Sharon, with all the lovingkindness in your heart, you should have taken your umbrella and hit that man over the head with it!"

* * * *

One fall I was teaching at the Insight Meditation Society, which is located in a rural area. Each morning I would go for a walk very early, just as it was getting light. This walk took me past the mobile home where Max lived. Max was a huge dog—he looked like a cross between a Doberman pinscher and a mountain lion. I started hearing reports that Max had grown agitated and aggressive, snarling at people and threatening to attack them. I had been experiencing a series of unfortunate events that fall, and I thought I might end this cycle of difficulty by being torn limb from limb by this dog.

Every day at dawn I would set out with a certain "Max consciousness," my fear growing with each step as I approached his territory. For many days Max had not been in the yard as I passed, but I was becoming increasingly tense about the prospect of an encounter. As the days went on, I found that my very first thought when I awoke in the morning centered on Max and my fear of him. I had read that His Holiness the Dalai Lama's very first thought upon waking is a prayer of love and compassion, dedicating all of the coming actions of the day to the benefit of all living beings. Starting the day as I was, in fear of Max, was beginning to seem pretty ignoble.

Finally, one morning Max was there. From far away I saw him sitting in the twilight. Fear rose sharply. I proceeded slowly, with each step seeing him as increasingly separate from myself and as a tremendous threat: "He's out there, he's very big, and he's getting closer." Finally I arrived. Max stood up. I stopped. We looked at each other. And then I blurted out the first thing that came to mind: "Max, Maxine is my middle name. People used to call me Max, too, you know!" We looked at each other for a few moments more, then Max sat down again, and I walked on.

From that point on I saw that love was a choice for me in many different situations. I developed a relationship to Max, a feeling of connection. He seemed like someone I knew, someone who might be in a bad state, who might even lose control and actually try to hurt me, but someone who was nevertheless a friend. I did not at all stop being careful. But Max ceased to be a terrible, alien creature, a great, hulking beast out there waiting to get me. He stopped being the "other."

·   ·   ·   ·

Whenever I teach lovingkindness retreats in an urban setting, I ask the students to do their walking meditation out on the streets. I suggest they choose individuals they see and, with care and awareness, wish them well by silently repeating the phrases of the practice, "May you be happy, may you be peaceful." I tell them that even if they don't *feel* loving, the power of their intention to offer love is not diminished. One retreat took place a few blocks from downtown Oakland, California. Since we were directly across the street from the Amtrak station, several people chose to do their practice on the train platform.

When a train pulled in, one woman from the class noticed a man disembark and decided to make him the recipient of her lovingkindness meditation. Silently she began reciting the phrases for him. Almost immediately she began judging herself: *I must not be doing it right because I feel so distant. I don't have a great wash of warm feeling coming over me.* Nonetheless, reaffirming her intention to look on all beings with kindness instead of estrangement, she continued, reciting, "May you be happy, may you be peaceful." Taking another look at the man, who was dressed in a suit and tie and seemed nervous, she began judging him: *He looks so rigid and uptight.* Judging herself, she thought, *Here I am trying to send lovingkindness to someone and instead I'm disparaging him.* Still, she continued repeating the phrases, aligning her energy with her deep intention: to be a force of love in the world.

At that moment the man walked over to her and said, "I've never done anything like this before in my life, but I'd like to ask you to pray for me. I am about to face a very difficult situation in my life. You somehow seem to have a really loving heart, and I'd just like to know that you're praying for me."

Down Under

Almost twenty years after I first began meditating, I found myself at a retreat being held "down under" in a convent tucked away in New South Wales, Australia. The site featured prim gardens, heavy mahogany furnishings, copious amounts of tea, roaming tabby cats, and not quite enough heat at night. The retreat was under the guidance of Burmese master Sayadaw U Pandita. For the previous six years, this venerated monk—head of one of the main monasteries in Southeast Asia—had been among my primary teachers, inspiring me by both his rigorous discipline and his profound wisdom.

I believed myself ready for what I knew would be a demanding yet liberating retreat. Perhaps reflecting the quaintness of the atmosphere, my inner world felt neatly contained, orderly. Whatever disturbances arose in my thoughts—administrative decisions to be made back home, communications to be smoothed out before any possible misunderstandings grew—seemed vague and distant, issues I could neatly tie up and stow away on a shelf to be dealt with later, at my leisure. However, underneath this casing of peace lay deep pockets of pain held in habitual abeyance, guarded by the thinnest of membranes.

During one early morning meditation I was sitting peacefully, watching my breath, feeling sensations move throughout my body, observing the lazy drift of thoughts coming and going in my mind. Suddenly everything abruptly shifted. I had never forgotten the circumstances of how my mother died, but with an immediacy that left no escape, I was engulfed in reliving what had happened that evening when I was nine years old and my mother began hemorrhaging. My heart pounding, my breath catching in my throat, the memory lifted out of the cells of my body, vivid, consuming.

This was more than I could handle sitting in the meditation hall, and I got up and went back to my room. I lay on my bed sweating, too stunned to cry, almost unable to breathe. The swelling of grief that had once closed off my heart drew tightly again. I found myself in a mapless terrain of suffering, a flat, uncontoured land where no change seemed possible. Haunted by my mother's death, I watched the world turn vague and very cold. The despair of feeling completely alone, the anguish and desolation of my childhood once again suffused all time and eradicated all space.

I tried to coach myself out of it. "Well, now you're an adult, and this just isn't like you anymore." I tried to counter my guilt about not saving her with rational arguments. "You were a nine-year-old child, you did the best you could." I tried to manipulate the feelings. "It's not really so bad, shape up." I contemplated fretfully, "Why is this happening to me? I've worked so hard. This is old stuff."

In the middle of this abyss, I remembered I had a scheduled interview with U Pandita. I opened my eyes and noticed it was almost time to go. Automatically, I pulled on my shoes and set off to see him. Outside the confines of my room, I looked around at the primal, elemental landscape. The sky was a viscous dome of saturated blue. The hard, clear subequatorial sunshine thrust the looming eucalyptus trees and convent buildings into sharp relief. Even the shadows were bold—where there was light there was light, and where there was none the darkness was distinct.

I walked into U Pandita's room, which was much like my own—a cavernous space, with a few pieces of heavy furniture and a threadbare rug. It had seemed picturesque; now it felt devoid of comfort. In accord with Asian custom, I bowed three times and then, sitting down, I hesitantly began to describe my experience to him. Such enveloping pain wasn't what I had anticipated for this retreat, and it wasn't at all what I believed should be happening after years of meditation practice. Embarrassed, I told him I had gone from anguish to a strange kind of constricted numbness. He listened carefully, looked at me calmly, and simply said, "Be mindful of the pain."

·   ·   ·   ·

One night I sat up late in the garden. The sky seemed too close, pressing down upon me, filled with stars that looked . . . wrong. The Big Dipper, the constellation I was most familiar with, was nowhere to be found. Instead, here in the Southern Hemisphere, the unfamiliar Southern Cross dominated the night. How would I ever find my way home again? In my early life I'd lost my family; now I'd also lost my footing on the path that had saved my life. I'd lost my comfortable center of gravity in the world. I was on my own, left sitting unhappy and lonely under a too close, alien sky.

A memory of Dipa-Ma arose in my mind. She certainly knew what it was like to have great heartache. Over the course of ten years, two of her three children died, one at birth, one after a few months of life. Her husband, whom she loved very much, had come home from work one day not feeling well and was dead by nightfall. In extreme grief, Dipa-Ma was unable to get out of bed, unable to eat, unable to care for her surviving child. Her doctor came to see her and warned that she might actually die of a broken heart if she didn't do something about the state of her mind. "Go learn how to meditate," he advised.

She was so weak the first time she went to the center that she had to crawl up the temple stairs to begin her meditation practice.

Dipa-Ma's practice enabled her to put the pieces of her experience together in a way that completely altered her life, so that her pain, instead of leaving her stranded in grief, opened her to intense compassion. Deep within herself and even within her suffering she found a power of love that wouldn't diminish, no matter what happened.

When I was preparing to leave India in 1974, I'd gone to see Dipa-Ma to get her blessing. Suddenly, in the midst of our conversation, she said to me, "When you go to America you should teach meditation." I was astonished and immediately protested, "No, I can't do that. I'm not at all qualified." She smiled patiently, as though at a child who has lost the point of a story, and answered, "Yes, you should teach. You really understand suffering. That's why you're qualified to teach." The notion that the unhappiness of my earlier life could serve as the distinction of my abilities seemed most peculiar. She hadn't said, "You have a full grasp of the Buddhist cosmology and all theoretical applications, therefore you should teach." Instead, her criteria were based in the power of moving through great heartache and, rather than being destroyed by it, coming to greater faith—faith in one's self, faith in the power of love, faith in the movement of life itself.

During Dipa-Ma's first visit to the United States, we had sat together under a starry sky as she eagerly sought to spot any differences from the skies of India. Even though her past had left her so bereft by the deaths of her children and husband, she had come out of the tragedy alive and open to life's new experiences. Dipa-Ma had found herself more truly than ever by finding faith and love, even in the crucible of her anguish. Sitting there alone now, under the Southern Cross, I thought if such extreme suffering could serve as the proximate cause of faith, then the suffering of my own despair must also contain a crack of light between shades of darkness. Remembering that the way out of the pain was through it, trembling, I sought the crack. I began to sense a gleam of direction.

When we see our pain, whether mental or physical, as a single, solid, monolithic entity, unyielding and oppressive, it is almost impossible to bear. Fighting a consolidated enemy, we feel overcome, helpless, stuck. But when we can be mindful of exactly what is happening, we begin to see that everything we experience is composed of many ever-changing elements. Instead of viewing pain as static and fixed, we begin to see its component parts. Physical pain may be composed of burning, throbbing pressure. Emotional pain such as anger may be made up of fear, hopelessness, frustration. Learning how to work with pain in this way, a musicologist once said, "We would call that 'taking apart the chord.' " When we take apart the chord of our pain, even though the experience may remain difficult, the pain becomes an alive system, with movement and variation and flux. Just as the world is breathing, the pain is breathing. It's inhaling and exhaling, and there is space between its arisings. Rather than feeling overcome and helpless in the face of a wall of pain, we can find hope, relief in that rhythm of change.

Over the next few days alone in my retreat room I rocked back and forth for hours, remembering, and crying. As I began to explore the ball of suffering in my stomach, mindfully taking apart the chord, I found notes of fear and grief and loneliness. I found sadness and resentment and a tremendous amount of guilt. I also found glimpses of space between them. As I let in each state, my body became less rigid, and my armor of despair began to soften. The world grew a little bigger than my suffering.

For the first time in what felt like weeks, I went outside for a walk. In the garden, several other meditators were silently walking. While I knew the particular stories of only a few people on the retreat, at that moment I knew with surety that there was pain ribboned through the lives of everyone I saw there, whether mild unease or severe distress, whether current sadness or potential sorrow.

I had seen suffering aplenty as people revealed their hearts and lives to me. From my very first months of teaching, when someone came for a meditation interview and told me about her parents hanging her in the shower and beating her when she was a child, my career had unfolded in witness of suffering: physical and sexual abuse, betrayals, illnesses, depression, loneliness, oppressive relationships, oppressive secrets, exhausting moral dilemmas. Dipa-Ma had been right in telling me that understanding suffering was a good qualification for a life of teaching. And knowing I was not alone in suffering was a good qualification for a life of practice.

· · · · · · · · · · ·

Chapter IX

The Diamond Sutra. The Diamond Business

Michael Roach

Michael Roach (b. 1952) was one of America's golden youth. He received the Presidential Scholars Medallion from President Nixon, and he graduated from Princeton University with high honors. While some of his classmates then went on to earn their Ph.D.s, he studied for his geshe degree—often called a Ph.D. in Tibetan Buddhism. After becoming a geshe, what are you able to do? In Michael Roach's case, apparently anything. Start off with no capital and quickly earn millions of dollars in the diamond business? For Roach that was a snap (see below).

Roach has become a human dynamo in the service of Buddhism. He is putting on computers 200,000 Buddhist texts, as the surest way to preserve them. (His personal laptop has more Buddhist books than the largest monastery library.) Among other activities Roach has established the following: the Asian Classic Institute to teach Buddhism popularly; the Diamond Abbey in New York state, to train Western nuns and monks; the Enlightened Business Institute to show businessmen how Buddhist ethics can be turned to profit. In the year 2000, this human whirlwind undertook a different sort of project—a traditional three-year meditation retreat in secluded isolation. Michael Roach furnishes a model of how to adapt ancient Buddhism to contemporary America, while preserving its traditional vigor and integrity.

In Part I of the following selection, Roach dictated an overview of his life and professional career (which has been twice profiled in Forbes *magazine) to Vickie Mackenzie. In Part II, Roach writes how business people can increase through Buddhism both their satisfaction and their profits.*

I

One day in July 1975 I was meditating and something very extraordinary happened. It was very special. I had a vision which was to do with diamonds. The diamond has a special meaning in Buddhism. In particular it represents absolute truth, or the philosophy of Emptiness. There are several reasons, but the most important is that the diamond is the closest thing to an absolute in the physical world. Nothing in the universe is harder than a diamond; nothing can scratch a diamond; a diamond is perfectly clear. If a diamond wall were built around us, we wouldn't see it, because it's perfect. Similarly, ultimate reality is around us all the time, we live in it. If we could see it, we would be very close to reaching Buddhahood, Enlightenment.

When I had that vision, I knew I had to be working in the diamond business. It was part of my spiritual development. I asked my lama, Khen Rinpoche, a great, high lama who before the loss of Tibet had been the administrator of the Tantric College in Lhasa, and afterwards was the abbot of Sera monastery in south India. The day after graduating from Princeton I had gone to live with him at his monastery in New Jersey, where he had been sent by the Dalai Lama. I was being trained in the traditional manner. That meant, in effect, that there were only two things you could do without asking your preceptor, clean your teeth and go the bathroom. A real lama is meant to help you with everything. Khen Rinpoche, who was always very practical, approved of my plan. "Grow your hair a little bit and buy a suit," he said. "Am I allowed to deal in money?" I asked. "Sure," he replied, "if it helps people."

Until that moment I had no interest in diamonds, no background in diamonds. My family is Irish. I was like Candide trying to join this business, which is run almost exclusively by Hasidic Jews and is very tight and closed. It needs to be, because you can steal a million dollars in your pocket. For that reason, diamond traders only employ their relatives. I applied to 30 firms and was rejected by all of them before I met an Israeli man who was opening a diamond business in the States. He didn't know anyone in the USA, so he took a chance with me. I told him I would do anything: I would be a messenger or clean the windows, but I needed to work with diamonds. He said OK.

He taught me from scratch. First he let me be a messenger. Then he let me touch diamonds, then he let me sort them. For the first year we worked an eighteen-hour day. I didn't sleep much. One thing, I'm celibate and I don't have the commitment of a family, so that saved a lot of time. My commute to New Jersey was three and a half hours round trip, which gave me time to study my Buddhism and say prayers. After that first year, when things settled down, my day was divided into waking up at 6 A.M., meditating for an hour, getting the bus and being at work by 9 A.M., at 5 P.M. going home. At 7 P.M. I'd have a class with my lama till 9 P.M. Then I'd meditate till 10 P.M. or 10:30 P.M. Simultaneously I was taking my Geshe degree, which necessitated going to India to debate with thousands of monks, literally. My company gave me chunks of time off to do that, but as the monastery was close to Bombay, a major diamond center, I'd combine it with business.

Shortly after starting the company my boss invited me to head up my division, which at that time consisted of two people. I made a deal with him. "I'll do it providing I can run it along my own principles—Bodhisattva principles [the altruistic ideal of only benefiting others]. You can't interfere so long as I make a profit." He agreed, and it worked very well. We started with $50,000, which we borrowed, and now we do $125 million a year and have about 900 employees. Until recently I was vice-president of the company in charge of the diamond importing. We have branch offices all over the world and play the markets in Tel Aviv, Brazil, Antwerp, Russia, Australia, South Africa, Zaire, Botswana and Bombay by phone and e-mail.

The first Buddhist principle I established was that of "exchanging self with others." The managers have to do this Bodhisattva thing of putting themselves in the other person's shoes. The idea is that whenever you are dealing with an employee, even the janitor, you only think of what they would like and what would benefit them from the situation. I'd instruct them, "Even if you're having a ten-minute conversation, think, 'What would help this person?'" I trained all my people this way and I never told them it was Buddhism. For five years no one knew I was a monk. I wore a suit, I didn't shave my head. I really wanted to move in the workplace, to make moral decisions there without them being labeled Buddhist. They knew I was making millions of dollars without knowing why.

Another principle is what is called in Buddhism *Lojong* or mind training. The idea is that whenever there's a problem you turn it into an advantage. You use it. The Kadampa Geshes developed this 1,000 years ago in Tibet. So, say we get an order from a big jewelry company for 10,000 diamonds which we would proceed to buy, and then the order gets canceled. The result is we're stuck with 10,000 diamonds. Instead of trying to sell them and take a loss, which is the normal practice, we would design a new piece of jewelry using exactly 10,000 diamonds, go to another customer and suggest they make whatever adjustments to the design they want. Inevitably we would actually make more money from the second deal than the first.

I have rules, too, for dealing with outsiders, such as the suppliers. The main one is total honesty. We never ever pay a payment late and never cheat someone out of a deal. If someone makes a mistake in our favor we phone them immediately and tell them the payment is, say, $2000 too little and please bill us correctly.

According to the theory of karma, if you behave like this you'll get richer and richer, which is what happened to us. By using Buddhist principles the place started to go like crazy.

My division, which now has around 200 people of eighteen different nationalities, runs like clockwork and is very harmonious. The reason why most businesses do not flourish is because of problems among the people inside. It's not the market. We work on the Buddhist principles of no anger, no jealousy. If someone was being jealous or angry I would take them out to lunch and give them Buddhist logic. There are lots of Buddhist arguments about how destructive anger and jealousy are. I spent a lot of money on lunches! On a mundane level the reason is that a mental affliction takes time. A good jealousy attack lasts twenty minutes. Anger takes two days—it ruins your concentration. Even after the object of your anger is gone and the argument is finished, you still think about it. So if you teach your employees not to get angry, their whole mind is freed for other things. It's the same with desire. If people's minds are free from desire for any object—food, sex, money, fame, whatever—then they actually save lots of hours of their lives, and so you can do lots of projects because you're not thinking about those things.

I pass on my techniques to other business people through a series of seminars called things like "Ancient Wisdom for Motivating Employees to Reach Business Success," "Two-Minute Office Meditations for Learning Business Focus" and "Doing the Right Thing: Increasing Profits Through Honesty and Ethics."

Another condition of heading up my division was that I took a month off twice a year to go on retreat. This is unheard of in New York corporations, where the annual leave is two weeks. I insisted my staff got a similar deal. All of my people who work in the computer office are required to break twice a year—for five- to six-week retreat. And they're paid for it. It's for the creativity. The level of creativity is extraordinary when they come back! They see things totally differently. One good idea, one good solution in the diamond business and you're talking millions of dollars. For example, we worked out a way to weigh the diamonds to 1/1000th of a carat, which saved one percent or $1 million. That's the budget for the whole office.

My boss initially complained about my methods: "The other divisions are getting angry because they don't get two months off." "Hang on, we've got a deal," I'd reply.

People often ask me what a monk is doing working in such a material-istic and lucrative field. My reply is that the reason I went into the dia-mond business had nothing to do with the money—it was due to the vision, and nothing else. It was a coincidence that I got paid for doing what I would have done anyway. I can say now that the purpose of that vision has and continues to be fulfilled completely and very nicely. The vision was 90 percent of the reason. The other ten percent was due to the fact that so many monks needed help. Back in Tibet, Sera monastery had 8,000 monks and only 108 made it to south India. They started all over by living in tents in the jungle. It was wild! People were being killed by ele-phants there.

If you have just the basic Buddhist vows, you can't work. Among the basic 250 vows that all monks take there is a rule that says I can't own anything except my robes. Nothing. So if someone gives me a piece of red cloth I can only hold it for ten days. If I don't make it into a robe within ten days I have to give it away. But with Bodhisattva vows that Tibetan Buddhist monks take, if someone offers you a warehouse of red cloth you keep it until such a time as you can use it to help other people. There's a big difference. If thousands of monks in India are dying you *must* work. You must try to find the most lucrative work you can.

Now I support 2,000 monks. I don't keep any money for myself. I donate my salary. I take enough to live on—the rest has been given to the monasteries and to Tibetan refugees. It goes directly to the charities. We have helped establish schools, water systems, buildings, temples, a library, a diamond factory. We are teaching computers to refugees—monks, nuns and lay people—in twenty different camps. We train them to input Buddhist scriptures. We then put these onto CD-ROMs and give them away. To date we've given away about 10,000. We take handicapped peo-ple, deaf people, teenagers at risk, we teach them how to type and pay them $1 a page. Every time a handicapped boy or a bad boy earns $1, we put $4 into a village food fund we set up, and so he is helping to feed everybody in the village. It's a real incentive. Everyone starts to love them—and they start to work hard.

People often wonder if spirituality is compatible with making money, having a comfortable house, a nice car. Generally the idea that a Buddhist is not meant to desire to own nice things and have a comfortable lifestyle is false. It's true that the Buddha said that most people if they have more material things will start to experience more suffering because there's the suffering of not having enough and the suffering of having it. But the Buddha also said that if you have a good attitude and are generous, then the more you have, the happier you will be. If you are constantly getting it and giving it away, it works very well. There's absolutely no problem with being extremely wealthy and being a Buddhist because you can do wonderful things. The greatest first tantric practitioners in India were the kings and the aristocrats—the Buddha constantly went after that sort of person because they were in a position to really help people. An important principle of Buddhism is that if everyone were a perfect Buddha, everyone would be wealthy. The idea that there's not enough to go round is only created by our negative thoughts. If we were all perfectly ethical there would be more than enough. There would be limitless money for every person on this planet.

The goal of Buddhism is that physically your body transforms into a body of light, your mind becomes omniscient and materially you have all the money you ever dreamed of. All Buddhas are incredibly wealthy. They own a lot and they use it. And there's no problem with that.

I love my work. It's very useful for a spiritual person to have a whole life around normal people. You get to understand the suffering that normal people go through—the stress that's involved in earning a living to feed your family. When I travel about as a big lama, no one criticizes me to my face. Everyone's always telling me what a wonderful person I am, and congratulating me on the things I do. But when I'm at work the boss screams at me. There's greed to deal with. There's the jealousy of my other vice-presidents to deal with. Your spiritual life gets challenged every few seconds. It's a laboratory for Buddhist practice which you don't get in a monastery.

There are also beautiful women to deal with. We would go to the Diamond Fair at Basel and there would be hundreds of exquisite women modeling the diamonds. Buddhist monks are given methods for dealing with that sort of situation should it arise. There's a famous work by Nagarjuna which suggests we see how the body is mortal—so, you visualize the woman getting sick or performing human functions like defecating. That doesn't work very well. The other way is to see the Emptiness of a person—to see that the woman has no inherent existence. That works better for me. I was not in robes, so if a woman seriously approached me I would have to tell her I was ordained. After that it didn't happen. I grew up in the USA where there's a lot of pressure to engage in relationships with the opposite sex. It's very much drilled into you since childhood, yet if you go to a monastery and stay celibate for decades, as I have done, you discover you don't need that sort of relationship. There are much higher things to be interested in.

Actually, as a young man I was very troubled about relationships—it was one of the main things that got me into Buddhism. My parents had a very tough divorce. I saw how impermanent relationships were. I saw the swing from deep love to deep hatred. Even my own experience with my girlfriend in high school showed me how you could go from loving someone one minute to disliking them the next. That deeply disturbed me. I wanted to know how people could do that. Buddhism says that the disintegration of relationships is caused ultimately by negative thoughts and that when you change your negative thoughts that disintegration doesn't happen any more. Most relationships, however, end in sorrow, and when they don't they are ended by death.

There are so many ways I have benefited from being in the workplace. The translation work I put out afterwards was much better. You learn, for example, how normal people speak. If you deal with business people all day, you get to know that. I also now know how to teach in normal American terms. We started the Asian Classics Institute, in the East Village, Manhattan, with six people; now 300 turn up. It's because the teachings are delivered in a language ordinary people can grasp. They're coming like crazy. We keep having to rent bigger places. We started in a Christian church, now we're in a basketball gymnasium. We do no advertising, they just come in off the street. They really want to know.

Positively what they're looking for is contentment—because it's totally lacking in New York. No one is content there; no one. Of all the places in the world, New York City is the hardest one to find happiness in. I'm not sure why. Maybe because we have everything. In the negative, the people who come to us are trying to explain the pain of human existence. They want to make sense of why people suffer, why they get old and die. I wanted to know the same things. The year I joined my monastery, my father, my mother and my brother all died. If you're brought up believing that God made you and that God is compassionate, then the question has to be asked why did he kill three people like that. I found that Buddhism dealt with the issue of death more thoroughly than Christianity.

Buddhism has a lot to offer. Mentally it makes you very happy. You remove your negativities, the qualities of your emotions improve and you become content. The individual becomes responsible for the individual's world, so any misfortune you might have is not blamed on an external force, like God. Rather it is due to your own state of mind. If you learn to observe your mind throughout the day, from hour to hour, and are very careful to be compassionate to other people, very, very careful to be good to other people, then the result after months or years is that your own mind becomes extremely contented. And that's what people want. So Buddhism works.

Ironically, watching out for other people's happiness becomes the best way of reaching happiness yourself. You would think that doing things for yourself would make you happy, getting things for yourself, but actually it's the reverse. It's so unexpected that most people never try it. Yet the more you try it, the happier you are.

There are certain techniques that can be used to foster mindfulness like this, other than meditation. My students and I do an exercise where we have a little book and every two hours we examine the state of our mind and jot down what it is. Actually this was invented by the Buddha, it's a deep tantric practice. You do this all of your life. Once you get good at it you can do it anywhere—even in an office in Manhattan with thousands of transactions going on and the pace so hectic that people are actually running up and down the aisles.

These days I am drawing away from the diamond industry. I just go back when they want me. I told them five years ago that I wanted to quit and it has taken me that long to get out. For a while I worked eight months a year, then six and last year I cut back to one month. Now I am concentrating on my teaching.

I will have spent seven years transmitting the Geshe degree to my students in New York, and one year reviewing it. Then I hope to build a place in Arizona to start a community there made up of serious practitioners who like to study and meditate. It will be a lifestyle which doesn't require them to be in a city. We're designing some adobes, and a meditation temple with a courtyard in the middle. It will be a large property. It looks like we might get 7,000 acres. I think western monasticism is going to consist of people living in communities like that, with monks, nuns and lay people who have made lifelong vows earning their living through computer-related skills. I'd also like to keep the center in New York open and to come back periodically to teach.

It has been suggested that westerners are so excited by their discovery of Buddhism that they are overly gullible and naïve. There might be a slight danger of that, but it's overstated. A person who's infatuated with Buddhism will come down after their honeymoon period to a true Buddhism. Westerners are actually the best Dharma students in the world. Here you have hundreds of millions of people who are well educated and who are not looking for their next meal. They have time and they're critical. They're not going to believe something unless you can prove it to them. My students are extremely cynical and skeptical; 75 percent of them have rejected something. This makes them perfect for Buddhism. There's a huge customer base for Buddhism in the West—in the diamond market you call it an overhang.

II

Money by itself is completely meaningless if we cannot enjoy its use. We also have to learn how to maintain a clear and healthy body and mind both in the office and out of it—how to keep our careers going year upon year with youthful vigor and creativity. Here at the end though we must speak about the inevitable; which is to say, regardless of how well you succeed in making money and then maintaining the clear heart to enjoy it properly, you must one day come to the end of your business, and even your life. In the Buddhist tradition, a businessperson is not really successful because he or she has made a lot of money, nor even because the person has made a lot of money and knows how to enjoy it fully. The end is as important as the beginning and the middle; you must be able to come to the end, the inevitable end, and look back on your life in business and say honestly that it was all worth it—that all your intense hours and years of effort have had some real meaning.

The decision to make sure that your business has some real meaning and benefit in the world cannot even come to you unless you are able to look at your life and your career from the perspective of its inevitable end. You cannot resolve to see that your life has meaning unless you are able to see yourself in the final hours of your life, unless you are able to put yourself in those future shoes, and practice looking back upon what you have done with your life. And so this story is about Shirley.

The day I walked into Andin [a start-up diamond company] for my first real job I ran into Shirley; it wasn't hard, because she was the only other employee at the time. I was just coming out of eight years of intense, single-pointed concentration on studies and meditation in a small monastery with my Lama; the noise and stench of New York City would literally make me nauseated coming in on the bus for nearly two hours every morning, but then to watch Shirley go through the day would counterbalance everything. She was a strong, proud Jamaican woman with flowing black hair and a smile the size of the room; growing up in Arizona, I had never met someone from the Islands and was entranced when I saw this living sunlight walk up and down the corridors, singing some beautiful song in a lovely British lilt. Shirley and her husband Ted quickly became like family; we struggled and worked overtime along with the owners, Ofer and Aya, as Andin took off, doubling and tripling in sales almost by the year, until reaching its current volume of more than $100 million per year. In time, both Shirley and I were running large divisions of the company: she the distribution, and I the diamonds.

Shirley's unshakable good humor and the love she poured out to all those around her were lengendary; we could work until one or two in the morning and she would be as cheerful at the end as she had been at the beginning of the day. A song was never far from her lips, even under the pressure of directing nearly a hundred employees and packing and shipping ten thousand pieces of fine jewelry per day, against impossible deadlines. She would be the first in and the last out, and would die for her people; this and other traits earned her the fierce loyalty and love of anyone who worked for her. The inner strength that shone from her eyes, and the deep convictions of her living Christianity, made her a rock of strength for all of us.

I remember when the first problem came; something was wrong with Shirley, people said, and did we want to go visit her at the hospital. This was one of those profound shocks you get when someone you thought was invincible proves to be more than fragile: the feeling I had when my mother got a large lump on her breast, or the time my father blacked out hunting and started falling down a mountain, with me the teenage boy trying to stop his huge body from rolling off a cliff. It turned out that Shirley had a fairly serious case of diabetes, but all would be well if she would take it easy a bit, eat well and regularly, swallow a few pills at the right time of day.

You have to realize that the company was burning up the market; we were invincible, running circles around a whole world that didn't seem to know how to do anything right. Shirley and I reached a point where we were playing with hundreds of thousands, or even millions, of dollars on an hourly basis. Our salaries grew nearly as wildly as our work and our staff—we became little gods in office kingdoms, discussing the future of a person or a whole room full of people over lunch, as if they were dolls or toy soldiers that we owned, and moved here and there at our whim. Andin was an all-consuming passion and mistress; the company made impossible demands of us and drove us to performances way over our abilities, only to reward us with money we had never had any dream of seeing. And Shirley began to stay later and later into the night, entranced in a way, as we all were to some extent.

Nothing was as important as work. She would miss a meal here, and then there, and then frequently. Maybe she would remember to take her medicine, and maybe not, but the monster shipment to J. C. Penney would go out without a minute to spare. The hours and the abuse of her body began to take their inevitable toll, but she refused to slow down. I think one of the most important corporate lessons I ever learned came to me around this time: Really good employees will continue to drive themselves until they hurt themselves, and it takes great wisdom and self-control on the part of managers to know when to force people to slow down, even when the operation will suffer as a result.

There came a time when Shirley wasn't well enough to run a large group of people, but out of pure affection the owners created a job—a customer service department—that she could continue with at a slower pace. And then she left and moved up to New Hampshire, to rest and begin expensive kidney dialysis treatments. Andin continued to roll and it was hard to keep in touch; my day was moving at a thousand miles per hour, sometimes three or four phone calls going on at once, gemstones flying through the division not in little envelopes but in garbage bags and bins—not in hundreds but in thousands and tens of thousands. Shirley's day though was slowing down.

The last time I spoke to her I accidentally called at the very moment she had returned from the hospital after both her legs were amputated.

She was, as always, incredibly cheerful and caring, talking more about me than about herself; and then for the first time wondering out loud what she would become. Within a short time she was dead.

With the news of her death, with the knowledge that the woman we had stood next to over the years, and shared every conceivable sorrow and joy with during most of our waking hours, was no more, and could not be with us again, we looked for the first time back on our lives at the company, with the eyes of a person who had reached a permanent turning point. It was inevitable that, for the first time, we would begin to ask ourselves if it was all worth it. It was fun; it was more than fun, it was consuming; but the illusion of grandeur and importance faded instantly against the fact of death, forced upon us by her permanent departure. The lusty war for money would never be the same again. Now it was something serious. Now it was something for keeps. We were spending real life here, and at the end we would run out of life. No one could continue to ignore the fact that—regardless of our company's growing power in the market, and regardless of the authority and money we ourselves accumulated in our positions as Andin grew—it would be no more than an ill-remembered dream only a few days after we retired. We were forced to question why we were there at all.

The Buddhist approach to business says that we should walk into the office this way every morning, with the question: "If I were going to die tonight, is this the way I would spend my last day?" This is not just a way to depress yourself, or some kind of morbid thinking. It's very practical; it frees you; and it makes for great business, business you can really be proud of when you come to the inevitable end of your business career and look back. Here's how it works.

There's a practice called "Death Meditation" in Tibetan monasteries. The idea you get in your mind when you hear this phrase is probably lying down on a cold piece of sidewalk somewhere and trying to imagine a lot of tubes up your nose, relatives crying at your side, and heart monitors going off with a beeping sound. But this is not the point at all. To put it simply, you just wake up in the morning and stay there in bed, lying down, without opening your eyes. And you say to yourself: "I'm going to die tonight. What would be the best thing to do with the rest of my time?"

A couple of things will go through your mind right away. It would be like having a surprise day off, and since you're going to die tonight, well, then, maybe try something you always wanted to do that was a little off-the-wall or maybe even a bit dangerous but—what does it matter, if you're going to die tonight? So I suppose you might get the urge to try skydiving that day, or maybe go sing in a karaoke bar, or get the most expensive tickets to a Broadway play (assuming there's a matinee).

The Death Meditation practice has to be done on a regular basis, over an extended period of time—and that's when it has its strongest effect. One result you'll find comes pretty quickly is that you streamline your life: You cut out the things that you own or do that slow you down. This is the beginning of a new kind of freedom, both physically and mentally. How many pairs of shoes do you have? And where are the pictures of your old vacations, the ones that you don't look at anymore? In your mind when you hear these questions you start picturing all the different shoes that you have: Your mind goes into your closet and looks at least at the ones you use most often. And then your mind goes to a cabinet or dresser somewhere and sees a few stacks of photo envelopes; goes inside one or two; sees roughly what a couple of the photos are of.

All this proves that, somewhere, on some level, you are keeping a mental inventory of all the things you own. Which also means that some part of your mind space is taken up with these details; remember that the mind is like the hard drive of a computers—it only has so much space. You know how computers start acting when their hard drives get near to full: programs stop working, everything gets slower, systems crash. And you know how fun it is to use a new computer with a lot of hard drive space—everything is flying. The idea of Death Meditation is to go from one to the other. A quick, dirty way to achieve this is to start throwing out things in your house that you don't need or use. This can be up to about 75 percent of the things there—a good rule of thumb is, have I really used this thing in the last six months or so? If not, throw it out.

As you practice this meditation longer, you'll start to do with your schedule what you've done with your things. If you were really going to die tonight, would you sit and read through the whole Sunday paper, or most of the magazines you subscribe to? Would you really surf around the TV looking desperately for anything of even minor interest? Would you still go out and spend an hour or two at lunch or dinner, gossiping about the other managers? Decide then: *If not on the day I die, then not now either.* Because, frankly, it may really be today.

At some point in this process you will begin examining your career itself. Is this really the job you'd want to be doing if you were going to die tonight? Is there something else you would rather be doing, but were afraid to try, because you weren't sure you could make enough money at it, or because you're afraid to try something that's completely new, or just because you're a little lazy to fully move on? Life really is very short, and your working years are very limited—your years of maximum energy and health and mental sharpness. Maybe it would be worth it to make a little less money, if you could live each day doing what you really felt was important.

At the final evolution of the Death Meditation, this kind of thinking flowers into an instinctive attraction to those things in a human life which really are of the greatest beauty and meaning. You have, through a process of internal thought and meditation, pushed your thinking ahead to what it will very likely be toward the end of your career and your life. You have already probably made a pretty good amount of money. You have met your own basic needs, even comfortably, and provided for those of your family. Occupationally you are at a place where, even though your physical energy and to some extent your mental powers may be a little less than they were at your peak, you have a wealth of experience that makes you capable of pulling off almost any kind of task successfully.

This is the point, mentally, when successful business people in their later years begin to be attracted to philanthropy. This is not happening because they have nothing else to do; rather, these people have picked up a kind of wisdom over the entire course of their life that has pinpointed the single most meaningful thing you can do with the money and power and experience you've accumulated. People like this are at the point we were talking about before: They are looking back on their career from the viewpoint of the end of career, and have begun the inevitable process of asking themselves, "Was it worth it?"

The idea here is to anticipate where you're going to be in a few years, and make some decisions now that will allow you to look back with total joy and satisfaction. The knowledge that you'll be able to do so makes not just the goal, but the entire trip—your entire career—infinitely more fun and interesting. So try the Death Meditation now; my guess is that you'll end up in the state of mind we call "exchanging self and others."

• • • •

This is perhaps the greatest secret of the ancient books of Buddhism: a simple, daily method to give your life and career meaning, so that they are more than just the gradual crumbling of power and wealth and vitality into old age and death. It just also happens to be the greatest management tool of all time. In the Diamond Division at Andin we typically had over ten different nationalities working together on the same floor: ruby and sapphire experts from Thailand; topaz people from Sri Lanka; emerald sorters from India; pearl sizers from China; gemstone matchers from Puerto Rico and the Dominican Republic; diamond buyers from Israel; stone setters from Vietnam and Cambodia; quality control and colored stone buyers from Barbados; buying coordinators from Guyana; and more. You can imagine what it sounded like to have ten different languages going in a stone sorting room at once; ten different exotic food smells emanating from the microwaves at lunch; ten different sets of cultural etiquette to be satisfied simultaneously: Don't point your feet at the Thais; don't offer a Gujarati anything to eat that grew underground; don't forget something gold for the bride at a Cantonese wedding.

But the division ran as one person, and one thing I can honestly say is that it was a true pleasure to work with every person there; despite our hugely different backgrounds (the most frustrating thing was that *no* normal American joke would seem funny to *everyone,* and since nobody had grown up in the United States you couldn't make references to old TV shows or songs or anything else), despite the obvious and also the unspoken gaps between us, we ended up with a deep feeling of mutual love and respect, which in turn made the division work like a well-oiled machine. A big part of this was simply *the absence of personal problems that could have happened but never did.*

I think we achieved this in a large part because of the initial philosophy of the division from the day it began—and the core of this philosophy was the ancient Buddhist practice of "exchanging yourself and others." If you really want your business or your department to be a success, I suggest that you try this practice; it's simple, extremely powerful, and costs you nothing. It's just an attitude that you start from the top—it begins with you, and then leaks down to the entire staff. No memos needed, no announcements, no meetings.

That thing that the Buddha invariably talked about—the wish for enlightenment—has the exchange of yourself and others at its core. It involves three essential steps, and the third of these steps includes the answer to the question about why the Buddha said "nobody gets there unless you get everybody there." This profound practice is over 2,500 years old; we'll present it here in the classical way, but with modern, real-life examples.

I like to call the first step the Jampa Method. Jampa is a shy, young Tibetan monk who lives in the little Mongolian monastery where I did a lot of my training, in New Jersey. He's the cook, mows the lawn, takes care of the older Lamas, and does a million other selfless tasks, constantly and quietly. He turns the Jampa Method on whenever a visitor shows up in the little kitchen next to the abbot's quarters. He does it to you and you never know. He opens the door with a big smile that covers your face with his sunshine, but he's already doing it. What's "it"?

Jampa was trained in our home monastery of Sera, now relocated in India after the invasion of Tibet, and he was trained by some of the best—by two high Lamas named Geshe Lothar and Geshe Thupten Tenzin. The minute you step in he has you down on a chair at the kitchen table, and he's puttering around the stove and the refrigerator to prepare you something to drink or snack on as you describe why you're visiting the monastery. While he walks around the room he watches your eyes and your body language. As your eyes scan the room, do they stop and rest on the kettle on the stove, or do they hesitate at the refrigerator when he reaches for the handle; that is, would you like something hot to drink, or something cold? There's a bowl of candy on the kitchen table, and a plate of cookies farther down, and the perpetual pot of soup on the stove—which one do your eyes come back to most often?

Within a few minutes, Jampa has figured you out completely: he knows whether you like tea or coffee, hot or cold, with milk or sugar or not, cookies or crackers or noodles, and a dozen other details about your likes and dislikes. The next time you show up, you'll find your favorite beverage on the table before you say anything, because he remembers— he makes it a point to remember. And he makes it a point because *he really wants to give you what you want.*

The Jampa Method is, in short, learning to be very observant of what others need and like. This is so you can give them what they want the most. This may sound a little naïve, but the simple exercise of taking the time to *educate yourself about what others like and want* has a profound effect on your entire business world. The nature of business, and the nature of corporate life, is that executives tend to concentrate on the immediate issues at hand for themselves—they are expected to perform as individuals, and they are rewarded as individuals. When was the last time you and *another* vice-president were given a holiday bonus to split between you for doing a good job together? This individual focus causes us then to concentrate on ourselves, at the expense of paying attention to others.

The Jampa Method, the first part of the exchange of self and others, takes us out of this exclusive focus on ourselves and starts us off on the process of being sensitive to others. This has all sorts of immediate benefits on the work flow, and on your finances. It also plants some of the most powerful and profitable imprints possible in your mind. Here's how we apply it in a corporate setting.

As you walk around your department, watch the people who work for you. Most of us make it a point to be an expert in the finances of running our operation; in the important occupational regulations affecting our business; and in the state of the suppliers who provide the services and materials we absolutely need to get our product out. The idea here is that you now consciously train yourself to be an expert in one more thing— and that's the likes and dislikes of the people around you. We're talking here about *everything,* every detail about what makes them happy: how they fix their coffee; what kind of cushion they like on their chair; what kind of pen they prefer; how many children they have, what the children's names are, and how they're doing; when was their last vacation, and where did they go, and how did they enjoy it.

Then go and sit down in your office and *memorize* these details for each of the people close to you. If you have to take some notes, then do so. I find a laptop computer very useful for this; you can pull the file up again on the way home from work and review what you learned. This exercise inevitably leads to some kind of improvement in your behavior toward the person, even if it's just handing them sweetener rather than sugar the next time you're standing next to them at the coffeepot. Deep down, people really notice this kind of thing; in a way, we're all like your dog at home—he knows it when a person who loves dogs walks in the room, and he knows it when a person who hates dogs walks in the room, and he acts accordingly, even before anything is said or done.

People have an instinct that informs them when you don't care that much about what they like or need, and they have an instinct for the opposite just as well. It may seem a little artificial at first to track their likes and needs so blatantly, but that's part of the process—it is, exactly, artificial at the beginning. Later it becomes second nature, but only because you've done everything artificially at first.

It is true that what most of your employees would really like is if you gave them a six-week vacation or doubled their salary. But these are not the kinds of likes and dislikes we're talking about. We're not suggesting that you make any major financial or personnel move here. Just that you watch and observe quietly, and within your immediate capacity supply those around you with what they seem to like the most. Inevitably the tables will start to turn, and they will get in the spirit of doing the same for you. Imagine the feeling of a whole division of people acting this way.

There was a point in my career at Andin when I realized, clearly, that the primary reason I was being paid such a ridiculously high salary was because I could get people to work together. I realized that the most important role I filled was simply that of an arbitrator between any two or three of the people who worked for me; that the most important hour for me in the entire day was lunchtime, when I would almost always be taking out two supervisors who couldn't get along with each other very well. This kind of friction bleeds a company silently but surely: Supervisor A has a little beef with Supervisor B, and avoids talking to that person unless it's absolutely necessary. A little issue comes up on an important order that can be handled easily in its early stages on Monday, but which will form into a disaster by Friday.

Supervisor A knows about the issue on Monday but doesn't say anything to Supervisor B, who could have fixed it easily. It's not the kind of issue that should have or would have been brought up on Monday at the staff meeting, but it is something that Supervisors A and B would have mentioned to each other if they were in the habit of hanging out at the water cooler together to shoot the breeze once in a while. What I'm trying to say is that a little good will among your staff members is worth much more money than you ever dreamed of. And the Jampa Method is the first step.

Again, no announcements or policy statements—you just start doing it, and others follow. I remember when His Holiness the Dalai Lama visited my home state of Arizona to give a series of talks, and one of my old high school friends had a chance to ask him a question: What's the best way to teach young children how to lead an ethical way of life? "At that age," said His Holiness, "it doesn't matter what you tell them to do. They will watch and imitate you; they will do what you do, and so you are faced with the hardest task of all—to be ethical yourself." You have to start spying on the people who work for you, a kind of very beautiful spying, to see what they like, what they find important in their own lives; and then go about helping them get it.

The second step in the practice of exchanging yourself and others is to pretend to put your mind in their body, and then open your eyes and look at you, and see what it is that you (they) would like from you (you). If you think this sounds confusing, try to imagine how hard it is to translate an ancient book on this subject from Sanskrit or Tibetan!

This step, called Switching Bodies, is a little deeper and harder than just watching the people around you to see what they like and don't like. I can remember trying it with a young man from Guyana who had just joined the division; he came recommended by a friend of his mother's, who already worked for us (people who work with stones always come on recommendation; there's not really any way to stop them from walking out with a few hundred at any given hour of the day, so they have to have a traceable history). We sat him down the first day in front of a huge pile of diamond chips and set him to counting out hundreds or thousands for specific ring orders.

By the end of the day I had learned a bit more about him; he was pleasant with the people around him, a fast learner, quiet, humble, and quick as hell. On the way out I learned one more thing: I looked into his face and saw a mix of enjoyment for the place and a twinge of despair at the thought of having to sit in a chair and count little rocks for the next few years of his life. And then I did the Switching Bodies thing, I put myself in his body, and looked at my face, and asked myself what I would like me (me) to say to me (him). So I said, "Come into my office in the morning and we'll see if we can't find you something a little more challenging." And I felt my eyes drop a little shyly, and a smile stretch across my (his) face.

From that moment on I was steadily putting my mind in his body; we got him (me) something that I (him) had always dreamed of—a chance to learn to work with computers. We put him under one of the best programming cowboys we had, and after he had proved his determination we helped him get through a series of college courses. In the diamond business, this kind of night school is traditionally a no-no: During the busy season, everyone's working very late hours, and even off season you don't want tired people messing up sensitive inventory systems or piles of diamonds. But every time I saw him I knew it was what I (he) wanted when I looked at my (my) face, and I knew the sense of fulfillment and accomplishment it gave, and we found ways to work around his (my) absence on school days. In the end he became the best programmer we had, and even more important an employee who knew we had done what we knew would be best for him, even when it hurt the company a bit. And in this way we had created a person who would really give when the crunch came, and who throughout the day would be looking for ways to help the company and those around him.

You can't put a price on these kinds of people, sprinkled around your department, constantly on the lookout for ways to smooth out problems with orders or systems or people before you ever hear about them. And when the day is over, when you reach the end of your own career and look back, it won't be the sales you made or the projects you completed or the P&L that you remember at all. It will be looking into the young man's face looking up at your own, and knowing you have given him something precious for his entire life. And if you keep up this kind of thinking, this kind of putting yourself into your employees' bodies and looking to yourself for help, you will find a profound kind of satisfaction growing within you, the kind of deep contentment that you have at very rare and special moments, except that—the more you keep this up—the more frequently the feeling comes to you. This in fact is a sign that your work *is taking on true meaning.* And it's important to point out again, I think, that this kind of thinking is not only *right,* but also *the most profitable,* as your department and your company begin to run themselves, begin to be run by people who really care, because you care for them as you would for yourself. Money and happiness. You can have your cake and eat it too.

We call this third step the Rope Trick. You can do it on any one of your employees; just walk up and stand next to an individual some day at her desk. Pretend that you have this huge Roy Rogers lasso in your hand, and that you drop it on the floor around the both of you—it surrounds you both. Now imagine that the two of you are, literally, one person.

You see, in the first two steps we did some pretty radical things about learning to watch and think about what those around us really like—we even got to where we could switch bodies with someone and look at ourselves and see what we (they) wanted most from us (us). *But there was still the distinction between "you" and "me."* It was a question of "me" watching "you," or "me" trying to get into "your" body. With step three we take the practice of exchanging yourself and others to a completely more radical level: You *are* your employee, and he or she is you: you are one person.

Anyone can see, with only a bit of thought, that the place where "I" ends and "them" begins is a very slippery matter. When mothers give birth to children, their sense of "me" suddenly gets stretched to cover another, tiny body: Do harm to *this* particular child, and you can expect *this* particular woman to react with all the passion that she would show if you attacked her own body. People with really bad cases of diabetes act the opposite: their feet form sores, and the sores become gangrenous, and the doctors tell them they either have to amputate the leg or die.

The minute you decide that losing your leg would be better than losing your life, you have in effect *shrunk* your definition or border of "me" to a smaller space than before. This proves that you have the power to expand or contract "me" to greater or smaller areas, so don't tell me it's impossible to do the Rope Trick and throw the rope around another person until you become one person. It's only the imprints from your past, your *habit and choice* of thinking of the edge of yourself as the edge of your skin or the edge of *your* stomach, that keeps you from making someone else you too. Imagine, just for a moment, what would happen if the entire world thought and acted as if everyone else were they themselves. We could bring everyone to total happiness, and "no one" would reach total happiness—because "everyone" would only be one of us: us.

Which brings us to your second objection, the second hesitation you must have in your mind about this whole proposal. Suppose I do do the Rope Trick; suppose I do take the border of "me" and stretch it around one or even more other people. Where do I draw the line? What's the limit? Life is hard enough as it is; it seems almost impossible to provide successfully for all the physical and emotional needs of a person who has even just a single body and mind—that is, my current me. If taking care of myself, if trying to keep my own body from falling apart, and keeping my own mind from breaking down every day or two, is such a struggle, then what hope would I ever have of taking care of one or more other people *as if they were truly "me"*? Where would I ever find the resources?

The irony here is that *the resources would come from the very act of expanding yourself to include others;* that is, the very ability to handle, physically and emotionally, the job of taking care of lots of people as if they were all "me" comes from *the true decision to do so.* If the whole idea of the hidden potential and imprints creating our very reality is true, then there can be no greater way *of creating wealth* than *sharing it indiscriminately.* Put simply, if the only way I can ever *see* a dollar is to have planted an imprint from *giving* a penny, then the very act of making sure that all those around me have money *as if we were, all together, a single person* would bring me almost limitless resources. Imagine, in short, a world where everyone considered everyone else his or her responsibility, as if everyone else were all "me." And there's no reason why they can't be.

Any intelligent person reading these lines right now can sense, can smell, that we're barking up the right tree. To overcome the tendency *not* to think of others, to spread your idea of yourself to include all your employees and everyone else around you, to work *not for the sake of others,* but as if *there were no "other"*—this would be real happiness, this would be true contentment. You know in your heart that it would be right, you know in your heart it would be right to start it now, and you know that, if you spent your whole career and your whole life this way, purposely trying to work for the good of those around you as hard as you work for yourself, that you could look back with pride, for this is the real meaning of a human life. This is the ultimate wealth.

Permissions

Grateful acknowledgment is made for permission to reprint the following selections.

ALEXANDRA DAVID-NEEL. Selections are from *Magic and Mystery in Tibet*, which is in the public domain. An edition is published by Dover Publications.

LAMA ANAGARIKA GOVINDA. Selections are from *The Way of the White Clouds*. Reprinted by permission of the Overlook Press.

JOHN BLOFELD. Selections are from *The Wheel of Life*. Reprinted by permission of Shambhala Publications.

PETER GOULLART. Selections are from *The Monastery of Jade Mountain* and *Forgotten Kingdom*. Reprinted by permission of John Murray (Publishers) Ltd.

JANWILLEM VAN DE WETERING. Selections are from *The Empty Mirror*. Reprinted by permission of St. Martin's Press, LLC.

Index

abhiseka, 94–95

Abo Rinpoche, 329, 330

Adi Buddha, 214

Afghanistan, 205, 326, 350

African Americans, 20–21, 23, 24, 266,
267–316

Agnai tsang, 54

Ah Heng, 126–28

Ah Lok, 133–34

Ajanta caves, 149

Ajo Rimpoché, 116

Akong Rinpoche, 325

Alabama, 269, 314

Alexander the Great, 180

Allione, Chiara Osel, 333–35, 336, 337

Allione, Costanzo, 332–33, 335–36, 338–39

Allione, Costanzo Kunzang, 333–34, 339

Allione, Tsultrim, 20–21, 24, 266, 317–42
　Buddhist centers founded by, 21, 320,
　　332
　Buddhist name of, 327
　as Buddhist nun, 21, 319, 330–31, 332,
　　336, 337, 340
　Buddhist studies and profession of,
　　319–20, 322–31, 337–42
　childhood and adolescence of, 319–25
　marriages and motherhood of, 319,
　　331–39
　teaching of, 332–33

writing of, 21, 320

Alpert, Richard (Ram Dass), 332, 351–52

Altar of Heaven, 180

Amchi, 107

Amish, 24

"Amsterdam Cop" mystery novels (van de
　Wetering), 236

amulets, 48

Andin, 379–82, 385–86, 389

angels, 173

anger, 373
　feigning of, 24, 279

animals, 80, 85, 112–13
　pet, 107, 273, 359–60
　sacrifice of, 44–45
　traveling with, 72–73, 115, 118, 150–57,
　　166–67
　treatment of, 153–55

anjali, 277

Ansi, 55

anthropology, 265

arhats, 210

Aric, 56

Aristotle, 312

arjopa, 63–65

Arya-kula (family of Buddha), 112

Asanga, 308

asceticism, 81, 90*n*

Asian Classic Institute, 369, 376–77

asparas, 150
Aspect, Alain, 357
Assyrians, 213
Atman (divine self), 243
Australia, 293, 361–63, 372
Avalokitesvara, 316
Aye, 313
Ayer, A. J., 235

Babylonians, 213
bamboo, 209, 210, 211, 217
Banaras, 270–71, 272, 277, 278
Bangkok, 20, 125–26
baptism, 282, 300
Bardo Thodol, 112
beauty, 167–68, 169–70, 204, 212
Being, 213, 214
Bell, Charles, 18
Bell, John Stewart, 357
Bengal, 40
Bernstein, Richard, 16
Bhagavad Gita, 29
Bhutan, 41, 184
Bhutan, Rajah of, 39, 103
birds, 112–13, 137, 205, 224, 301–2
Birmingham, 269
Biwa, Lake, 259–60
Black Panthers, 20, 269, 284
Black Student Alliance, 270
Blofeld, John, 17, 18, 20, 33, 123–200,
        265
    Asian travel of, 147–200
    as British Cultural Relations Officer,
        182–84
    Buddhist studies and profession of, 23,
        30–31, 32, 34, 125, 129–47, 172–84,
        186–87, 190, 193–200
    Omei pilgrimage of, 182
    Western education of, 125
    works of, 16, 125, 126
Bodhanath, 271, 272, 274, 290–91
Bodhgaya, 20, 297, 327, 328, 351–55, 358,
        359
bodhicitta, 91–92
Bodhidharma, 245–46
Bodhisattva Lights, 160
bodhisattvas, 22, 82, 85, 133, 169, 174, 178,
        179, 284–85

images of, 127, 150
    power of, 135, 138
    principles of, 371–72
    vows of, 82, 104–5, 284
bodhi tree, 353–54
Bokhara, 205
Bolshevik Revolution, 17, 205
Bombay, 320, 372
Bongdzera, Duchy of, 227, 230
Boulder, 332–33, 335
Brahmins, 98
breath control, 58, 65, 66, 356
    exercises in, 57, 62, 67, 256
Brest-Litovsk, treaty of, 205
Buddha, 17, 21, 40, 82, 135, 137, 179, 213,
        214, 230, 260
    aura of, 89
    birth of, 105n
    earthly career of, 102, 244, 327, 328,
        353–54
    golden face of, 82
    of Heavenly Spheres, 215
    of this Illusory World, 215
    images of, 82, 83, 85, 88, 95–97, 103, 125,
        149–50, 210, 215–16, 226, 283, 295,
        321
    meditation by, 244
    Primordial, 214, 215
    teachings of, 352, 378
    worship of, 91
Buddhism:
    African Americans and, 20–21, 23, 24,
        266, 267–316
    American, 20, 126, 266–394
    Brotherhood of, 258
    canon manuscripts and sacred texts of,
        30, 93, 96, 98, 99, 137–38, 350,
        369
    communities dedicated to, 19, 192, 281,
        332
    contemporary, 19–24, 263–394
    diet and, 44–45, 175
    doctrines of, 23, 44–45, 50–51, 60, 93,
        101, 175, 179, 197, 243, 358,
        369–75, 385–94
    Eightfold Path of, 236, 238
    essence of, 203, 245–46
    ethics of, 369, 371–72, 375, 379, 382

experience vs. theory in, 93–94, 95, 101, 170
Hinayana teachings in, 142
initiation into, 93–95, 140–41, 142–47, 174, 184, 195–200, 281–82, 329, 330
knowledge and study of, 15–19, 21–25, 29–34
Mahayana system of, 135, 142, 192, 216, 265, 273, 284–85, 293–94, 308
multiple sects and interpretations in, 60, 125, 135, 138–39, 142, 146, 172–73, 184, 199
as process, 286
"Red-Cap" Sect of, 194
ritual in, 88–89, 107, 116–18, 135, 137, 140–47, 162–66, 175–81, 186–87, 195–200
sacred feminine principle of, 21, 320
sacredness of nature in, 112–13, 114–15
Southern, 138, 139, 142
spread of, 149
Taoism vs., 203, 211–15
Third Noble Truth of, 354–55
Three Jewels of, 280–81
Western, 18–21, 30–34, 126, 129
women and, 16, 18, 21, 23–24, 29–76, 266–316, 319–66
see also specific Buddhist sects
Buddhist centers, 21, 126, 266, 325, 332, 345–46
Burma, 135, 165, 356–57
Burnouf, Eugene, 18
butter-lamps, 85, 88, 89, 101, 143, 170, 186, 226
Byzantine sects, 168

Calcutta, 102–3, 134, 146, 320–21, 358–59
California, University of (Santa Cruz), 307, 310
calligraphy, Chinese, 128, 129
Cambridge University, 125, 166
Canterbury Tales (Chaucer), 151
Capri, 107–10
Carthusians, 52
Castaneda, Carlos, 294
Ceylon, 17, 39, 79, 135
Chad, Dr., 304–6
Chan, "Old Foxy," 140, 141

ch'ang, 187
Chang, Dr., 175, 182
Changtehkuan, 227–28
chela, 87, 91, 93–96
    relationship of guru and, 94–96, 119–20, 159
Cheng, Old Uncle, 141–42
Chengtu, 182–84
Chiang Kai-Shek, 158
Chicken Foot Mountain, 224
Ch'ien Lung, Emperor, 129, 157, 180
children, 83, 92, 138, 142, 314
China, 17, 32–34, 48, 62, 125, 126–84
    British Embassy in, 182–84
    Canton province of, 128, 132
    caravan travel in, 150–57
    Communist revolution in, 125, 181, 203
    food and restaurants in, 148–49, 152, 193, 208, 210–11, 226
    Japanese invasion of, 158–59, 181
    Kansu province of, 73
    Kokonor province of, 171, 173
    Kuomintang government of, 181
    Likiang district of, 224, 227, 230
    Northern, 147, 156
    People's Republic of, 156–57
    rural, 53, 150–57
    Shansi province of, 149
    Southern, 198
    Szechuan province of, 73, 134
    Tibetan border with, 32–33, 73–75, 205
    Tibetan invasion and occupation by, 119–20, 184–85, 284, 285
    Western, 125, 134
China Sea, 148
Chinese Buddhism, 17, 125, 126–29, 149, 175
    Tibetan Buddhism vs., 146, 172–75, 184
Chinese language, 135–36, 157, 161, 195, 205
    Cantonese dialect of, 134, 136, 140
    Mandarin dialect of, 131–32, 133, 136
Chinese medicine, 127–28, 130
Chinese New Year, 130
Chinese proverbs, 261
Ch'ing Hai (Blue Sea), 171
Chöd, 338–42
Chogtses, 89, 90, 101, 102

chorten, 156, 162–64
Christianity, 17–18, 22, 208, 218, 377
    missionaries of, 113, 139, 169, 173–74, 209
    sacraments of, 144–45, 282, 300
    scriptures of, 139, 288
Chungan, 208–9, 211
civaram, 88
civil rights movement, 269–70, 275, 284
clairaudience, *see* mental telepathy
clairvoyance, 79–80, 204
    see also mental telepathy
Colorado, 320–35
Colorado, University of, 320
communism, 119
    Chinese, 125, 181, 203
    Russian, 17, 203, 205
compassion, 92, 214, 277, 279, 286, 316, 377
consciousness, 115, 356
    enlightenment and, 91
    expansion and development of, 215
    higher states of, 87, 93–94, 147
    see also mental states
conversion, 212
cooperatives, 203
Cornell University, 270, 284
Crawford, Pamela, 327–28

Dainshin River, 71
dakini principle, 336
Dalai Lama, Thirteenth, 18, 30, 38–43, 57,
    102, 103
Dalai Lama, Fourteenth, 22–23, 105*n*,
    283–85, 319, 323–24, 328, 350, 354,
    359, 370, 389–90
Daling, 43–48
damarus, 80–81, 99, 106
dam-ts'hig, 94
Darjeeling, 38, 184, 198, 273
darshan, 98
David-Neel, Alexandra, 19, 20, 21, 29–32,
    35–76, 265, 266
    adopted son of, 51, 55, 61, 62, 64, 71–72
    Buddhist studies and profession of, 18,
        23, 29–30, 33–34, 37, 40–43, 48–52,
        60, 66
    childhood of, 22
    contemplative and ascetic life of, 49–53,
        69

Dalai Lama visit with, 30, 38–43
    death of, 19, 38
    disguises and religious garb of, 37, 60
    hermit's life of, 49–53, 69
    marriage of, 23
    psychic phenomena witnessed by, 53–75
    royal romance of, 23, 30
    skeptical nature of, 32, 37, 59–60
    Tibetan language mastered by, 37, 40,
        52, 56
    Tibetan travels of, 19, 30, 32, 37, 53–75, 79
    Western education of, 29–30
    works of, 16, 18, 32, 37, 236
Davis, Angela, 307–8
Dawasandup (translator), 40–43
Death Meditation, 382–85
Defense of Poetry, A (Sidney), 25
deities, 135, 138, 139, 224
demons, 135, 169, 220–23, 338–39
depression, 206, 237, 259–61, 333, 335,
    362–63
devas, 150
Dharamsala, 271, 277–78, 281–85, 323–24,
    350–51
Dharma, 15, 25, 104, 125, 164, 169, 176,
    190, 281, 293, 305, 337
    mastery and transition of, 91, 378
    power of, 298, 358
    wheel of, 328
Dhauladhar Mountains, 350
dhoris, 185
Diamond Abbey, 369
Diamond Sutra, 215, 266
Dingo Khentse Rinpoche, 319, 330
Dipa-Ma, 363–64, 366
dohas, 323
dokpas, 61, 64*n*
Dolma, 101
Dolomites, 156
dorje, 43
Dorjé Chuncheh Rimpoché, 32, 130–46,
    184, 199
    death of, 140
    teaching of, 132–41, 144, 146, 174
Dorje Khandro, 301
Dorje Sampa, 296–97, 298
Dreaming Me (Willis), 269
dreams, 115, 119, 329

Duality Principle, *see* Yin and Yang
dubthab, 73
Dudjom Rinpoche, 319
Dungkar Gompa (Monastery of the White
    Conch), 82–97, 104, 105–7, 120
Durrell, Lawrence, 19
Dzog Chen, 336

ego, 76*n*, 80
Egyptians, 213
Einstein, Albert, 357
emotion, 93–94
Emotional Intelligence (Goleman), 351
Empty Mirror, The (van de Wetering),
    235–36
Enche Kazi, 105
England, 125, 129, 131, 194
English language, 92, 126, 133–34, 136, 140,
    186, 191, 195–96, 206
Enlightened Beings (Willis), 292
Enlightened Business Institute, 369
Enlightened Ones, 84, 85, 174, 214
Enlightenment, 85, 91, 94, 135, 167–68, 170,
    173, 176, 197, 238, 239, 255, 370
Everest, Mount, 69, 137, 328
evil, 169, 213–14, 309
Ewing, Joan Rousmaniere, *see* Allione,
    Tsultrim
exorcism, 114
    Taoist, 217–24

faith, 22, 24, 160, 170, 334, 340, 352, 355
Faith (Salzberg), 346
Farina, Dick, 288
fasting, 324
fire-*puja*, 299, 300–301
flowers, 130, 132, 133, 139, 155, 156, 180,
    204, 210, 211, 224
food:
    in China, 148–49, 152, 193, 208, 210–11,
        226
    famine and, 205
    in Japan, 241–42
    lack of, 205
    in Sikkim, 190, 193, 199–200
Forbes, 370
Forgione, Francesco (Padre Pio), 22
Forgotten Kingdom (Goullart), 17, 203

Forster, E. M., 16
fortune-tellers, 219
Foundations of Tibetan Mysticism (Govinda),
    80, 192*n*
Fourfold Invocation, 190
Four Hindrances, 137
France, 20, 275
Francis of Assisi, Saint, 19, 100, 302
"From the Pre-Socratics to Wittgenstein"
    (Willis), 312, 314
fundamentalism, 24

Gabet, Father, 50
Gandhi, Mohandas K. "Mahatma," 31, 230
Gandren Oral Tradition, 292
Gangtok, 51, 101, 105, 106, 120, 185, 186–87
Gautama, Buddha, *see* Buddha
Gaya, 103
Gelukpa Monastery, 271, 272–77, 278–79,
    292, 295
geshe, 21, 80, 92, 107, 119, 369, 371, 378
Ghengiz Khan, 161
Ginsberg, Allen, 332–33
Glimpse of Nothingness, A (van de
    Wetering), 236
Gobi Desert, 57, 147
God, 24, 173, 213, 243, 377
Golden Dragon Medical Hall, 128
Goldstein, Joseph, 345–46
Goleman, Daniel, 351
gomchens, 33, 43–53, 64
    see also hermits
gompas, 118, 271, 298, 309
Gonsar Rinpoche, 277, 282
Gonsar Tulku, 323
Goullart, Peter, 18, 31, 32, 33, 201–31, 265
    Buddhist studies of, 18, 32, 203, 211–16
    childhood and adolescence of, 204–5
    Chinese exile and citizenship of, 203–4,
        205–8
    death of, 34
    education of, 204–5
    UN work of, 204
    works of, 17, 34, 203, 204
Govinda, Lama Anagarika, 17, 21, 31–34,
    77–121, 265
    Buddhist studies of, 18, 20, 32, 33–34, 79,
        82–121

Govinda, Lama Anagarika (*continued*)
  childhood writings of, 108–10
  reincarnation belief of, 105–11, 119–21
  Tibetan travels of, 21, 79–107, 111–21
  Tomo Géshé Rinpoché and, 79, 84,
      86–98, 119–21
  works of, 16, 79–80, 192n
Great Wall of China, 147–48, 155, 161
Green, Dolly, 287–88, 291
Guru-bhai, 97, 115–16
gurus, 227
  definition of, 86–87
  relationships of *chelas* and, 94–96,
      119–20, 159
  teachings of, 91–96
  Tibetan, 20, 84–121
Guyana, 385, 390
Gyalwa, 322, 324, 328
Gyelwa Ensapa, 292–93

Han dynasty, 161
Hangchow, 206, 208
Hanlin Academy, 142
Han-san, 257–59
happiness, 200, 204, 213, 377, 393
healing, 22, 97–98, 100, 113
hermitages, 67, 69, 81, 82, 209, 227
hermits, 15, 33–34, 43–53, 175, 189
  blessings of, 81–82
  Buddhist studies with, 33–34, 37, 48–52,
      69–70
  endurance of, 65–67, 69, 81
  food and shelter of, 46–47, 48–52, 65–66,
      67, 69, 81, 82
  silence and solitude of, 47–48, 49, 51–52,
      69, 80–82, 101
  superstitions about, 50
Hesse, Hermann, 20
Himalayas, 15, 37, 46, 52, 97, 111–12, 118,
      120, 156, 190–92, 322, 350
Hindi language, 193, 195, 277
Hinduism, 29, 40, 98, 193, 215, 243
Hitchcock, Maxine, 321
Hitchcock, Victress, 320–22
Hodgson, Brian Houghton, 30
Hoffman, Ernst Lothar, *see* Govinda, Lama
      Anagarika
holy water, 176, 222

Hong Kong, 126–46, 204, 320
Hong Kong University Medical School, 127
houkous, 228
Huc, Father, 50
huching violins, 210
humor, 280, 324
hungpao, 208

I Ching, 126
idolatry, 209
Ignorance, 214, 230
incense-sticks, 102, 143, 215
India, 21, 24, 33, 38–43, 53, 79, 99–104, 118,
      119, 120, 134, 204, 256, 269, 319–21,
      323–25, 328–30, 345, 349–59
  Bashar State in, 98–99
  Buddhist refugees in, 205, 288, 319, 350
  colonialism in, 29, 39
  Kashmir State in, 184
  Tibetan border with, 100, 111–19, 184
Indian Buddhism, 21, 24, 30, 103, 149, 213
Insight Meditation Society, 21, 345–46,
      359–60
Introduction a l'histoire du Buddhisme indien
      (Burnouf), 18
Italy, 20, 333–39

Jade Emperor's Mountain, 208–9, 211
James, William, 9
Jampa, 386–88
Jampa Method, 386–88
Jampel Gyatso, 292
Japan, 19, 33, 48, 130, 335–61, 265, 266
  invasion of China by, 158–59, 181
Japanese language, 235, 242
Jerusalem, 208
Jesus Christ, 18, 100, 113, 211, 230, 244, 288
Jigme Nagawang Kalzang Rimpoché,
      105–7, 119–21
  imprisonment and release of, 119–20
  spiritual education of, 107, 119
Joan of Arc, 19, 31
Jung, Carl, 24

Kachenla, 82–86, 89, 92, 97, 101–2
Kadampa Geshes, 372
Kailas, Mount, 98, 114
Kalgan, 148

Kalimpong, 39–43, 51n, 120, 139, 198
Kanchi, 294, 300, 302, 303, 304, 305
k'ang, 148, 152, 157–58
K'ang Hsi, Emperor, 157
Kanjur, 98
kaoling, 147
karma, 92, 174, 184, 213, 214, 243, 334, 372
Karmapa, Sixteenth, 319, 326–27, 328, 329, 330
kasa, 166
Kathmandu, 20, 269–77, 297–300, 321–22, 324, 325–28
kattas, 283
kazi, 188
Kennedy, John F., 20, 347
Kent State University, 284
Kewzing, 45
Khampas, 63, 119, 285
Khamptrul Rinpoche, 319, 331
kha-tags, 74
Khen Rinpoche, 370–71
Khunu Rinpoche, 354–55
Kimdol, 322–23
King, Martin Luther, Jr., 269
Kloppenburg, Aloka, 332, 333, 336
Kloppenburg, Paul, 331–32
Kloppenburg, Sherab, 332, 333
koans, 242–44, 245, 246, 248, 258
Kobe, 256
Kopan, 270, 271, 272–73, 278, 289–90, 295–96, 309, 310, 328
Korea, 158
Kronfield, Jack, 345–46
Köros, Csöma de, 50
Kouecifo, 222–23
Kowloon, 140
Kuangchi Moup'ang Monastery, 172–75
Ku Klux Klan, 269, 309
Kum-Bum Monastery of, 53–57
Kuomintang, 181
kusa grass, 176, 296
Kushog Lama, 156, 157, 166, 170–71, 172, 175–76, 177, 179–80
kyilkhov, 74
Kyoto, 19, 20, 33, 235, 259–61
Kyoto, University of, 243

Lachan, gomchen of, 48–52

David-Neel's spiritual training with, 30, 33–34, 37, 50–52
hermitage of, 49–50
Ladakh Monastery, 184
Ladenla, Sardar Bahadur, 103
Lakshman, 294–95, 296, 300–301, 304
Lamaism, see Tibetan Buddhism
lamas, 23, 31, 32, 40–46, 47–48, 223–31
ceremonial garb of, 88, 117, 143, 151, 158, 176
female, 43, 60
instruments accompanying invocations of, 80–81, 88, 99, 228
Mongolian, 92–93, 95, 156
psychic powers of, 117
spiritual training with, 70–71, 115–19, 132–41, 146
Tibetan, 31, 52–57, 115–19, 130–46, 156, 192–93
Land of the Lamas (Goullart), 17
Lao-tse, 127, 142, 213
Lao Wêng, 153
laughter, 139, 167, 171, 282
Lawrence, Brother, 22
Lee, Abbot, 208
Lee, Madame, 225
leeches, 189, 190
Lhasa, 53, 56, 79, 80, 92, 107, 119, 156, 158, 180, 227, 370
David-Neel's journey to, 19, 30, 37, 62, 71
palace and court of Dalai Lama at, 39
Li, Mr., 136, 138, 140, 175, 182
Liao, General, 183
Liberation, 214, 307–14, 354
Lichun, Abbot, 217–24
Light, 81, 82, 94, 121, 139, 173
Li Gotami, 98, 118
Lincoln, Abraham, 31
Little Owl (van de Wetering), 236
Living Buddhas, 132, 157, 170, 171, 177–78, 308
London, 235, 236, 325–26
Lothar, Geshe, 387
Love, 85, 92, 94, 97, 215, 216, 337, 359–60
lung-gom, 57–58, 79
lung-gom-pas, 57–65
fleetness and endurance of, 58, 59, 61–62, 63, 64–65

lung-gom-pas (*continued*)
  testing of, 62–63
  training of, 57–58, 59, 62–63, 64
  trances of, 59–60, 61, 64–65

Machig Lapdron, 340–42
magic, 31, 43, 50, 103
  black, 58, 113, 132, 137, 219, 256
Magic and Mystery in Tibet (David-Neel), 16,
    18, 32, 37
Mahabodhi Temple, 353–54
Mahamudra, 292–95, 329
mahjong, 157
mala, 354
Ma Lama, 158, 159, 170, 179
Malaysia, 204
Manali, 328–30
Manchu dynasty, 156, 157, 158, 166–67
Manchuria, 151
mandala, 175, 324
Mani Bhadra Monastery, 159–61
Mani Kahbum, 112
Manjusri Bodhisattva, 164, 168–69, 172,
    173, 176
mantras, 84, 85, 93, 117, 163–64, 220,
    315–16, 324, 329, 354
  Dorje Sampa, 298–99
  power of, 86, 87, 316
Mao Tse-tung, 125, 203
marijuana, 271
Marpa, 340
Marxism, 203
Max, Sister, 311
Maya, Queen, 105
meditation, 66, 80, 84, 87, 96, 97, 99, 112,
    135, 168, 186–87, 215, 216, 328
  challenge and rigors of, 240–53, 300–307
  on death, 382–85
  Great Seal practices of, 292–307, 329
  on Great Void, 139
  interruption of, 59–60
  koans of, 242–44, 245, 246, 248, 258
  one-pointed, 70–71, 117, 168–69, 197
  places of, 86, 99, 112, 325, 332
  postures of, 89, 103, 104, 140, 235–36,
    240, 246–47
  powers of, 139

  prerequisites of, 92, 297–300
  silence and, 102, 300, 301, 302, 329
  study and practice of, 21, 31, 33, 67, 68,
    86, 89, 92, 93–94, 95, 146, 184, 196,
    216, 227, 240, 242–53, 292–307, 322,
    329, 331–32, 345–46, 349, 350–52,
    356, 358, 361–66
  time periods of, 244–53
  traditional methods of, 93, 132, 298
  see also mental concentration; trances
Mekong River, 66
mental concentration, 57, 65, 66, 79–80, 88,
    116, 173, 220, 250
  deep, 222–23
  one-pointed, 70–71, 117, 168–69, 197
  spiritual and psychic training for, 70–71,
    255–56
  ten-stage exercise in, 67–69
  see also lung-gom-pas; meditation; mental
    telepathy; *tumo*
mental states, 377–78
  emotion and, 93–94
  higher, 87, 93–94, 146
  positive, 92
  subconscious, 107–8
  see also meditation; Nirvana
mental telepathy, 69–75, 93, 95–96, 137–38,
    194–95
  experiments with, 70
  mastery of, 70–71
  receivers of, 70, 71, 108
  unconscious, 70, 71
  volitional perfect concentration and,
    70–71
metaphysical research, 218
Migyur, 56–57
Milarepa, 49, 58, 69, 175, 292, 311,
    340
Milton, John, 319
Mind, 138–39, 214
  intellect and, 243, 281
  Oneness of, 168–69
Mingzing, Abbot, 209–16
miracles, 22, 37, 113
missionaries, 113, 139, 169, 173–74, 209
Moksha, 215
monasteries, 21, 30, 41, 50, 56

education and study in, 80, 92, 107,
192–200
Lhabrangs in, 89–90
shrine-rooms and private quarters in,
89–90, 97, 101–2, 193
Taoist, 208, 211
Tibetan, 63, 80, 82–97, 140, 184, 192
Westerners' visits to, 50, 53–57, 82–83,
174–75, 193–200, 236–61
Wu T'ai Shan, 155–61, 164–66, 170–81
Zen, 19, 33
Monastery of Jade Mountain, The (Goullart),
17, 203
Monastery of the White Conch (Dungkar
Gompa), 82–97, 104, 105–7, 120
Mongolia, 39, 55, 148, 156, 162, 170
Mongolian language, 165, 166, 167
Mongols, 55–57, 131, 132, 148, 151–52,
154–55, 159–68, 175
monks, 43, 192–93, 216
"flying," 37, 57–65
rituals of, 83–86, 88
robes and togas of, 54, 55, 60, 88, 90,
353, 354
Taoist, 208, 217–18
mou, 176
mudras, 85, 144
Muhammad, 31, 100
Munindra, 359
music, 93, 94, 112, 165–66, 190, 227
musical instruments, 80–81, 88, 144, 145,
150, 165, 178, 210, 228
Muslims, 188
Mussulmans, 173
My Journey to Lhasa (David-Neel),
37
mysticism, 146, 237
Christian, 302
secrecy and, 65, 74–75
stages in, 75–76
teachers of, 70
Tibetan practitioners of, 45, 52, 65, 69,
103, 320
trances and, 45–46
words and terminology of, 65, 66, 76,
192, 322*n*
mythology, 22, 24

naljorpas, 40–43, 44, 45, 68
Namgyal, 111–16
Namgyal Monastery, 283
Namkhai Norbu Rinpoche, 320, 334–35,
336
nam-thar, 311
Nank'ou, 147
Naropa, 311
Naropa Institute, 332, 345
National Endowment for the Humanities,
292
nature, 203, 204, 213, 301–2
Nehru, Jawaharala, 120
Nêng Hai, Abbot, 170–75, 181, 182–84, 198
Nepal, 30, 40, 46, 184, 269, 270–86,
288–300, 321–23, 326–28, 336
Netherlands, 235
New Delhi, 350, 351–52
New York, State University of (Buffalo), 24,
348–49
New York, N.Y., 377–78, 379–82
New York Times, 16
ngags, 59
ngagspa, 73–75
ngondro, 329
nierpa, 54, 55
Nirvana, 146, 164, 170, 173, 213, 215, 243,
253, 258
nomad herdsmen, 58*n*, 59, 61, 80–81
nuns, Buddhist, 21, 300, 311, 319, 328, 329,
330–31, 332, 336, 337, 340, 353, 354,
369
Nyingma Lamas, 112

"Old Manchuria," 151, 152, 154–55, 159–61
Omei, 182
opium, 152–53, 157
Oracle of Lhasa, 105, 106
Oracle of Nachung, 105, 106
Orphanage and Home for Unwed
Mothers, 321
ouija-boards, 107–8, 206
Ovid, 18

Pabong Monastery, 63, 64
Padmasambhava, 75–76, 112–14, 199
Pakistan, 204, 350

Palden, Lama Thubten, 297, 298
Pali, 92
Palmo, Tenzin, 15
Panchen Lama, 83
pangchinmei, 228
Paradise of the Great Bliss, 45
Patan, 296
peace, 90, 110, 144, 213, 286
Pegyai Lama, 53–54
Peking, 31, 55, 92, 147, 148, 158, 159, 160,
    161–62, 182, 184
    Lama Temple in, 156
Penang, 210
Perfection, 169–70, 172
Perry, Diane, *see* Palmo, Tenzin
Peter, 253, 260
philosophy, 235, 236–37, 243
    Western, 311–13
Phiyang Lama, 115–18
phurba, 60
Pio, Padre (Francesco Forgione), 22
Plato, 312
Polo, Marco, 17–18, 19
Poo, 100, 111–19
Power of Nothingness, The (David-Neel), 236
Practice of the Presence of God, The (Brother
    Lawrence), 22
Prajna, 168
prayer-carpet, 88
prayers, 84, 85, 86, 118, 216, 219, 354, 359,
    360–61
prayer-wheels, 98, 162–63, 170
priests, 203, 208, 217–18, 220–23, 241
Princeton University, 20, 369, 370
Psi, 204
psychic research societies, 70
psychic states, 21, 115
    development of, 63, 64–65, 70–71
    energy currents and, 70–71
    investigation of, 70, 75
    see also lung-gom-pas; meditation, mental
        telepathy; trances; *tumo*
psychiatry, 218, 243
psychoanalysis, 238
psychology, 113, 114, 351
P'u Hsien (Personification of Divine
    Action), 160

P'u Lotao, *see* Blofeld, John
Purple Bamboo Grove Monastery, 29
P'usa Ting Monastery, 156–59, 162,
    164–66, 170, 175–78

Rabten Geshe, 277–78, 279, 281–83, 284,
    323
Rachevsky, Zina, 272, 273–75, 328
racism, 269, 270, 275–76, 277, 279–80,
    309–10
radongs, 88
Rajgir, 103
Raksha, 169
Rakshi, 66
rakshi, 303, 306
Ralpachan, King, 112
Ram Dass (Richard Alpert), 332, 351–52
Rampur, Maharaja of, 98–99
Rangoon School, 93
Reality, 212, 213, 215
Reincarnation, 23, 90, 104, 105–11, 177–78,
    213, 214, 243, 326
    previous lives and, 53–55, 56–57, 106–7,
        289–92, 358
    of Tomo, 104, 105–7, 119–21
relaxation, 299–300, 301–2, 304, 329
religion:
    conversion and, 212
    faith and, 22, 24
    fundamentalist, 24
    theology and, 23
resurrection, 113
ribus, 97–99, 119
Ricard, Matthieu, 21
rinpochés, 22, 134, 352n
Roach, Michael, 19, 20–21, 24, 266, 369–94
    Buddhism promulgated and supported
        by, 369, 374–75, 376–78
    Buddhist studies and practice of, 370–94
    childhood and adolescence of, 369, 376,
        380
    diamond business career of, 369–81
    Western education of, 369
Rohatsu, 244–53
Roman Catholic Church, 174, 180
Rome, 333–35
Rooks, Conrad, 273

Roosevelt, Franklin D., 31
rosaries, 131, 170, 193, 324, 354
Royal Nepalese Airlines, 272
Russia, 55, 205, 372
Russian Revolution, 17, 203, 205

sadhana, 83, 103, 115, 325–26
"Sadhana of All the Siddhis, The"
    (Trungpa), 325–26
sadhu, 271
Sagamon Barcon, 17
   see also Buddha
saints, 95, 100, 113, 171, 173, 292
Sakya-Gompa, 117
Sakyong, gomchen of, 47
salvation, 213
Salzberg, Sharon, 20–24, 266, 343–66
   automobile accident of, 355–57
   Buddhist studies and practice of, 23–24,
      345–46, 349–55, 358–66
   childhood and adolescence of, 23–24,
      345, 346–49, 355, 362
   meditation center founded by, 21,
      345–46, 359–60
   meditation retreats of, 351–55, 361–63
   teaching of, 345–46, 359–60
   Western education of, 23–24, 345,
      348–49
   works of, 346
Samandabhadra Bodhisattva, 160
Samarkand, 205
samsara, 270
Samteling Monastery, 296, 297–98
Samyas Monastery, 291
Samye Ling meditation center, 325
Sangha, 190, 280
Sangharakshita Thera, 120
Sangri Khamar, 340
Sangsara, 172–73, 175
Sanskrit language, 29, 30, 144, 195, 196,
   271, 390
Sanskrit University, 271
Saraha, 323
Sarawak, 204
Sarnath, 102, 103, 271, 328
Satipatthana-Sutta, 93

satori, 245, 255
Satseto, Mount, 228
Sawamura, 323, 324
Sayadaw U Pandita, 356–58, 361–63
science, 23, 218, 219, 236–37, 358
Scotland, 325, 330
séances, 107–8, 206
Seattle, 332, 333
September 11, 2001, terrorist attacks of,
   320
Sera Monastery, 107, 119, 370, 374, 386–87
sesshins, 244
Seventh Day Adventists, 265
sexuality, 325, 330–31
Shakayamuni Buddha, 17–18, 91, 95–97,
   100, 112, 113
   see also Buddha
Shalu gompa, 64
Shanghai, 203, 205–6, 210, 218
Shangri-La, 155
Shangri Moupo lamasery, 224–31
Sherab, 116, 118
Sherpas, 289, 328
Shigatse, 83
Shipki-La, 111
Shirley, 379–82
Siam, 165
Siberia, 205
Siddhartha, 273
siddhi, 95
Sidkeong Tulku, Prince of Sikkim, 43, 44,
   45–47
Sidney, Phillip, 25
Sikkim, 18, 43–48, 53, 120, 184–200, 328,
   330
Simla, 111
Sinai, Mount, 213
Singapore, 34, 204, 210
slavery, 275–76
Snow Mountain, 230
so-cha, 84–85
Soldeb, 118
sonam, 272
Song of the Mahamudra, The (Tilopa),
   329
Songtsen, King, 112
Soochow, 205, 206

Sōphē, 168
Sorbonne, 29–30
South Korea, 265
spirit(s), 24, 203, 214, 216
    animal, 44–45
    manifestations of, 218–19
spiritists, 107–8
Spirit's Retreat Monastery, 210
Sri Lanka, 385
stigmata, 22
stupa, 271, 272, 321–22, 325, 328
Suchow, 56
Sudden Infant Death Syndrome (SIDS),
        334–35
Sumaru, Mount, 137
superstition, 53, 54, 57, 58, 114, 132, 219
sutras, 170, 226, 228, 240–41, 258, 266
Suzuki, Shunryu, 322*n*
Swayambhu ("Monkey Temple"), 321
Swayambhu Monastery, 324, 325, 326–28
Swayam bhunath, 297
Switching Bodies, 390–91

Tagan, 73
Taj Mahal, 149
takuan, 241
Tali, 224
Tangku Rimpoché, 186, 192, 193–96,
        197–200
    character and personality of, 193–94,
        199–200
Tangu, 48
Tanjur, 98
Tantric Buddhism, 37, 115, 227, 276, 292,
        306, 323, 326, 329, 378
Tantric College, 370
Tantric Mysticism of Tibet (Blofeld), 126
Tao, 213, 214, 215
Taoism:
    Buddhism vs., 203, 211–15
    Changtienssu, 212
    Chengyi, 212
    doctrine of, 213
    Lungmen, 211, 212
    monasteries of, 208, 211
    nature and, 203, 213
    philosophical basis of, 212, 213–15

Tara Mandala, 320
Tashiding Monastery, 186, 192–200
Tashiding Mountain, 187, 191–200
Tashi Jong, 328, 330, 331
Tashi Lama, 83
Tat'ung, 148, 150, 161
tea, 193, 322
    Chinese, 130, 190, 210
    hot-buttered, 71, 72, 94–85, 101, 161
    red, 148
Teichman, Eric, 183
temples, 82–84, 86, 89, 98, 155, 169, 186
    maintenance of, 83–84, 90*n*, 97
    rituals in, 88–89, 107
    sacred objects in, 99, 103
Ten Thousand Things, 214
Tenzin, 289, 292
Tenzin, Geshe Thupten, 283, 387
Teresa, Mother, 321
Thailand, 190, 385
thankas, 102, 112
Theravadin Buddhism, 79
Three Gems, 138
Three Precious Ones, 162
Throne of the Almighty, 218
Thubden Sherab "Geshela," 92–93, 95, 98,
        116, 118
Tibet, 18, 19, 30, 44, 53–75
    Central, 97
    Chang thang region of, 58, 97
    Chinese borderlands of, 32–33, 73–75, 203
    Chinese invasion and occupation of,
        119–20, 184–85, 284, 285, 386
    David-Neel's travels in, 53–55, 79
    Eastern, 63
    foreigners barred from, 30, 37, 79
    Ga region of Kham in, 63
    horseback travel in, 72–75, 115
    Indian border with, 100, 111–19, 184
    isolation and silence of, 71, 79–80
    Kunka pass in, 73–74
    Mongolian border with, 171
    Ngari province of, 56, 57
    Northern, 58, 66
    secret lore of, 69–75
    Southern, 80, 97, 104
    Thebgyai territory of, 61, 64

Tomo Valley of, 104, 120
Tsang province of, 63, 64
Tsaparang district in, 118
vanished culture and society of, 32–33, 118–19, 370
Western, 97–100
Tibetan Buddhism, 18, 22, 23, 24, 33, 37–76, 79–121, 125, 126, 130–47, 164
Chinese Buddhism vs., 146, 172–75, 184
diaspora of, 319
early history of, 112–14, 289, 291
Gelugspa (Yellow-Hat) sect of, 143
great teachers of, 319–20, 329–30
Kagyu sect of, 326, 327
Kargyupta Order of, 117
Nyingma Order of, 117, 290
pilgrimages in, 339–42
religious books on, 112
Western knowledge of, 15, 21, 79–107, 111–21, 296–316, 345–66
Tibetan language, 37, 38, 40, 45, 52, 56, 66, 84, 85, 157, 165, 167, 279, 289, 328, 390
Tibeto-Sanskrit language, 144, 195, 196
Tientsin, 159, 174, 175
Ti-Gah Chö-Ling (Kalimpong), 39–43, 51*n*, 120, 139, 198
Tilopa, 329
Time, 21
Tisong Detsen, King, 112
Tista, 185
tjap tjoy, 241
Tokyo, 237
Tomo Géshé Rimpoché, 32, 80–82, 86–121
blessing and healing gifts of, 81, 86, 90, 95–100, 114, 119
character and personality of, 90–91, 94–96, 100, 102, 103–4
death of, 90, 94, 100, 104–5
early hermetic life of, 80–82, 97–98
fame of, 95, 98–101, 102–3, 119
Indian pilgrimage of, 99–100, 102–4, 114
Lama Govinda and, 79, 84, 86–98, 119–21
monastic education of, 80
physical appearance of, 90

reincarnation of, 104, 105–7, 119–21
teachings of, 91–92, 93–96, 116
yogic powers of, 93, 95–101, 103
torma, 143
trances, 45–46, 59–60, 61, 64–65, 66
interruption of, 59–60
trapas, 72–73
Travis, John, 327–28
Trikaya (Trinity), 215
Trisong Detsen, King, 291
Trungpa, Chögyam, 236, 320, 325, 326–27, 330, 332, 345
Truth, 137–39, 168–69, 170, 173, 174, 175, 236–37, 286
tsa, 68
Tsai Tahai, 127–33, 136, 140–43, 194
tsampa, 65, 117, 291
Tsangpo River, 340
Tsaparang, 115
Tsépamé (Buddha of Infinite Life), 117
tsé-ril, 117
Tsewang ceremony, 116–17
ts'hang-khang, 86
tsok-loong, 303–6
Tsongkhapa, 281, 292
tulkus, 53–55, 57, 105, 119, 327
Tulsig Rinpoche, 290–92
tumo, 37, 65–69
definition of, 66
exercises in, 67–69
probation and initiation in, 66–67
training in, 66–69
Turkestan, 148, 205
Turkey, 326

Ukraine, 205
Ultimate Journey (Bernstein), 16
uma, 67–68
Umdze, 88
United Nations, 125, 204
United States, 20, 126, 330–35
Universe, 214–15, 238, 302
universities, monastic, 80, 92, 107, 370
upasaka, 281

vajras, 90, 101, 106, 321
Vajrasattva, 296–97

Vajrasattva Buddhism, *see* Tibetan
    Buddhism
van de Wetering, Janwillem, 18, 19, 20, 31,
    233–61, 265, 266
    Buddhist studies of, 33, 34, 235–61
    depression and personal struggle of, 236,
        256–61
    public talks and teachings of, 34
    works of, 235–36
Varanasi, 271
Varieties of Religious Experience, The
    (James), 9
Vashon Island, 332
Vatican, 180
Vision, A (Yeats), 24
visualization, 65, 66, 139, 301, 302, 329
    ten-stage exercise in, 67–69
Vladivostok, 205
von Stael-Holstein, Baron Alexander, 92
von Veltheim-Ostrau, Baron, 103–4

Wallace, B. Alan, 21
Wang Lama, 158, 159, 170, 179
Wangyal, Tenzin, 22
Wat Chalerm, 198
Way of the White Clouds, The (Govinda), 16,
    79
Weber, Max, 31
Wên Shu (Personifiation of Divine
    Wisdom), 164, 168–69, 176
Wesleyan University, 270, 288, 310
Wheel of Life, 214
Wheel of Life, The (Blofeld), 16, 125
Wheel of the Law, 89
Willis, Jan, 20–21, 23, 24, 266, 267–316
    Buddhist studies of, 269–316
    Buddhist teacher of, *see* Yeshe, Lama
    childhood and adolescence of, 269, 270,
        277, 286–88, 309–10
    civil rights activism of, 269, 270, 284
    Dalai Lama's meetings with, 283–85
    former life revealed to, 289–92
    Great Seal retreat of, 292–307
    hair of, 286–88, 291
    impact of racism on, 269–70, 275–76,
        277, 279–80, 309–10
    teaching of, 269–70, 288, 308, 310–13

Tibetan name of, 280–81
    works of, 269, 292
wine, 205, 215, 225, 226
wisdom, 137–38, 167, 168–69, 170, 173,
    176, 181, 213, 220
Women of Wisdom (Allione), 21,
    320
World War I, 48, 203, 204–5
World War II, 125, 203, 235, 237
Wu T'ai Shan, 147, 150, 155–81
    battlefield of, 181
    five sacred peaks of, 155, 177
    Holy Week in, 166–67, 175–81
    monasteries and temples of, 155–61,
        164–66, 170–75, 180

Yamanataka, 169
yamên, 170
Yeats, W. B., 24
Yeshe, Lama, 24, 269–70, 328
    character and personality of, 274, 276,
        277, 279
    death of, 311, 314
    exile of, 269
    teaching and guidance of, 271–81,
        284–86, 289–90, 292–301, 305–14,
        316, 319
Yi-Gah Cho-Ling Monastery, 89–97,
    101–2
Yin and Yang, 127, 214
yoga, 115, 298, 351, 352
yogis, 41, 311, 326, 329
    powers of, 81, 85
Yongden, 55–56
    David-Neel's adoption of, 51
    David-Neel's travel with, 55, 61, 62, 64,
        71–72
Yuenfoungsze lamasery, 224–31
Yünkang caves, 149–50

Zen Buddhism, 142, 146, 173–74, 175, 184,
    198
    monasteries and temples of, 19, 33,
        233–61
Zen masters, 237, 238–39, 254, 257–59, 261
Zen Mind Beginner's Mind (Suzuki), 322*n*
Zopa, Lama, 273, 274, 295, 328